THE SUNDAY TIMES
DIY and
DECORATING

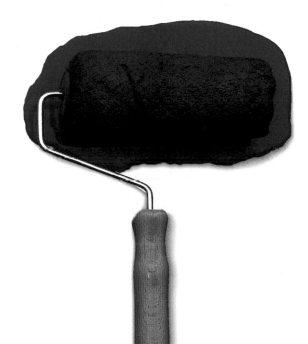

THE SUNDAY TIMES
DIY and
DECORATING

Contents

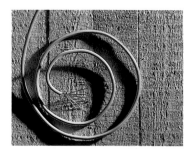

Lighting 162

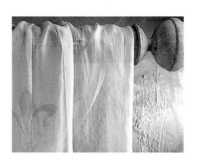

Soft furnishing 218

Storage 174

The exterior 240

Colour 192

Introduction

Today, the materials and equipment that go into making and maintaining a comfortable and attractive home are within everyone's reach. Choosing do-it-yourself and decorating items, in the day of the DIY superstore, has never been easier, or more enjoyable.

The do-it-yourself industry's success is due to the recognition by manufacturers and retailers that a 'professional' standard of work, when it comes to home maintenance and improvement, is no longer the preserve of the full-time craftsman. Tools and materials that were once the preserve of builders, joiners and other trades now have no more mystique than a paintbrush or a roll of wallpaper.

But of course there is more to decorating and DIY than mere merchandise. Paints and wallcoverings may be easier to use than they've ever been, but how do you choose the right colours, patterns and finishes for the effects you want to create? Is there a set technique for papering round a doorway? Which do you paint first, the walls or the ceiling? And while power tools might make light of a job such as preparing timber for a shelving system, what arrangement will best suit your needs, and what methods of construction are most appropriate to your type of home?

In other words, while good materials are a big part of the story, bright ideas and basic skills are no less important. And that is what this book is all about. In plain words and clear illustrations, *The Sunday Times DIY and Decorating* explains the principles of interior decorating and home DIY, giving guidance on tools and materials, techniques and tricks of the trade, to working efficiently and safely – all with that vital objective, the professional finish, in prospect.

Whether you are a complete novice or a more experienced handyperson intent on more ambitious decorative effects, this book will serve to excite your interest, and to bring new tasks and more advanced techniques within your scope. Sections of the book range from using colour and pattern to repairing and preparing surfaces, creating all kinds of decorative finishes, improving flooring, lighting and storage – and even the shapes of your rooms.

In every case, the sections take a step-by-step approach, offering ideas, outlining the items you will need and illustrating the methods by which you can achieve the best possible results. This is a book to inspire as well as to inform, to read at leisure as well as to follow project by project. Whatever types of jobs around the house you are contemplating, if the appropriate section gives you the confidence as well as the practical advice you need to tackle it, then this book will have achieved its purpose.

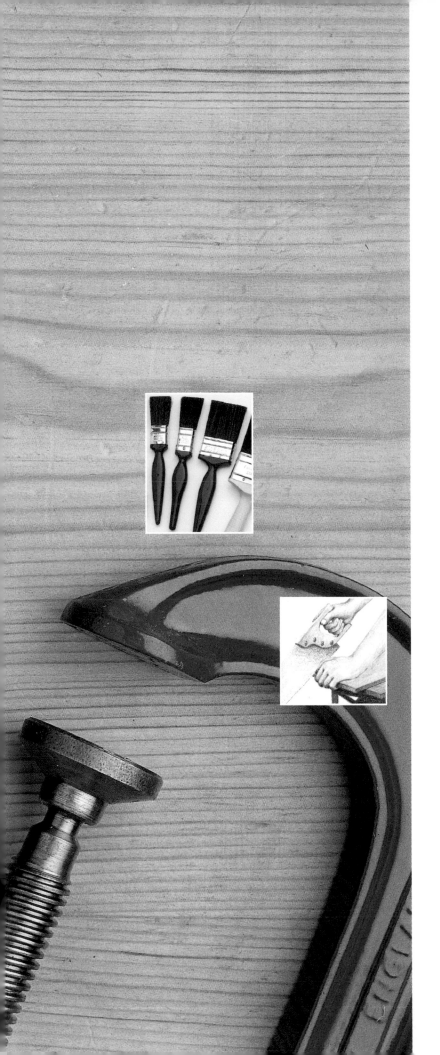

BASIC
EQUIPMENT

Tools you need

The right tools for the job greatly simplify the task in hand and ensure the best possible results. Some tools are expensive, but you must weigh their cost against the savings you will make by not paying someone else to do the work for you. Always buy the best tools you can afford; good, well-cared-for tools will last, so think of them as an investment.

Sharp scissors, chisels and knives give a clean cut and are safer to use than blunt ones. For general use, do not buy a made-up tool kit. These often include a number of tools you will never use. Be selective and choose tools according to the work you plan to do.

Clean tools immediately after use. A wipe with an oily rag ensures metal surfaces stay rust-free. Never let sharp tools rub against each other – this is the most common cause of blunted cutting edges.

A soft hold-all is best for transporting tools. Wooden, metal, or plastic tool boxes are heavy and cumbersome.

Be safe

- Keep hands away from the direction of any cut. Where possible, clamp work to free both hands to hold the tool correctly.

- Always unplug power tools when they are not in use, and store them out of reach of children. Wear protective clothing where recommended (*see p. 20*).

A basic tool kit

You will find many of the following tools useful for everyday household tasks. Power tools and specific tools for decorating and other special tasks are described in detail on later pages (*see p. 12–17*).

Portable workbench This provides a working surface and highly adaptable vice, and can be used as steps or as one of two trestles.

Tool carrier A lightweight carrier for tools required for the job in hand.

Steel rule For use as an accurate cutting guide and marking straight lines.

Metre rule Plastic rules are lightweight and the folding wooden types are convenient to use and store.

A BASIC TOOL KIT

1 Heavy-duty craft knife
2 Floorboard saw 3 Tenon saw
4 Mini hacksaw 5 Mole grips (self-grip wrench) 6 G-clamp 7 Adjustable spanner 8 Pincers 9 Pliers
10 Fine-nose pliers

Spirit level For checking horizontal and vertical surfaces before fixing them in place. A long one (typically 60cm (24in) long) makes checking accuracy over a long span easier, but a short spirit level is useful when working in a confined space.

Tenon saw For fine cutting smaller timber sections. This one is 13pt – the pt, or point, refers to the number of teeth per 25mm (1in) of blade.

General purpose (GP) saw Used for cutting both metal and wood. Copes well with old and reclaimed timber that may contain nails or screws.

Floorboard saw Specially designed for floorboards, the curved cutting edge makes it easier to cut a board without damaging the adjoining ones.

Mini hacksaw Different removable blades mean this can be used for cutting metal, wood and even tiles.

Cross-cut handsaw Used for cutting large timber sections.

Screwdrivers Blade sizes differ according to screw sizes. Heads are available for single-slot or cross-slot (Phillips) screws. A good-quality ratchet or spiral-ratchet screwdriver will save a lot of effort in turning, and is a worthwhile labour-saving tool.

Bradawl Used to make a starter hole for a screw.

Electrician's screwdriver The handle is specially insulated to protect the user against accidentally touching a live wire.

G-clamps Used for holding work in position. They come in a range of sizes, the most common being 10cm and 20cm (4in and 8in).

Mole grips Snaplocks onto objects, leaving your hands free.

Pliers Used for improving grip on small components and bending wires. The toothed jaws have a curved section for gripping round objects, and wire-cutting blades. Fine-nose pliers are used for manipulating small, hard-to-reach objects. They are also called needle-nose pliers.

Pincers For pulling nails.

Craft knife With disposable blades.

Adjustable spanner With 24mm (nearly 1in) opening for routine plumbing tasks.

Chisels Choose the finer, bevel-edged type for working on wood. Sizes include 6mm, 12mm, 18mm and 25mm (¼in, ½in, ¾in and 1in). Cold chisels, which come in a similar range of sizes, are used for stone or brick.

Hammers A lump hammer is used for heavy-duty work, a pin hammer for tapping in pins and tacks, and a claw hammer has a claw on the back for drawing out nails.

Soft-face mallet Used when it is important not to leave any mark on metal and wood surfaces.

Try-square For marking right angles.

File For smoothing. Typically 12mm (½in) round.

Steel measuring tape Typically 3.5m (12ft) or 5m (16ft) in length. Check that the tape is marked with both metric and imperial measurements.

Glue gun Filled with special adhesive and sealant for quick repair work.

Shaping tool or Surform A rasp-like tool available in a number of sizes and shapes, for shaping wood.

1 **Soft-face mallet 2 Lump hammer**
3 **Claw hammer 4 Pin hammer**
5 **Cold chisels**

6 **Single-slot screwdrivers**
7 **Cross-slot screwdrivers**
8 **Bradawl 9 Steel rule**

10 **Spirit level 11 File**
12 **Steel tape measure**
13 **Wood chisels**

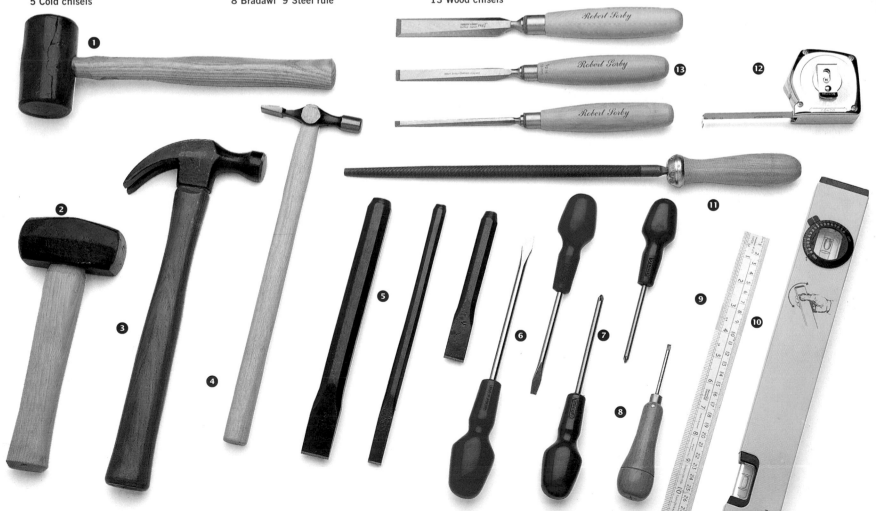

Painting tools

The way you apply paint is largely a matter of personal choice. You can use brushes and/or a paint-roller – a tool developed for the amateur user of emulsion paint. The paint pad has its advantages, too.
There are also a few vital special items, including triangular shave hooks and flexible scrapers for removing old paint; masking tape for protecting surfaces not to be painted; paint shields in metal or plastic to restrict paint to the area being painted; tack or tacky rags to pick up dust; clean, lint-free rags; paint stirrers (there is one usable with a power drill); and paint kettles.

Use a paint kettle to keep the bulk of your paint free of contamination. It also makes carrying paint – especially up ladders – much easier, since not all paint tins have built-in handles.

Brushes

For a good finish, choose brushes with genuine bristle or with the best-quality synthetic bristle. As a rule, costlier brushes do give the best results. Use inexpensive brushes, though, for outside work, such as applying preservatives to wooden fencing or painting masonry.

Brushes that are well cared for improve with use. Loose bristles are shed and the tips become nicely rounded. Start a brush on primer and undercoat, then use it for fine finishing as it ages.

Useful brush sizes include an angled 18mm (¾in) cutting-in brush and 12mm, 25mm, 50mm and 10cm or 12.5cm (½in, 1in, 2in and 4in or 5in) brushes.

Radiator brush This is a brush with an extra long metal handle that can be bent to allow you to paint behind radiators.

Rollers

Rollers are used with a paint tray and offer an easy way of applying paint to large, flat areas without leaving defined brush strokes. They are best suited to applying water-based paints, which you can easily clean off the roller. When using solid emulsion paint, lift the roller direct from the container. Roller types include:

Foam With easy-clean removable sleeve. It does not give the finest finish and will tear when used on rough surfaces.

Mohair Very close pile on a hard roller, giving a fine finish to smooth surfaces. Not suitable for textured surfaces.

Shaggy pile Deep, floppy pile makes it suitable for textured surfaces. Can also be used to apply textured paint.

Radiator roller A thin, deep-pile roller on a long wire handle to reach behind radiators and other awkward spots.

Texturing roller Specialized roller used to produce a rag-rolled or other textured effect.

Paint pads

These pads of fine mohair pile stuck to a layer of foam, bonded to a metal or plastic handle, are light and easy to use. Sizes range from 25mm to 15cm (1in to 6in); some have a hollow handle to take the end of a broom handle for painting tops of walls or ceilings without steps. Suitable for smooth or textured surfaces, but not rough finishes. A pad does give a very fine finish when gloss-painting flush doors.

Clean pads immediately after use, with water where water-based paints have been used. Note that proprietary cleaners can attack the adhesive holding the mohair to the foam.

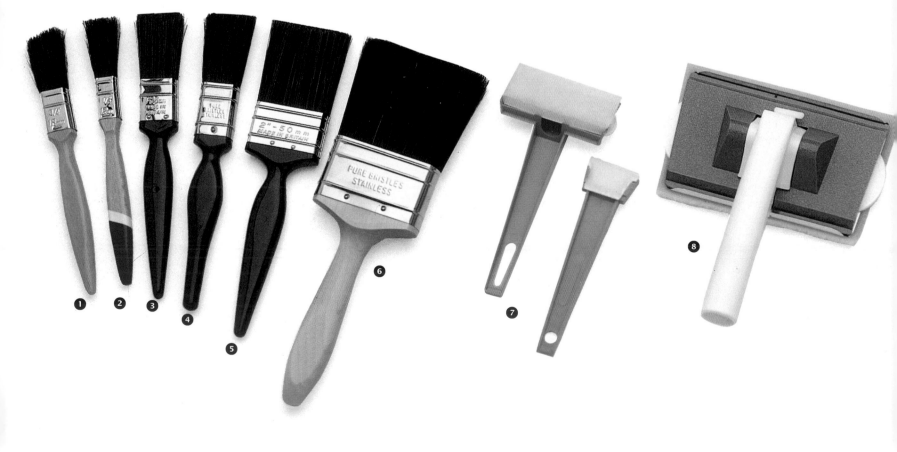

1 18mm (¾in) cutting-in bristle brush
2 12mm (½in) bristle brush
3 25mm (1in) synthetic no-loss brush
4 25mm (1in) bristle brush
5 50mm (2in) synthetic no-loss brush
6 Emulsion brush 7 Paint pads
8 Paint pad with edging rollers at side
9 Foam roller 10 Textured roller for
textured paint 11 Radiator roller
12 Paint tray 13 Roller with shaggy pile
attachments 14 Mohair roller
15 Deep-pile roller

Wallpapering tools

No expensive or specialized tools are required for hanging wall and ceiling coverings. A pasting table makes it easier to apply paste to long lengths of wallpaper or other material, and make sure that the scissors or knife you use to cut the wallpaper to length are sharp.

Tips

- When hanging delicate wallpapers, you may find that a clean foam paint roller does a better job than a brush when it comes to smoothing down the newly hung paper. Apply only the lightest pressure to avoid marking the paper.

- When using a platform to stand on, adjust its height so that you can stand comfortably without having to bend your neck or stretch your arms too far above your head.

Depending on the job, you may need a certain number of specialist tools for applying wallcoverings. The following is a checklist of the basic essentials:

Pasting table A sturdy, purpose-made pasting table is a wise investment. Easy to move, store and put up, it provides a stable surface of ideal dimensions and makes pasting very much simpler. Alternatively you can use a flush door laid over trestles.

Bucket Use a clean plastic bucket for paste, with string tied across the top between the handle joints. You can then rest the pasting brush across the string when it is not in use.

Scissors You will need a pair of long decorating scissors, and a small pair for trimming.

Craft knife For use with a metal straight-edge or cutting guide to trim vinyls and heavy papers. Scissors are best with thin, wet paper.

Pasting brush Choose a brush at least 10cm (4in) wide, and keep it only for pasting.

Smoothing brush Also known as a paperhanger's brush, this has stiff but soft bristles and is used to brush trapped air out to the edge of paper and press the wallcovering into place. Always keep it clean and dry.

Sponge Essential for wiping away any surplus paste while it is still wet.

Seam roller Use this small wood or plastic roller to press down seams once the wallcovering is up. Don't use it on embossed papers or you risk making 'tramlines'.

Plumb line and weight This is used to produce true verticals. It is an essential piece of equipment for starting every wallpapering job. A builder's line will hang better than ordinary string.

1 **Smoothing brush**
2 **Steel tape measure** 3 **Scraper**
4 **Decorating scissors** 5 **Seam roller**
6 **Sponge**

Pencil Use an HB or softer lead for marking the paper clearly. Oversharp or harder leads can tear more delicate papers.

Steel tape These measures are typically 3.5m (12ft) long, which should be adequate for measuring the height of normal walls. Longer measures are widely available.

Rule It is important to have a rule long enough to span the roll's width – normally about 53cm (21in). A retractable rule may tear the paper, so it is better to use a fixed rule.

Set square A large plastic square (or any improvized square) is useful for checking that your cuts are consistently at a 90º angle.

Sanding pad Keep one to hand for sanding away any scraps of old wallpaper or lining paper you may find on a stripped wall just as you are about to hang the new paper. Likewise, a sharp **scraper** is a useful standby.

Clean rags Choose rags made of lint-free cloth, such as old sheeting, for wiping the pasting table as the job progresses. Other material may leave fibres on the table.

Water trough For ready-pasted wallcoverings you need a water-resistant trough in which to soak the cut sections.

Steps You will need at least one pair of steps in order to reach the tops of the walls or ceiling.

1 **Heavy-duty craft knife**
2 **Steel rule** 3 **Plumb line and weight**
4 **Lining paper** (*see p. 122*)
5 **Pasting brush**

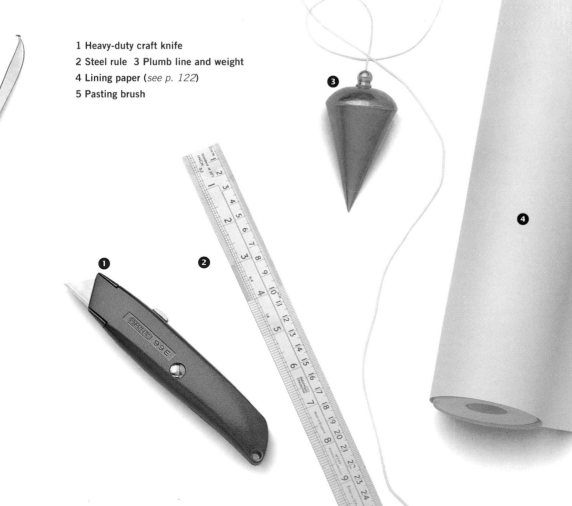

Power tools

There seems to be a power tool for just about every imaginable DIY task. Certainly the electric drill has become indispensable, and many other power tools are a great help in making work easier and the results more accurate. Choose dedicated tools rather than just a basic drill to which lots of attachments can be added. Tools specifically designed for the job will have the right range of speeds, and they will be well balanced and easy to use. For particular jobs, such as sanding floors, you may need to hire special equipment.

Safety

As a safety precaution when using any mains-operated power tools, fit an RCCB (residual current circuit breaker). This device will cut off the power supply in microseconds in the event of a fault or accident involving a leakage of electricity to earth. After the fault is repaired, resetting the device is easy.

Electric drills and screwdrivers

Many power drills have a hammer action, which enables them to penetrate dense masonry, timber and softer metals. The action is one of pumping the drill bit back and forth to increase the bite. It can be engaged or disengaged as necessary.

Simple drills are commonly geared to provide two speeds at the chuck, but the important feature to look out for is a variable speed facility, usually operated by the trigger. As you squeeze the trigger in and out the speed alters progressively between slow (important when starting a hole) and the maximum (which can be variably set on some more expensive models).

Another common option is a reverse gear, which is most useful for screwdriving. It enables you to withdraw screws as well as drive them in.

As well as screwdriver blades, other useful drill options include circular sanding discs and wire brushes for cleaning and removing rust.

Electro-pneumatic drills, incorporating powerful hammer actions, are for tough masonry jobs. But they are large, have only a single speed and are expensive. They are best hired when needed.

Cordless drills offer convenience and are easy and safe to use outdoors. But note that they are considerably less powerful than mains-powered tools.

Power drill chucks For longer life and easy working, tighten the key in each of the three holes in turn. To remove the chuck for fitting accessories, insert the key normally and tap it smartly, but gently, with a light hammer or a piece of wood. If the chuck sticks, put the short end of a hexagonal Allen key in as if it were a drill, tighten up, and tap the key.

Electric saw

Jig saws are invaluable for general cutting of timber and sheet materials. The best jig saw will have a reciprocal blade (which cuts on both the upward and downward stroke) and blowing action to clear the cutting line of

1 Power drill

2 Masonry bit

3 Twist bits

4 Radiator cleaning bit

5 Cordless drill/screwdriver

6 Screwdriver bits and extension

7 Countersink attachment

8 Polishing pad

9 Sanding sheets

10 Rotary sanding/polishing attachment

sawdust. Scroll action is another refinement, enabling you to make tight curved cuts by turning the blade and not the whole tool.

Circular saws are useful for cutting sheet materials and timber in a straight line. These are not as versatile as jig saws – and they are considerably less safe to use. Different blades are available for cutting a variety of materials.

Electric sander

Rotary sanders are attachments for power drills. Glasspaper is fitted to a simple sanding disc or, for a better finish, a foam drum sander. A foam drum sander gives a good finish on both flat and shaped surfaces.

An orbital sander is a dedicated power tool, which drives a rectangular pad (to which the sandpaper is fixed) in small, rapid orbits. Use gentle pressure (always with both hands on the tool) to produce a smooth finish in quick time. Coarse, medium and fine grades of glasspaper are available cut specifically to fit orbital sanders. When you have completed sanding a floor with an industrial appliance, an orbital sander will give a smooth finish and is particularly useful for edges and corners of floors. Most sanders will work on wood, plastics, metals or fillers, so long as the abrasive is suited to the surface you are sanding. A random orbital sander uses circular, grip-on pads and works in eccentric movements.

Small sanders, shaped rather like little irons, are useful for fiddly sanding jobs as the pointed 'nose' can reach into corners and cope with crevices that a full-size rotary or orbital sander cannot.

Hot-air stripper

This is a convenient alternative to a blowlamp for softening and stripping old paint, particularly oil-based paint from woodwork. You can use a blowlamp which works off bottled gas, or a hot-air gun which is powered by electricity. This is more suitable near glass as there is less likelihood of damage. See p. 87 for care when using hot-air strippers and blowlamps.

Hire or buy?

Many decorating and DIY jobs can be made much easier with professional equipment, which you can hire for a reasonable charge based on the length of time you borrow the item. Charges for delivery and collection – which may be unavoidable for really heavy equipment – need to be taken into consideration, too, when calculating the cost.

For large projects of long duration, it may make better sense to buy special equipment, such as a cement mixer or platform tower. Compare retail prices with hire catalogue rates. Bear in mind that you can always sell equipment in good condition after you have finished the work.

If you have never used an item of equipment before, get as much advice as possible before starting work – especially on safety aspects.

1 **Orbital sander**

2 **Random orbital sander**

3 **Jig saw**

4 **Hot-air stripper with scraper attachment**

Steps and ladders

For all interior decorating work, having the right tools, observing basic, common-sense safety precautions and making sure that you have easy access to the work to be done are all vital considerations. Many decorating accidents inside the home are completely avoidable and are due to simple carelessness about basic points of safety.

Comfort is another important consideration. Standing on the rungs of a ladder for lengthy periods of time, for example, will soon become hard on the instep, and may result in accidents as you shift about. However, working from a solidly built, static platform surrounded by a safety rail is easy, safe and more comfortable, and better-quality workmanship is likely to result.

Using steps and ladders

- When decorating inside on steps, ensure that they are fully extended and stable. And if you are working from a ladder in, say, a high stairwell, ensure the ladder is safely anchored and that the feet are at a distance from the wall equal to about a quarter of the height of the ladder itself.

- Always wear strong shoes (not boots) with grip soles. Standing on the rungs of a stepladder in trainers will soon cause your feet to ache. When you are climbing a ladder, hold onto the rungs, not the stiles, since this makes the ladder better balanced. Carry any tools and equipment in your overall pockets, or wear a special tool-carrying belt, so that both your hands are free to grip the ladder.

- When you are painting on steps or a ladder, right-handed people should work from right to left; the opposite is the case for left-handed people. By adopting this working practice, you will always be moving the steps or ladder away from the freshly painted area.

- Never go higher than the third rung from the top of a ladder or you will have nothing to hold on to. Do not stretch too far out to reach a work area – this is both dangerous and tiring. Only work within comfortable reach and move the steps or ladder to new areas whenever necessary.

Steps It is wise to own at least one pair of steps. For indoor decorating work the steps should have five treads or more, a platform, and a grab rail. Aluminium steps are much lighter than timber ones, but are not as stable as wood.

Working platform For comfortable ceiling work there should be about 75mm (3in) between the top of your head and the ceiling. Make a platform from two pairs of steps, or a pair of steps and a stout box, with a scaffold board running between them. You can also hire trestles for the same purpose.

Staircase platform Designed to be used in confined spaces, you can hire a platform in sections for easy home assembly. Alternatively, improvise with a ladder section against the wall, and steps (or a box) on the landing, with a scaffold board running between the ladder and steps.

A dual-purpose adjustable ladder used with a scaffold board on stairs.
Note: the ladder must be tied securely to the stairs. Screw two heavy-duty metal eyes into the staircase and tie the ladder to them with strong rope or cord.

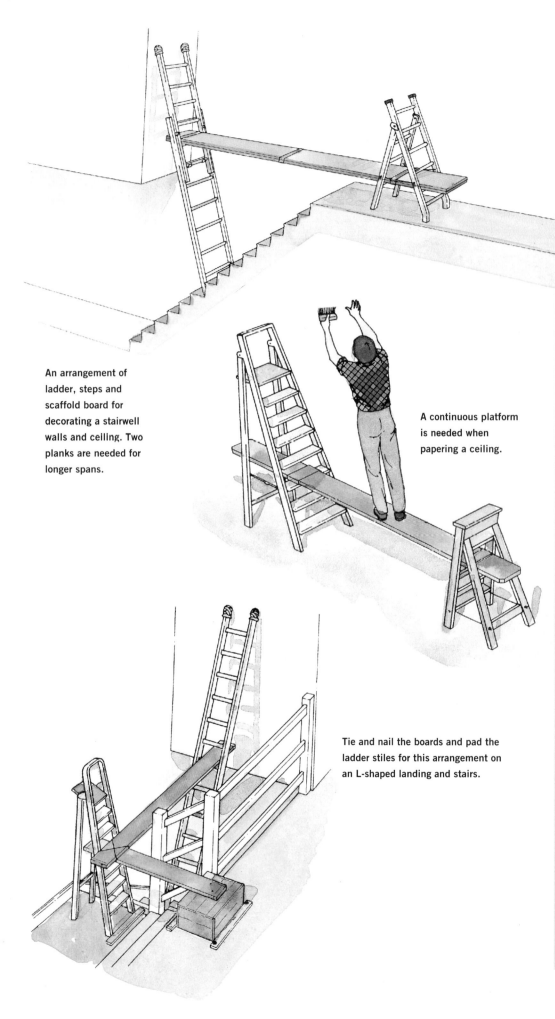

An arrangement of ladder, steps and scaffold board for decorating a stairwell walls and ceiling. Two planks are needed for longer spans.

A continuous platform is needed when papering a ceiling.

Tie and nail the boards and pad the ladder stiles for this arrangement on an L-shaped landing and stairs.

Scaffold tower

A scaffold tower is far safer and easier to work from than a ladder because it is more stable. It also provides access to a larger working area. Although a tower is used mainly for exterior jobs, it can prove just as useful inside tall rooms and, particularly, in stairwells.

Scaffold poles in many different sizes can be bought or hired and they come with very clear instructions on how they should be safely erected. Pay close attention to the details for locking sections together and double check that the frame is completely vertical. Use a spirit level and the adjustable feet to get the base frames level. Some scaffolds for indoor use come with castor-like wheels, which you must lock securely once the tower has been pushed into its correct position to prevent it shifting about.

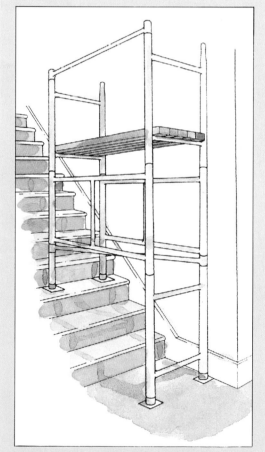

A scaffold tower can be built straight up to a considerable height for exterior work, or indoors on a staircase.

Safety at work

Using tools and materials correctly is vital not just for producing good results, but for your own safety. As well as taking common-sense precautions when doing electrical and plumbing jobs, always follow manufacturers' instructions when using power tools, or applying hazardous substances – and wear the recommended protective clothing. When using chemical products indoors, make sure that the room in which you are working is well ventilated. Once your work is finished, leave the windows open for a few hours to allow all the fumes to escape.

1 **Dust mask** 2 **Safety goggles**
3 **Respirator** 4 **Ear protectors**
5 **Heavy-duty rubber gloves**
6 **Leather gloves**

Wear heavy-duty gloves to protect against cuts when using dangerous tools and materials such as glass. PVC gloves give protection against chemicals and grease.

Ear protectors make noisy tools more bearable, and protect against damage to your hearing, and goggles and masks are vital protection for eyes and mouth.

Protective clothing

The dangers of DIY may not always be as obvious as you might think. A spinning circular saw, a blowlamp or a high ladder are self-evident hazards, but the effect of a dropped club hammer, the fumes from a tin of adhesive or the fine dust thrown up when sanding paintwork may seem hardly worth considering.

But the danger from these items can be very real. A heavy hammer falling just a short distance can break bones in a foot that is inadequately protected. A flying particle of rust or paint is like a shard of glass and can damage your eyes, while inhaling fumes from some adhesives and corrosive liquids can have serious health effects.

Wearing appropriate clothes and, when necessary, safety clothes is essential. Loose clothing, scarves, necklaces and ties are all potential hazards since they can become tangled in moving parts of machinery. If you have long hair, tie it back when using tools.

Footwear Wear safety boots with reinforced toe-caps when working with heavy building blocks or bricks – or hammers. Wear strong shoes when working from a ladder.

Gloves Wear heavy-duty industrial gloves in leather when working with dangerous tools or materials. Lighter PVC gloves protect against oils, greases and most chemicals, while natural rubber gloves – stronger than most washing-up gloves – withstand chemicals and resist tears and abrasions. Knitted gloves with a latex-reinforced palm and back are good for carrying glass and metal.

Face masks To avoid inhaling airborne particles and fumes, a dust mask or respirator is vital. The simplest mask consists of a filter holder that moulds to the shape of your face and takes a replaceable cotton gauze pad to cover the nose and mouth.

Respirators are robust, being made from moulded rubber or plastic. They have an exhalation valve and a replaceable cartridge filter that resists organic vapour and paint spraying. You have to fit the appropriate filter for the substance being used.

Safety glasses Typical jobs requiring eye protection are sanding, painting a ceiling with a textured compound, spraying paint and most metalwork tasks. Whenever you are using chemicals, make eye protection a priority.

In their simplest form, safety glasses are like standard spectacles but with impact-resistant lenses. More sophisticated versions have ventilated side protection and non-fogging lenses. Safety goggles are the most robust, with safety lenses housed in a flexible PVC frame. Gas welding goggles have a shaded lens.

Ear protectors Foam earplugs with a connecting cord for easy removal are relatively cheap and give protection against noise levels above 80 decibels. More expensive – and more effective – are ear capsules or muffs, usually mounted on an adjustable headband, with interchangeable ear pads.

Safety helmets A safety helmet is generally needed only for a sizeable DIY demolition or building project. You might prefer to hire a hard hat rather than buying one.

Overalls If you don't have old clothes to wear for painting and other work, a polypropylene suit is ideal. It protects your clothes, doesn't weigh you down and is rip-resistant. Some styles have elasticated sleeve-cuffs and deep pockets for tools and materials.

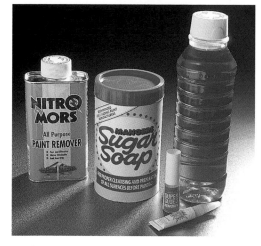

Carefully read and observe the manufacturer's safety instructions before using any product.

Chemical products

Adhesives, corrosives and other chemical products used in DIY work include many substances both harmful to the touch and capable of giving off fumes and causing dizziness and injury if inhaled. Most important of all, keep children away from these materials – which often come in bright and appealing containers and can all too easily be mistaken by a young child for something containing sweets.

Always read the warnings which, by law, appear on the packaging. Do this before you open the container, let alone start using it. Fumes arise immediately certain chemicals are exposed to the air – and if you are in a poorly ventilated space and have a particular sensitivity to any of the compounds involved, you could be putting yourself at risk.

Ventilation When recommended, open wide all the windows in the room. It is probably best to close internal doors to prevent fumes carrying to other parts of the house. Leave windows open for a couple of hours after the work is complete to make sure all the fumes have dissipated.

Volatile fumes may ignite if exposed to a naked flame, so follow the instructions to extinguish any pilot lights in boilers or stoves – and, of course, don't smoke.

Fumes permeate clothes so, when you have finished for the day, change into something clean and hang your working clothes out in the open for a couple of hours before washing them.

Superglues Cyanoacrylates, or superglues, are extremely powerful. A container can burst and squirt liquid into your face, so wear a mask and safety glasses. Familiarize yourself with the first-aid advice printed on the container in advance.

Any substance that gets on to your skin – adhesive, preservative or paint-stripper – must be washed off immediately. Hold the affected part under running water. If the irritation or pain continues later, seek medical help.

Poisoning If swallowed, some liquids can cause severe sickness, permanent disability or even death. Store all chemicals in their original containers under lock and key and out of children's reach.

Never mix different household cleaners – a chemical reaction can result and cause poisonous fumes to be given off.

Safe disposal

- Keep domestic and garden chemicals securely locked away, especially if children are present.

- Store liquids below solids so that if a bottle leaks, the liquid cannot flow onto the packets of solids and cause a chemical reaction.

- Check 'best before' or expiry dates of materials you are using to ensure they are still safe.

- Dispose of old materials through the appropriate local authority services.

- Do not throw old paint, chemicals or noxious substances into domestic household refuse, which may be collected and returned to land-fills in the earth. These substances can contribute to contamination of land, ground water, rivers and the sea through leakage or breakage. Contact your local authority for advice, if unsure.

 **Harmful**
These substances are dangerous to the skin. Irritants give off vapours or gases that are dangerous to inhale.

Toxic
This covers solids, liquids or gases that are dangerous if swallowed or inhaled, even in tiny quantities.

 **Highly flammable**
Depends on a liquid's ability to form a vapour. Nail polish remover is very flammable.

Explosive
Explosive materials such as fireworks must be stored in a cool, dry place away from naked flames.

 Corrosive
Both acids, such as vinegar, and alkalines, such as washing soda, are corrosive. Never mix the two together.

 **Oxidizing**
Hydrogen peroxide and weed killer are common oxidizers. These release large amounts of oxygen to fuel fires.

Using tools

Buying the best tools you can afford and looking after them properly is common-sense advice. There is no doubt that good tools used well will produce top-quality work. However, it does not matter how much you pay for something if you fail to use it properly. You will not produce good work and, more importantly, you may endanger or harm yourself.

Hold a saw firmly with your index finger pointing in the direction of the cut.

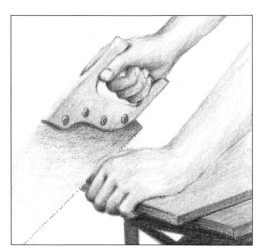

Keep a firm grip on the wood when starting, and saw gently to stop the blade jumping.

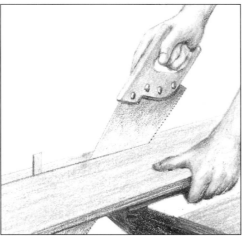

Support one side of the wood securely and always cut on the forward stroke.

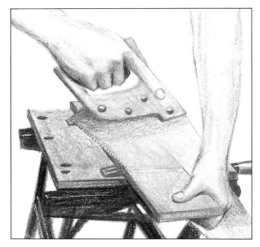

Support the offcut when close to finishing to prevent the saw suddenly breaking clear.

Cable and pipe detector

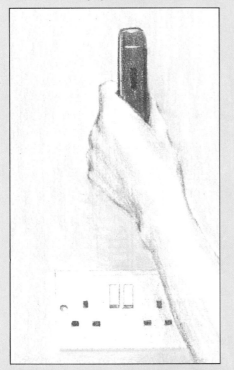

Concealing cables and pipes beneath the surface of plastered or partition walls is a neat solution. The safety rule when routing concealed cables and pipes is that they should always run either vertically or horizontally, never diagonally. This ensures that anybody making fixings into the wall in the future knows where to expect them to be.

However, unless you know for a fact where pipes and cables are, using a cable and pipe detector will prevent any nasty surprises.

Hand tools

Keep all your tools sharp, clean and in a good state of repair, and store them in dry conditions where there is no danger of rust forming on them. Bear in mind that a blunt or damaged tool, such as a saw or a chisel, is not only harder to use and will not produce top-quality results, but it is also more dangerous – both to yourself and, potentially, to anybody else in the immediate vicinity.

Whenever you are going to use a saw, first firmly secure the piece of work to a bench. Position the work so that the cutting line just overhangs the edge of the bench. This ensures that it has maximum support and also prevents the piece whipping about as you saw. Position yourself so that the saw becomes an extension of your arm, with your index finger pointing in the direction of the cut. Draw the saw gently and cleanly back and forth, cutting on the forward stroke only. Toward the end of the cut, support the offcut to prevent the saw blade suddenly breaking clear and ripping the wood. If you have to put a lot of force behind the saw in order to get it to cut, then your saw needs to be sharpened.

A craft knife is an essential part of a tool kit. Make sure that the blade is sharp and that you use the correct type of blade for the material being cut – whether it is paper, floor tiles or carpet. Remember to keep your fingers well away from the line of the cut, and do not exert too much pressure or the blade may slip sideways. Knives with retractable blades are much the safest to use, and the types that feature snap-off blades ensure that you always have a sharp edge to work with. Dispose of old blades safely by wrapping them in thick card.

Chisels can be very dangerous tools if they are blunt or misused. You should first secure the piece of work and then use a mallet to strike the handle of the chisel to take away the bulk of the wood. For the final paring away of the wood, it is best to use hand pressure only. Use the fingers of your other hand to steady and guide the blade where you want it to cut.

Always ensure the piece you are working on is clamped firmly in position when using a power saw.

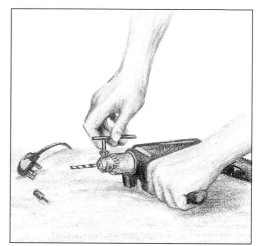

Before adjusting a power tool, unplug it from the mains. Make certain that blades and bits are correctly fitted before using it.

When chopping with a chisel, guide it between your thumb and index finger for accurate paring of the wood.

Power tools

Electric tools add power to your elbow, bringing all kinds of jobs within the range of amateur DIY enthusiasts. But beware – as well as making your life easier, they can also be lethal if not used properly.

Always keep young children and pets well away from the area in which you are operating power tools. When young children are in the house, unplug the tool if you leave the room, even if it is for only a minute or two. When carrying a power tool, never hold it by its cable – this can easily cause wiring problems resulting in an electric shock.

A few points to note are that you should always engage the safety guard when working on a power saw, and you must keep both of your hands and the power cable behind the saw's line of operation. Don't apply force to a power tool in order to speed up its operation. If you are drilling or sawing, then make sure that there is nothing underneath that may be damaged by the tool or cause damage to it.

When changing a power-saw blade or drill bit, the first rule is always to unplug the tool from the mains. A distraction at the wrong moment, such as a knock at the front door, could divert your attention and you could accidently switch it on while holding it.

If you are using a power tool above ground level, make sure that the ladder or platform is solidly positioned. If possible, enlist the help of somebody below to switch on the

power only when you are comfortably in your working position. Remember that the flex can become tangled up, causing you to fall, so never let anyone stand below you as you work.

Always make sure that your piece of work is well anchored to prevent the power tool slipping. Use workbench clamps or a vice. In other situations where clamps or a vice cannot be used, such as when you are working on a door *in situ*, for example, either close the door tight or wedge it securely open underneath to prevent it moving.

Make sure that the chisel blade is sharp and clean. Keep your guiding hand behind the leading edge so that it is out of danger if the chisel unexpectedly slips.

Working safely

- Before starting any task, ensure you have not only all the materials and tools you need, but also any safety equipment (*see p. 20–1*). It is not clever to work without masks and safety goggles, and simple gadgets such as RCCBs (*see p. 16*) can quite literally be life savers.

- When using an electric tool for the first time, understand exactly how it works and try it out first on an offcut of material to assess its power and manoeuvrability.

WIRING and PLUMBING

Wiring safety and materials

Electricity is potentially deadly, so safety is the by-word when it comes to carrying out any electrical work in the home. The following pages describe some of the most useful repairs and improvements you can make to a domestic wiring system, from connecting up a plug to making a simple extension to a lighting circuit, but it is most important that you use only the correct materials and tools when carrying out this work, and have in mind the vital common-sense do's and don'ts noted in the box below.

For clarity, the earth wires in many of the wiring diagrams on the following pages are shown as the single colour, green. The actual insulation is coloured with green and yellow bands.

The right equipment

The essentials for basic electrical work include plugs, plug-in adaptors and flexible cord (flex for short) that connects appliances to the mains, plus the cable with which all the circuits are wired up.

You will use three-pin fused 13-amp plugs and adaptors, with 3-amp fuses fitted to plugs on appliances rated at less than 690 watts. Choose tough plugs with resilient covers on portable appliances and items such as power tools.

If you cannot avoid using adaptors, never plug in more than one and double check that powerful appliances such as heaters do not overload the socket.

Always use three-core flex unless the appliance is double-insulated – it will carry the double-square symbol – or is of non-metallic construction. Always ensure the cable is of the correct rating for your particular circuit, and that all the bare earth cores are covered within electrical wiring accessories by a length of

Do's and don'ts

- **Don't** attempt electrical work unless you know what you are doing and are confident you can carry it out safely.

- **Do** turn off the main system on/off switch before starting any wiring work.

- **Don't** touch any electrical fitting or appliance with wet hands, and never take a portable appliance into the bathroom on an extension lead.

- **Do** unplug appliances before attempting to inspect or repair them.

- **Don't** omit earth connections when wiring appliances.

- **Do** double-check connections.

- **Do** warn children of the dangers of electricity, and protect them by fitting shuttered socket outlets.

- **Don't** position lights or other appliances where this means having long, trailing flexes that somebody could trip over.

- **Do** use only the correct equipment for any work you are carrying out.

green and yellow PVC sleeving. Remember never to use flex as a substitute for cable in permanent wiring situations.

Light switches and sockets are available in many different forms. The simple on/off switch – usually operated with a rocker action – is wired into a lighting circuit to control one or more room lights. Plate switches have one, two, or more individual switches, known as gangs. The basic switch with just two wiring terminals provides 'one-way' switching – making it the only control point for the light it serves. A switch with three terminals can be wired for two-way switching – linked to another switch to allow lights to be controlled from either switch.

Socket outlets are available as singles, doubles and triples, switched or unswitched. The faceplates may have neon indicators to show if the power is on. Fused connection units are used to provide a permanent flex connection for large, fixed appliances.

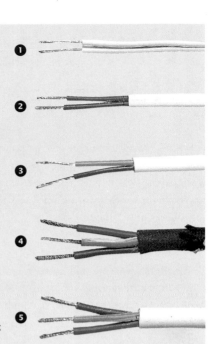

Wire types and appropriate uses

Flex, for connecting appliances to the wiring, has either two or three conductors, all insulated: brown for live, blue for neutral, and green-yellow for earth. Two-core flex is for wiring appliances without an earth terminal, such as non-metallic light fittings. Always use three-core flex where an earth connection is required.

1 Bell wire 2 Flat 2-core flex
3 Round 2-core flex
4 Fabric/rubber-covered 3-core flex
5 3-core flex

1 Cable and pipe detector
2 Insulation tape
3 Wire cutters/strippers for differing conductor sizes
4 Electrical screwdriver

5 Connector blocks 6 Cable clips
7 Circuit tester for tracing faults
8 Plug fuses 9 Fuse wire
10 400/230 volt test lamps (to test continuity) not illustrated

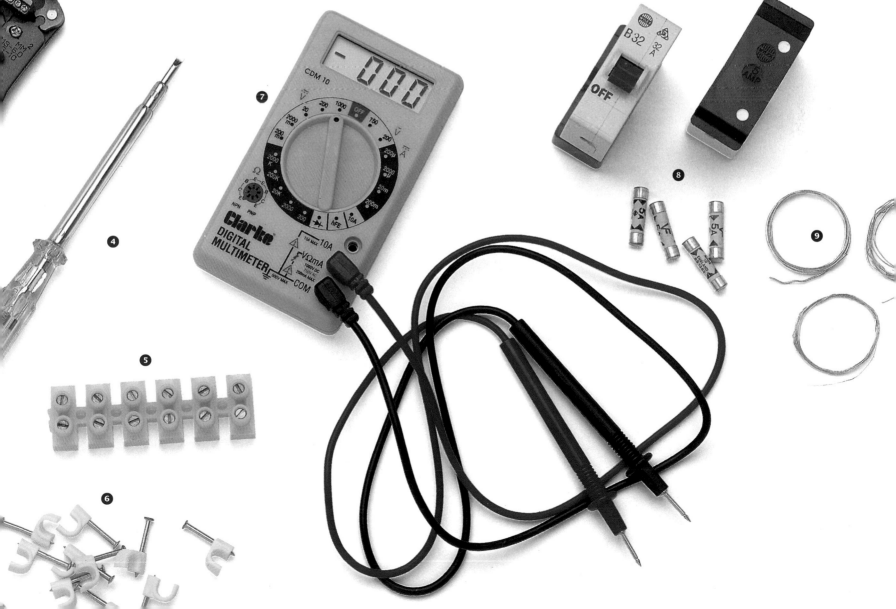

How wiring works

Knowing how electricity works makes understanding your wiring system easier. In a sense, electricity flows between two points, like water through a pipe. The force of flowing water can provide the power to make things work – to turn a waterwheel, for example. So does electricity, creating light and heat when it passes through a lamp, or rotation in an electric motor. In each case, what causes the flow is a difference in pressure between the two points.

Electricity can provide power only if it has a circuit to flow around. In the home, the circuit starts at the incoming supply cable, which contains two conducting cores. Think of the electricity as entering your home via the live core and leaving via the neutral, or phase, core. Each wiring circuit is tapped off the incoming supply, and reconnected to the returning neutral core when its work is done.

Electricity can escape from its circuit so if you touch a live conductor, electricity passes through your body to earth. This is why the wiring system is connected to earth, so that current can flow away safely if anything goes wrong.

Basic Circuits: Lighting

Lighting circuits are wired radially, the 1mm^2 cable starting at the 5-amp fuse or miniature circuit breaker (MCB), running to each lighting point and terminating at the most remote one. There are two wiring systems:

Loop-in circuits The cable loops from one lighting point to the next, with each switch cable wired into its ceiling rose or fitting. Roses have three sets of terminals. The live cores on the circuit and switch cables all connect to the centre bank. The circuit cables' neutral cores go to one of the outside terminals, as does the neutral core of the flex to the light fitting. The black sheathed core of the switch cable (tagged with red tape for identification) is connected to the other outside terminal, as is the live flex core, so that operating the switch breaks the flow of current to the light but does not interrupt the supply to the next rose in the circuit. There is a separate fourth terminal for the earth cores of both cables.

Junction-box circuits The cable runs from box to box, at each one connecting to the light, with another cable running to the switch. Each box contains four terminals, wired as in a loop-in rose: the circuit and switch cable live cores to the first terminal, the switch black sheathed core and light cable live cores to the second, all neutrals to the third and the earths to the fourth.

Spurs Both loop-in and junction-box circuits may have spurs, often to feed remote lighting points. The spur is usually connected at a three-terminal junction box, with all live cores to one terminal, all neutrals to the second, and all earths to the third.

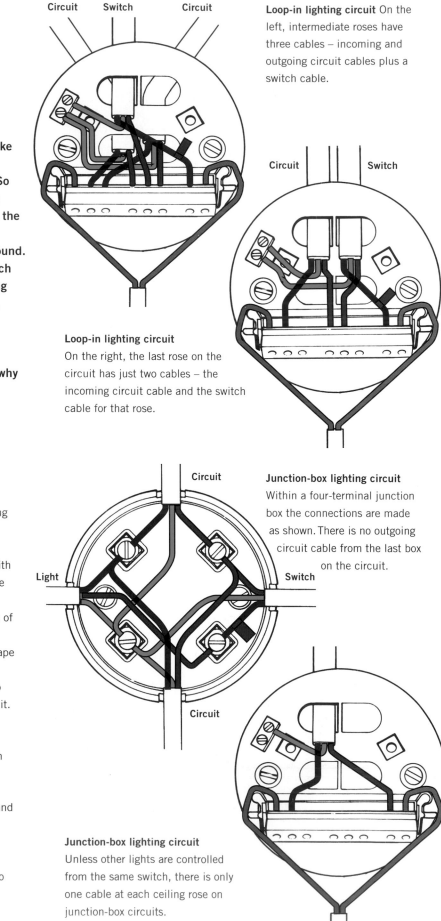

Loop-in lighting circuit On the left, intermediate roses have three cables – incoming and outgoing circuit cables plus a switch cable.

Loop-in lighting circuit On the right, the last rose on the circuit has just two cables – the incoming circuit cable and the switch cable for that rose.

Junction-box lighting circuit Within a four-terminal junction box the connections are made as shown. There is no outgoing circuit cable from the last box on the circuit.

Junction-box lighting circuit Unless other lights are controlled from the same switch, there is only one cable at each ceiling rose on junction-box circuits.

Basic Circuits: Power

Power circuits supply current to socket outlets with one, two or occasionally three sockets designed for plugs with three rectangular pins. Each plug contains a cartridge fuse designed to cut off current to the appliance if it develops a fault. Fuse ratings are usually 3-amp (colour-coded red) for appliances consuming up to 720 watts, and 13-amp (brown) for more powerful appliances. Modern power circuits are wired up in one of two ways:

Ring circuits The cable runs from the fuse round the circuit and back again, so current can flow round in either direction. Within reason, there is no limit to the number of outlets the circuit can supply, either on the main circuit or on spurs (see below). Wiring regulations state that each ring circuit should serve a maximum floor area of 100sq m (1075sq ft), and that the number of spurs should not exceed the number of socket outlets on the ring itself. Ring circuits are wired in 2.5mm² cable and are protected by a 30-amp fuse or MCB.

Radial circuits Similar to lighting circuits, these take cable from the fuse to socket after socket terminating at the most remote one. If 2.5mm² cable is used, the circuit has a 20-amp fuse or MCB and serves a maximum floor area of 20sq m (215sq ft). If 4mm² cable is used, the circuit must be protected by either a high breaking capacity (HBC) cartridge fuse or an MCB (not by a rewirable fuse) rated at 30 or 32 amps; the floor area served must not exceed 50sq m (540sq ft). Any number of sockets may be installed, and spurs may be added as long as they do not outnumber the sockets.

Spurs These may be connected to the circuit at sockets on the main circuit or via three-terminal junction boxes, rated at 30 amps, cut into the circuit cable. The spur must feed only one outlet. Cable cores are wired like to like (see illustration below).

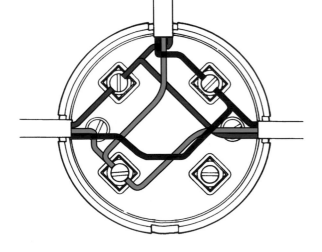

Ring or radial circuit
Spur cables can also be connected to ring or radial circuits at convenient points using 30-amp, three-terminal junction boxes. Cable cores are linked like to like.

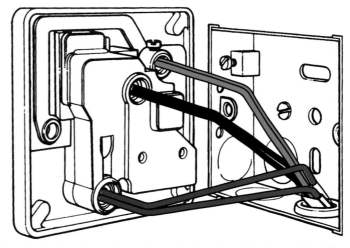

Ring circuit A socket outlet on the main ring circuit has two cables. The cores should be twisted together in pairs as shown, or may be uncut and crimped into a U-shape.

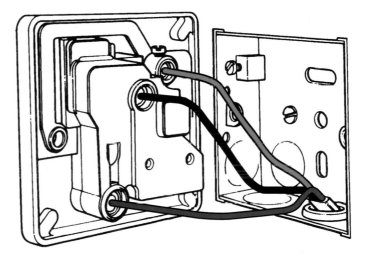

Ring or radial circuit A socket outlet supplied as a spur has just one cable. Wiring regulations stipulate that spurs may feed only one outlet.

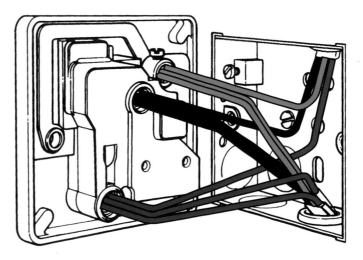

Ring or radial circuit Spur cables can be connected directly to the main circuit at a socket. There are three cables at such a socket, which can supply only one spur.

Simple wiring tasks

Two of the most basic wiring tasks that are undertaken about the home are fitting a new plug and wiring up a pendent light fitting. Although simple tasks, whenever dealing with electricity, make sure to use the right materials and make all connections firm and secure.

With post terminals, a screw secures the core.

With stud terminals, the core is held by a washer.

Snap-down terminals hold the core in place.

Wiring a plug

The plug is the all-important link between an electrical appliance and the mains and must be wired up correctly. The cores must be linked securely to the right terminals – brown to live (the fused terminal), blue to neutral and green-yellow to earth – and the cord grip securely engaged to prevent tension on the cores. The plug must always be in good condition; if it is cracked or parts of the casing are missing, it is all too easy to touch live parts as the plug is handled, with potentially fatal results. Always fit the right fuse: a red 3-amp fuse for appliances up to 690 watts, a brown 13-amp fuse otherwise.

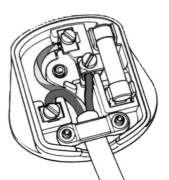

Most plugs are fitted with a bar-type cord grip. It is worth checking that these grips remain secure, as they can become loose.

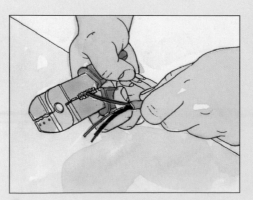

Jaw-type cord grips clamp on to the flex as the plug is closed up. They are simpler and more reliable than the bar-type cord grip.

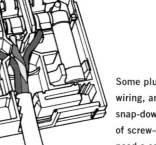

Some plugs are made for easy wiring, and are fitted with snap-down terminals instead of screw-down ones, which need a screwdriver.

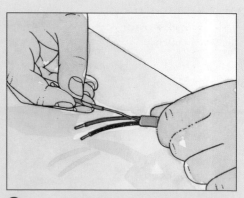

Round-pin plugs, now rarely used (a wiring system with round-pin sockets is probably in urgent need of replacement), usually have no fuse.

Stripping cable sheathing

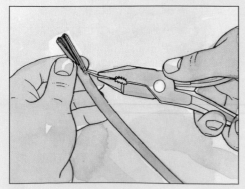

❶ To strip cable sheathing, either slit it with a knife or grip the earth core with pliers and pull this to split the PVC.

❷ Use adjustable wire strippers to remove the core insulation, with the jaw separation matching the core diameter.

❸ Before connecting the cable to a wiring accessory, always cover the bare earth core with sleeving.

Wiring a pendent light

Flex also connects pendent lampholders to their ceiling roses. Use round PVC-sheathed two-core 0.5mm^2 flex without an earth, unless the lampholder is metallic, when three-core flex with an earth must be used. For lampshades weighing more than 2kg (4½lb), fit 0.75mm^2 flex instead.

Within the ceiling rose, strip back the insulation on the flex cores to allow them to be connected to the switch live and circuit neutral terminals, and loop each core over the support hook to prevent any strain on the connections. At the lampholder, again carefully strip the cores, connect them to the lampholder terminals and loop them over the support hooks. Remember to thread the flex through the rose and lampholder cover before making the final connections.

Luminaire support couplers

These are special plug-and-socket connectors that take the place of the conventional ceiling rose. The flex from the pendent lampholder is wired to a specially designed plug that engages in the ceiling-mounted socket. This means the light can be unplugged at any time and taken down very easily for cleaning or repair, for example, or when the room is being redecorated. The circuit cables are connected to the socket part of the coupler in the same way as for a ceiling rose.

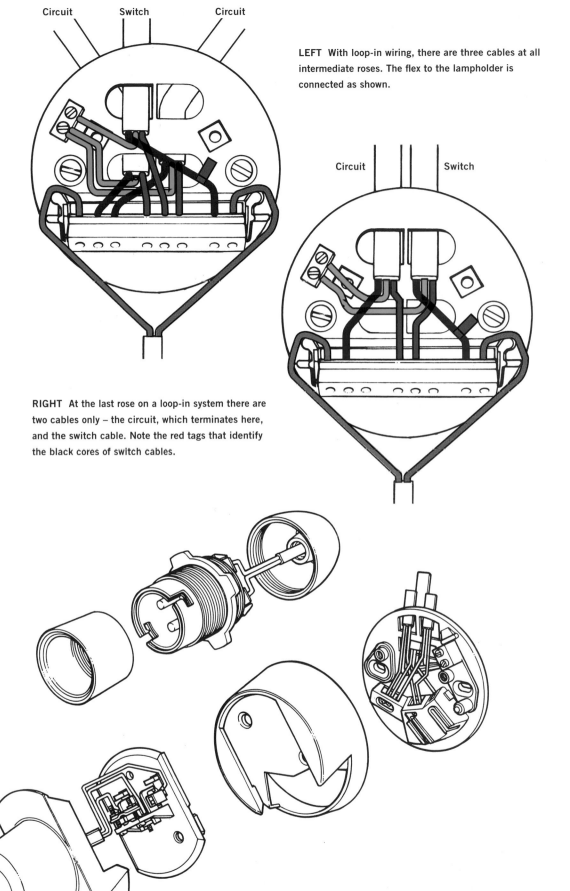

LEFT With loop-in wiring, there are three cables at all intermediate roses. The flex to the lampholder is connected as shown.

RIGHT At the last rose on a loop-in system there are two cables only – the circuit, which terminates here, and the switch cable. Note the red tags that identify the black cores of switch cables.

ABOVE RIGHT Pendent lampholders consist of a cover, the lamp socket itself and a protective shroud to shield the contacts.

BELOW RIGHT A luminaire support coupler has a ceiling-mounted socket and cover, into which a special plug carrying the flex and lampholder fits.

More simple wiring tasks

Converting existing single sockets into doubles is often a better option that using double and triple adaptors, which are not only unsightly but also potentially dangerous if overloaded. Surface-mounted sockets are extremely straightforward to install, while flush-mounted sockets require more general DIY abilities.

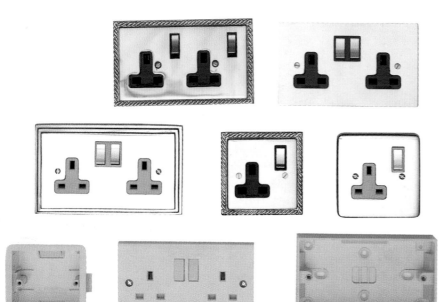

Socket outlets usually come with switches and sometimes with neon indicators, and in a range of finishes including white and coloured plastic, brass, chrome and enamelled steel.

Converting sockets

If your home has single sockets and you would like to replace one or more of them with a double, this is a relatively easy job involving no new wiring work – the power supply is simply disconnected from the old socket and reconnected to the new one, which is then fitted in its place.

Do make sure, however, that your wiring is in good condition and can carry the extra load. In older homes with radial power circuits that have not been rewired, you must not fit modern 13-amp sockets to cable that originally supplied 2-amp or 5-amp round-hole sockets. If your existing sockets are wired with rubber-sheathed cable, it may well need replacing – so seek professional advice.

If you have surface-mounted single sockets, you can simply exchange these for surface-mounted doubles with new boxes, but you may prefer to flush mount your new sockets. You will have to make recesses behind old surface-mounted sockets – or remove existing one-gang flush-boxes – to accept the new double boxes. Check first where the cable enters the box, so you do not chop through it while enlarging the hole if it enters from either side.

Carrying out the work

Once you have decided how you intend to make the changeover, buy as many new sockets and mounting boxes as you need. Check whether the earth cores within your existing sockets are covered with PVC sleeving; if they are bare, buy some green/yellow earth sleeving. Fit a length to each core as you reconnect the cables to your new sockets.

Start work by turning off the power to the circuit you will be working on. Undo the screws holding the faceplate of the first socket to its mounting box and gently ease it away from the wall. If the walls are painted, you may find the socket is stuck to the surface by paint along its edges; run a craft knife around the faceplate to minimize the risk of pulling any paint way.

Disconnect the cable cores from their terminals on the back of the single socket. The next step depends on whether the old socket was flush or surface mounted, and which option you have chosen for the new socket.

Converting single flush sockets

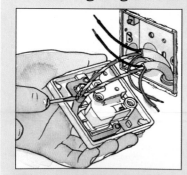

❶ Turn off the power supply to the plug. Remove and disconnect the old faceplate.

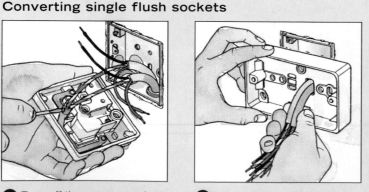

❷ Remove a knockout in the back of the new box, and draw the circuit cables into the box through it.

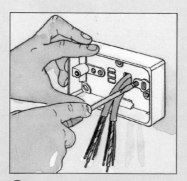

❸ Position the new box over the old flush one, and use the old faceplate screws to fix it to the lugs.

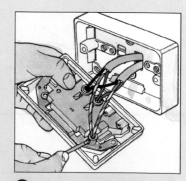

❹ Connect circuit cable cores to the new faceplate. Restore power supply. Test each socket for continuity (see p. 33).

Dimmer switches

Dimmer switches allow you to vary the brightness of the lights they control. Installing one in place of an existing switch simply involves disconnecting the switch cable and reconnecting it to the dimmer. Remember, however, that ordinary dimmers will not dim fluorescent lights; you need a special type. Also, dimmers operate properly only between a lower and upper wattage limit, so you must check that the one you intend to buy matches the wattage of the light(s) it is to control.

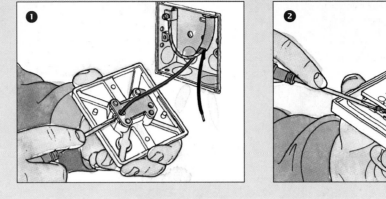

1 To fit a dimmer in place of a plate switch, turn off the power and remove the faceplate so that you can disconnect the cable.

2 After checking that the dimmer will fit the existing mounting box, reconnect the cable cores to the dimmer terminals. Restore the power supply.

Converting single flush to double sockets

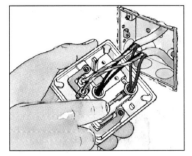

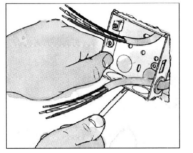

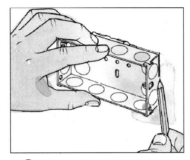

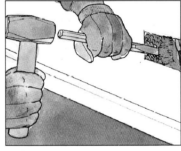

1 Turn off the power supply to the plug. Unscrew the old faceplate, then disconnect the cables.

2 Undo the screws securing the box in the recess. Then cut round it with a knife to free it and carefully ease it out.

3 Hold the new double box in position and mark its outline on the wall. Position it to avoid damaging the cables.

4 Honeycomb the masonry with drill holes. Then use a cold chisel and club hammer to enlarge the recess.

For a surface-to-surface socket conversion, unscrew the old box, remove it and fit the new one in its place after removing a knockout for the cable(s). For a flush-to-surface socket conversion, position the new socket box over the existing one and secure it in position. For a surface-to-flush socket conversion, remove the old box and make a recess in the wall large enough to take the new socket mounting box. For a flush-to-flush conversion, remove the old box and enlarge the existing recess in the same way, to take the new box. With the box conversion complete, loosen the terminal screws on the new socket, and connect the cores to their correct terminals: live (red) to the terminal marked L; neutral (black) to N and earth to E. Fit a length of green/yellow PVC sleeving over the earth core first if it is not already sleeved. Attach the faceplate.

Testing for correct continuity Always turn the plug to the off position while inserting and removing probes. Insert the negative probe of the continuity tester into the left neutral socket and the positive probe into the right live socket. The lamp should light up. Repeat with the negative probe in the neutral socket. The lamps should light up.

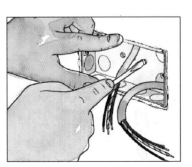

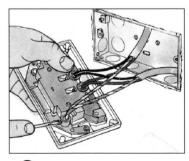

5 Remove a knockout from the flush box, fit grommets and feed in cables. Fit the box and secure it with screws.

6 Reconnect the cable cores to the terminals on the new faceplate, then secure the faceplate on its box. Restore power supply. Test for correct continuity on each socket. (*See left*)

Extending a lighting circuit

Adding one or more extra light fittings is straightforward using junction boxes – provided your wiring has the spare capacity.

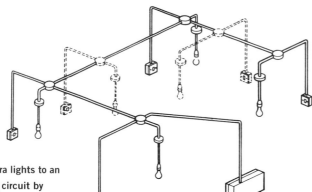

You can add extra lights to an existing lighting circuit by cutting junction boxes into the main circuit cable and running new cables to the extra light and switch.

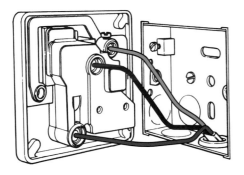

LEFT At the new one-way switch, connect the cable cores to the faceplate and box. Note the red insulation-tape tag identifying the neutral core.

RIGHT Connect the cables to the new switch and light at a four-terminal junction box.

FAR RIGHT Complete the wiring by connecting the light cable and flex at the new ceiling rose.

To supply additional light fittings, you can cut into an existing lighting circuit at a convenient point and connect the ends of the cut cable in a 5-amp junction box. You can do this in two ways.

The first is to use a three-terminal box to connect in the spur cable. You then run the cable to wherever it is needed and provide the required switching connections at that point.

The second method is to use a four-terminal box for the connection to the existing circuit cable, and connect in the switch cable for the new light in this junction box. You must connect into the circuit itself, not into switch cables or into cables running from four-terminal junction boxes to individual light fittings. Be quite sure you identify the correct cables. Switch cable from new junction boxes should have their cores tagged with red insulation tape for identification.

The second point is that you cannot extend a lighting circuit indefinitely. Each circuit on a modern system is protected by a 5-amp circuit fuse, so can supply a maximum wattage of 1200W. Each lighting point is deemed to consume 100W, so the number of lighting points is limited to 12 – though in practice it is generally no more than eight. If your circuits are already up to capacity, you have no option but to provide power for the new lights from another circuit with spare capacity.

Quartz lamps range from 300W to 1000W per fitting. It is therefore recommended that a registered electrical contractor carry out this work.

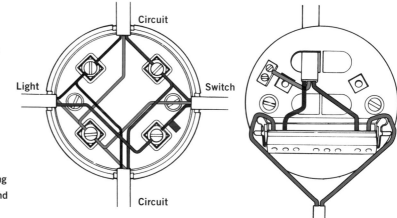

Circuit

Light

Switch

Circuit

Installing a new junction box

1 Turn off the power supply to the lighting circuit. Lay the cables to the new rose and switch, and fix a batten between the joists where you want the box to be.

2 Screw the junction box to the batten. Cut the circuit cable, prepare the cores and connect up. Prepare the light and switch cables, sleeving their earth cores.

3 Connect the new light and switch cables, and tag the switch cable's black core with red tape. Ensure all cables are secured with cable clips. Screw on cover. Restore power.

Installing new light fittings

The light fittings in many homes are nothing more adventurous than pendent lampholders hidden inside an array of decorative lampshades. However, with such a wide range of decorative light fittings now available, you can easily replace your roses and lampholders with something rather more attractive.

Wiring up a light

Some types of light fitting, such as flush-fitting lights, have a terminal block on their baseplates designed for direct connection to the lighting circuit cable. Others usually have a length of flex attached, which you have to connect to the circuit cable.

Your first step in either case is to turn off the power supply to the circuit you are working on. If you are fitting a light where none exists, run in the new supply as described previously and bring the spur cable to the point where the new light will be mounted. If you are replacing an existing rose, unscrew its cover and note how many cables are present. One cable means the light is wired from a four-terminal junction box, while two or more mean that loop-in wiring has been used. In the latter case, label the black switch cable with red tape before disconnecting the cores from the rose baseplate, so you reconnect them correctly to the new light. If there is more than one cable, the black core from the switch is a live core (the switch line), not a neutral.

Now remove the old rose. If there is just a single cable and you are mounting a fitting with an integral terminal block,

connect the cable cores to the terminal (they will be marked L for live, N for neutral and E for earth), and screw the fitting firmly to the ceiling.

Fitting a conduit box

For other wiring arrangements you need to make the cable connections in a conduit box in the ceiling. This is then concealed by the light's baseplate – some fittings are designed with screw holes at 50mm (2in) centres, allowing them to be screwed directly to the thread lugs at each side of

Assemble a new pendent lampholder in this sequence, passing the flex through the lampholder cover before connecting its live and neutral cores to the lampholder terminals.

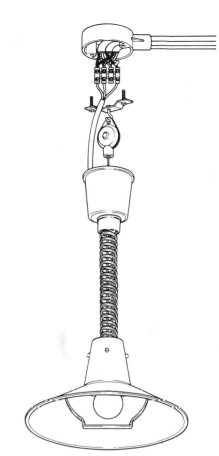

Many fittings come with a short length of flex, and you must connect this to the circuit wiring using connector blocks housed within a recessed conduit box.

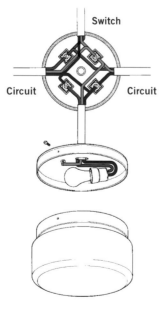

For light fittings with a built-in terminal block, run cable to them from a four-junction box, wired up as shown, and connect the cable cores directly to the fitting's terminals.

the conduit box with M4 machine screws. To mount the box, you need access to the void above the ceiling. The box should be screwed to a batten fixed between adjacent joists so that the lip of the box is flush with the ceiling surface. The batten also gives support for the light fitting itself if it is not being mounted on the conduit box. Place the batten over the desired light position, then cut a hole in the ceiling, secure the batten, and screw the box to it. Feed in the supply cable and connect it to the flex on the light fitting – red (live) to brown, black (neutral) to blue, and earth to earth – using connector blocks. If you are replacing an existing

loop-in rose, you need four connector blocks to allow for the switch cable. Link the cable cores to the flex, as shown below.

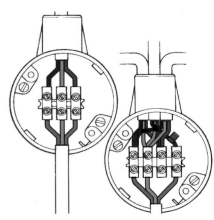

Use four-terminal connectors for loop-in wiring connections, and three-terminal connections with junction-box wiring, wired up as shown here.

Electrical problems and simple repairs

The heart of the modern wiring system is what most people refer to as the fuse box. It is more correctly called the consumer unit, however, and it comprises a one-piece enclosure housing the system's main on/off switch and the individual fuses for all the circuits in the house. In older homes, the on/off switch may be in its own enclosure, with cables running from it to separate metal fuse boxes, one for each circuit. If your system is like this, it may need rewiring – take professional advice.

Safety hints

- If you appear to have a supply fault, call your local electricity company (emergency number should be listed under Electricity in telephone directories).

- Disconnect appliances from the power supply before attempting any repair. Before inspecting wiring, make sure the relevant circuit has been turned off.

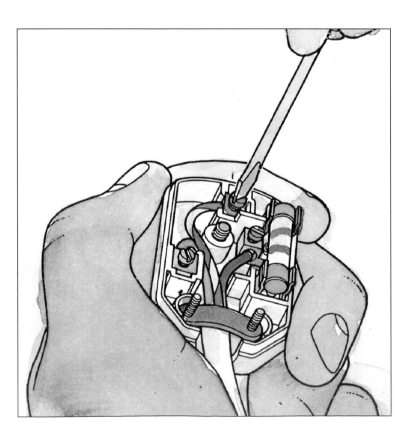

LEFT Check and if necessary remake connections within the appliance plug.

Fuses and MCBs

Inside the consumer unit is a series of fuses or, on a modern system, small switches called miniature circuit breakers (MCBs). Each of these protects an individual circuit in the house supplying lights, socket outlets and large appliances such as electric cookers.

Each fuse or MCB is rated to suit the demands of the circuit. Light circuits, for example, take relatively little current so are rated at 5 amps; power circuits take more, and are generally rated at 30 amps; cookers may be rated at up to 45 amps. Each fuse or MCB will be labelled with its current rating or colour-coded for identification.

On modern systems you may also find a separate component called a residual current device (RCD), housed within the consumer unit or in a separate enclosure beside it. This detects faults in the system and cuts off the current almost instantaneously.

Tracing electrical faults

When an electrical appliance will not work, or all the lights go out, don't panic! There is usually a logical explanation. You need to work methodically through the checklist on these pages, mentally ticking off possible causes as you eliminate them until you find the trouble.

1. Appliance fault When an appliance stops working, unplug it immediately. If there is no obvious fault – such as a damaged flex – try plugging the appliance into a socket on a separate circuit (on another floor, for example). If it works, the fault is at the original socket or on its circuit – see fault 3. If it does not work but another appliance does at the same socket, the fault is with the appliance.

Open the appliance plug and check that all the flex cores are properly connected to their terminals. Tighten or remake connections as necessary. If this does not work, replace the fuse with a new one of the correct rating.

Finally, check the flex cores using a continuity tester, and fit a new flex if necessary. If all these checks fail to find the fault, take the appliance to a service engineer.

2. Pendent light fault When a pendent light stops working and it is not simply the bulb, switch off the power to the circuit and open up the ceiling rose and lampholder to check for loose connections. Check the flex continuity between lampholder and rose with a continuity tester and replace it if necessary.

3. Circuit fault If a whole circuit fails, switch off all lights or disconnect all appliances on it. Turn off the power at the main switch on the consumer unit and replace the appropriate circuit fuse or reset the MCB. Restore the power and go around the circuit, turning on lights or plugging in appliances. Note which, if any, blow the circuit or trip the MCB, and isolate it for repair. If the circuit is still dead after you have replaced the fuse or reset the MCB, turn off the power and check circuit continuity by opening faceplates, junction boxes, and so on. Remake any faulty connections.

Where the cause of the circuit fault is obvious – perhaps you have drilled through a cable, for example – turn off the power, expose and

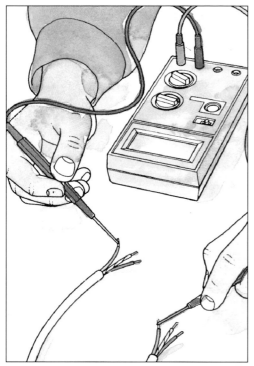

LEFT Use a test meter to check continuity in flex cores, by touching the probes to each core.

BELOW With MCBs, you cannot reset the switch until the circuit fault has been fixed.

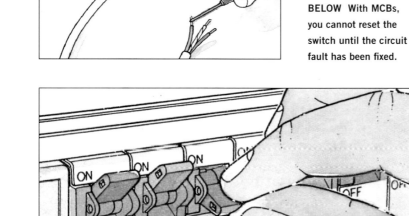

replace the damaged cable, then remake the connections inside a junction box. If your system has MCBs and you cannot reset any that have tripped to the off position, the fault is still present. Call an experienced electrician if you cannot locate it.

4. System fault If the whole house is without electricity, check with neighbours to see if there has been a power cut. Bear in mind that a single-phase supply fault may affect only one house in three, so your immediate neighbour may still have an electricity supply if it comes from another phase. Next, check your own consumer unit if you have a residual current device (RCD) protecting it, and attempt to reset it if it has tripped to its off position. If you cannot reset it, the fault is still there, and you should call an electrician. If there is no RCD fitted and the supply is still off, even if your neighbours' supply is on, then contact your local electricity company.

Replacing fuses

When a circuit fuse blows, you must either replace the wire in the fuseholder or fit a new cartridge fuse. With rewirable fuses, you must use wire of the correct rating for the circuit, so make sure that you have a supply of spare fuse wire for every power rating used in the house. *Never* repair a fuse with any other metallic object.

It is a good idea to keep a spare correctly wired fuseholder for each fuseway. This way, you can restore power immediately and then mend the fuse later. Keep a torch near the consumer unit in case the lighting circuit trips.

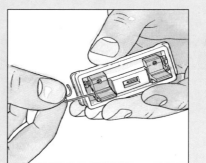

❶ If a rewirable fuse blows, turn off the power and pull out the fuseholder. Unscrew the terminals. Remove the burned wire.

❷ Thread in new wire of the correct rating and fix it to the terminals. *Never* use any other metallic object as a fuse.

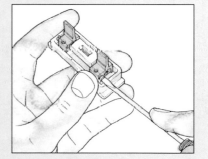

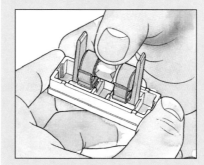

❸ With some cartridge fuseholders, the fuse is a simple push-fit. Fuses of different ratings are different sizes.

❹ Sometimes, the fuse is held between wraparound terminals, so you must dismantle the fuseholder to fit the fuse.

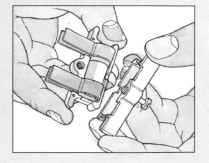

Plumbing tools

Successful plumbing is only possible with the right tools, equipment and materials – but that does not mean you have to acquire a collection anything like as comprehensive as the kit carried by a professional plumber. Most plumbers will admit, anyway, that there are a lot of tools they use only rarely. Now that these specialist tools are available for hire, and that modern fittings have done away with the need for a good many more, the essential tool kit looks relatively modest.

The main kit illustrated on the right includes the full range of tools likely to be required for most plumbing and central heating projects. For the straightforward tasks described in the following pages, however, the tools in the 'emergency' kit should be quite adequate.

The emergency kit is a basic set of tools that no household should be without. By taking on such tasks as changing a tap washer, then moving on to a more advanced job, such as plumbing in a replacement kitchen sink, you should gain confidence and discover that there is no real mystique in basic plumbing. Anybody with even modest ability should then be able to go on to collect a few more tools, and tackle some larger projects.

Emergency kit

For the sorts of plumbing problems that are likely to occur at some point, such as a burst pipe or overflowing tank, every household should have these essential tools and accessories to hand:
- Pipe repair kit
- Claw hammer
- Screwdriver with blade selection
- Tap and ballvalve washers
- Combination pliers
- PTFE tape
- Garden hose (for draining system)
- Length of wire
- Piece of rubber (an old hot water bottle does nicely)

Plumber's tool kit

The tools shown below should cover just about every eventuality. Among them are several that are needed only for very special tasks. Study your project to find out what is involved, and decide which, if any, tools you would be better off hiring.

- **Pipe cutters for copper tubing**
- **Junior hacksaw for cutting pipes in position**
- **Claw hammer**
- **Club hammer**
- **Single-slot screwdriver (medium)**
- **Single-slot screwdriver (small)**
- **Electrical test lamps**
- **Cross-slot screwdriver (medium)**
- **Cross-slot screwdriver (small)**
- **Adjustable grips**
- **Stillsons (can be hired)**
- **Blowlamp**
- **Heat-resistant mat**
- **Steel tape**
- **Flat file (small)**
- **Electric drill**
- **Masonry bits**
- **Hole saw (multibladed)**
- **Electric jig saw**
- **General purpose hand saw**
- **Open-ended adjustable spanner**
- **Bending springs (15mm and 22mm)**
- **Spirit level (small)**
- **Sink plunger**
- **Combination pliers**
- **Crowsfoot basin spanner**
- **Radiator valve key**

Some tools such as the power jig saw and hand saw might perform many of the same tasks. However, if you are cutting a hole in a worktop, for example, the jig saw will be indispensable (though you might only wish to hire one for the purpose).

Accessories

There are several items and materials that should form part of your basic plumber's kit alongside the tools. These include:

PTFE (Polytetrafluoroethylene) tape A non-sticky film used for winding round and sealing threaded joints.

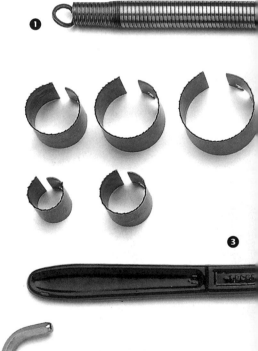

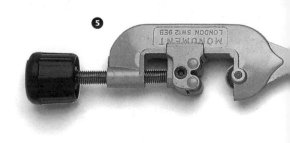

1 Bending spring 2 Multiblade hole cutter attachment for electric drill 3 Adjustable grips 4 Skeleton gun and silicone sealant 5 Copper pipe cutter 6 Basin wrench or spanner 7 Boss blue 8 PTFE tape 9 Radiator valve key 10 Immersion heater spanner

Boss blue A sealing compound approved for use on drinking water supplies. It is a useful standby for troublesome joints.

Lead-free solder Used for end-feed fittings. Solder ring fittings already have solder in them and do not require extra.

Flux A paste used to help solder run easily around a joint when it is heated with a blowlamp.

Steel wool Used to polish copper pipe before it is soldered.

Silicone sealant (Fernox XLS) Used for sealing pressure joints and a variety of emergency repairs.

Silicone lubricant Used on push-fit rubber seals.

Pipe freezing kit To isolate a point in the pipe in order to make an emergency repair, a freezing spray is used to solidify the water temporarily. This saves having to drain the whole system.

Hire tools

The range of tools available for hire is constantly expanding, so it is worth checking what is on offer at your local hire shop. Listed here are some of the tools that make plumbing projects easier.

If you have never used a particular tool before, make sure you are certain about how it works. This is extremely important when you are using electric tools that are more

powerful than you are used to. Always wear recommended safety items, such as eye protection and a dust mask.

Pipe benders The hand-held model bends 15mm and 22mm pipe only.

Immersion heater spanner For removing or fitting immersions into cylinders. Never use a wrench for this.

Drain-unblocking equipment Hiring rods can be very much cheaper than calling in a specialist firm.

Electric rotary hammer This can be used as a breaker or, with a change of bit, as a powerful hammer drill for drilling through masonry for pipe runs.

Blowlamp Used for soldering work.

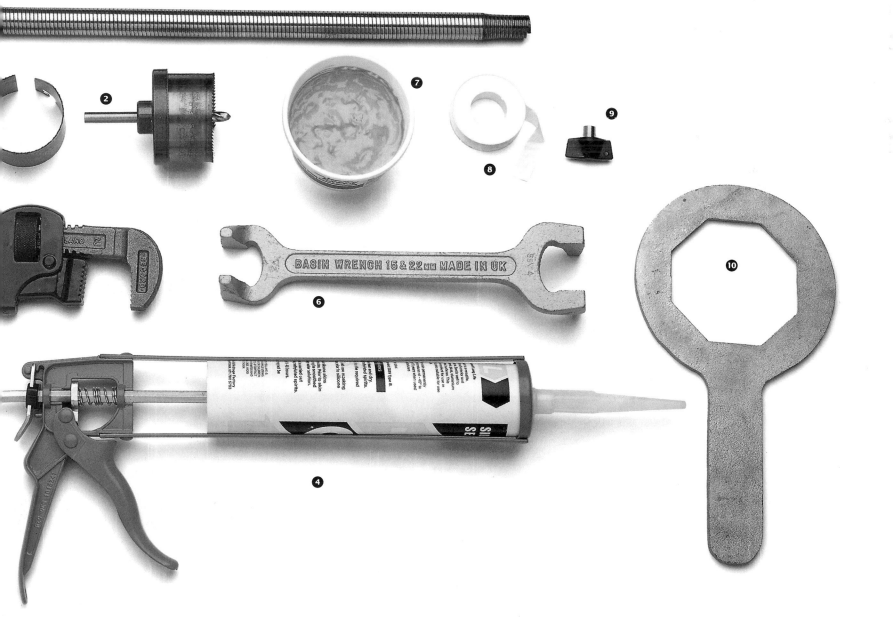

Understand your system

The pipes supplying water and heating to a house are often a complete mystery to those living there. But you should at least know where the main stopcock is. Having some idea of the water supply's and heating system's workings will certainly help you to deal with any professionals you may call in – and perhaps save you from being deceived into believing a job is more expensive than it really is.

The mains supply

The service pipe brings water in from the main in the road. The short section of pipe from the road main to the water company's underground stopcock on or near your boundary is their responsibility. From that point on, the pipe belongs to the property owner. Any leaks in that section must be repaired by the householder.

Modern service pipe is made of medium-density polyethylene (MDPE), which can be used to replace sections of old pipe. Adaptors are available to join all types of old pipe, including lead, galvanized iron and copper.

Under present regulations, pipe should be laid 75cm (30in) deep, but in the past pipes were sometimes installed only 30cm (12in) from the surface – so you may come across one when digging. If you are unsure about the exact location of the pipe, ask your local water authority.

Leaks

Suspect a leak in the underground pipe if you hear a rushing noise from the internal plumbing when you are not using any water in the house.

The service pipe enters the building through the foundations and comes up

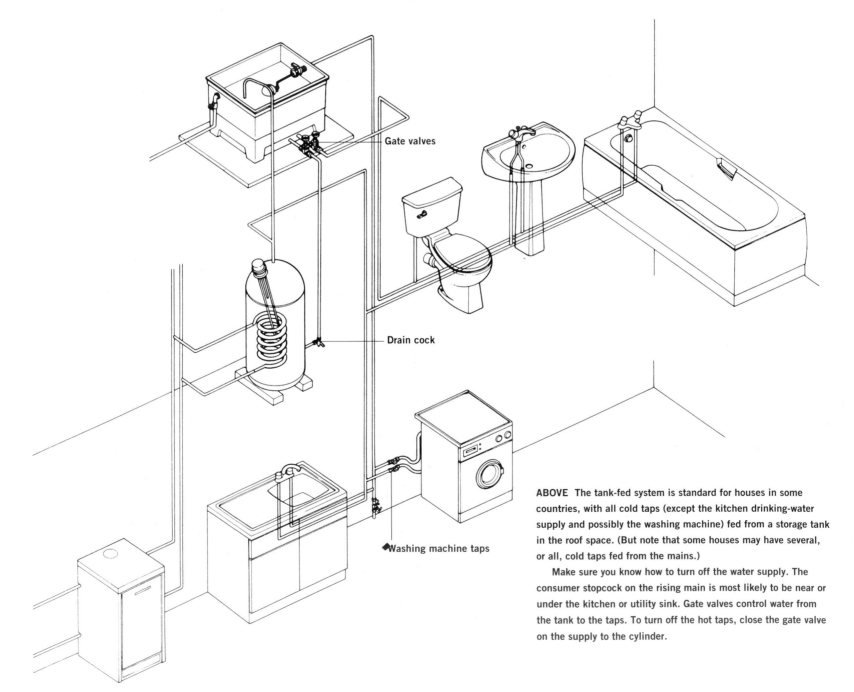

Gate valves

Drain cock

Washing machine taps

ABOVE The tank-fed system is standard for houses in some countries, with all cold taps (except the kitchen drinking-water supply and possibly the washing machine) fed from a storage tank in the roof space. (But note that some houses may have several, or all, cold taps fed from the mains.)

Make sure you know how to turn off the water supply. The consumer stopcock on the rising main is most likely to be near or under the kitchen or utility sink. Gate valves control water from the tank to the taps. To turn off the hot taps, close the gate valve on the supply to the cylinder.

BELOW The mains-fed system, usual in flats, is supplied from a main rising under, or close to, the sink, controlled by a consumer stopcock. The cold water goes direct to all cold taps and to a multipoint water heater, which in turn supplies all the hot taps.

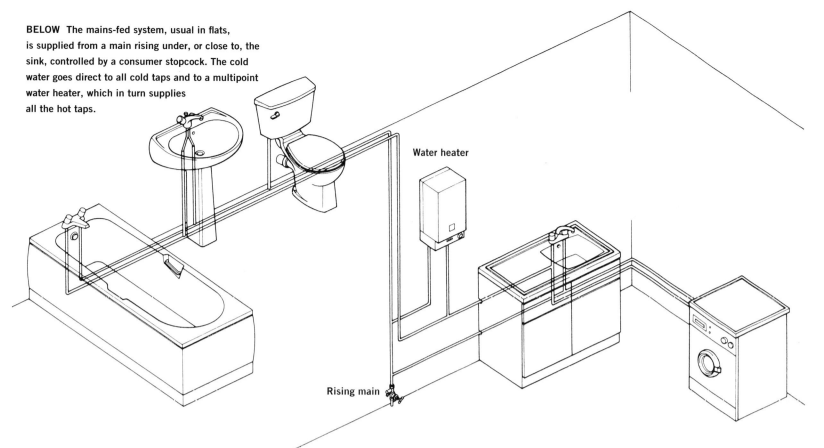

Water heater

Rising main

through the floor to a stopcock. This is the most important shut-off point and should always be accessible. Make sure you and everyone else in the house knows were it is.

Tank-fed system

The most common system in some countries is the indirect one. Apart from the kitchen cold tap and perhaps a washing machine, which are supplied direct from the mains, all taps are fed from a large storage tank.

The water going into the tank is controlled by a ballvalve, which shuts off the supply when the level is high enough. The tank, being higher than the plumbing outlets, provides a constant pressure or 'head' for the taps and toilet cistern.

Water pressure is governed by the height of the cold water tank, and this is therefore a critical factor when it comes to installing a shower. If space allows, the tank can be raised up on a strong platform in the roof space to improve water pressure.

Another factor affecting the flow of water to the taps is the condition and size of the pipes. If the pipes are badly scaled or corroded, the effective bore could be

dramatically reduced. Airlocks or spluttering can result if the hot water cylinder is not replenished fast enough by the feed from the cold tank, possibly due to a build-up of scale or corrosion.

The hot taps are fed via a copper cylinder, which may be heated by a boiler or an electric immersion heater.

The cold water enters the cylinder at the bottom and, because it is fed by the higher tank, maintains a constant pressure in the cylinder. As the water is heated, it rises inside the cylinder, so the hottest water is always at the top. A feature of this system is the cylinder vent, which must remain open to act as an escape route for air and overheated water.

The fact that water finds its own level is used to advantage in this system. Usually, the water in the vent pipe will rise and fall with the water in the storage tank. It is only when a thermostat fails that the water in the vent pipe rises over the top and gushes into the tank. If this happens, the water heater must be turned off immediately. Do not close any valves and run water through the hot taps to cool things down.

Insulate all pipework in the loft against the cold. A frozen vent and cold feed can cause a cylinder to collapse or explode.

Mains-fed system

This system is often used in flats, where no stored water can be accommodated. The incoming water is controlled by the consumer stopcock, which shuts off both the hot and cold water for the flats.

Cold taps, the washing machine, toilet and cold supply to the shower are fed from the mains. Isolating valves should be incorporated for servicing appliances without the need to shut off the water to the building.

The hot water is supplied through a gas-fired multipoint instantaneous water heater or, in more recently built or converted flats, an unvented cylinder.

Any shower should contain its own flow stabilizers. A non-return valve (which is also known as a double-check valve) must be fitted on a flexible shower hose if there is any possibility that the shower head may be under water. This is to prevent the contamination of the mains drinking water through back siphonage.

Emergencies and repairs

When water starts pouring through the ceiling, it is tempting to panic and to call in a 24-hour emergency plumber, who may or may not come at all, let alone in time to prevent the drama turning into a crisis. Whatever the case, it obviously makes sense to be able to cope with the first stages of such an emergency yourself, and perhaps to carry out a temporary repair that will save the situation until you can call in a reliable professional at a more regular hour.

Stopping the flow

The conventional ways of stopping water flowing through the pipes are shown on the left, but stopcocks and gate valves are notorious for not working when you need them to. If they don't, here are some alternative methods of stopping the water.

1 Use a bottle cork in the cold tank outlet to stop the water.

2 Drain the tank through the taps and turn off the cold supply at the main stopcock.

3 If you need to empty a tank because a gatevalve has jammed closed, use a hosepipe to siphon the water out.

4 If you cannot turn off a supply to a ballvalve, place a piece of timber across the tank and tie the arm to it with strong string – or hammer a nail into an overhead rafter and tie it up to that.

5 If an indoor stopcock will not stop the water, turn off the supply at the water company's stopcock at your property's boundary. If you do not have a suitable key, you can make one from a length of stout wood, cutting a V-notch in one end for tap-head stopcocks.

6 For square-head stopcocks, use a piece of steel pipe made slightly oval at the end to squeeze over the spigot.

Dripping taps

Before carrying out any work on taps, turn off the water supply. Most dripping taps can be cured simply by fitting a new washer. If this fails, it is likely that the brass seating inside the tap is damaged. You can buy plastic push-in seatings or grind the existing brass with a special tool. If the taps are old and worn, it may be time to think about fitting new ones.

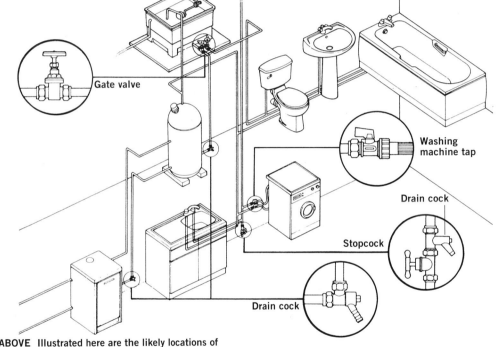

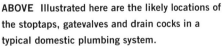

Gate valve

Washing machine tap

Drain cock

Stopcock

Drain cock

ABOVE Illustrated here are the likely locations of the stoptaps, gatevalves and drain cocks in a typical domestic plumbing system.

Pipe-freezing kit

Pipe-freezing kits are useful for stopping the water if there is no other way. If you use them for routine jobs, such as renewing radiator valves, make sure you have all the necessary tools and materials to hand before you start.

For emergency work, flatten the pipe with a hammer or stop the flow with a push-fit cap. Wrap the freezer muff around the pipe and insert the nozzle into the muff. Make sure there are no gaps at the top and bottom where freezant may escape. Protect your fingers from chemical burns. Give the recommended number of squirts. There is no point in overinjecting, because the pipe can only absorb at a certain rate. Wait several minutes until you hear ice forming inside the pipe, then gently release the stop end or open up the pipe. If water starts to flow, stop it immediately and give another spray or two. Wait for a few more minutes, then try again.

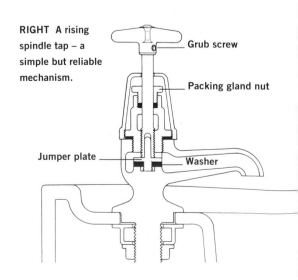

RIGHT A rising spindle tap – a simple but reliable mechanism.

Grub screw

Packing gland nut

Jumper plate

Washer

Rising spindle tap

The older style tap has a spindle in the middle that rises as it is turned on. If water is coming out through the top of the tap around the spindle, it means the 'gland packing' has worn. It is simple to cure once you have removed the shroud and handle.

If the tap only needs rewashering, it is not essential to remove the shroud, provided that you can get a spanner underneath it to undo the head gear.

1 Always put the basin or sink plug in to prevent small screws from being lost.

2 Remove the small grub screw from the tap head and then lift the head off.

3 If the tap head is jammed, turn the tap to full on and undo the shroud. Place an open-ended spanner under the shroud and turn the tap to off. The tap head should lift off as it closes down.

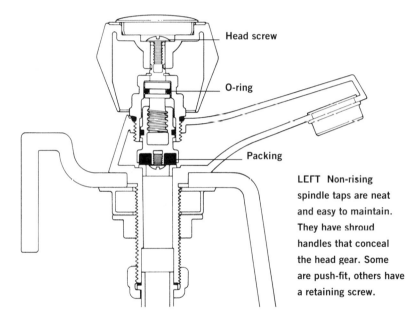

Head screw

O-ring

Packing

LEFT Non-rising spindle taps are neat and easy to maintain. They have shroud handles that conceal the head gear. Some are push-fit, others have a retaining screw.

Non-rising spindle tap

There are two types of non-rising spindle taps: conventional washered types, and quarter-turn ceramic disc taps, which never need rewashering. Rewasher conventional ones as for rising spindles.

Modern quarter-turn taps are fitted with ceramic discs that are claimed never to wear out. But it has been known for drips and dribbles to occur – and the only cure is to replace the cartridge. Manufacturers will usually supply replacements parts. Be sure to ask for the correct side, since they are left- and right-handed.

Supa taps

These can be rewashered without turning off the water. You need a special washer and combined jumper plate. Since the sizes have changed, take the old one along as a pattern.

To remove the washer, hold the nut at the top of the tap with an open-ended adjustable spanner and turn the tap as if you were turning it on. The spout will come away and, apart from a gush, the water will be sealed by a self-closing valve. Tap the antisplash nozzle on a hard surface and the washer will come out.

Replacing a washer

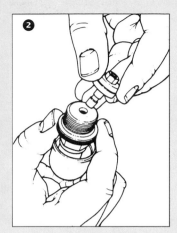

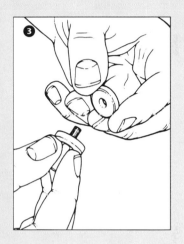

1 Loosen the head of the tap and remove it. There should be no need to dismantle the shroud.

2 Remove the old, worn washer from the end of the jumper plate.

3 Finally, push the new washer into place and reassemble the tap.

To renew gland packing

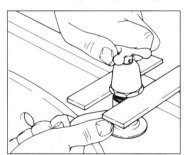
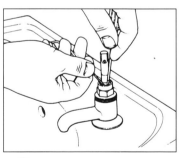

1 Free a tight rising spindle handle first, by turning the tap to on and undoing the shroud. Then place an open-ended spanner or any other supporting item under the shroud and turn the tap to the off position. The tap head should then lift off quite easily as it closes down. Undo the gland nut at the top of the spindle and slide it off.

2 Pull some PTFE tape into a string or alternatively use special impregnated packing material, wrapping it round the spindle and pushing it down into the tap with the blade of a small screwdriver as you go. Lubricate the thread with some silicone jelly before refitting the gland nut. Make sure that you do not overtighten the gland nut.

Heating systems

If anything, a leak in a 'wet' central heating system is even more daunting to deal with than a leak in the domestic water supply. Today's heating systems rely on a pump to propel extremely hot water around the system at considerable speed. A burst pipe in such a system can lead to a dramatic spout of water, possibly including a quantity of sludge that has built up in the pipes – which will do very little to improve the appearance of your interior décor.

ABOVE To drain a central heating system, attach a garden hose to the main drain cock near the boiler or on the lowest radiator in the system. Open the valve with a key or with an adjustable spanner.

Fixing a damaged pipe

The most likely cause of a disaster such as a leaking central heating system is accidentally driving a nail through a floorboard into an unanticipated pipe. However, there may be other causes – a joint may have given way, for example, or, in a roof space, a pipe may have burst due to freezing. But now that the worst has happened, what do you do to minimize any further damage?

The first step is to switch off the heating system immediately, and then make sure that only you – and not the time clock or the thermostat – can turn it back on again.

To prevent the leak simply drawing on more and more water, the second step is to close the main water feed to both the heating system's feed and expansion tanks. Either shut the feed valve on the mains, if there is one, or tie the float arm to a piece of wood spanning the tank so that the ballvalve is closed.

Next, investigate the cause of the leak. If it is a punctured pipe, don't pull out any offending nail, since this could make the situation worse by producing an even larger puncture. Instead, lift the adjacent floorboard to gain better access to the damaged area, and then try to manoeuvre a baking tray, or any other receptacle, under the breached pipe to collect the water.

If you can gain access to the pipe, hammer it flat, either side of the leak, to stop any residual flow of water.

Once you have stanched the flow of water, you can set about making a permanent repair to the pipe. You must first close off the flow, either by draining the system or by freezing the pipe (above the leak), for long enough to

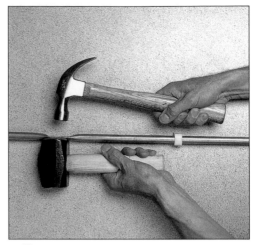

❶ With the pump turned off, stop the flow of water by hammering the pipe flat on either side of the leak.

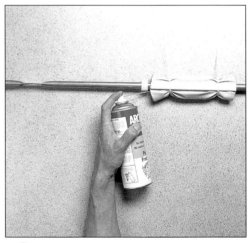

❷ Use a pipe-freezing kit to form an ice plug upstream of the burst. (*See p. 42 for the technique.*)

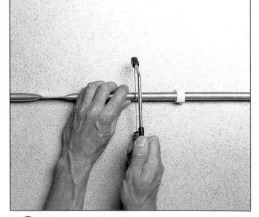

❸ With a small hacksaw, cut through the pipe next to the ice-plugged section, either side of the leak.

Home heating repair kit

One of the most common problems with a central heating system is a burst or damaged pipe. The first priority is to stop the flow of hot water to the leaking section. This will prevent any further damage to walls and carpets from the hot water. The next stage, replacing the damaged section of pipe, is reasonably straightforward (*see right*). You will need:

- Pipe cutters for copper tubing
- Junior hacksaw for cutting pipes in position
- Claw hammer
- Club hammer

- Pipe-freezing kit
- Wire wool
- Plastic pipe connectors
- Tape measure

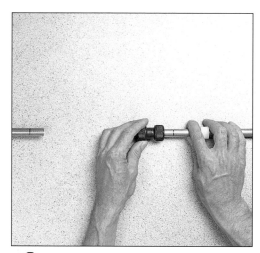

4 Clean the pipe ends with wire wool and fit the hand-tightenable plastic connectors to both ends.

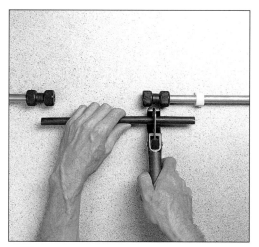

5 Carefully measure up the length of replacement pipe needed, cut it to size and smooth the ends.

6 Slip the replacement pipe into place and tighten up the connectors. Remember to fit the earthing strap.

effect a repair. (*See p. 42 for hints and tips on using a pipe-freezing kit.*) To drain the system, find the primary draincock, which will be either at the base of the boiler or nearby at the lowest part of the central heating return pipe. You simply attach a length of garden hose to the draincock's outlet, open the valve and drain the water into a gully. You will have to open the radiator air vents, starting at the highest point in the house and working downward, to prevent water being held inside by vacuum.

Replacing a section of pipe

To make a permanent repair to a burst copper pipe, the damaged section must be cut back to a sound length and replaced. Copper pipe that has been frozen is likely to be enlarged to a considerable degree, and you may have to cut it back further than you envisaged. The only way to tell is to keep cutting and trying until you reach a section that will accept the new joints.

Repair kits come in all shapes and sizes to tackle a variety of pipes and situations. No single repair kit will cope with all types of burst, so it helps to have the basic tools and then improvize as necessary.

Leaking radiators

Sudden leaks sometimes occur in radiators as a result of corrosion. The only safe long-term solution is to replace them with new ones. In the meantime, however, it is possible to continue to use the central heating system if you can isolate the leaking radiator.

To do this, turn off the handwheel valve on one side of the radiator. On the other side you should find the lockshield valve, which is basically the same as the one you have already turned off except it has a different head. If a screw is fitted in the plastic head, undo the screw first then pull the head up and off.

Turn the valve spindle using a pair of pliers or by substituting the other head. Pencil on the skirting board the number of turns it takes to close so it can be reopened by the same number later (this is important as the flow-rate into the radiator is crucial to the correct functioning of the central heating system).

ABOVE Isolate a leaking radiator by closing both valves. Once the radiator has been taken out of service, you should still be able to use the rest of the system until the fault is corrected.

Heat-saving tips

- A central thermostat maintaining all the individual room radiators at the same temperature is wasteful if you have little-used rooms in the house. In these rooms, fit thermostats to each radiator so that they can be set to a more modest background heat.

- Make sure all central heating pipes are lagged to stop heat being wasted.

- Reflective foil on the wall behind each radiator will reflect extra heat back out into the room.

Tanks and ballvalves

The ballvalves that control water flow into toilet cisterns and storage tanks can be the most troublesome of all plumbing fittings. Despite a number of recent improvements, the perfect design is still in the future. Few households escape the symptom of the dripping overflow – and if this tell-tale warning is ignored, in the hope that it will go away, the result may be a full-bore gush of water requiring urgent action.

The first place to look for the cause is a worn washer, but if replacing this does not cure the problem, look for wear, scale, grit, a leaking float or hair-line cracks in the nylon seating.

Most minor problems can be solved with a few tools and little know-how, but if the valve is old and worn it is usually better to replace it. This is usually straightforward, as long as the union is compatible.

Checking the float
Check the float by shaking it. Any sound of water means there is a leak. Replace it by unscrewing it from the end of the float arm and fitting a new one of the same size.

Removing the ballvalve
Working on a ballvalve is a lot more convenient if you remove the whole assembly first by undoing the union nut. It can then be examined for any other defects, such as blockages, scale and a damaged seating. If the fibre sealing washer has perished, fit a new one before replacing the valve. If the valve is badly worn, fit a new one on the old union.

Types of ballvalve
There are three main groups of ballvalves in general use.

Portsmouth Made mostly of brass and used in storage tanks and toilet cisterns, these are found in older homes, and are now obsolete. Replace them during routine maintenance – before they fail. In a hard water area, change the complete valve, not just the washer. Turn off the water (*see* **1**), undo connection to water pipe, undo clamping nut, remove valve, insert new valve, tighten clamp nut, reconnection to water pipe.

The high-pressure type is used on the mains, the low-pressure on tank-fed supplies. The water flow is controlled by a piston that holds a small rubber washer against a seating. If it becomes worn or damaged by grit, the replaceable seating can be a cause of overflows.

New type (British Standard Part Two)
The improved standard design now fitted on new installations to comply with current regulations has no moving parts in contact with the water and it is, therefore, less likely to suffer from hard water scale. The overhead discharge tube also means that there is less risk of the outlet becoming submerged – a potential hazard if stored water comes into contact with mains drinking water. Rewashering is also easier and can often be carried out without tools of any description.

Torbeck/hush-flow This plastic valve is fitted on some makes of toilet, as it is almost silent in use. It is available as a side entry or standpipe fitting, depending on where the water enters the cistern. The float arm has a tiny rubber washer on the end that blocks a small weep hole in the front of the valve. This then forces the water to return on itself and close the valve washer by water pressure alone. Inside the valve is found a fine gauze filter, to prevent dirt from damaging the delicate mechanism.

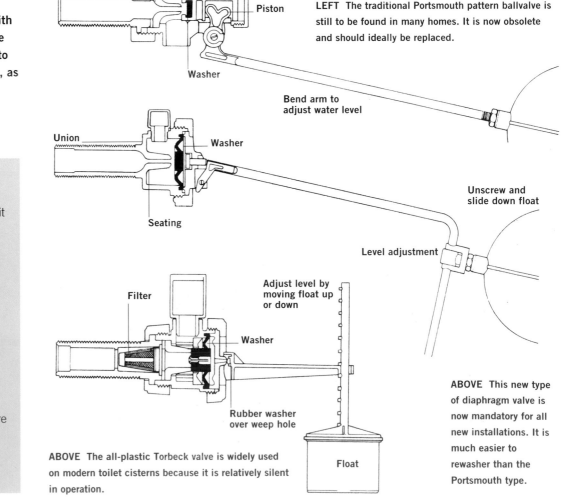

LEFT The traditional Portsmouth pattern ballvalve is still to be found in many homes. It is now obsolete and should ideally be replaced.

ABOVE This new type of diaphragm valve is now mandatory for all new installations. It is much easier to rewasher than the Portsmouth type.

ABOVE The all-plastic Torbeck valve is widely used on modern toilet cisterns because it is relatively silent in operation.

Leaking tank

A leaking galvanized tank should be replaced as soon as possible with a new lightweight polythene tank, but since this is a fairly large project, a temporary repair might be needed until you can manage the whole job.

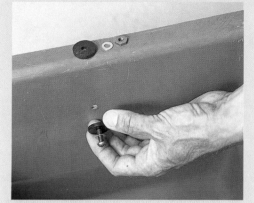

1 Drain the tank. Plug a hole by drilling through and inserting a bolt with rubber and metal washers on either side.

2 Use two-part epoxy resin putty-type sealants to make temporary repairs in awkward corners.

3 If the leak is near to the top of the tank, bend the ballvalve arm down to keep the water level below it.

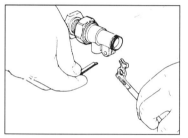

Portsmouth valve
1 First, turn off the water supply. Unscrew the end cap nut and remove the split pin, so that you can lift the float arm away from the valve.

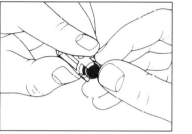

2 Remove the piston and unscrew the section with the washer, using a pair of grips. Push out the washer. Fit a new one and clean off any limescale from moving parts before reassembling the valve.

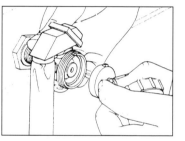

Torbeck valve
1 Unscrew (anticlockwise) the large nut on the front of the valve and gently pull away the whole front assembly, complete with float arm.

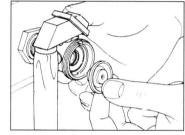

2 Remove the valve washer (note how it fits over the steel pin). Clean the gauze filter, fit a new Torbeck washer, and reassemble. Hold the float down to discharge air from the supply pipe.

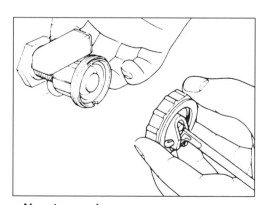

New type valve
1 Unscrew (anticlockwise) the large knurled nut visible on the front of the ballvalve. You can now remove the float and arm intact.

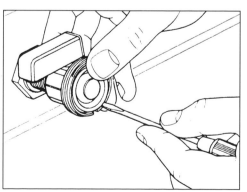

2 Very carefully ease out the large black washer now visible in the front of the ballvalve. Use a small screwdriver for this if necessary.

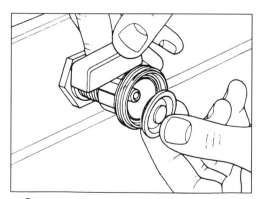

3 Fit an identical new washer in place, ensuring that the new washer is facing into the valve the same way around as the one it replaces.

Making joints in pipework

The level of skill needed to join and bend pipes is much less than it used to be. Once the techniques have been mastered, a whole range of projects is suddenly opened up.

It is best to gain confidence on a smaller project, such as fitting an outside tap. Provided the instructions are followed, perfect leak-free joints should be achieved every time.

If a joint does leak, don't just smear sealants around fittings – look to see what is wrong. Water can run down pipes and drip from the outside of sound fittings. If this is difficult to see, wrap tissue around the pipes and fittings and wait to see where the signs of moisture show.

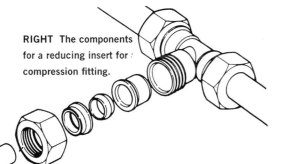

RIGHT The components for a reducing insert for a compression fitting.

Compression joint

Compression joints

Brass compression joints can be used on metal or plastic pipework. The joint is formed by the compression of a brass or copper ring around the pipework as the nut is tightened. If the joint needs dismantling, you simply undo the nut.

Preparation

With all joints, preparing the pipe end is important. If joining to an existing pipe, remove all surface traces with emery cloth. If plastic pipe is involved, push a metal stiffener into each end of the pipe.

Reducing inserts

The reducing insert is a kit that replaces the existing ring in the compression fitting and makes it possible to fit a smaller pipe. This can save time and trouble, especially if you find a fitting unsuitable.

Since the seal is brass against brass, smear a little sealant around the inside mouth of the fitting before assembly.

The reduced end is like a standard compression fitting and the pipe can be inserted in the usual way.

Solder joints

These copper fittings, which carry their own solder in rings just behind each opening, are the preferred way of making joints in domestic water and heating systems. They do require heating with a blowlamp, which can be hazardous in confined spaces. For small jobs, such as connecting a new sink or replacing a leaking joint, compression joints are probably more practical.

Preparation

Pipework must be dry, and pipe ends and the insides of fittings must be shiny and free of burrs. Polish away any tarnish with steel wool.

Flux

This helps the solder run evenly round the joint. Self-cleaning flux avoids the need for polishing, but it does no harm to clean anyway. Apply the flux sparingly with a small brush (not your finger) around the inside of the fitting and the outside of the pipe. Clean the pipe and joint of any excess flux with a damp cloth.

Assembly

When assembling the joint ensure that the pipes go right up to the internal stops. Then heat each end with the blowlamp until a continuous ring of solder appears around the fitting's mouth. Leave the joint to cool. If it leaks, drain, reclean, reflux and reheat. Extra solder can be melted on the hot end.

Safety

When working with a blowlamp, protect all inflammable surfaces with a heat-resistant mat and keep both a bucket of water and a fire extinguisher handy. If you burn your hand, plunge it in cold water and keep it there until the pain goes. For anything other

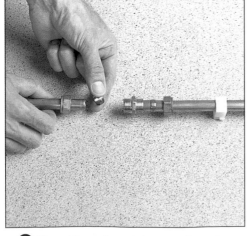

1 Thread the nuts and rings over the cut pipe ends and push the pipes into the fitting. Ensure they meet the internal stops.

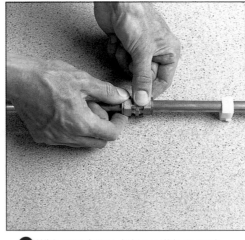

2 With experience, it is possible to push the pipe without dismantling the joint, but be sure it goes right in before tightening.

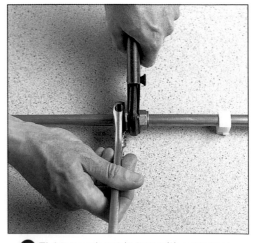

3 Tighten each nut in turn with a spanner until it feels firm. Do not overtighten – one turn past hand-tight is about right.

than a superficial burn, seek immediate medical assistance. Never leave a lit lamp unattended, even for a few seconds to answer a knock on the door or a ringing telephone.

Making joints in a waste pipe

There are three different types of joint used on plastic waste pipes. To be completely compatible, and problem free in the future, your new pipe and fittings must all be from the same range as the existing waste system. Check compatibility carefully before buying additional fittings.

Cleanliness

All pipes must be clean and cut squarely at the ends. Pipe used in push-fit joints must be slightly tapered at the end with a file to prevent dislodging the rubber seals. Solvent-welded pipe and joints should be cleaned with the chemical sold with the system.

Expansion joints

Plastic pipes expand when hot. To prevent buckling, an expansion joint must be used on lengths over 1m (39in) that have two fixed ends. Pipes must be supported by clips at 50cm (20in) intervals to prevent sagging. On vertical runs, clip every 1.8m (6ft).

Solvent weld
❶ Clean mating parts with chemical cleaner or roughen with glasspaper.

❷ Apply a coat of maker's recommended solvent weld to both surfaces.

❸ Push the pipe into the socket, twisting it slightly to ensure a good seal.

Push-fit
❶ Clean and taper the pipe end to a 45° angle using a deburring tool.

❷ Smear silicone lubricant on the rubber seal before assembling the joint.

❸ Mark the pipe with a pen. Withdraw it 3mm (⅛in) for expansion.

Mechanical
❶ When purchased, the tapered ring is often jammed inside the fitting.

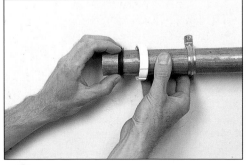

❷ Thread on the back nut, the anti-rotation ring and the rubber seal.

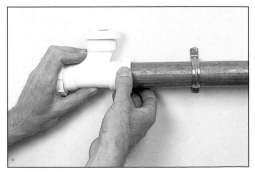

❸ Insert the pipe and tighten the nut by hand only; grips may distort it.

Fitting a kitchen sink

Whether swapping over a sink in the same position or fitting a totally new kitchen, one of the most important tools you will need is a tape measure. With sinks coming in so many shapes and sizes, you need to be absolutely sure that the model you want is right for the location.

The plumbing supplies for any sink are the same up to the point at which they connect to the taps and waste – thereafter they may vary a great deal. Fortunately, there is now a range of waste kits available that make the job a lot easier than attempting to marry up ill-suited components.

This plumbing can also be utilized to plumb in a dishwasher or washing machine – the connections are almost identical. Labour-saving quick-fit devices for taking water both in and out mean that the kitchen can soon be in full working order.

Hints and tips

- Avoid awkward working positions by making all the connections to the sink, including fitting the taps, before you put the sink into its base unit.

- When working under the sink connecting up the hot and cold water supply pipes and the waste pipe, remove the base unit doors and any internal shelves to give yourself more room to work in.

- All metal pipework in the house must be earthed. If in any doubt about the sink's earthing, consult an electrician.

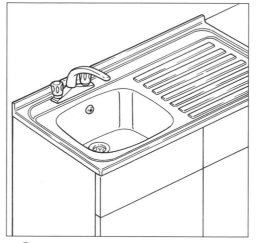

1 Roll-top, or 'sit-on', sinks are made to fit on and cover the top of the base unit. If you intend to fit this type of sinktop onto a unit that has previously been fitted with an inset sink (or vice versa), make sure to check that the base unit is suitable. It may be necessary to replace the base unit altogether if you are changing to a different type of sink design.

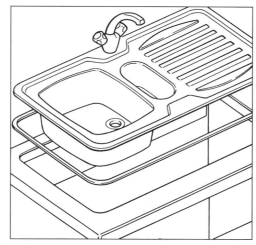

2 Inset sinks drop into the worktop attached to the base unit. When cutting a new worktop to accommodate the sink, measure up very carefully, since there will be only a narrow area of top around the sink – especially if the taps are to be mounted in the worktop behind the sink rather than through the sinktop itself. Using the template provided with the sink, draw the outline on the worktop. Drill a starting hole just inside the cutting line and cut carefully around with a power jig saw. The sink can then be secured firmly to the worktop on a sealing strip by clips to the underside of the worktop.

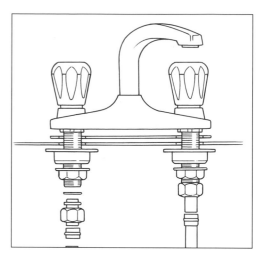

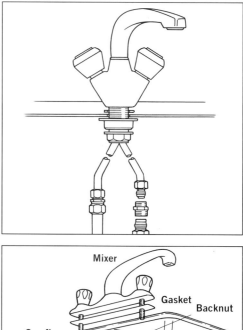

Mixer
Gasket
Backnut
Overflow
Compression fitting
Water supply
Slotted waste
Washer
Backnut
Bottle trap

1 To fix a mixer tap into a two-hole sink, secure the top hat washers immediately beneath the sinktop by the backnuts, pulling the top down onto its rubber seal.

2 With a one-hole monoblock tap, use the compression fittings supplied with the tap.

3 All connections for taps and their plumbing assemblies and wastes are available as kits, complete with directions.

Plumbing in a new sink

1 Wind PTFE tape tightly around the waste outlet thread. If the flange has not been supplied with its own plastic or rubber washer, use plumber's putty to make the seal.

2 Fit the waste pipe through the sink's outlet hole. Apply jointing compound to the washer and pass it over the outlet thread. Press the waste outlet into position with the smeared side down.

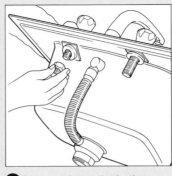

3 Line up the outlet in the collar of the overflow hose with the slot in the waste. Fit the backnut into position over the outlet and tighten it up using a spanner to hold everything firmly in place.

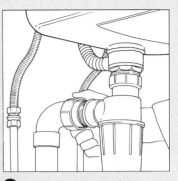

4 Fix the other end of the overflow hose to the overflow outlet in the top of the bowl by screwing the thread of the small grate and chain stay into the overflow end.

5 Position the tap, slip the top hat washers over the inlet tails, and screw on the backnuts. If not connecting directly up to existing pipes, then connect pliable pipe of the appropriate length.

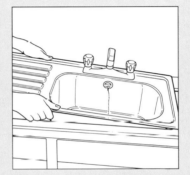

6 Set the sink onto its rubber seal in position on the worktop. Before connecting the sink up to the plumbing, clip the sinktop firmly into place so that there is no movement possible.

7 Connect with compression fittings to the existing supply or manipulate the new pliable pipes so that they meet the supply pipes. Screw on the bottle trap and connect the waste pipe.

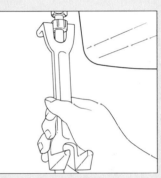

8 To work on inaccessible connections, particularly when loosening old pipework, a basin wrench can be an invaluable tool for turning nuts where other spanners cannot reach.

Sinktops

A huge range of different styles, colours and finishes of sinktops is available. As well as single-bowl/single-draining types, there are single-bowl/double drainers, and double-bowl/single-drainers in stainless steel, coloured enamels and acrylic. There are also 1½- and 2½-bowl models to choose from. Round sinks are designed to fit into a worktop and don't have an integral drainer at all.

LEFT A single-bowl/single drainer.

BELOW LEFT A round sink gives you a large bowl without taking up much worktop space.

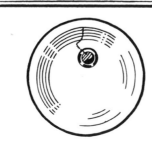

ABOVE A single bowl/double drainer which has a small drainer for cutlery.

LEFT A double bowl/single drainer incorporating a small sink for washing cutlery.

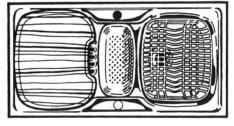

Fitting a bathroom

Replacing bathroom fittings should be a straightforward task if you are connecting your new bath and basin to existing plumbing. Before choosing new equipment, it's worth checking how the plumbing is set, and opting for tap arrangements that will obviate changes to the hot and cold water supplies.

TOP RIGHT
Monobloc bidet mixer with adjustable nozzle and pop-up waste.

ABOVE Gooseneck rigid riser shower head with adjustable rose.

ABOVE RIGHT
Wall-mounted thermostatic shower mixer.

BOTTOM RIGHT
Rigid riser with shower rose, handshower kit and cradle.

FAR RIGHT
Wall-mounted thermostatic shower mixer tap.

Fitting a bath

You need plenty of space in which to assemble a bath.

❶ Fit the frame first, then the waste, and finally the taps and hand grips if supplied.

❷ Screw the trap to the waste and the flexi-connectors with the washers to the taps.

❸ Level the bath with a spirit level. There is no need to worry about a slope to the waste – it is built in.

❹ Mark the positions of the waste pipe connection to the trap and the two supply pipe connections.

❺ Draw a line on the wall along the top edge of the bath and remove the bath from the room.

❻ Measure down from the line to create a channel of the same width as the bath edge.

❼ Gently cut away the plaster line along the channel so the bath can be set slightly into the wall.

❽ It is a good idea to screw a horizontal batten to the wall along the lower edge of the letting-in channel. This helps prevent movement and gives extra support to the edge frame. Bring the bath back into position.

❾ Fit the waste and overflow, with the large rubber washers on the undersides, and the thin ones inside the bath. If this produces a lip around the plug hole, remove and seal on a bed of silicone.

Preparing the floor

Baths usually have instructions on fitting the legs or cradles. Check all fixing screws to ensure that the frame will support the weight of a full bath. Screw the feet onto timber bearers for extra strength. This is essential on chipboard floors. The bearer must straddle the joists to spread the load.

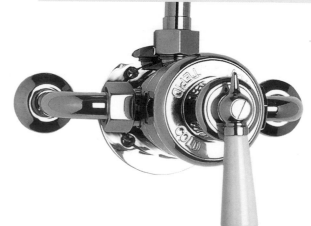

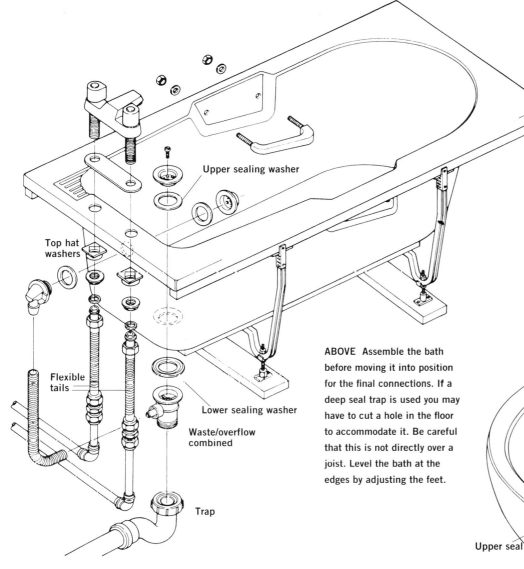

ABOVE Assemble the bath before moving it into position for the final connections. If a deep seal trap is used you may have to cut a hole in the floor to accommodate it. Be careful that this is not directly over a joist. Level the bath at the edges by adjusting the feet.

Fitting a basin

Make sure you have all the clips and brackets to secure the basin. Never rely on the plumbing to hold a basin in position.

❶ Fit the slotted waste with the rubber washer supplied, or silicone mastic, under the metal flange. The slots should about line up with the integral overflow. Tighten the backnut gently on to the washer.

❷ Insert single taps in their holes as shown in the illustration, with an antirotation washer above the china and a plastic nut below. Use flexible connectors bent gently by thumbing round so they follow the line of the basin. Single-hole mixer taps have protective washers above and below the china.

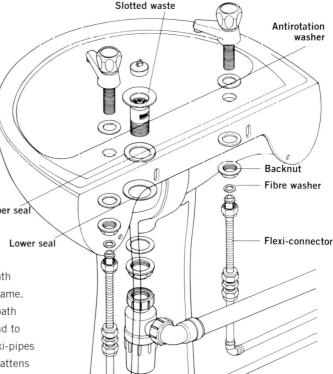

Connecting up to plumbing

❶ Flexi-connectors allow you to tighten the supply joints before the bath is in position, so you don't need special spanners to reach up behind the bath. The connections are usually 22mm compression joints, but if plain-end connectors are used, push-fit joints can be used.

❷ Push the waste pipe into the trap end and connect it up to the remaining run.

❸ The bath is now ready for testing. Run cold water through it and examine the waste run, then put in the plug and fill up to the overflow pipe. Pull the plug and test the waste again. Finally, fill the bath and make final adjustments to the feet and mark out the wall brackets.

Bath shapes

Although there is a great variety of bath shapes, fitting them is basically the same. Some corner baths with taps on the bath require plumbing to be brought around to accessible connection points, but flexi-pipes greatly simplify this task. Always fit battens right into the corner, to prevent the back edge sagging and collecting water.

ABOVE RIGHT A basin comes with a choice of one, two or three tap holes, each needing a different tap arrangement. Three-hole taps connect to the pipes like two-hole taps, but have flexible connecting tubes below the basin to take water to the spout.

RIGHT Fit the tap with an anti-rotation washer on the upper side. A top hat washer can be used on the underside to give the nut a broader holding area and further reduce movement.

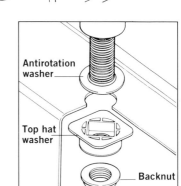

Blockages and airlocks

The sudden unwillingness of water to drain away is disconcerting, but usually has a simple cause. To cure the problem, you probably need only some basic equipment.

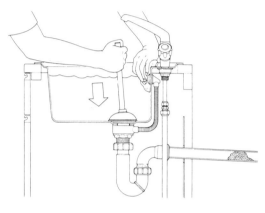

ABOVE To clear a blocked waste pipe with a plunger, first cover the overflow with a wet cloth. Then move the plunger sharply up and down.

Using a sink plunger

The volume of water filling a blocked fitment and waste pipe works in your favour when using a plunger, so don't bail it out. It might even help to fill it up a little, particularly with a bath. Water is not compressible, so any force applied to one end of a full pipe by plunging must be transferred to the other end to work on the blockage, provided it has no escape route.

The most common mistake is to leave the overflow pipe empty and the grille uncovered. The considerable push/pull forces built up by plunging will be wasted if they have an easy escape route up the overflow or along an air-filled pipe.

Hold a rag firmly over the overflow or, if it is a double sink, the other waste hole as well (a three-handed job). Then place the plunger over the waste hole and work it up and down vigorously. If you prefer, a special blockbuster gun can be used instead of a plunger, but keep the overflow and any other exits firmly covered.

Blocked toilet

Before starting, remove any carpet around the toilet, or put down some old rags than can be thrown away. You will need an old mop or plunger. Make an emergency plunger from a plastic bottle cut in half, with a broom stick in the neck of the bottle.

Use the plunger or old mop to force the blockage around the bend and follow with several buckets of warm water.

Strong caustic soda or similar drain-clearing chemicals can sometimes be successful at clearing minor blockages.

Airlocks

Air tends to rise in pipework. If it has no means of escape it will stay in the highest part of the system and cause an airlock.

Mains plumbing There is sufficient pressure to force air back down the pipes and out through taps. You will see this if you drain the rising main and then turn it back on again. There will be a lot of gushing and spluttering at the taps.

Tank-fed systems The pressure of the air is not usually enough to clear an airlock. In a well-designed system all pipes are laid so that air will be able to escape through taps or the feed and vent pipes. Where the layout of the building makes high spots unavoidable, small air cocks are fitted.

Purging air

The quickest and easiest way of clearing airlocks is to blow them through with mains-pressure water by connecting a hosepipe between a mains cold water tap and the tap affected by the airlock.

Turn on the airlocked tap first, then the mains tap. Depending on where the airlock is, the water will have to be directed along that particular pipe run. You will need a helper to hold the hosepipe while you go around turning on and off bathroom taps to try to release the air.

If the airlock is on the hot pipe, it might also help to block the cylinder vent with your thumb for a minute or so, but do not attach any plumbing fittings to this pipe since it is an essential safety release.

Central heating pipes

Often, airlocks occur when a radiator is taken off for redecorating. When it is reconnected and filled it ceases to work.

• Turn off all radiators except the airlocked one. Turn on the system and adjust the pump speed to maximum. Leave it running for a few minutes to see if it heats up.

• Loosen a radiator valve union nut and drain off a few litres of water, keeping the other valve closed. Repeat this with the other valve open and this one closed.

Radiator bleeding

Over a period of time air gets into radiator systems and forms a cold patch at the top of radiators. To bleed a radiator, turn on the system and turn any radiator thermostats to their maximum setting, With a bleed key, open the valve of each radiator to release the air. As soon as water flows tighten the valve. As you work, hold an old towel beneath the valve to catch the water. Return the thermostats to normal. It is advisable to bleed radiators at the start of autumn.

LEFT If a sink blockage is caused by congealed fat, try gently warming the trap and waste pipe with a hair drier.

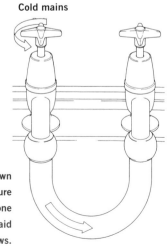

Cold mains

RIGHT Airlocks can be blown through with mains-pressure water, but this must be done according to the provisions laid down by water by-laws.

Working safely

Apart from the inherent risks of using power tools, there are dangers from the electrical and water supplies running through many parts of the house. Piercing a power cable or a heating pipe carrying scaldingly hot water with the pressure of a pump behind it are the kind of accidents every DIY enthusiast dreads – yet even professionals make this type of error.

Drill into masonry only once you are confident there are no cables concealed beneath the surface – and wear goggles to protect your eyes from flying grit.

When using a blowlamp to carry out plumbing work – or paint-stripping – always use a heat-resistant mat to prevent adjacent woodwork catching fire.

Under the floor

Conscientious electricians, heating installers and plumbers often mark on floors where they have run cables or pipes beneath. Equally, they will position the wires or pipes correctly, halfway down the depth of floor joists where they have to cross them, so that they lie well below the floorboards or chipboard sections.

Unfortunately, not all tradespeople – or the previous occupiers of your home who were perhaps keen on DIY – are necessarily so considerate. So, if you are planning to nail or drive screws into a timber floor and you are in any doubt whatsoever about the position of power or water circuits, lift the appropriate section of floor and check it out before you start.

Even if you are laying grippers for a carpet using nails that pass just a short way through the boards, make sure that there is no cable or pipe lying immediately beneath the surface of the floor. Extremely bad practice though it is, it is not unknown for electricians and plumbers (skilled or otherwise) to lay their circuits at door thresholds in just such a manner.

If you have cause to run cables or pipes across joists and prefer to notch the joists, it is safe to do so provided you cover the run with a stout metal plate screwed flush with the top of the joist over the notch.

In the walls

The presence of an electric cable in a solid wall is usually obvious. It is either running down to a switch or wall light, or up to a socket. But beware the installer who, for some unguessable reason, may have approached the task from an unusual angle.

There may be pipes within walls, too, leading to radiators on certain designs of central heating systems.

If you are in any doubt, you can locate objects such as cables and pipes with an inexpensive metal-detecting device. Move this slowly over the area in which you plan to drive a nail or drill into, and it will emit a sound or show an indicator light if there is any buried metal present.

Again, if you are installing new wiring in a wall, be sure to run it vertically to the fitting or switch, and protect it with metal conduit before replastering.

First aid

In the case of anything more than a minor accident, see a doctor.

Burns and scalds

Hold minor burns and scalds under cold water until the pain eases, and then apply a light, sterile dressing. Use only medically approved creams or lotions. If the burn appears serious or the skin is badly broken, seek medical advice.

Electric shock

The risk of serious injury is worse when water is involved. If the victim is still in contact with the current, try to separate them from it using a non-conductive object – a wooden broom for instance – or switch the current off. Do not touch the victim until you have done this. Call an ambulance if the victim is unconscious. Give artificial respiration if you know how.

Although it is important to offer first aid immediately to anybody who has had an accident, such as an electric shock, do not endanger yourself in the process.

STRUCTURES

Walls

The different methods and materials used in the construction of walls often depends on the age of the building, when alterations or extensions (if any) were made and whether the walls are external or internal.

For the purposes of decorating it is hardly important to know how walls are built for they are usually covered internally with a layer of plaster or plasterboard, which presents a smooth surface for painting or papering. All types of wallcovering – from wallpaper and vinyl to hessian, cork and ceramic tiles – can be fixed with special adhesives, as long as the plaster is firm and sound. But for fixing anything heavier it is important to know what lies beneath the plaster so that you can make the right choice of fixing (*see p. 60–1*).

ABOVE Stripping off the interior surface of plaster on walls exposes the underlying brickwork. Once cleaned, repointed, if necessary, and sealed, an exposed brick wall makes an attractive focal point for a room.

External walls

The outside walls of a house are usually built with a double thickness of bricks or blocks. Originally, walls would have been solid but, in the 1920s, cavity walls were first introduced and these are now standard in houses built since that decade. These double walls improve insulation and reduce the risk of damp. The inner leaf may be constructed of brick, block or a 10 x 5cm (4 x 2in) timber frame. The inner sides of brick and block walls are usually plastered, but a timber frame is covered on the outside with exterior grade plywood and on the inside with plasterboard.

Solid walls

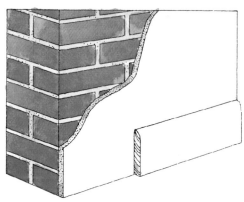

Plastered brick Normally found only in houses built before the 1920s.

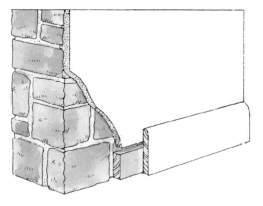

Plastered stone Normally found only in houses built before the1920s.

Cavity walls

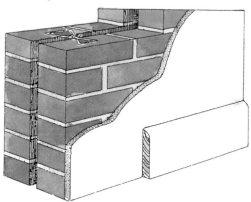

Plastered brick inner leaf Two leaves of brick separated by a 5cm (2in) gap.

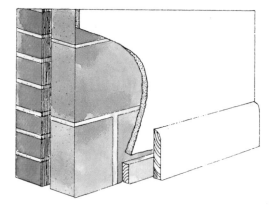

Plastered block inner leaf An outer leaf of brick and an inner leaf of block separated by a 5cm (2in) gap.

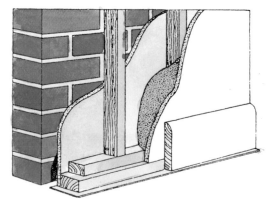

Timber frame inner leaf Outer leaf brick or block, inner leaf of 10 x 5cm (4 x 2in) timber frame clad on the outside with plywood and inside with plasterboard.

Internal walls

The walls within a building divide the interior space up into individual rooms, hallways, corridors, cupboards and so on. These walls may be built from a number of different materials depending on the age of the building, and they may be either of solid or hollow construction. Some interior walls are also load-bearing. When struck with the heel of your hand, a solid wall sounds and feels solid, whereas a hollow wall makes more of an empty sound.

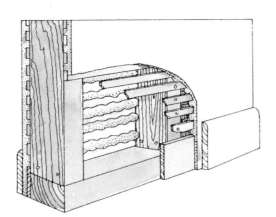

Lath and plaster stud Normally found in houses built before the 1920s. Plaster is pressed onto thin timber laths, which are nailed across timber uprights.

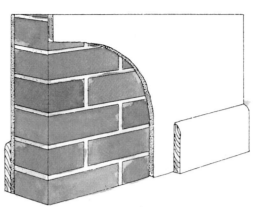

Plastered single skin of brick Ordinary bricks covered with about an 18mm (¾in) layer of plaster.

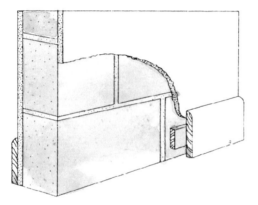

Plastered concrete block Lightweight building blocks covered with an 18mm (¾in) layer of plaster.

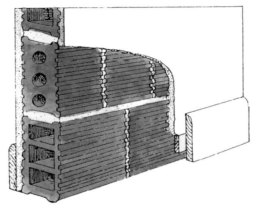

Plastered hollow clay block Lightweight hollow building blocks covered with an 18mm (¾in) layer of plaster.

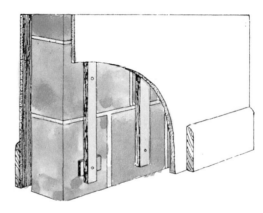

Plasterboard-lined block or brick Sheets of 9.5 or 12mm (⅜ or ½in) thick plasterboard fixed onto the wall or held on vertical timber battens.

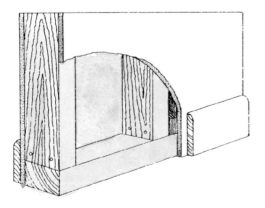

Plasterboard stud Sheets of 12mm (½in) thick plasterboard nailed onto timber studs, usually 7.5 x 5cm (3 x 2in), and spaced at 40cm (16in) intervals.

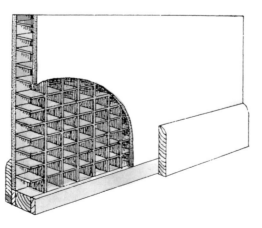

Cellular-core wallboard Cardboard honeycomb sandwiched between sheets of 18mm (¾in) plasterboard fixed between 3.8cm (1½in) timber studs 40–60cm (16–24in) apart.

RIGHT (FROM TOP) Cellular-core wallboard (useful for sound insulation); foil-coated plasterboard (the metallized backing is vapour resistant and provides thermal insulation, making it suitable for internal lining as it prevents condensation inside structural walls or ceilings); and standard plasterboard (used for partition walls and ceilings).

Fixings

All walls appear to be 'solid' to the person whose task it is to fix shelf brackets or other items to them with nails or screws. But in reality, when attaching anything more than a lightweight picture to a wall, for which a hook is usually adequate, it is necessary to find out what the wall behind the surface skin of plaster is composed of. If it is brick or stone, it will be too hard for you to be able simply to hammer ordinary nails into it, as you can with early forms of insulating block – known as breeze block. These insulating blocks have the texture of particles of ground coke. You can tell if you are working on a breeze block wall if the dust that comes out when you drill into it is dense black or dark grey in colour.

Heavy objects, such as mirrors, shelving, kitchen cabinets and timber cladding, must be securely fixed in place to the underlying structure with screws or nails; for plasterboard, special fixings have been devised that grip onto the board itself.

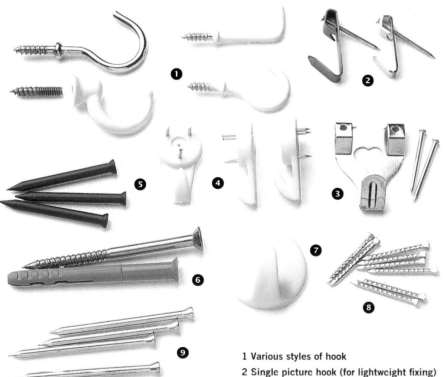

1 Various styles of hook
2 Single picture hook (for lightweight fixing)
3 Double picture hook (for heavier objects)
4 Plastic nail-in hooks 5 Plastic nails
6 Hammer-in plug and screw (insert screw into plug, and hammer assembly into hole)
7 Self-adhesive hook 8 Terrier nails (with ribs for extra grip) 9 Masonry nails
10 Hooks with eyes

Fixings for walls

Simple fixings may be made to timber and breeze block with ordinary nails. When faced with harder materials, however, you will need to drill a hole and plug it, in order to make a firm and secure fixing.

Bits designed for drilling into masonry are tipped with tungsten carbide. If the bit is blunt, if deep holes become choked with dust or if the drill is used at too high a speed, this can become sufficiently hot to remove the tip completely. Use a low drill speed if possible and withdraw the bit from the hole every 12mm (½in), with the drill still running, to clear out the hole. Use a hammer action on brick or block walls.

Breeze block can be difficult to drill accurately because the irregularly sized particles tend to cause the bit to wander, making holes oversize and off-centre. The only solution is to drill oversize holes, about 12–16mm (½–⅝in), push in a length of dowel, and screw into that. If this is not tight enough, cement the dowel in first and let it set.

Steel reinforcement rods may be present near the surface of concrete blocks. If you encounter one of these, there is no alternative other than to re-site the fixing or screw a wide batten to the wall and fix into that.

Fixing holes must be at least 38mm (1½in) deep in order to penetrate through the plaster and at least 25mm (1in) into the solid part of the wall. For a heavy-duty fixing, such as a bracket for a bookshelf, it will be necessary to have 50mm (2in) of the screw thread in the solid part of the wall.

Plugs Plugs are made from wood, fibre or plastic. Plastic is the most common material and is generally satisfactory in brick, stone and concrete. Many manufacturers make one-size plugs for any screw size between No. 6 and No. 12, which means that all the holes for these can be drilled with a single bit – a No. 12 or No. 14. If the plug is shorter than the hole, turn the screw once or twice into it then tap the screw lightly into the wall before using the screwdriver.

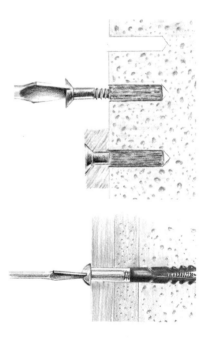

Expanding bolts For very heavy loads, such as those taken by pivoting support brackets, expanding bolts are your best choice. These have a soft iron plug around the stem, which expands to make a tight fit as the bolt is tightened in the hole.

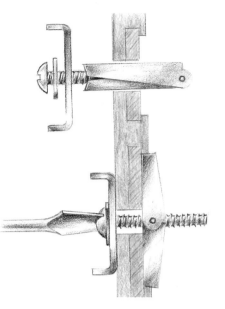

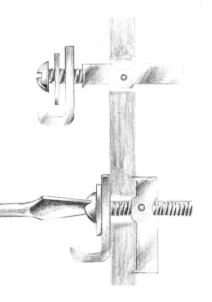

Hollow wall fixings For hollow walls, those made of plasterboard or wallboard, there are two main types of fixings for heavy loads – gravity toggle fasteners and spring toggle fasteners. Both consist of a bolt with a specialized nut that folds down the shank as it is inserted through the object to be hung and the board. Once released, however, the nut opens out and grips onto the blind side of the board as the screw is tightened. These fixings are strong and spread the load over a wide area. Large toggle fasteners can even support the weight of central heating radiators. These fixings are permanent, however, and once used they cannot be reclaimed.

Screw anchors Lighter fixings into hollow walls can be made with any of several types of plastic screw anchor. As the screw is tightened, the anchor opens and grips the blind side of the panel. Some screw anchors open like umbrellas, but work on much the same principle. Yet others resemble masonry bolts but are split in such a way that the plug around the stem collapses as the screw is tightened to form

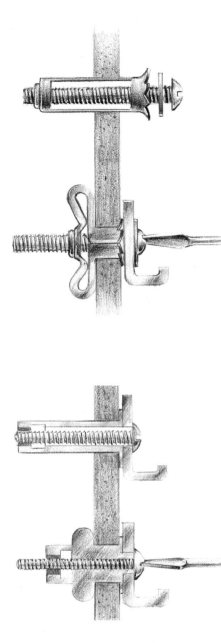

a mushroom-shaped nut. These fixings can be reclaimed and used again if necessary.

Adhesives

Glues that advertise themselves as replacements for screws and nails sound like a DIY dream come true. Although it is true that modern adhesives can perform miracles in certain situations, you should be at least a little cautious about using them instead of nails and screws. This is because a bond is only as strong as its weakest element – the strongest adhesive will not be enough if the paint it is spread on comes away from the plaster by the weight of a shelf. If you use adhesive over a broad expanse of wall, however, it is unlikely to let you down. Make sure you degrease the surface to which you are applying adhesive, using white or methylated spirit. You can also use a strong detergent, but then you must rinse and dry the surface. Neoprene-based adhesives, which can be squeezed from a tube or gun, are available for fixing thin wall panels. These take up minor irregularities in the wall surface, up to about 6mm (¼in).

Hints and tips

- If you have a large number of screws to plug into masonry walls, you can save a lot of time and trouble by using a tap-in screw/plug system.

- Screwing into a tightly fitting wall plug can sometimes be extremely difficult. If so, place a little soap, light grease or a silicone lubricant on the screw ends before starting.

- No matter how much care you take when drilling, you often end up with oversized holes in masonry and breeze blocks. If the looseness is only slight, insert spills (splinters of wood or twists of paper) or matchsticks around the wall plug to take up the slack.

- When fixing objects to ceilings, it is important to discover where the joists are located. Once these have been found,

you can then drill directly into them and screw in woodscrews without having to use toggles or other types of fixing designed for hollow panels. If it is not obvious where the joists are located – paler strips on the paintwork or slightly different sounds in response to knocking lightly on the ceiling are often tell-tale signs – drill a series of tiny holes through the plasterboard until you meet some resistance. Refill the holes with filler.

A partition wall

A room that is too large for its requirements often can be successfully partitioned to create two smaller, more manageable spaces that can be used for different activities. Constructing a partition wall yourself may seem like a major undertaking, however, and one that requires considerable knowledge and skill. Happily, the task is much simpler and more straightforward than you might initially think – all that is required is a timber stud framework covered with plasterboard. Bear in mind, though, that such a wall is simply a partition and is not load-bearing.

BELOW A large room may sometimes be put to better use if it is divided into different activity areas. In the example illustrated here, a partition wall – made up from sheets of plasterboard – has been built in order to create an attractive study/home office at the rear of a living room.

Materials and techniques

Making a frame out of 75 x 50mm (3 x 2in) timber is straightforward. The framework must be fixed to the ceiling joists, which is not a problem where the partition is at right angles to them. If it runs parallel, it is best to locate it directly under a joist. Alternatively, noggings can be installed between the joists, but this will probably involve lifting carpets and floorboards in the room above. Noggings are short bracing pieces of wood fixed crossways between joists or vertical studs.

The tools required for building the frame are a hammer, screwdriver, drill, spirit level, and plumb line and bob. A footlifter, a rounded triangular section of timber cut from 25cm x 50mm (10 x 2in) softwood (see p. 64), is useful for lifting the plasterboard off the floor as you fix it.

Buy a ready-made door, if one is required, rather than trying to construct one yourself. Match the door frame and architrave to other doors in your home.

Plasterboard is normally available in sheets 1.2 x 1.8 or 2.4m (4 x 6 or 8ft) long, in thicknesses of 12mm (½in) or 9.5mm (⅜in). The length of board needed depends on the height of the room. Thicker sheets of plasterboard are more expensive to buy but require fewer supports as they are much stronger.

Working with plasterboard requires few tools: a fine-toothed saw or a sharp heavy-duty craft knife and straight edge. Holes for light switches and socket outlets need to be marked on the plasterboard with a pencil and cut out with a padsaw or keyhole saw before being fixed in place. Fix the plasterboard to the framework with galvanized plasterboard nails and hide the joins with joint tape and filler.

Constructing the framework

First, mark on the ceiling exactly where the wall, and door if required, are to be located. Using a spirit level against a straight piece of timber or a plumb line, mark a line on the floor exactly below that on the ceiling. A continuous length of timber, the sole plate, broken only for the door opening, is fixed along the centre line on the floor. It is nailed or screwed to the floor at 60cm (24in) intervals, two fixings at a time. The sole plate can be fixed directly to floorboards, but securing it through to joists will make the structure stronger.

Now fix the head plate: fix a continuous length of timber to the ceiling line, driving through the ceiling into the joists. The head plate should be broken only if the ceiling is very low or the door exceptionally high. Once the sole and head plates are in place, fix the vertical studs between them. Place these at 40cm (16in) intervals for 9.5mm (⅜in) thick board or 60cm (24in) intervals for 12mm (½in) thick board and at each side of any opening. Skewnail the studs, using two nails per fixing.

For extra strength, fix noggings halfway up the studs, as well as where they are required for supporting heavy fixtures, such as a washbasin or large mirror.

Fixing the plasterboard

Cut plasterboard 25mm (1in) short of the partition's height and hold it firmly against the ceiling while it is being nailed to the framework. Fix the boards with galvanized plasterboard nails at 40cm (16in) intervals and 12mm (½in) from the edge. Drive each nail until the head dimples the board's surface but does not tear the paper lining.

1 Mark the position of the new wall on the ceiling using chalk. Also mark on the position of any door required.

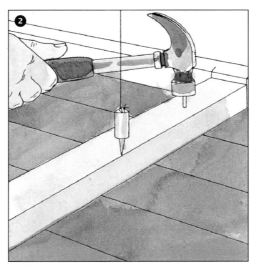

2 Use a plumb line to mark the position of the new wall on the floor, then fix the sole plate in place, using nails or screws driven into the joists if it is a wooden floor.

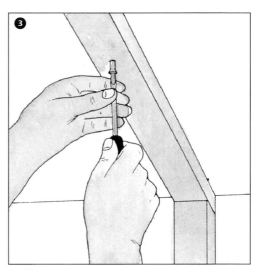

3 Use long screws to fix the head plate securely into the ceiling joists supporting the plaster, then attach a vertical stud to the wall at either end.

4 Cut vertical studs precisely to length so that they are a tight fit when in place between the head and sole plates.

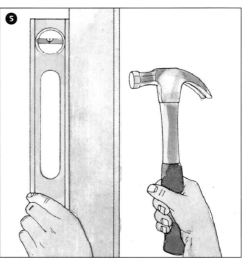

5 Tap each stud into place with a hammer and check with a spirit level to make sure that it is vertical.

Cutting plasterboard

Cut sheets of plasterboard with the paper lining face downward. Use a sharp, fine-toothed saw for long lengths of plasterboard. Alternatively, for short lengths you can use a sharp knife to score deep lines in the material and then snap off the waste over a straight edge. Cut out holes for switches with a padsaw or keyhole saw after first drilling a starting hole. Sand the cut edges lightly to remove any paper burrs.

6 Use an offcut of timber to support a stud so that it does not slip while you nail it to the sole plate.

7 Supporting noggings can meet each other exactly or be slightly offset. Support each nogging with an offcut while nailing.

8 If a door frame is required, the top should be cut into the studs so that it is firmly supported at either side.

9 Use glassfibre for sound and thermal insulation, especially between a bathroom and bedroom.

10 When fitting the plasterboard into place, slip a footlifter made of wood under the board to help hold it at the correct height while you fix it in position.

11 Nail the sheets of plasterboard to the battens using plasterboard nails.

Locating joists

To locate the joists in a top-floor room, you need to climb up into the attic space and take a look. In a boarded attic or in an upstairs room, you need to note where the nails are that fix the floorboards to the underlying joists. If the boards are covered, tap the ceiling in the room below with your knuckles. A 'solid' sound and feel indicates the presence of a joist. Alternatively, you will have to make a series of small test holes with a drill to find the joists and then fill them again afterwards to repair the damage.

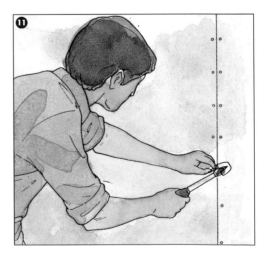

Disguising the joints

To hide the joints between the pieces of plasterboard to produce a smooth, professional surface that can then be painted or papered, the following materials are required:

- **Jointing compound**

- **Jointing tape**

- **Steel float**

- **Filling knife**

- **Jointing sponge**

1 To fill the joints between the pieces of plasterboard, first apply jointing compound to the tapered edges using a steel float.

2 Next apply jointing tape, pressing it down with a filling knife so that it is well embedded in the jointing compound.

3 Use the steel float once more to apply another band of jointing compound, about 20cm (8in) wide.

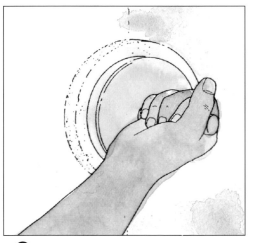

4 Feather out the edges of the jointing compound with a moist sponge. Allow the compound to dry thoroughly.

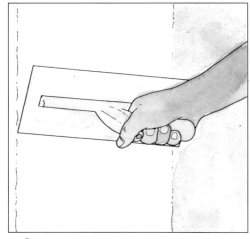

5 Finally, apply another band of jointing compound, this time 30cm (12in) wide.

Screen walls

Although they don't offer much benefit in terms of sound insulation and, often, they cannot be used as structural partitions, screen walls are a quick and relatively inexpensive method of dividing up a large space. In this way, different uses can be made of what was formerly a single-activity room.

As well as the traditional Japanese style of screen wall, freestanding 'flats' can be used, or a studwork and plasterboard partition can be constructed, which is capable of supporting bookshelves and pictures.

ABOVE Here, a traditional Japanese type screen has been made out of a black wooden frame and textured glass.

BELOW A free-standing screen divides the space and offers different ways to vary the arrangement of the room.

Ceilings

Although they are an integral part of a room's structure, ceilings tend to be ignored until they start to cause problems or they are in need of decoration. Fortunately, major problems are few and usually the most that is required before repainting or papering is for a few hairline cracks to be filled in. However, by simply adding moulded decorative features to a ceiling, you can introduce a little style and distinction and perhaps bring harmony to a room.

Investigating a false ceiling

If you have inherited a lowered ceiling you may be tempted to take it out, especially if it was done with outmoded materials such as polystyrene tiles. Before demolishing it, however, try to find out why it was done. It may have been for practical reasons, or it may just have been to reduce the height of a tall room. In a ground-floor room, taking up a few floorboards in the room above may reveal the state of the old ceiling. An upstairs room will need to be checked from the attic. You will also need to see if any wiring or plumbing runs through the cavity between the old and new ceilings: if it does, removing the lower newer ceiling may end up being a longer and more complicated job than you had anticipated.

Problems with ceilings

Ceilings are constructed in one of two ways. Traditional lath-and-plaster ceilings are still found in many older houses and continue to do good service. These were made by nailing narrow strips of timber, known as laths, close together across the joists of the floor above to provide a key for the plaster, which often contained horsehair. Modern ceilings are of a more simple construction. They are usually made from sheets of plasterboard nailed directly to the joists. The joints between the sheets of plasterboard are then filled with plaster filler.

While plasterboard ceilings rarely cause any problems, the older lath-and-plaster ceilings tend to crack and sag as the house settles, and generally require more repair work.

Repairs are usually straightforward, consisting of cleaning out a crack or hole and making it good with cellulose filler. Large areas of damage will have to be patched with new material, however, and an old ceiling that is sagging excessively usually needs to be taken down and replaced with a new plasterboard ceiling. This is not a difficult job, but it is extremely messy and dusty. If the room is very tall, you could consider constructing a new ceiling just below the old one to avoid the need to take the old ceiling down.

Cracks and bumps in a ceiling are not always ominous. Narrow cracks may simply have appeared as a result of plaster shrinking. See whether they get any wider before taking action. A bulge could be sagging plaster – or just that the paper has come adrift from the ceiling.

Stains on a ceiling can sometimes 'bleed' through new decoration. If this is the case, you will have to seal the ceiling with either aluminium prime-sealer or a proprietary stain block.

Ceiling types

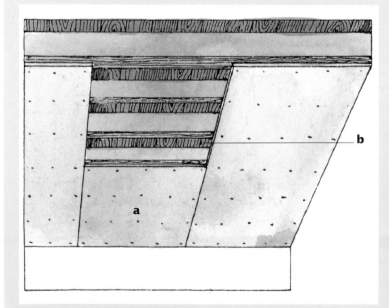

Plasterboard Sheets of plasterboard (**a**) are nailed to the undersides of the ceiling joists (**b**) and the joints between the boards are smoothed with plaster filler.

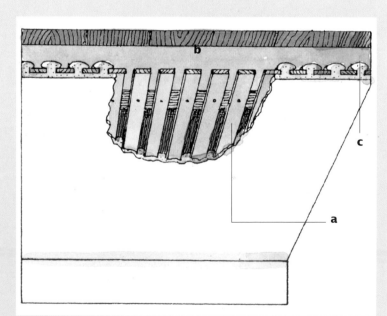

Lath and plaster Timber strips known as laths (**a**) are nailed to the undersides of the joists (**b**). Plaster (**c**) can then be spread on the underside of the laths and forced between them.

Lowering a ceiling

Removing a ceiling is extremely messy, and replacing or even replastering one is a job for an expert. An alternative is to construct another one below the original. A drop of just a few inches is enough to hide surface-mounted water pipes, or an old ceiling in poor condition. If you have very tall rooms you may want to lower the ceiling by a significant amount to make the room seem cosier and easier to heat, but beware of spoiling the room's proportions.

If the original ceiling is old and sagging, make sure you remove any loose plaster that could eventually break away and fall, damaging the new ceiling below.

The new ceiling is constructed on battens fastened into the ceiling joists, not just the old ceiling, so first ascertain the position of the joists (*see p. 64*) and mark them. Cut battens to fit and screw them into place. Construction of the new ceiling is then very much like a partition wall (*see p. 62*). You will definitely need help with manoeuvring sheets of plasterboard into position, even if you cut them into more manageable portions, so get someone to help you.

Your new ceiling does not have to look like a conventional plastered ceiling. A finish that would suit a minimalist or modern look also avoids the trouble of covering up the joins in the plasterboard sheets. Paint or stain narrow lengths of wood (matt black or navy are particularly effective) and nail these neatly in place over the plasterboard at about 60cm (24in) intervals in both directions to form a chequerboard pattern. Some panels could be sand-blasted glass instead of plasterboard, lit from behind.

If suited to the style of room, wooden boards are an alternative to plasterboard. These could be streamlined tongue-and-groove, shiplap (charming in a clapboard cottage) or rustic square edge, like floorboards. And like floors, ceiling boards can be stained or painted in any number of imaginative ways.

A romantic solution Where practicality is not a prime consideration, swathes of fabric can provide a highly romantic solution to disguising a sound but ugly ceiling. Rather than fixing battens all across the ceiling, all it requires is a wooden plate or square of battening fastened firmly to the centre of the ceiling and battening around the walls at a suitable height, rather like a picture rail. Use a staple gun to attach lengths of fabric to the battening around the walls and then gather them up to the ceiling like an exotic tent.

ABOVE LEFT Tiles are useful for hiding a poor ceiling and for adding insulation. In the example here, the tiles are mounted in a lightweight frame.

ABOVE A new ceiling has been added to this dining area to match the style of the built-in units, window frames and furniture.

Detector alarms

Smoke alarms and carbon monoxide alarms are simple to install and can give invaluable warning should a fire break out or a heating appliance malfunction. Most are battery-operated and come with advice on the most effective positioning: usually on the ceiling at the bottom and top of the stairs. Those that are particularly sensitive to humidity are not suitable for kitchens or bathrooms.

Mouldings

Horizontal moulding that separates a ceiling from the walls is often referred to as cornicing or coving. It has a dual role in that it decoratively disguises the right-angled join between adjacent surfaces and successfully covers any cracks that may appear along it.

Many older houses are fortunate to have ornamental plasterwork on their ceilings, but prefabricated coving – available in many styles – can easily be installed to add a little sophistication to any room. Even plain rounded coving will go a long way to finishing off the ceiling perimeter of a fairly ordinary room. Rolls of decorative strip can be bought to add pattern and colour to plain coving. Additionally, a ceiling rose, a centrepiece of decorative plaster, can be fitted in the middle of a ceiling to set off the coving.

Gypsum plaster coving

Gypsum plaster coving is normally available in 1.8m (6ft) lengths, either 10cm (4in) or 12.5cm (5in) wide – although longer lengths can be specially ordered. Like polystyrene coving, gypsum plaster coving is also fixed with a special adhesive, but good wall and ceiling plaster surfaces are essential. Cutting mitres for the corners can be tricky, but plaster coving is always supplied with a template. It is wise to practise cutting mitres on timber offcuts before tackling the coving itself.

Polystyrene coving

Expanded polystyrene coving is usually available, either plain or patterned, in 1m (39in) lengths, about 10cm (4in) wide. Internal and external corner pieces are also available with many types, avoiding the need for cutting complicated corner joints, but you will need to check that the room is square. The advantage of expanded polystyrene is that it is very lightweight and needs only to be fixed with a special adhesive. Plaster-coated polystyrene is also readily available in a range of styles.

RIGHT Coving provides a decorative transition from wall to ceiling as well as hiding any unsightly cracks.

BELOW A range of different decorative mouldings is available, made of plaster, plastic, resin or polystyrene. Choose the style and depth of moulding that best suits the style and decorative theme of individual rooms in your home.

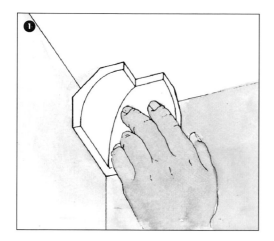

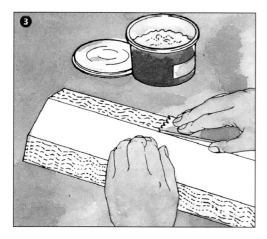

❶ Start by fixing the corner pieces. Spread adhesive on the angled back of a corner piece and push it gently but firmly in place.

❷ Measure the distance between two corner pieces and cut a length of coving to fit with a trimming knife.

❸ Apply adhesive on the angled back of the coving. Gently press and smooth in place. Remove any excess adhesive with a damp rag.

Centre mouldings, or roses

It was common for Victorian and Edwardian houses to have plaster centrepieces on the ceilings of one or more of the principal rooms. Although many of these have been removed, they are once again finding favour among a new generation of home owners.

Reproduction roses can be installed to complement decorative coving. They are fixed with adhesive in the same way as coving, but may need supporting until this has set. Large centrepieces should be fixed to the joists with brass screws driven through the plaster and their heads covered with filler. A hole may have to be drilled through the rose to accommodate the wire for a central light fitting.

Wooden mouldings

These come in a variety of profiles, from simple half-rounds, to complex classical and geometric shapes, in widths from 6mm (¼in) up to about 50mm (2in). They are an attractive alternative to plaster mouldings, particularly in a cottage or modern setting, and can also be used for dado rails, edging shelves made from blockboard or MDF, or adding interest to plain doors or furniture.

Restoring old plasterwork

Much decorative plaster in older houses has suffered from decades of overpainting and sometimes neglect and physical damage as well. It is often surprising how sharp and attractive the original detail still is once the layers of paint have been cleaned off. Cleaning old plaster caked with distemper is a labour of love, however, requiring long patient hours wearing down the layers with an old toothbrush dipped in water and a pointed implement, such as a skewer. Once the paint has been cleaned away, any cracks and chipped detail need to be filled. Before decorating, wash the moulding and apply a stabilizing primer. A moulding that has been overpainted with other types of water-thinned paints, such as limewash and cement paints, can simply be scraped and brushed with a stiff-bristled brush, and then wiped with white spirit. Any sections of excessively damaged plaster mouldings can be repaired by specialist firms, who can also replace mouldings that have been completely removed.

Floors

Floors, like ceilings, tend to be taken for granted until a problem occurs or a new surface is required. Then, knowing how the floor has been constructed will enable you to sort out any problems. Basically, there are just two types of floor – suspended timber and solid concrete – although some very old houses still have original stone or brick floors laid directly onto soil or sand.

Little can go wrong with a well-constructed solid floor. Made from a concrete slab laid over a layer of hardcore, such a floor is usually found on the ground level of modern houses and recently built extensions to older ones. The slab is topped by a damp-proof membrane, which blocks rising damp, and finished with a fine concrete screed. Solid floors rarely contain pipes or cables.

Timber floors are commonly found in the upstairs rooms of houses of all ages and usually on the ground floor of older properties. Traditionally, they comprise timber boards, plain or tongue-and-groove, nailed onto floor joists supported either by metal brackets, known as joist hangers, attached to the outside walls of the house or by low walls. Today, sheets of chipboard often replace the floorboards of old. Electricity cables and pipework often run under timber flooring.

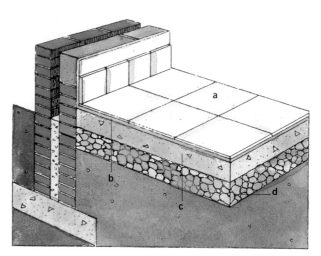

Solid floor Flooring tiles (**a**) are here laid on the cement screed, which is protected from rising damp by the damp-proof membrane (**b**). Beneath this is the concrete slab (**c**) on a layer of hardcore (**d**).

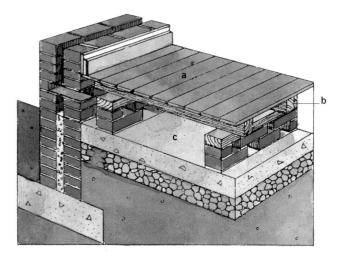

Timber floor Downstairs floorboards (**a**) are nailed to joists (**b**), which, in turn, are supported by low walls; in some floors the joists are supported by joist hangers. The gap (**c**) is for air circulation to keep the timber dry.

ABOVE Original floorboards, well sanded and sealed, can become a decorative room feature in their own right. These have been painted in an antique white emulsion to soften their effect and enhance the neutral tones of the room.

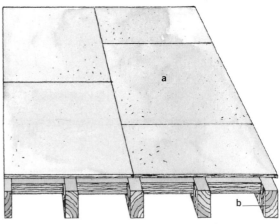

Upper floor Chipboard panels (**a**) or floorboards are nailed onto the joists (**b**), which may receive intermediate support from partition walls as well as from the outside walls of the house.

Preparing the floor

Before a covering can be put down onto a floor it must be clean, dry and smooth.

Solid floors

If the floor is dry and smooth but dusty, vacuum and then seal it with one part PVA adhesive to four parts clean water.

Any dampness must be treated before a new covering is laid. Where damp is coming up through the floor (test for this by laying polythene over it for a few days) it will ruin any new covering. You may be able to treat damp with a bitumen paint, but if you are in any doubt seek specialist advice.

Remove projecting nibs of concrete with a steel chisel or a bolster and a club hammer. Small areas of damage can be patched with a cement-based filler or mortar, but if the surface is crumbling and dusty, the best solution is to cover it with a new screed using a self-levelling compound. This works on the principle that a liquid always finds its own level. Clean the floor, then make up the levelling compound, according to the manufacturer's instructions. It should have a stiff pouring consistency. Then all you need to do is pour it all over the floor, where it will fill all gaps and cracks. Roughly trowel the compound over the whole surface and leave it to level itself out and dry.

Handy tips

- Before you start, ensure you are equipped with a face mask and ear protectors – sanding machines are extremely noisy, especially in a confined space, and the fine sawdust that they throw up soon gets into your nose and mouth.

- Start with the coarsest grade of sandpaper, change to medium and finish off with the finest grade.

- After you have vacuumed up all the sawdust, wipe over the floor with white spirit to pick up fine particles that may not show but will spoil the look of the finished floor.

Timber floors

Old tacks and nails must first be removed or hammered down below the surface using a nail punch. Loose boards, which squeak and may warp, should be nailed down securely; use screws to force a warped edge back into its original position.

If the floorboards are uneven over the entire floor, there are two solutions. First, lay sheets of hardboard over the entire floor – smooth side up unless you are laying carpet tiles. This will seal gaps and cracks, but has the disadvantage of making any pipes or cables under the floor difficult to get to. Second, the floor can be sanded smooth using a hired industrial floor sander and small belt sander (*see right*).

Small holes can be filled with wooden plugs or wood filler, but saw out and replace large areas of damage. To lift a board, punch the nails through and prise it up with a claw hammer and bolster. Tongue-and-groove board must be sawn along the join with a padsaw to cut through the tongue.

Sanding a wooden floor

Even quite badly damaged or neglected wooden floors can be brought back to an attractive state. Mechanical sanders, which can easily be hired, make this task considerably easier, although some hand finishing may be necessary. All you will need is a hammer, a nail punch, a mechanical sander, a belt or disc sander, plus sanding belts or discs.

1 Punch all nail heads well below the surface of the floorboards before beginning to sand them.

2 Start by running the sander diagonally across the line of the floorboards. This will flatten any warped boards.

3 Finish the main part of the floor by running the sander up and down the boards until the surface is even.

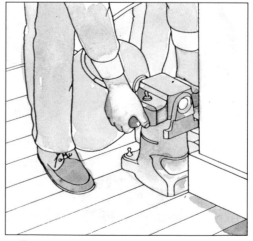

4 Use a heavy-duty disc sander in the inaccessible areas and then remove all traces of dust. The floor can now be sealed.

Doors

Doors can make a great contribution to the overall appearance of your home, so their type and style need to be chosen with care. Internal doors that harmonize with the mood and decoration of the interior make a substantial impact on the whole atmosphere. The front door, especially, needs to match the style of the house. External doors should not only look good, however, they must also be solid enough to withstand inclement weather, providing an effective seal against wind and rain as well as heat loss. In addition, they must be sufficiently secure and well made and fitted to deter any opportunistic burglars.

ABOVE Internal doors are usually painted white or varnished. This door in natural varnished wood tones with the polished wood floor of the landing.

TOP RIGHT An elegant decorative glass panel set into an old pine door; the bold, free-style flowers soften the look of the door.

TOP FAR RIGHT A solid, old studded wooden door provides a feature in the corner of this room.

Flush doors

Flush doors consist of a cellular core arranged within a framework of solid timber rails (horizontals), stiles (verticals), and a lock block sandwiched between two panels. Bonded together with resin adhesive, these materials make lightweight yet strong doors. The panels are usually flat, but are sometimes shaped to look like panelled doors. Some are inset with glass.

Fire-check flush doors have a core of fire-resistant material giving 30–60 minutes of fire resistance. These are required by law in certain situations, such as access to an integral garage or where a house has been converted into flats. It is also sensible to fit a fire door to the kitchen.

High-security flush doors, on the other hand, are designed to withstand heavy blows, even from a sledgehammer.

All types of flush door are available for exterior or interior use. Facings are either prepared for painting or come in a wide choice of veneers for sanding and lacquering.

Panelled doors

Traditional panelled doors are now regaining popularity, especially for exterior doors. The rails and stiles are mortised and tenoned with a wide rail for a letter plate. Hardwood doors usually have four or more raised and fielded (sunken border) panels and are usually stained and sealed. The panels of softwood doors, which are designed to be painted, are normally exterior grade plywood.

Hanging a door

If replacing a door, you may need a helper to hold the door in position as you check it for fit and attach the hinges to the frame.

The first task is to remove the protective plywood that is covering the stiles. Then try the door in the opening to see where it has to be trimmed; it may be necessary to support it on wedges at the correct height and it must be perfectly level. Mark where the door is too big for the opening, allowing a maximum 1.5mm ($\frac{1}{16}$in) gap all around and 3mm ($\frac{1}{8}$in) at the bottom. Remove the door and saw off any major excess across the bottom, and plane the edges to fit. The hinges need to be recessed. Fit one screw in each hinge and then try the door. If necessary, adjust the depth of the hinge recesses.

If an external door frame has a water bar at the bottom, the door should close up against this, which might involve cutting a rebate or step on the inside edge of the bottom rail of the door. This is best done with a circular power saw and the waste cleared with a chisel.

1 Ask a helper to hold the door in position against the frame while you mark in pencil where it needs to be trimmed.

2 Shave off excess wood so that the door fits with a 1.5mm (1⁄16in) gap all around and 3mm (1⁄8in) at the bottom. Reposition the door in the frame to check the fit.

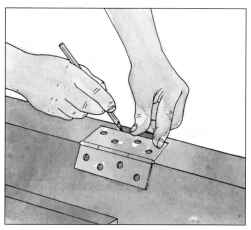

3 Mark positions for three 10cm (4in) butt hinges on the hanging side of the door, drawing around the hinges.

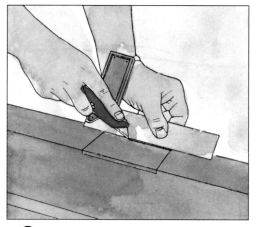

4 Use a sharp knife to score the outline of the hinges.

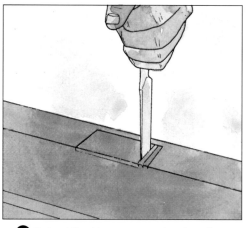

5 Cut out the hinge recesses by chopping across the grain at close intervals, using a wide chisel.

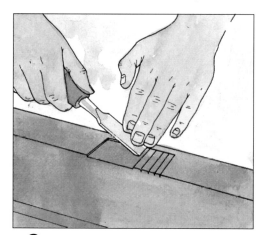

6 Turn the chisel bevel down to remove the chopped wood and level the base of the recess.

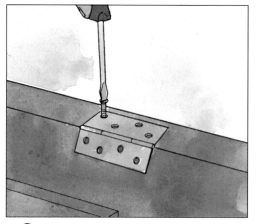

7 Drill pilot holes for the screws before driving them home.

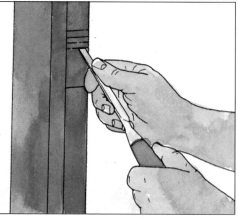

8 Place the door in the frame, using wedges if necessary to get the correct height. Mark the hinge positions on the frame and then cut the recesses.

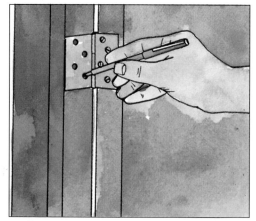

9 Mark the positions of the screws and drill pilot holes. Drive home one screw only in each hinge and try the door for fit before driving the remaining screws home.

Security

The openings through the outside walls of a house represented by the external doors are an obvious point of weakness, unless those doors are well made. But even the strongest of doors will offer little resistance to a hefty and determined kick if the frame on which it hangs is in poor condition or the hinge screws are rusty or have not been set deeply enough.

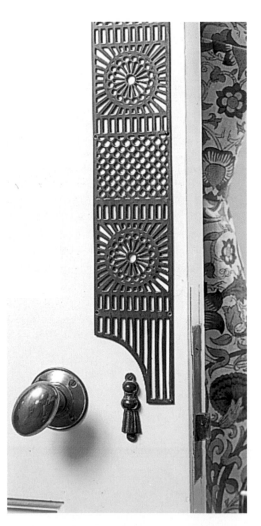

ABOVE The appearance of old doors in period houses can be spoiled by the addition of modern door furniture. If you are fortunate to have the original locks, it is well worth the time and effort to refurbish them if they are in need of repair.

Making doors secure

Having checked that the frames are in good repair and well anchored to the wall, and that the hinge screws are robust enough, you can assess the type of locks your doors are equipped with. It is usually recommended that a front door is fitted with two deadlocks: one mortise lock and one rim lock. A mortise lock is housed in a mortise cut into the door stile and incorporates a key-operated deadbolt. A rim lock, or rimlatch, is fitted in two parts, the body of the lock to the inside surface of the door and the key cylinder in a hole cut through the door. Rim locks are easier to fit than mortise locks, but they are visually more obtrusive.

Security bolts are also a good idea. They are extremely effective against forced entry and are easy to install. Two heavy-duty bolts should be fitted to any external doors of the house, including both front and back doors. Fit them to the top and bottom rails of the doors in addition to a standard mortise lock or rim lock.

Some advisers suggest installing security or rack bolts on internal doors, with the proviso that they are used at night once you have gone to bed. The theory is that intruders who get into a room from outside are then limited to that room unless they force an internal door, which would be very noisy. It would be inadvisable to use these bolts during the day when you go out, since a burglar would know you were out and try to break the door down, causing extensive damage inside.

Hinge bolts, fitted to the hinge side of the door to strengthen it, are easy to install and very effective. The bolts are screwed into the edge of the door and fit into recesses drilled in the frame when the door is closed. Fit two bolts on each door.

A viewer fitted through the front door at eye level allows you to see doorstep callers before opening the door. This is a particularly good device for elderly or vulnerable householders. A sturdy security chain fitted inside the door with strong screws is also recommended; it allows the door to be opened slightly without the risk of it being pushed right open. Some chains have an alarm fitted that sounds if the chain is forced.

Fitting a cylinder rim lock

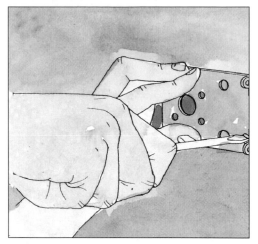

❶ Drill a hole through the door for the cylinder using a flat bit or hole cutter. Then fix the lock mounting plate in position.

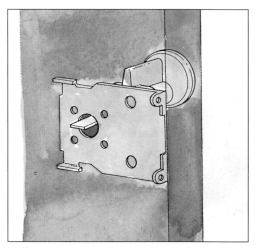

❷ Fit the cylinder from the outside and cut the connecting bar to the correct length with a hacksaw.

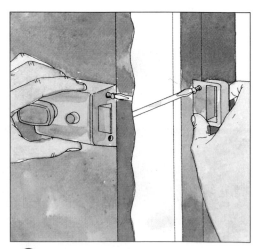

❸ Secure the lock to the mounting plate and screw the strike box to the frame.

Fitting a rack bolt

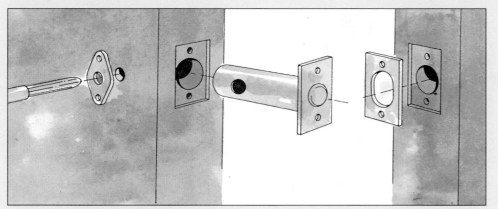

The lock is fitted into a hole drilled into the edge of the door stile and a small recess is cut to take the fixing plate. The keyhole is drilled from inside the door. Once the bolt is fitted, a mating hole can be marked on the doorframe and drilled out.

Fitting a hinge bolt

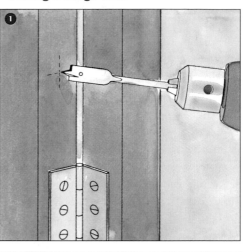

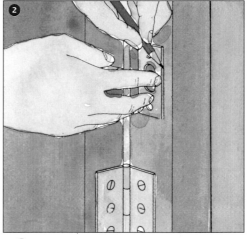

1 Drill a hole in the door edge to the correct depth and tap in the bolt.

2 Mark and drill a mating hole in the frame. Mark and cut a recess for the locking plate and screw it in place.

LEFT There is no reason why door furniture cannot be decorative and in keeping with the style of the door and house. There is a huge choice of letterboxes, knockers and house numbers as well as decorative hinges, studs and escutcheon plates for keyholes. It is possible to find excellent reproduction brass door furniture in many retail outlets. These examples would be perfect for using on doors dating from about the early 19th century onward to the present day.

RIGHT For genuinely old doors, or if you just want to give your front door a period feel, there is a good range of cast-iron door furniture and elaborate hinges available.

Windows

The principal functions of windows are to allow light into the house when shut and to provide ventilation when open. Cracks and crevices are integral to the design of windows, but when these are subjected to heat, cold and moisture they become liable to draughts or rot. A regime of regular maintenance, such as filling cracks and abrasions, rubbing back and painting, will go a long way to ensuring that your windows give you long and trouble-free service.

Like doors, windows represent the weak points in the solid structure of the walls of a building – they must move effortlessly yet be capable of sealing a large opening. They are, therefore, vulnerable to forced entry and you need to make every effort to make them as secure as possible without spoiling their appearance.

BELOW Windows are an integral part of the character of a building, and you should think long and hard before replacing them. This is a traditional multi-paned sash window with a concertina-type internal shutter.

Types of window

A window consists of panes of glass set into a frame of wood, metal or extruded aluminium, which may be coated in plastic for protection. The glass panes may be single or double glazed with sealed units that provide good insulation. They are also available in a variety of different gauges, with the heavier gauges offering most resistance to being broken. Secondary glazing consists of additional panes added to the window recess after its construction to cut down on heat loss and draughts, or to minimize sound intrusion from busy roads or children playing nearby, for example.

Window design has changed through the ages and many older houses retain their original windows. Assuming that these are well and regularly maintained and painted, they should continue to do good service almost indefinitely.

Modern windows are made in a variety of styles to suit various tastes, as well as in traditional styles to suit the architecture of earlier buildings. Each type of window has a different mechanism and serves a slightly different function.

Traditional windows

Older houses tend to have vertical-sliding sash windows, which were first introduced in about the 17th century. These windows do not intrude into the room when opened and their two-piece design allows stale air to be drawn from the top opening while fresh air is sucked in through the bottom opening.

The drawback with sash windows is that their many moving parts require a fair amount of maintenance, and the sliding channels can become jammed if they are carelessly painted. The traditional wooden sash window has a deep box frame, while modern wooden or aluminium ones, which are fitted with spring-assisted spiral balances, are of slimmer construction.

Modern windows

Casement windows are the most common design being installed in new houses today. Casement windows consist of an opening sash, which is hung either on one side of the frame or from the top. Windows often incorporate a sash of each type as well as a fixed light. Standard sashes close flush with the window frame, but storm-proof designs have projecting rebated sashes.

Another type of modern window design is the pivot window, so called because it turns about a central anchor point. This type of window is extremely useful for certain applications, particularly as rooflights in loft conversions. Louvre windows are another form of pivot window. These consist of a series of unframed rectangles of glass held at each end in pivoting alloy carriers. The long edges of the glass panes are ground and polished. Often used as ventilators, they are difficult to draughtproof and offer poor security.

Weather-resistant windows

Metal and plastic windows are generally more weather resistant than timber ones and, consequently, need less maintenance and repair. Unless they are galvanized or regularly painted, however, mild steel windows are vulnerable to rust.

Vertical sliding sash windows (left)

Commonly referred to as sash windows or double-hung sash windows, this type of window was traditionally made with a box frame to house the pulleys, sash cords and counter weights. The sashes are held in place by the outer lining of the box, a parting bead and an inner staff bead; the beads are removed to service the sash mechanism. Pockets, removable pieces of wood set in the lower part of the stiles, give access to the weights. A window fastener is fitted where the bottom rail of the outer sash and the top rail of the inner sash meet when the window is closed.

Aluminium and plastic windows (above)

Aluminium and rigid plastic-framed windows are often installed to replace old wooden and metal-framed ones. Both types of material are extruded into complex sections that hold sealed double-glazed units and draughtproofing material. They are fitted into wooden subframes, usually by specialist companies, and are virtually maintenance free. They do not require stays to hold them in an open position.

BELOW These traditional sash windows have been fitted with textured glass in the bottom panes to inprove privacy in this bathroom.

Casement windows (below)

In construction, a traditional casement window resembles a door in its frame. The side jambs are mortised and tenoned into the head at the top and the sill at the bottom. The frame may be divided by a vertical mullion and a horizontal transom. Side hung sashes may be fitted with butt hinges or 'easy clean' extension hinges, which allow better access for cleaning the outside surface from the inside. The window is secured with a fastener attached to the stile on the opening side. A casement stay fitted to the bottom rail holds the window open.

Pivot windows (above)

This type of window is similar to a casement window, but instead of being side hung, the sash rotates on a pair of pivot hinges to allow cleaning from the inside. If required, the window can be fitted with a safety roller arm to limit its opening to 11.5cm (4½in). Specialized pivot windows are commonly used in loft conversions, where they are set into the pitch of the roof.

Glazing and security

A broken window needs to be repaired promptly both as a security measure and to keep the weather outside, where it belongs. Carefully clear up and safely dispose of all broken glass. Wear leather gloves and clear away any shards from the window sash, working down from the top of the frame.

Security locks

Windows are weak areas in home security, but they can be made less vulnerable. Ground-floor windows should be fitted with key-operated locks, as should upstairs windows. Make sure the key is accessible to occupants, in case of emergencies, but it should not be visible to anybody looking in from the outside.

The window mortise rack bolt, fitted into the edge of the frame with the bolt being shot into the sash, is a good choice for timber casement windows. Large side-hung casements will need two bolts. Top hung sashes can be fitted with these locks, but they can also be fitted with window stay locks. These can be used to lock the window in a closed position or slightly open. The casement window lock, which is screwed to the opening sash and to the window frame, locks automatically when the window is closed.

Sash windows can be secured by bolts inserted through their meeting bars to lock them shut, or sash stops to prevent windows being opened more than is required for ventilation.

CASEMENT LOCKS, FROM TOP
Catch-type lock, stay bolt,
screw-down stay lock,
push-bolt lock, stay lock,
child safety stay lock

Replacing a pane of glass

The first thing to do with a broken window is to clear up and carefully dispose of all loose and broken glass. As a safety precaution, it is best to wear thick leather gloves when handling this material and clear away any shards from the window sash, working down from the top of the frame. If there are any stubborn or large pieces of glass still firmly attached to the window frame these can be removed by running a glass cutter around the perimeter of the pane and gently tapping out the glass with a hammer. In case of splinters of glass flying up, it is also advisable to wear some form of eye protection.

With all the glass removed and safely disposed of, you can now turn your attention to the window frame itself. As a first step, you will need to chop out all the old putty with a hacking knife or an old chisel. Look out for the original glazing sprigs. If these are still in good condition they can be carefully removed and reused to hold the new pane of glass in position. Alternatively, buy 16mm (⅝in) long replacements. Metal window frames use clips instead of glazing sprigs; mark their positions around the rebate as you remove them.

Where lengths of wood beading hold the glass in place and form the decorative finish for the pane, remove these carefully for re-use, as well as the pins that held them in place.

Now you should be able to see the unobstructed window rebate into which the glass fits. The rebate should be brushed clean of all dust so that the new putty will adhere.

Measuring and fitting

The replacement glass must be cut exactly, allowing a 3mm (⅛in) gap all around for expansion, and using the shortest distance between opposite sides of the frame. Measure each way in three places and take the shortest distance. If the frame is crooked or awkwardly shaped, make a cardboard template as a cutting guide.

Buy the right putty for the frame: linseed oil putty for timber, metal casement putty for metal frames. If the putty is hard, roll small pieces in your hands until it softens. You can add a little linseed oil to linseed oil putty, and wet your hands to prevent the putty from sticking as you work.

To fit the new pane, run a continuous bead of soft putty, about 3mm (⅛in) thick, into the rebate and press it in with your thumb. Next, press the pane onto the putty, with the 3mm (⅛in) expansion gap all round, applying pressure to the edges only. The sprigs now need to be driven in flush with the glass, about 15cm (6in) apart, to hold the glass securely. Replace the clips in their original positions.

Finishing off

Run another strip of putty around the outside of the glass and smooth it at an angle with a wet putty knife to match the surrounding windows, trim off surplus putty with the knife on both sides of the glass. Running a brush dipped in water all over the bevelled putty will make it stick to the glass, creating a tight seal. The putty should be allowed to dry out thoroughly for one or two weeks before repainting. Alternatively, if the window is to be edged with pieces of wooden beading, apply a smaller bead of putty on the outside of the glass and press the beading pieces into it. Knock small pins carefully through the beading to hold it in place, avoiding the edge of the glass.

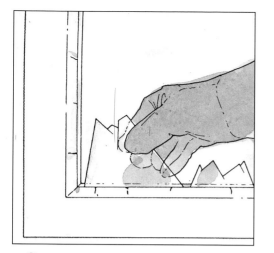

1 Clear the frame of any remaining broken glass; wear thick leather gloves and eye goggles for protection.

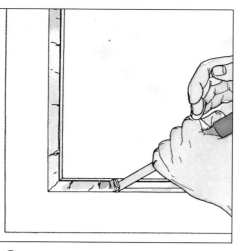

2 Remove hard putty with an old chisel and take out any glazing sprigs. These can be reused if they are in good condition.

3 Brush the window recesses, or rebates, clean of any dust and debris to allow the new putty to adhere properly.

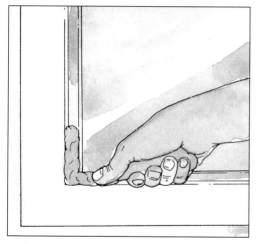

4 Run a bead of softened putty, about 3mm (⅛in) thick, right around the window frame rebate.

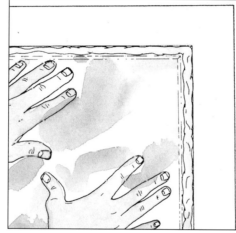

5 Position the new pane of glass into the rebate, pressing it carefully around the edges only.

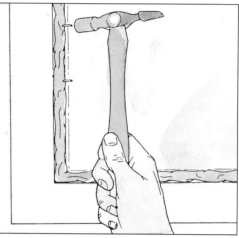

6 Tap the glazing sprigs in with a small hammer or the side of a square-edge chisel to secure the glass in place.

7 Press another bead of softened putty around the outside edges of the glass and bevel it neatly with a wet putty knife.

8 If using beading to hold the pane, mitre the corners and pin it in place. Punch the pin heads below the surface for a neat finish.

SASH LOCKS, CLOCKWISE FROM TOP Locking bolt, locking catch plate, easy-fit screw-in bolts, push-bolt stop

Stairs

Intricate though their construction often is, staircases are rarely the cause of any serious concern to the householder, although they may require some routine decorative maintenance from time to time. The most common problems are to do with squeaking treads. Because the staircase is one of the most perilous areas in a home, it is important to repair any problems that do arise as soon as they are noticed to avoid the possibility of an accident. Fortunately, most defects can be rectified fairly easily.

1 Cap   2 Newel   3 Landing   4 Handrail
5 Balusters   6 Nosing   7 Riser   8 Tread
9 Wall string   10 Well trimmer   11 Apron lining
12 Nosing   13 Drop   14 Outer string
15 Newel   16 Going   17 Rise   18 Skirting
19 Half landing   20 Line of spandrel panels
21 Landing joists   22 Landing trimmer
23 Floor joists

Replacing a nosing

Worn nosings are potentially dangerous and should be repaired or replaced. Cut off the damaged section using a padsaw or jig saw. Fit a strip of wood the same depth as the tread and the same width as the other nosings, and glue and screw it in place. The screws must be deeply countersunk to allow you to shape the nosing with a small plane or spokeshave to the required profile. Finish off with abrasive paper.

Stabilizing a newel

Tightening a moving newel post involves lifting a floorboard to reach where it is screwed to the floor joist. Try tightening the screws or make a new, firm fixing by installing two bolts through the base of the post into the joist. Also check the joint between the newel post and the outer string; if it has moved, the treads and risers might pull away. Brace the post with wood blocks glued and screwed to the inner face of the string and the post.

Repairing handrails and balusters

Wobbly handrails can be made firm by tapping small glued wedges into the loose joints or driving in screws at the appropriate points, countersinking and plugging them to hide the repair. Broken balusters can often be repaired by gluing and clamping. If not, a new baluster will have to be installed. First, place the lower end into the mortise in the string and then screw the upper end in place beneath the rail. Sections of damaged handrail can be replaced with pieces of matching profile fixed with special bolts. Alternatively replace the whole of the handrail.

Fixing a wall string

Where treads and risers pull away from the wall string, a gap up to 18mm (¾in) can be filled. Tap narrow wedges between the wall string and the wall to force it against the treads. Cut the tops of the wedges flush with the string and screw through the string into the wedges. Fill the gap between the wedges with filler.

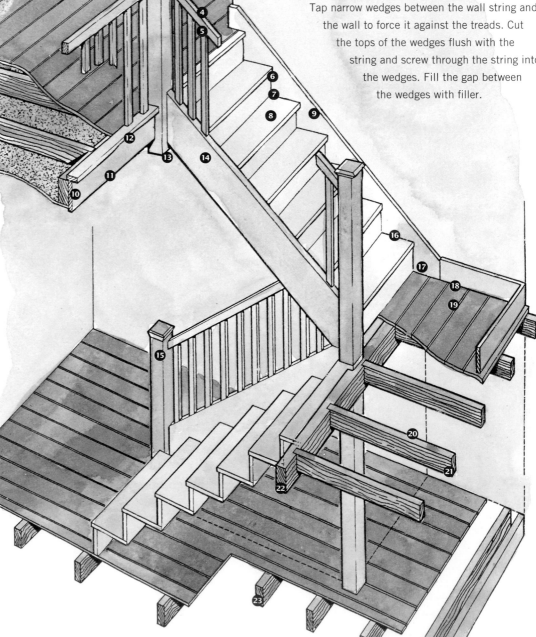

Curing a squeaky tread

Noisy stairs occur when pressure is applied to a tread that has moved in relation to its riser. If the underside of the staircase is exposed, glue and screw wooden blocks into the angles between the tread and the riser, or you can fix metal shelf brackets into the angle to hold the pieces firmly together.

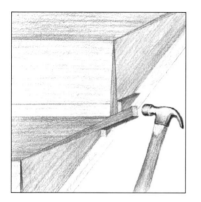

Where the underside of the staircase is covered, attempt the repair from above. Work a chisel into the crack between the nosing of the tread and the riser and squirt woodworking adhesive along the gap. Spread it evenly with a knife blade and then screw the tread firmly down onto the risers.

The rear joint cannot be opened up so easily, but try to squirt adhesive in and don't use the stairs until it has dried. As a last resort, fix small angle brackets to draw tread and riser together.

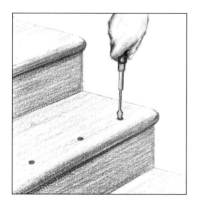

BELOW Spiral stairs are probably the most space-efficient starirways and are useful wherer there is no nearby load-bearing wall. RIGHT Decorative wood panelling can be used instead of balusters between the handrail and outer string. BOTTOM This modern house has a very low-maintenance stairway with its supports built into the walls and unusual tiled risers.

Fireplaces

Fireplaces give rooms a focus, and a fire in the grate adds warmth and comfort, creating an inviting atmosphere. An unsightly fireplace can be removed, or a missing one installed with one from a vast range of secondhand and reproduction fire surrounds – but an original fireplace that belongs to the period and style of the house should not be unnecessarily removed.

Removing a fire surround

1 A tiled surround is held against the wall by fixing lugs on each side. Saw off the heads of the securing screws, lever the surround forward and lower it to the floor. Then prise up the hearth stone. If the surround rests directly on the floor, you will have to remove the hearth first.

2 A cast-iron or marble fireplace has resale value, so remove it carefully so that you can reuse or sell it. Again, the surround will be held with metal lugs. Cast-iron fireplaces can be very heavy and may need two people to move them. The cast iron may also be brittle and can crack, so handle carefully.

3 Timber fireplace surrounds are usually fixed to battens nailed or screwed to the wall. The screw heads fixing the surround in place will be covered with filler, making them hard to locate. The tiled section will probably be held by lugs fitted to the top and sides and screwed into the brickwork.

ABOVE LEFT AND RIGHT Whether elaborate with built-in shelves or starkly plain and unadorned, whether made of wood, cast iron, brick or tiles, a fireplace helps to bring a room alive. Even when it is not in use, a fireplace immediately becomes a central focus. Once alight, an open fire represents an invitation to sit and relax, and just watch the flames.

Restoring a fireplace

With the advent of alternative forms of heating, many fireplaces were removed and their chimneys sealed. Fortunately, chimneys can be re-opened and fire surrounds reinstated. This may involve some building work to adjust the opening to fit the new fireplace.

Anyone without a chimney need not be denied the pleasure of a handsome fireplace in their living room fitted around an imitation fire. And those who hanker after the companionable flickering of a living flame can install a sealed balanced flue gas fire, which does not require a chimney. If only a real fire will do, a sectional fireplace opening can be built and connected to a lightweight preformed flue or chimney, which rises above the roof running either outside or through the house. This will require a concrete slab foundation to take the weight of the chimney and fireplace and to provide a noncombustible area reaching into the room. The slab must be a minimum of 12.5cm (5in) thick and extend at least 50cm (20in) into the room and 15cm (6in) each side of the fireplace opening. The slab should be topped with a decorative hearth at least 47mm (1⅞in) thick and extend at least 30cm (12in) in front of the fire.

Removing an unwanted fire surround is a straightforward job, but may require some muscle and, if it is to be re-used elsewhere, some care. Fire surrounds are usually attached to the chimney breast by a fixing lug either side near the top; large surrounds may have more lugs. Timber fire surrounds are usually fixed to battens.

If the hearth and fireback are in good condition, all that is required is to repair any damage and make a smooth surface for the new surround. The opening may have to be modified, however, to take the new fire surround and a new fireback cast from reinforced concrete. If this is too large a job for you to tackle, employ an expert instead. If you discover there is a lot of debris at the bottom of the chimney, it is a good idea to have a specialist in to inspect the chimney to ensure it is sound before continuing with the work.

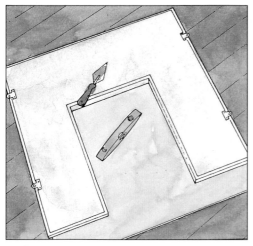

1 It may be necessary to have cast a new concrete fireback reinforced with 6mm (¼in) diameter steel rods.

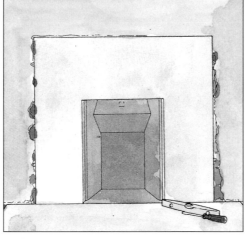

2 Place the replacement fireback over the opening and screw it to the wall using mirror plates.

3 Screw a 50 x 50mm (2 x 2in) batten to the underside of the mantelshelf to act as a support.

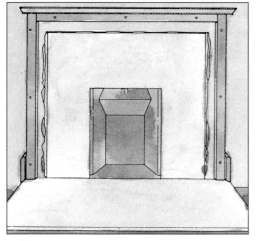

4 Fix the side and mantelshelf battens to the wall to frame the opening. Mark the fixing holes and check the shelf is level.

5 Cover the front face of the fireback with tiles of your choice.

6 Screw the fire surround boards to the corner blocks, working from the rear.

7 Position the assembled fire surround on the wall battens and screw it in place.

8 Fix any additional mouldings to the front and sides of the boards, following the manufacturer's instructions.

9 Stain and varnish the fire surround and allow it to dry before lighting your first fire in the grate.

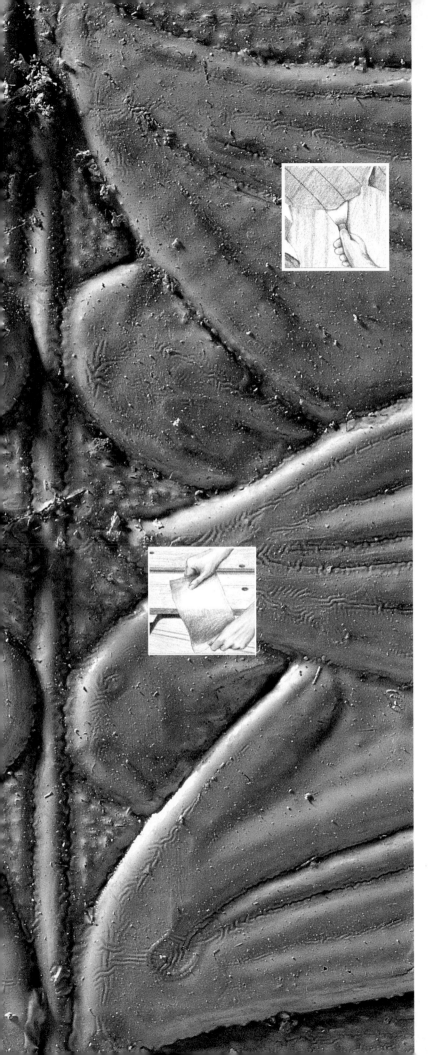

PREPARATION

Stripping and cleaning

When preparing painted surfaces for redecoration – whether walls, woodwork or floors – you don't need to remove the old paintwork if it is in good condition. It is sufficient to wash down the surface with a strong solution of sugar soap to break any glaze and remove grease to which the new coat will not adhere. Then simply rub over the surface with a flexible sanding pad to improve the 'key', and dust it down before applying the new paint.

If the existing paintwork has been badly applied or consists of so many layers that it causes windows and doors to stick, then you should remove the paint. Surfaces that have been poorly painted, or overpainted several times, can take on a treacle-like appearance, robbing architraves and mouldings of their fine detail. Plaster ceiling roses look particularly unattractive when they have been painted once or twice too often.

You may have to strip the paint in order to use one of the new microporous finishes that require direct contact with bare wood. Be cautious about stripping back wood in order to stain and varnish it, however. A great deal of sanding is necessary to remove all of the primer from the pores of the wood; if any remains, the stain will look rather patchy.

ABOVE The quality of any redecoration depends on how well the room has been prepared. First, clear away all movable furniture that will only get in the way, and cover any surfaces, such as the floor, that you want to protect. If old wallpaper is involved, this may need to be stripped back. If painting on top of existing paint, make sure the surface is sound, free of dirt or grease, and that it has a good 'key'.

Stripping radiators

It is wise to strip paint from radiators before repainting them, since they will lose their heat efficiency if covered with too many paint layers. Special radiator paints are available that do not discolour when heated.

Chemical stripping

Chemical stripping can be expensive when large areas are involved. The secret is to be patient while the chemical works – otherwise you may have to apply more coats to get down to the bare wood or metal. Protect your eyes and hands while working, and keep the stripper away from plastic or other vulnerable items.

There are two main types of chemical stripper. One is a liquid that you apply with a brush and scrape away when the paint bubbles and breaks up. The other type is a paste that you trowel on and allow to set before lifting it away with the point of the trowel. The latter is best for mouldings and textured surfaces, since it lifts paint out of hollows.

Be sure to neutralize the stripper after use, carefully following the manufacturer's instructions. This process involves washing the surface with plenty of water, probably with a little vinegar added.

Doors, unglazed sashes and other large items can be taken to specialists for stripping, usually in a tank of caustic soda. However, this involves a risk of the wood discolouring, and the joints in woodwork may open up as any glue or filler dissolves.

Heat stripping

Most paints soften quickly when you apply heat with a blowlamp or hot-air gun, but take great care not to overdo it since the paint may ignite. Do not use newspaper on the floor to catch the hot, flaking paint because of the risk of fire. Have a bucket of water conveniently to hand just in case of emergencies. Hold the scraping tool so that the stripped paint cannot fall onto your hand. Cotton gloves provide adequate protection. Use a flame-proof deflector, such as a pane of glass, to shield areas adjacent to where you are working.

Chemical stripping

1 Chemical strippers that are brushed onto old paintwork may take off several layers of paint at a time.

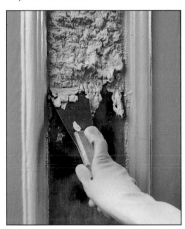

2 Once the paint has bubbled, use a scraper to remove the old paint. If many layers of paint are involved, more than one application may be needed.

3 Once the surface has been stripped of all paint, it must be thoroughly cleaned with water to remove chemical residues.

Safety hints

- Don't try to remove very old paintwork with glasspaper. The paint may contain lead and you risk inhaling it along with the dust. Moreover, the friction from rubbing down will soften the paint and clog the abrasive. Sand only after stripping is over.

- If you are stripping very old paintwork with a blowlamp or hot-air gun, make sure the area is well ventilated.

- Dry scraping is possible using a Skarsten scraper for convex surfaces, such as banister handrails. Use a shavehook on finer mouldings. Be sure to protect your eyes and hands, and wear a simple face mask when removing old paint using these tools.

- Protect any exposed skin and your eyes when using chemical stripping agents. These products usually contain caustic chemicals, which could cause minor burns or localized irritation to the skin.

Using a blowlamp

A blowlamp burns liquid gas either from a small container attached to the torch head or from a larger cylinder connected to the torch by a tube. The flame can be extremely hot, so keep it moving all the time to avoid scorching the wood or cracking glass.

Using a hot-air gun

This tool resembles a powerful hair dryer, blowing a jet of air through a very hot electric element. Having no flame, it is safer than a blowlamp, but this can be deceptive since you don't see anything emerging from the gun. It can become sufficiently hot to char wood and crack glass, so treat it like a blowlamp.

Stripping around door handles

You will achieve a neater finish if your remove door handles, and any other door furniture, prior to stripping. If for some reason a metal door handle cannot be removed, use a thin piece of plywood to shield it from the direct heat of a hot-air gun or blowlamp. Chemical strippers may not affect the metal, but test them first on a small area that

cannot be readily seen – such as the inside surface of the door handle.

Using a heat stripper

'Burning off' sounds rather alarming, but it is the professional's way of removing paint from woodwork; it is not suitable for use on painted plaster and metal.

The idea is to use heat to soften the paint so that it can be scraped off, rather than actually setting fire to it. However, it does require care. To burn off a small area of defective paint you can use a hot-air gun or a blowlamp with an attached container of butane gas. For larger areas, professional-sized equipment can be readily hired.

Hold the gun or blowlamp in one hand and a scraper in the other; keep the gun or lamp and scraper moving together. Use a shavehook for scraping mouldings. Try not to scorch the wood or dig into it. If you are burning off window frames, keep the heat away from the glass. After you have removed the paint, rub the wood down with medium-grade glasspaper following the direction of the grain, paying particular attention to any mouldings.

Wallcoverings

If you are planning to redecorate a papered wall or ceiling – whether with emulsion paint or a new wallcovering of some description – it is often essential to remove the existing wallpaper first in order to achieve a smooth and professional-looking finish. However, some wallpapers can successfully be coated with emulsion paint and, provided that the surface is perfectly sound, all you need do is sponge it down with a mildly soapy water solution to remove the film of dirt and grease to which the new paint will not adhere, and redecorate on top.

Easy-strip wallcoverings, which consist of a thin, decorative top layer you can detach from the backing layer, must be removed entirely if you intend to paint the wall. The backing layer of these papers (including vinyls) is not suitable as a base for painting, although it may be satisfactory to use as a lining paper for a new wallcovering.

Sometimes it is possible to paint over decorative wallcoverings, but it makes sense to experiment first by trying out the paint on a small area and allowing it to dry thoroughly. The covering may be affected by the water content of the paint and bubble up. If so, you will have to strip it all off.

Dealing with different coverings

If you have to soak a wall or ceiling covering before you can remove it – which is normally the case – you can save yourself a lot of time and effort by using a steam wallpaper stripper. Domestic models are available at a reasonable price. If only a small area of wall or ceiling covering needs to be removed, however, and you are not likely to use it again in the near future, it may be best to hire a steam stripper.

Standard wallpaper To remove most wallpapers, use a steam stripper or soak the paper with a mild mixture of warm water, liquid detergent and a little wallpaper paste. The paste is used to hold the water on the paper. Leave the soaked area for 20–30 minutes before starting to lift the covering with a flexible scraper.

Duplex paper Treat this type of covering in the same way as you would standard wallpaper, but allow a longer soaking time.

Heavy paper Embossed and washable papers are, in particular, always difficult to strip. Roughing the surface with a coarse abrasive or scraper, such as a Skarsten, will help steam or water to penetrate the paper and loosen the paste beneath. Allow plenty of soaking time.

Painted paper You will have to break down the surface of the paper with a coarse abrasive pad soaked in water before stripping. It is best to avoid using a wire brush – this may leave tiny metal strands embedded in the plaster of the wall, leading to rust spots later on. Soak the abraded wall with water and then strip.

Stripping standard wallpaper

 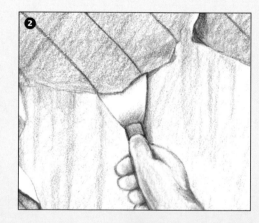 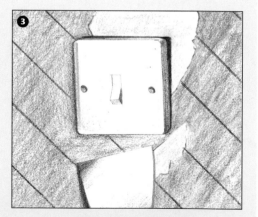 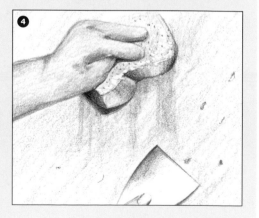

Look carefully at the condition of the wallpaper. If the surface is well stuck down and sound, you may not need to remove it before redecorating (*see above*).

1 Thoroughly wet the surface of the wallpaper, using a standard sponge or a plant mister.

2 Allow enough soaking time so that the paste starts to dissolve before you try to remove the paper. Test a small area first. Then work your scraper underneath the paper and lift it away from the plaster. If you wait too long, however, the paper will dry out and the paste will re-adhere.

3 Water and electricity can be a fatal combination. As a precaution, turn off the main power when stripping around a light switch or power point and try to strip the paper without water.

4 Stubborn patches of paper and paste may require a second soaking.

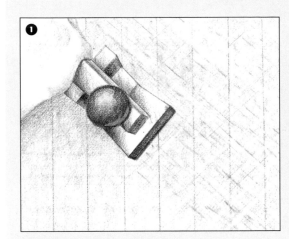

Washable wallpaper

Washable wallcoverings, other than those with separate backing papers, can be difficult to remove. Abrade the surface to allow water to penetrate and loosen the old paste. Use a serrated scraper to score the surface covering.

❶ To allow water to penetrate the washable plastic coating, first break up the surface using a

serrated-edged scraper. A coarse grade of glasspaper is also suitable, although it may quickly clog and become unusable.

❷ When the surface is roughed up, soak the paper liberally with a weak solution of warm water and washing-up liquid. Use a sponge to force the water well into the wallcovering before you attempt to scrape it off.

Vinyl/easy strip

Many vinyl papers are easy to strip since the top layer pulls away intact, leaving the backing paper stuck to the wall. Loosen a corner of the vinyl at the foot, then pull the strip away, holding the vinyl out from the wall as you pull.

Easy strip You can strip this type of wallcovering simply by pulling the top decorative layer away from its backing material, which, if it is thoroughly stuck down, you can paper – but not paint – over. If you do want to paint the surface of the walls, soak the backing paper with water and it should strip off relatively easily.

Vinyl Standard and blown vinyl wallpapers have a backing layer too and you can treat them in the same way as easy-strip papers.

Hessian Pull the layer of hessian away from the wall to separate it from its backing paper. Take care, however – hessian is popularly used as camouflage for badly flawed wall surfaces. If the plaster is in poor condition, the pulling action may make the situation worse by removing or loosening the plaster. Investigate the state of the walls in several small areas before you start to strip off hessian.

Lincrusta This type of covering is stuck in place using an extremely strong adhesive and it is, therefore, difficult to remove. Use hot water and a scraper to ease the sheets of lincrusta from the wall, taking care not to pull away the plaster with it. Soak and then remove any remaining adhesive that is still stuck to the wall.

Cork wall tiles Use a flexible scraper with force to lift away the cork tiles, then soak the exposed adhesive with water or use a hot-air stripper or blowlamp to soften the remaining adhesive. Take care not to damage the wall plaster.

Expanded polystyrene tiles Use a flexible scraper to ease expanded polystyrene tiles away from the wall or ceiling. Then, when every scrap of polystyrene has been removed, use a hot-air stripper or a blowlamp to soften the exposed adhesive before removing it with a flexible scraper or sharp shavehook. Be careful to protect your eyes, hands and hair, especially if you are working on a ceiling.

Stripping ceilings

Most domestic steam strippers are perfectly safe to use because their water reservoirs contain only cold water – the steam is produced at the faceplate. (This isn't always the case, however, so make sure you understand your stripper before you use it.) Press the steam stripper against the paper using one hand and hold a scraper in the other. As the steam penetrates the paper, it will start to lift away from the plaster. Use the scraper to encourage this process. Get as close to the surface you are stripping as possible. Holding the steam stripper at arm's length soon becomes tiring.

Repairing walls and ceilings

Once you have stripped and cleaned the walls and ceiling, you need to examine them for any defects, such as cracks and gaps in the plaster. Most such problems should have become evident during the preparation stages; some others, however, may not initially be obvious. The most common of these is 'blown' plaster, which occurs when patches of plaster lift away from the underlying wall. When rapped with your knuckle, blown plaster has a distinctive hollow sound. Ideally, you should hack out this defective plaster and patch with fresh material.

Although replastering an entire room is a major job – one that requires considerable skill and professional expertise – it is relatively easy to undertake minor repairs yourself.

ABOVE For paint to be effective it needs to be applied to dry, sound plaster. Plaster that is damp is likely to result in the problems illustrated here.

Filling a small crack

1 Start by carefully raking out any loose material from the crack, using the corner of your filling knife or a narrow wallpaper scraper.

2 Using a small paintbrush, wet the crack with water. This stops the plaster from drying out the filler too quickly, causing it to crack or fall out.

3 Now fill the crack by drawing your loaded filling knife across it, at right angles to the crack. Repeat until the crack has disappeared.

4 Fill the crack slightly proud of the surrounding plaster. Leave it to set and, when it is hard, sand it back flush using a medium grade of glasspaper.

Repairing Walls

Small cracks If the cracks are small, fill them with a cellulose filler. Work the filler into the cracks with a flexible filling knife, leaving it just proud of the surface of the wall. When set, smooth the filler down with a medium-grade glasspaper and sanding block.

Large cracks With large cracks, your preparation must be thorough. Dig out all loose and crumbling material, right back to sound plaster. Damp the hole with a water spray or a wet paintbrush and fill with a plaster repair filler. Take the filler just proud of the wall's surface and then sand it level when it has set. If you are not using a ready-mixed product, be sure to use clean water to mix the plaster and clean the mixing platform or bucket after each mix. Any residues of set plaster will reduce the setting time of subsequent mixes and may weaken them.

If the cracks are particularly wide or deep, fill them in stages. Each layer should be no more than about 12mm (½in) deep. Score the surface of each layer to provide a key for the next layer, which you apply when the previous layer is set but not completely dry. With the final undercoat set (allow 1–2 hours) and scored, apply the finishing coat of plaster flush with the original wall surface. When smoothing the finish plaster, it may help to dampen the surface slightly, but don't overwet it or it will become dusty.

The filling material is likely to absorb more paint or wallpaper paste than the original plaster, so prime it with one or two coats of universal primer or emulsion before starting to redecorate.

Cracks at doors and windows Where the wall abuts door and window frames, cracks in the plaster are commonly caused by the movement of the woodwork with temperature and humidity changes. Clear any loose material out of these cracks with the point of a small trowel. Then fill these cracks – and any gaps along the skirting boards – with an acrylic sealant, which grips better than a cellulose filler.

Filling a deep crack

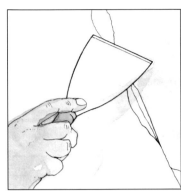

1 Use a filling knife to widen the crack and then remove all loose debris. Dampen the crevice with water and fill it just proud of the surface of the wall or ceiling.

2 When the filler is dry, sand it smooth. A deep crack may need a second application of filler. When it is dry, sand the surface flush with the surrounding plasterwork.

Patching plasterboard

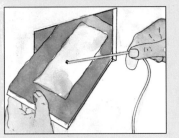 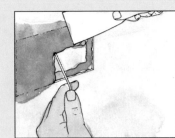 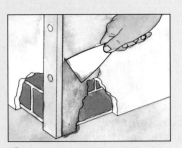

1 Cut a piece of plasterboard just larger than the hole. Tie string to a nail and feed it through a hole in the centre. Dab the edges with plaster.

2 Insert the new piece through the hole and pull the string tight while you fill the recess in front with plaster. When the plaster is set, cut the string and fill the hole.

3 To repair a corner, pin a batten on one side flush with the corner and fill the opposite side. When set, move the batten and repeat on the other edge.

Types of plaster

Undercoat plaster For deep or wide cracks and holes, first apply an undercoat plaster. On absorbent surfaces, such as brick or lightweight block, choose a browning coat. If you are plastering over concrete or stone, use a bonding coat.

Finishing plaster For the final layer, apply a lightweight finishing plaster, such as a premixed gypsum plaster to which you need only add water. This is more convenient than plasters that have to be mixed with sand.

DIY plasters Special plasters have been developed for DIY use. They require no undercoat and you can apply them up to about 50mm (2in) thick, directly onto brickwork or similar walls without the sagging you would get with

traditional plasters applied this way. These plasters are, however, more expensive than the traditional ones.

Some DIY plasters have the advantage of staying workable for quite a long period, giving you plenty of time to bring your patch to a satisfactory finish. When the surface is completely dry, you can decorate it in the same way as conventional plaster.

One brand of ready-mixed plaster gives a skim finish that is ideal for levelling rough surfaces. You apply it either with a brush or a spreader (enclosed in the pack along with the plaster) to no more than a thickness of about 3mm (⅛in). You can skim this material onto plaster, plasterboard, bricks or lightweight blocks, and its slow drying time gives you ample opportunity to bring it to a good finish.

An alternative sealant is expanding foam filler, which you inject down a fine tube into the gap, where it expands dramatically. Once set, it is easy to cut and shape to form a surface ready for sanding smooth and decorating. Expanding foam filler is particularly useful for packing awkward-shaped holes.

Deep holes If you have to fill a large cavity in a wall left by the removal of a drainage outlet, or perhaps a banister rail, it is not a good idea to pack it with filler. This is wasteful, and the filler may crack unless you apply it in a laborious series of layers. Instead, where possible, pack the hole with broken brick or stone and push cement in to fill the gaps and firm it all up – small bags of ready-mixed mortar are convenient for these minor jobs. Once you have packed the hole to within 50mm (2in) of the wall surface, you can apply an all-in-one DIY plaster.

For plastering large areas, it is a good idea to nail temporary guide battens to the wall. These enable you to bring all the plastered surface to the same level. When the plaster has set, remove the battens and fill the grooves level with the rest of the job.

Weak spots Cracks between walls and ceilings rarely stay sealed, whatever material you use. This is a weak area where any slight movement of the building will re-open the cracks. An expanding foam filler is the easiest material to use, but the best solution to a very noticeable gap is to hide it with a decorative coving in expanded polystyrene or plaster.

Replastering Large expanses of wall in very poor repair and areas of blown plaster must be stripped back to the brickwork and replastered.

Plastering

Unless you are skilled, it is unlikely that you will want to undertake replastering an entire room. You may, however, feel confident enough to tackle a large area of damaged or missing plaster where a window, door or fireplace has been blocked off. For such a job, it is easier for the beginner to achieve a smooth, flat finish with either a ready-to-use DIY plaster or a traditional type (*see p. 91*).

Your preparations for plastering must be thorough. Remove all loose and flaking plaster. If the reason for the original plaster failing is due to dampness then you must find the cause of the problem and cure it – otherwise the same fate awaits the new patch.

Once you have cleaned away all the loose material, wet the wall and apply the plaster. When you have applied about a 12mm (½in) undercoat, use a fairly wide straight edge to level it off. Work the straight edge up the wall using a sawing action.

The undercoat should finish about 3mm (⅛in) below the level of the surrounding plasterwork. This gap allows you to apply a fine finishing plaster flush with the surrounding surfaces. Use a little water with the top coat to give it a polished appearance.

Repairing a lath and plaster wall

1 Provided the laths are secure, you can fill holes in a lath and plaster wall as you would a solid wall. Reinforce broken laths first using expanded metal mesh, stapled in place.

2 Dampen the laths and apply a plaster undercoat. Make sure that the plaster is forced between the laths for good adhesion. Key the undercoat, allow to set and then apply the finishing coat.

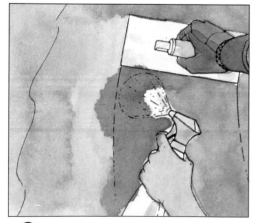

1 Use a wood or plastic float to apply the undercoat, working upwards.

2 Draw a wooden straight edge, spanning the patch, upwards to level the surface.

3 Draw a scratcher over the drying undercoat to give the surface a good key.

4 Use a steel float, aided by a light spraying of water, to give the top coat a fine, polished finish.

5 You will have to reinforce a large corner repair. Here angle bead is used, held in position by blobs of plaster.

6 Plaster the walls in turn, working away from the corner. Leave the nose of the bead exposed to form the corner's apex.

Ceilings

Once the ceiling has been stripped (*see p. 89*), fill any minor cracks with cellulose filler, as for walls (*see p. 90*). You may find that a large crack runs right across a ceiling, opening and shutting as the house moves slightly with the changing seasons. This type of crack is virtually impossible to seal and, unless you want to replace the ceiling, you may have to disguise it with ceiling tiles.

Plasterboard ceilings are particularly prone to forming cracks in the finishing coat along the joins between the pieces of plasterboard. To minimize this, newly plasterboarded ceilings should be formed with small 'lath' sections of board, and a plaster undercoat as well as a finishing coat applied. You can decorate the ceiling with a thick, textured paint to cover up these fine cracks. However, if you prefer a smooth finish, your best chance of a lasting repair is to work a fine-surface filler – or even a finely textured paint – into the cracks and smooth off with a dampened sponge.

Stains On a ceiling, stains will sometimes bleed through new decoration if they are not treated beforehand. Seal the stained area with either an aluminium primer-sealer or with a proprietary stain block. Stain sealers are now available in easy-to-use aerosol form.

Textured surfaces If you wish to remove a textured coating from a ceiling, beware: the coating may well have been applied by a previous occupant of your home – or for that matter by its builder – to conceal a ceiling in poor condition.

If you want to remove a textured coating, use a steam stripper to soften the compound, or apply one of the special stripping preparations that are now readily available. Either way, you will not find it to be an easy task, since you will have to scrape the compound away a little at a time and then wash the ceiling clean.

Plasterboard cracks

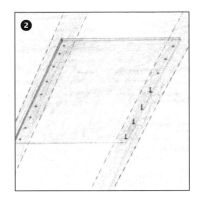

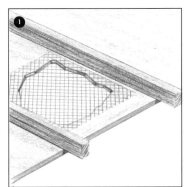

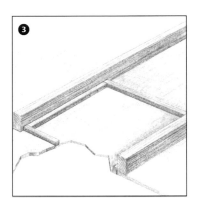

1 When you have to fill a large hole in a plasterboard ceiling, use expanded metal mesh stapled behind the hole. The mesh forms a backing to which the filler can adhere.

2 It is relatively easy to mend a hole that spans the ceiling joists. The resulting patch should make a neat, easily concealed repair that can simply be redecorated.

3 Where the old ceiling plaster thickness cannot be matched, fixing a framework of battens to the joists will help to compensate. Nail the side battens to the joists first, and then carefully tack cross battens on their ends.

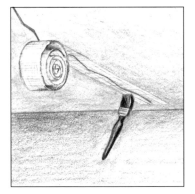

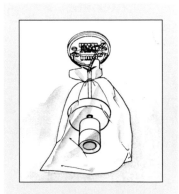

Hairline cracks

1 The first step in repairing a hairline crack is to widen it slightly using the corner of a stripping knife or wallpaper scraper. Unless you do this, it will be impossible to work sufficient filler into the crevice to repair it.

2 After you have widened the crack and removed any loose debris from it, the crack should look like this detail in cross section – a slightly V-shaped crevice. The wide end of the V will be on the outer surface of the wall.

3 Work cellulose filler into the crack using a filling knife. When the filler has set, rub it smooth and flush with the surrounding plaster. To prevent the crack reopening, fix a scrim mesh across the crack and cover with lining paper.

Protecting a light fitting

To protect light fittings while working, turn the power off and encase the flex and fitting in a plastic bag held in place with adhesive tape.

Floors

Whether you plan to lay a new floor covering or to make a decorative feature of an exposed floor, careful repair and preparation are vital. The floor should be as level as possible, clean, dry and smooth. Smoothness is important, since any projections will quickly ruin a covering.

Checking the floor

- To help find small nails and tacks left in floorboards, slip an old nylon stocking over your hand and run it lightly over the boards.

- To check if the boards are uneven, lay a straight batten across the run of the boards. Draw the curtains or turn out the lights, then shine a torch behind the batten. Light will shine under the batten where the floorboards undulate.

- Where the boards are badly worn, try lifting them and turning them over instead of buying new ones.

Solid floors

If a floor shows signs of dampness, it is important to deal with it. A minor case of rising damp might be cured by coating the floor with a special latex waterproofing compound, but a floor that is really damp will have to be dug up and replaced with a new concrete base, damp-proof membrane and screed. If the damp is simply the result of moisture condensing on a cold surface, this usually clears up when the floor covering is laid.

Where the floor is just dusty, vacuum the dust, then treat the floor with a coat of PVA adhesive, diluted one part adhesive to four parts clean water. This will seal the surface and prevent further dust arising.

If the floor has projecting nibs of concrete, remove these with a bolster and club hammer. If the floor is uneven, it is best to use screeding compound to level it. You can buy this either as a powder that you mix with water, or ready-mixed in a tub.

Clean the floor thoroughly, then use a little of the compound to fill any holes and cracks. Allow these repairs to set before you apply the screeding compound over the whole area. Simply pour out the compound onto the floor, brush or trowel it out and leave it to find its own level.

Concrete or tiled floors

Bare concrete floors or securely fixed old quarry tiles can be painted with a special flooring paint designed to stand up to rough

wear and tear. But do make certain that the floor is clean and dust free before starting. If it is dusty, treat it in the same way you would a solid floor, sealing it with a solution of one part PVA adhesive to four parts water. If the floor is in poor condition, however, coat it with a screeding compound to provide a new, firm and level surface.

If you have an old property in which flagstones have been laid directly on the earth, and these are causing damp problems, you will need to seek professional advice. Lifting the stones to attend to the damp problem and then relaying the stones requires specialist skills and equipment. Flagstones that are dry but merely unsightly can be cleaned and their surface polished to a pleasing finish.

Timber floors

It is just as important for a timber floor to be smooth and sound as a solid one, so examine it carefully before laying any type of floorcovering over the top. Remove any old tacks and unwanted nails and hammer down any floor nails that are standing proud of the floorboards.

If the floor is uneven, then you have two options. The first is to lay sheets of hardboard, rough-side up, over the whole floor (lay hardboard smooth-side up only if the floorcovering is recommended for laying that way). This seals any gaps and cracks between floorboards and improves the evenness overall. It also has the advantage of

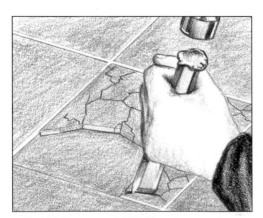

Repairing a ceramic floor
1 Break up the damaged tile with a hammer and chisel and remove pieces with a small cold chisel. In case of splinters flying up, wear safety goggles at all times.

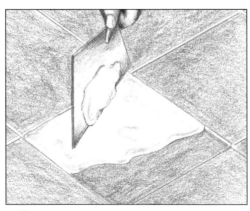

2 Once you have removed all splinters of old tile, use a trowel to spread a layer of ceramic floor tiling adhesive in the hole you have created. Level the adhesive and make sure coverage is even.

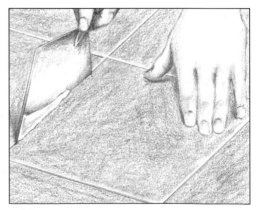

3 Press the new tile into position and scrape off any excess adhesive with the trowel. Read the manufacturer's directions regarding drying time, and avoid walking on the tile until the adhesive has set.

Repairing and replacing floorboards

Good-condition floorboards are essential even if you intend to lay a floorcovering on top of them. Uneven boards will cause any surface covering to wear out that much quicker, and loose floorboards will squeak every time they are walked on.

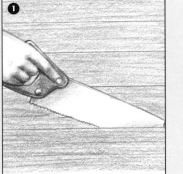

1 If you have tongue-and-groove floorboards, you will first have to saw through on either side of the board to free it from its neighbours and allow you to work on it.

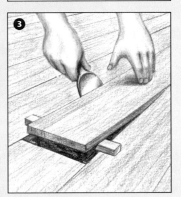

2 To lift an ordinary floorboard, insert a floorboard bolster in the crack between the boards and lever upward with the help of a claw hammer.

3 Once the floorboard nails have come free from the joists, use a scrap of wood to hold the board while you work towards the other end with the bolster.

4 You will need to support a cut floorboard after it has been replaced. To do this, nail a small piece of scrap timber to the side of the floor joist.

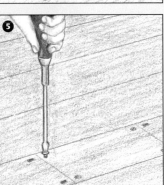

5 To allow easier access to pipework or wiring in the future, screw the patch back in place rather than using nails.

Laying hardboard

Hardboard gives an even surface and prevents dust rising up between the boards.

1 Before laying the sheets, condition them by brushing water onto the mesh side.

2 Pin the sheets with their long sides parallel to the floorboards, staggering the joins in each row.

adding to the floor's soundproofing quality. A disadvantage is that adding a covering of hardboard makes it difficult to get under the floor at any future date if you need access to pipework or wiring.

The second option is to rent an industrial floor sander from your local hire shop and sand the floor smooth (see p. 71). The sander will have a dust-collecting bag. Fine dust will escape, however, so you should still wear a dust mask, eye protection and old clothes or coveralls while sanding.

Before sanding, it is vital to punch all nails well below the surface of the floor. The machine is capable of grinding the floor down by a considerable depth, and any protruding nail will tear the paper belt.

Wherever possible, running the sanding machine in the direction of the wood grain will produce a better finish, and always progress from coarse to fine sanding belts. You may also need to hire a small belt sander to get into corners and close to the walls where the large sander won't fit. As an economic, if laborious, alternative, you could scrape the edge areas of the floor with a Skarsten scraper and then finish off with a sanding block.

Once sanding is complete, sweep the floor and vacuum it thoroughly before applying any finish. Using a damp cloth will help to settle fine dust.

If you plan to leave the floorboards exposed, you will need a good-quality finish.

Apply the sealing coat as soon as possible, before the boards have a chance to become dirty, choosing a seal that is formulated to withstand heavy wear. Some sealing products are sold as floor seals, others as varnishes, so read the information on the packaging.

When applying the seal, work the first coat into the wood with a pad made up from an old handkerchief or sheeting material filled with cotton wool. This acts as a key for further coats (which you can apply with a brush) and it ensures that the seal does not flake away.

If you wish to stain – or paint – the floor, there are many methods involving separate stains or dyes and combined formulas that stain and seal (see p. 150).

Woodwork and metalwork

The care and attention you put into the preparation stages of treating wood and metal surfaces prior to decoration pay big dividends. Treating old or damaged wood or metal not only gives it a professional appearance, it also means less on-going maintenance and redecoration in the future.

Preparing bare wood

1 The first preparatory stage is to sand the wood, working along the grain with successively finer grades of abrasive paper.

2 If the abrasive paper clogs, clear it by drawing the uncoated side to and fro over the edge of a table or your work bench.

3 Treat sound knots with one or two coats of shellac knotting to seal in the resin and stop it oozing through the paint film.

4 Fill any cracks or dents in the wood with cellulose filler if you intend to paint it. Use matching wood stopper prior to varnishing.

5 A coat of wood primer seals the surface and acts as a key for the subsequent coats of paint.

6 When the primer is dry, apply a layer of undercoat. Wait until this is dry and finish with a top coat.

Woodwork

Timber doors and windows, and their frames, are subject to penetrating or rising damp – inside as well as outside. If you find areas of paintwork where there are hollows in the wood surface, or paint has flaked away, push into it with a sharp knife blade. If it sinks in with little resistance, the wood is rotten and there is no point redecorating until you have repaired it.

The first step is to lift out all the rotten material using a narrow chisel, cutting back to sound wood. If the gap left is large, cut and shape a new piece to fill. However, before you fit this, make sure the area is dry. If it feels damp, speed up the drying process with the aid of a hot-air gun or blowlamp.

Hardening and filling When the area is dry, apply a proprietary wood hardener to all the wood in the area of the repair. Be generous – allow it to soak right into the wood fibres and dab it in with a brush. For extra protection you can drill a number of holes, about 3mm (⅛in) in diameter, in the nearby wood and tip hardener into them. It will take about 6 hours to set, and will strengthen any soft fibres and prevent the ingress of more damp.

Next, use a two-part wood repair paste to fill the hole. Check the instructions for the ratio of catalyst in one tube to repair paste in the other. Mix them together well, until they take on a uniform colour, then fill the hole using a small trowel or filling knife. Leave the filler just proud of the surface and, when it is hard (in about 20 minutes at normal room temperature), smooth it flush with glasspaper. Always work in the direction of the grain of the wood to avoid ugly surface scratches.

The drying time of filler is about halved if you are working outdoors in very warm weather.

If you plan to paint the wood afterwards, then any two-part woodfiller will do the job. If, however, you intend to stain it and finish off with a seal or varnish, then make sure you choose a filler that will take stain. Some fillers will not, and you will end up with ugly blotches where the stain has been repelled.

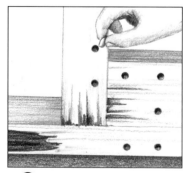

1 To protect wood around doors and windows, drill holes in the timber wide enough for wood-preserving tablets. If the wood subsequently becomes damp, the tablets release a fungicide that inhibits rot.

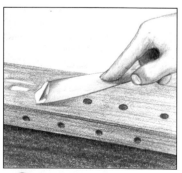

2 Fill the holes with an exterior-grade wood filler. Push the filler well into the holes, and clean up with a scraper or filling knife. Leave the filler just proud of the surface and sand it flush once it has hardened.

Surfaces	Primer to use
Unpainted softwood (new or stripped), composite boards	Ordinary wood primers, all-purpose surface primers or primer/undercoat
Resinous softwood and hardwood	Aluminium wood primer
Insulation board	Stabilizing primer
New plastering, plasterboard, rendering or brickwork	All-surface primer under resin-based paints; no primer needed under emulsion
Porous or powdery plaster, rendering or masonry	Stabilizing primer
Old wallpaper	Treat metallic inks with knotting liquid
New iron and steel	Calcium plumbate primer outdoors; zinc chromate primer indoors
Bitumen-coated metal	Aluminium spirit-based sealer
Galvanized iron and metal	Calcium plumbate primer
Aluminium	Zinc chromate or zinc phosphate primer (not lead-based primers)
Copper and brass	No priming necessary
Lead	Allow to weather before painting; no priming necessary
Ceramic tiles	All-surface primer or zinc chromate metal primer
Plastic, glass fibre	All-surface primer

Preventing further damage To protect vulnerable areas of woodwork – such as sills, which are affected by condensation or rain – drill holes in the timber and insert special wood-preserving tablets. These will dissolve and release a powerful fungicide should the wood become damp. Set them just below the surface and fill the hole above with wood filler.

Having made good the damaged area, check carefully to see how it became damp in the first place. If condensation is the problem, ventilation may need improving. If damp is rising, you may need to renew the damp-proof course. If water is penetrating, you may need to replace window putty or re-seal around frames to keep it out.

Replacing wood If the damaged area is greater than is practicable to fill, cut out and replace the damaged timber. Remove all the affected wood and shape the surrounding area so you can match it with new wood. Apply wood hardener to any remaining soft fibres.

Treat exposed wood with a clear wood preservative and, if you are planning to paint, use pretreated wood to fill the hole. Otherwise, treat your shaped piece with clear wood preservative before fitting it in place. It is best to cut the repair piece slightly too high so you can plane or

sand it flush with the surrounding wood. Drill your repair wood to take rustless (zinc) screws, which you should countersink about 6mm (¼in) below the surface. Once you have drilled the repair wood, apply a liberal coating of waterproof wood adhesive – not forgetting the drilled holes – then screw the piece into place. Fill the screw holes with a two-part wood filler and leave it to harden.

Finishing off When the adhesive has set, smooth any projecting wood with glasspaper until it is flush with the surrounding areas. Unless you have been very accurate, you may find slight gaps in places between old and new timber. If so, fill these gaps with wood repair paste, allow it to set completely and then smooth it back with glasspaper. You could use a wood stopping for this filling work, but if you do, be sure it is a weatherproof grade. Always use the correct mix: never use interior fillers for exterior repairs.

If damage is extensive, you may need a joiner to carry out major repairs. And if you find that wood has dried out and crumbled and there are signs of whitish strands that give off a musty smell, suspect dry rot. Call in a specialist treatment company at once.

Metalwork

Indoor metalwork, such as stair balusters and fireplace surrounds and inserts, can be unsightly if they have been painted and the surface is flaking. Paint that has been applied so thickly that it spoils the outline of decorative wrought iron is also unattractive. Remove excess or flaking paint manually with a wire brush or with a cup or wheel brush attachment on a power drill. Always wear face protection. If repainting, use a metal primer on the cleaned surface first.

Once metal has started to corrode, the process will continue and accelerate, unless it is properly treated. Where you find rust, indoors in bathrooms or on leaky radiators, or outdoors on decorative ironwork or guttering, use a wire brush to remove all traces of it. Finish off with wire wool to clear away any fine dust from the surface.

After that, paint over the whole affected area with a rust-neutralizing primer – or a decorative rust-resisting enamel paint of the type used for radiators, which does not need a primer coat – and allow it to dry completely before applying the top coat.

BELOW Neutralize rust by using a primer that reacts with the rust and forms a barrier between the metal and the moisture-laden air.

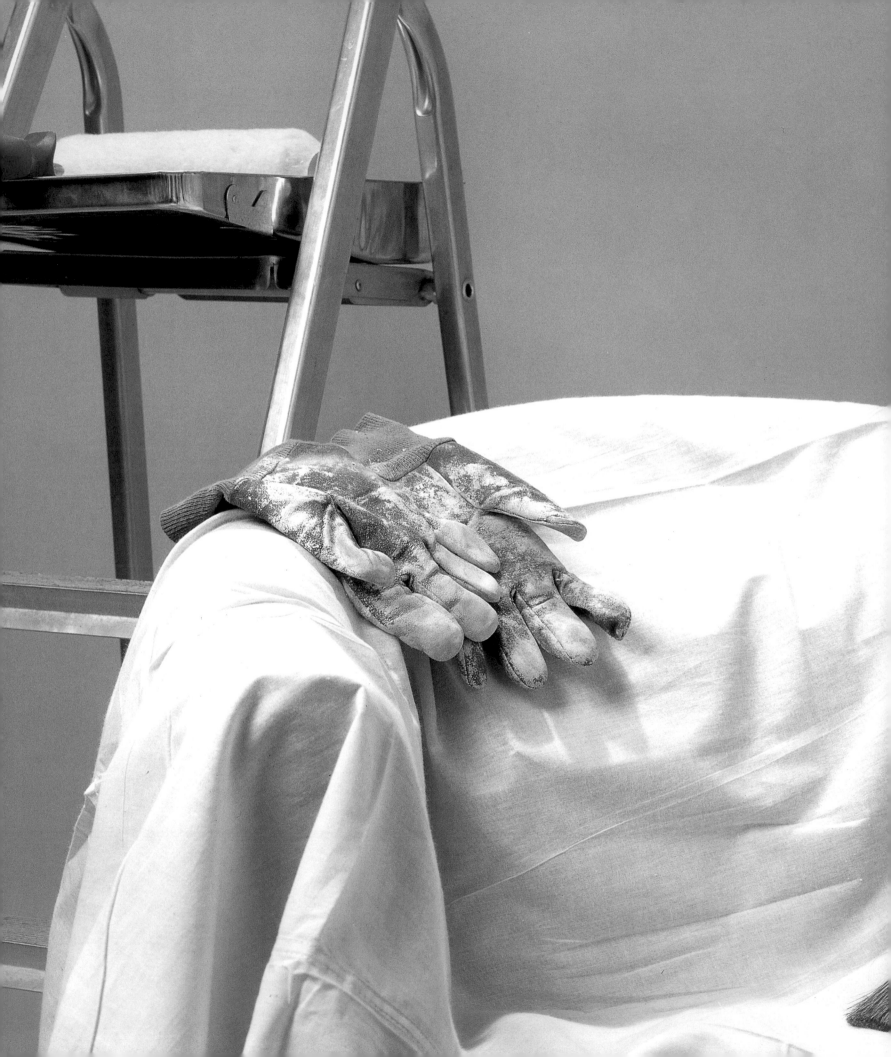

PAINT, WALLPAPER and TILES

Choosing paint

Choosing paint is both simpler and more complicated than ever before. Developments in paint technology have made paints easier and cleaner to use, and they are designed to meet all the many different requirements of the home decorator, from paints that cover in one coat to specialist effects that were once the province of the expert. The difficulty comes in deciding which colour and finish you want from the thousands available.

Types of paint

Traditionally, painting wood or metal involves a three-step application of primer, undercoat and top coat. Walls and ceilings are much simpler, however, requiring only one to three coats of emulsion paint, plus a primer on bare plaster or an undercoat before a change from a darker to a lighter shade. Many modern paints now combine two or more of these steps, making life much easier, so your choice will depend to a large extent on the type and condition of the surface you are painting and on your personal preference.

Special paint effects

Paints and glazes for graining, verdigris or bronzing, crackle glazing and numerous other interesting effects are widely available from craft shops. Should you want to create various antique effects on wood, to simulate age, or treat a surface such as a vase, lamp base or table top to imitate marble you will find a wide range of special products to choose from. Rag-rolling, sponging and bag-graining and similar techniques are described later in this chapter. It is also possible to achieve special effects using regular paints.

Primer This seals a surface to prevent subsequent layers of paint sinking in and disappearing. Primers are made for wood, metal and plaster, while universal primers are designed to suit all three surfaces. There are also aluminium primers for surfaces that need a high level of protection and rapid drying quick primers. It is a good idea to work with the same brand of primer, undercoat and top coat, since they will have been formulated to work together.

Undercoat A paint formulated to obliterate the previous colour and give body to the next coating. Some gloss paints are self-undercoating

Emulsions Mostly used for walls and ceilings. As it is water-based, emulsion is quick-drying, easy to use (and to rinse out of brushes) and reasonably odourless, but is not suitable for bare wood, since it may cause the grain to rise. Emulsions come as liquid, thixotropic or non-drip (a gel-

like consistency that should not be stirred) and semi-solid in a tray, to use with a roller. The widest choice of colours is found in vinyl matt and vinyl silk finishes. Mid-sheen emulsions labelled for kitchens and bathrooms will stand up better to washing down and condensation, and there are extra tough, scrubbable paints in colours that appeal to children. At the other end of the scale, there are several ranges of non-vinyl emulsions that produce the soft, almost

chalky finish of old paints; these are particularly good for old houses, but more difficult to clean.

One-coat emulsions These have extra covering power and will save you time, but perhaps not money. The choice of colours is not always as great.

Oil-based paints These provide a more durable surface than emulsion and are mostly used on wood and metal. Liquid gloss, when properly applied,

Using aerosol paints

Paint in aerosol cans is ideal for small areas, touching-up or repair jobs, stencilling and painting awkward objects such as the many different surfaces and twists and turns of wrought iron railings or gates. The range of colours is not as extensive as you will find for traditional paints, since the more subtle tones are not available.

Aerosol paints are not intended to be used for painting large areas. Shake the can well before use and hold it at the recommended distance from the surface.

Apply the paint in parallel bands, never in an arc. Apply only a very thin coat, allow it to dry and then build up further coats afterwards.

Because aerosol paint is released as a fine spray, objects are best taken outside for painting to avoid coating other nearby surfaces. Choose a still day to avoid too much paint drift. Protect the area around the object being painted with old sheets or newspapers. If you do have to work indoors for any length of time, it is best to wear a protective mask.

BELOW FROM LEFT TO RIGHT Undercoat primer, universal undercoat, liquid gloss top coat, non-drip gloss top coat, vinyl matt emulsion, textured emulsion, red masonry paint, rust-resistant paint

will produce a perfectly smooth and very hard surface, but is more prone to drips and runs; the jelly-like non-drip version gives nearly as good a finish. Oil-based paints also come in matt and various low-shine finishes, typically called eggshell, satin or silk. When painting bare wood you will need to use a primer first. If painting over another colour, a self-undercoating paint should cover the old colour without the need for a separate undercoat. Water-based paints are being made to replace these solvent-based paints.

Microporous paints Originally made for outside woodwork, these soak into the wood and act as a preservative. They also allow the wood to 'breathe' so you do not get any cracking or peeling. They cannot be applied over other paints, so you will need to strip back to bare wood before use.

Enamel and lacquer paint A finely ground paint with a high-gloss finish. No primer or undercoat is needed on wood or metal. Safe in a nursery.

Radiator paints Radiator enamel is formulated to maintain its whiteness where ordinary oil-based paint would crack and yellow with the heat of a radiator. Other heat-resistant paints are available in a limited range of colours.

Textured paint This special paint or compound is spread in a thick layer to hide joins in plasterboard. Lay the paint on thickly with a textured roller or use an ordinary roller and, before the paint starts to dry, use a rubber-bristled stippling brush to produce a variety of different effects. It is a permanent form of decoration and hard to remove.

Rust-resistant paint An enamel-formulated paint that inhibits the penetration of rust. No primer or undercoat is needed. Available in a smooth or indented 'hammered' finish.

Quantities and application

Before you start work, you will need to think about the surface you are painting and how many coats of paint it will require. This will be affected by the porosity of the surface to be painted as well as its overall texture.

Household paints are generally sold in 500ml, 1 litre, 2½ litre and 5 litre tin sizes. A few paints, such as white emulsion and paints for exterior walls, come in larger sizes. Smaller quantities – for example, 250ml, 100ml and 50ml – are available in some brands.

There is nothing particularly difficult or technical about painting but it is not worth taking short cuts. Paint applied to an unstable or greasy surface will quickly flake off, untreated knots in wood (*see p. 108*) will soon show through as brown stains, and you willl never disguise the drips or sag marks in paint that has been put on too thickly in an effort to get the job done quickly. Take your time.

1 Strain the paint into the kettle before starting. Load the brush by dipping it in to about half the depth of the bristles.

2 Squeeze out the excess paint by pressing the bristles gently against the inside of the paint kettle.

3 Apply the paint in parallel strips a short distance apart, working along in the direction of the wood grain.

4 Without reloading the brush, draw the bristles across the grain to spread the paint over the uncoated area.

5 Finish off by brushing the paint film lightly along in the direction of the grain. Draw the brush out towards the edge of a surface to avoid affecting the colour with a build-up of paint.

Calculating quantities

To cover a smooth, sealed surface, be guided by the coverage indicated on the can. As a general guide, 1 litre of paint covers an area as follows:

General-purpose primer	10–12 sq m	(11–13 sq yd)
Gloss paint	15 sq m	(17 sq yd)
One-coat gloss	10 sq m	(11 sq yd)
Emulsion paint	10–14 sq m	(11–15 sq yd)

To work out the area you have to cover, measure all around the room (or just one long wall and one short wall and double the answer if the room is a simple rectangle with no recesses) and multiply by the height. This will give you a number in square metres or yards. Subtract 1.8 sq m (2 sq yd) for each door. Measure the width and height of the windows (ignore any small ones) and also subtract their area. Remember to multiply by the number of coats the walls will need.

For standard windows with several panes, simply multiply the width of the overall frame by the depth, and treat it as a solid area. For large picture windows, make the same calculation but deduct 50 per cent. For metal windows, deduct 25 per cent. For flush doors, multiply the height of the doors by the width and add a further 10 per cent for the edges. For a panelled door, add 25 per cent. A little extra paint stored in a marked jar is useful for touching up in the future.

Preparing paint

Make sure the tin is free of loose dust and dirt before opening the lid. Check on the tin to see whether the paint needs stirring. If it does, use a length of wood. If you are using liquid paint, decant some into a paint kettle. This is a much less cumbersome way to carry paint around as you work. Paint kettles are also useful because should the paint become contaminated in any way, then only the paint in the kettle is affected.

How many coats of paint?

The number of coats you apply depends on the existing colour (if any), the type of surface you are working on, and the quality of the paint you are using. It is always better to apply two, or even three, thin coats of paint than a single thick one of topcoat. Always bear in mind that you cannot rush the job, and you must wait for one coat of paint to dry completely before applying another.

Painting interior walls

Choose your decorating tools according to the finish you require. For a smooth surface, use a brush, a foam or mohair roller or a paint pad; for a deeper texture, or to cover a rough surface, use a brush or a shaggy pile roller (see p. 12–13).

You will always produce a better finish if you apply two thin coats rather than one thicker one.

If you choose to work with a brush, choose the widest you can comfortably hold. Begin at the top of a wall and run bands of paint downward in vertical strips, leaving a slight gap between the bands. Then brush across the wall to blend the bands of paint, finishing with light, vertical strokes of the paintbrush.

Rollers and pads are easiest to use with shallow rectangular trays. Most have a built-in shelf or, for pads, a rolling edge, against which you can squeeze off the excess paint. If you decide to use a roller, begin by working the roller in all directions and finish off with light strokes in a single direction. It is best to work over a small area at a time. Don't roll too quickly or the paint will fly off the roller. Allow the roller to shed all its paint before reloading it. Don't paint too thick a coating; instead, work two (or more)

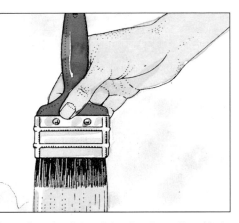

When using a brush to paint walls, choose the widest brush you feel comfortable with. Start at the top of the wall and work downwards. When using a matt emulsion, finish off with criss-cross strokes; with satin emulsion, use light, upward strokes.

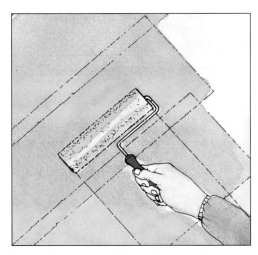

Run a roller over the wall in a criss-cross pattern, being careful to merge the joins and fill in any gaps. Finish off using a small brush around the wall edges.

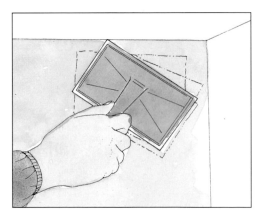

Use a paint pad in much the same way as a roller, applying paint in a criss-cross pattern. Paint pads are especially useful for running along wall edges.

thin coats as you would with a brush.

To use a paint pad, work the paint in all directions. Note that a pad applies a very thin coat of emulsion only and so you will have to repeat this process to give two or even three coats – especially if you have a base colour to hide. Whatever painting tool you use for the main area of walls, you will need a small paintbrush for the edges.

Emulsion paint dries quickly so you will not have to wait too long between coats.

Painting ceilings safely

Although you can paint a ceiling from a step ladder, it involves a lot of tiring leg work since you have to climb up and down to move the steps. It is much simpler to make a platform (see p. 18–19). Erect the platform so that your head is about 75mm (3in) beneath the ceiling.

Painting woodwork

If using an oil-based paint, first seal bare wood surfaces with a wood primer. When it is dry, rub this layer down lightly with fine-grade sandpaper, dust off with a lint-free rag, and apply a layer of undercoat (to give body to the final coat), unless you are using a paint that combines undercoat and topcoat.

To cover a sound painted surface, you can dispense with the primer. If painting over a different, especially a darker, colour, use a self-undercoating paint or as many coats of undercoat as necessary.

Apply the paint following the grain, working in strips. Next, work the brush across the grain and then, with light strokes, follow the grain as you did on the first application to ensure even coverage and a smooth finish. Always brush out towards an edge – for example, of a door frame – to prevent the paint forming an unsightly ridge.

When using a microporous paint you may not need a separate undercoat; some are primer, undercoat and topcoat in one. If you do need an undercoat, ensure you choose a microporous formulation, as the qualities of a microporous paint that allow the wood beneath to 'breathe' will not work over a regular paint.

Masking paintwork

A little time spent masking around glass window or door panes will save you a lot of time and effort afterwards. Run strips of masking tape around the edges of the glass where they meet the woodwork. Leave a narrow margin of paint on the glass to form a seal. Use a small brush, holding it like a pencil, and apply paint in the direction of the grain. Peel the tape off as soon as the paint is dry – otherwise it is difficult to remove.

Brush care

You need a selection of different sizes and shapes of brush for many home decorating jobs, but good-quality brushes are expensive to buy. However, if you take the time to look after them properly, they become better and better tools the more they are used and they will give you good service for many years.

Hardware stores, DIY shops and many large department stores stock a variety of brush-cleaning appliances. These are designed to hold brushes just clear of the bottom of the container so that the bristles don't become bent and damaged. But if you have many brushes to clean, these can work out to be expensive.

As a less-expensive alternative, you can make an effective brush-cleaning device using an old jar of a size appropriate to the brush you want to clean. Suspend the brush in the jar using a piece of string and a long nail, making sure the bristles are held clear of the bottom. Remember to change the cleaning solution regularly.

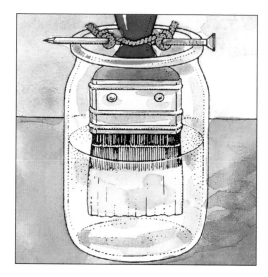

Storing paint brushes

When you have finished cleaning a brush and while it is still damp, slip an elastic band over the brush tip to hold the bristles firmly, but not tightly, together. Provided the elastic band is not too tight, it will ensure that the bristles keep a good shape, with no stray whiskers. When all the brushes are completely dry, place them in a sealed polythene bag to keep them free from dust, and store them so that their bristles stay flat.

Paint care

Rather than discard leftover paint once you have finished a decorating job, you can store any excess by transferring what is left in the can into small, screw-top jars. Choose jars of the right size so that the paint fills them right to the top. If all air is excluded, the paint will keep almost indefinitely like this

and can be used later for touching up any damaged areas. If you leave leftover paint in the bottom of its original container it will soon evaporate.

Paint that has been stored for some time can be affected in two ways. First, if there is a brown liquid floating on top, just stir it thoroughly back into the rest of the paint. It should recombine quite easily. Second, if a skin has formed on the surface, cut around this with a knife and scrape away any paint on the underside and return it to the can. Strain the paint before reuse, either with a paint strainer or by passing it through a clean nylon stocking. Fix the stocking loosely over the can with an elastic band and push the nylon down into the paint, then dip the brush into the nylon and the paint will seep through it.

If an emulsion can has become rusty on the inside, carefully transfer all the unaffected paint into a clean container and throw away any contaminated paint and the original container.

Handy hints

- Generally, it is all right to apply oil-based paint over existing emulsion, provided it is sound. Applying emulsion over oil-based paint is less satisfactory. Instead, use an oil-based mid-sheen or matt paint.

- Batch colours may differ slightly on standard paint colours bought off the shelf, so buy a little extra at the start of a job. This way you won't run out and have to go back for more, only to find the new batch is a slightly different colour.

- Try not to start with a new can of paint in the middle of a wall or ceiling in case of colour variation.

- If you find yourself running out of paint, stop at a convenient corner, angle, or other natural feature while you still have paint left.

Painting in progress

Ideally you should decorate during daylight hours to take advantage of the natural light. If you paint under artificial lighting you may overlook gaps in the coverage. For best results, paint an interior in a strict order, from the highest to the lowest point. For doors and windows, the sequence of painting is described on the following page.

Order of painting

1 Start painting at the window end of a ceiling (1–5).
2 Prime and undercoat frames, doors and skirting.
3 Paint walls, large ones first (1–4).
4 Top coat frames.
5 Top coat doors.
6 Top coat skirting.

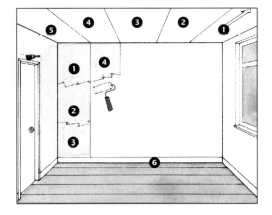

To paint any room always start with the ceiling, since paint will inevitably drip or be splattered onto the walls. In an average room with a window and a door, begin painting the ceiling at the window end and work across the ceiling covering the surface in parallel bands approximately a metre or a yard wide until you reach the door end (*see numbers 1–5 on the diagram above*). Work an area that is comfortable to reach from your standing point, whether you are on a makeshift platform or a stepladder. If there is a ceiling rose or a light fitting in the middle of the ceiling, you should paint neatly around this with a small paintbrush and then continue painting in parallel bands.

The next step is, if necessary, to apply primer and undercoat to the frames of the door and window and allow to them to dry out completely (*see p. 106*), preferably overnight.

Next paint the walls or any other large surfaces in the room. Start in the top left-hand corner of one wall and work with a brush, roller or paint pad covering an area of about a square metre or yard at a time. Work your way down the wall from the ceiling to the floor in vertical bands (*see numbers 1–4 on the diagram above*). Continue to paint the rest of the first wall and then the remaining walls in this order. Complete one wall in full before you begin the next. To paint around a window, first paint around the window frame with a small brush and then fill in the surrounding wall space with a larger brush, roller or paint pad. Once this is done, give the frames of first the door and then the window a topcoat. Then paint the door of the room and add any covering to the floor last. Paint the coving and skirting boards after the ceiling and walls are completely finished.

ABOVE The decorative topcoat of paint for a door should be applied as the last stage of painting a room, unless you intend to paint the floor as well.

Handy hints

- Before you use a new brush, or one that has been stored for any length of time, manipulate the bristles by rubbing them briskly in the palm of your hand to loosen and remove any dust and broken bristles.

- If you plan to use a number of different colours of paint, line your paint kettle or roller tray with layers of kitchen foil, pressing it well down so that it takes the shape of the container. By doing this, when you come to change paint colours you can simply remove the top layers of foil and the container is clean and ready to accept the next colour.

- If you are painting a room with more than one colour, use a different brush for each colour. This will save you a lot of time cleaning brushes.

Painting interior doors

Whatever type of door you wish to paint, you should first remove as many fittings as possible, since handles, escutcheon plates and hooks are all difficult to paint around. The ideal way to paint a door is to unhinge it and lay it flat over a pair of trestles. In order not the damage its surface, pad the trestle tops with old rags or magazines. Follow the instructions for preparing and painting wood (*see p. 103*).

Select your tools for the job carefully according to the surface of the door. Use a wide brush for a flush door and a small brush for the decorative moulding of a panelled door. With all types of door, paint the edge opposite the hinges last in the sequence so that you always have something to hold on to until the final stage.

To paint a flush door, mentally divide up the surface area into small sections (*see diagram below*). Try to work quickly to avoid tide marks or visible joins. Use a 75mm (3in) wide brush and begin at the top left-hand corner (or top right if you are left-

handed), covering to about half the width of the door (1). First, work using vertical brush strokes and then brush across these with light horizontal strokes. Complete the other sections (2–6) in the same way. It is important to work the brush strokes consistently so that the finish of the door will

be even. To complete the edges of the door (7), use a small brush. Paint the frame of the door (8) last with a small brush.

For a panelled door, the sequence is a little more complicated (*see below*). First, paint the mouldings around the panels (1) and then the panels themselves (2). Start with the upper panels and work from top to bottom. Begin each panel at the top and work downwards, painting vertical brush strokes followed by light horizontal ones.

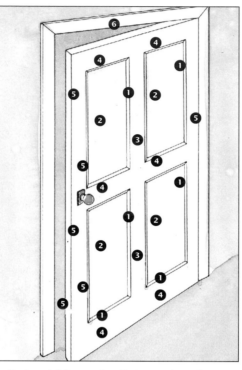

Next, paint the section that runs down the middle of the door dividing the panels (3). Continue by coating the horizontal rails, starting at the top and working down (4). Complete the outer vertical strips and then do all the door edges (5). Lastly, paint the whole door frame (6).

Painting interior windows

To protect the panes, mask the glass just inside the frames with tape, leaving a 3mm (⅛in) margin to allow a thin line of paint to overlap the glass and form a seal.

To paint a sash window (*see diagrams above right*), push the rear sash down and the front one up so that at least 20cm (8in) of the lower rear sash is exposed. Paint the bottom rail of the rear sash and as much of the exposed upright sections as possible (1). Pull the rear sash up so that it is almost shut and paint the rest (2). With the front sash

slightly open, paint its frame (3). When both sashes are dry, paint the surround, shut the window and paint the exposed part of the runners, but not the cords. Paint the sill last (4).

With a casement window (*see below*), fix the window slightly ajar. First, paint the rebates (1) and then the horizontal and vertical crossrails (2). Paint the horizontal top and bottom sides and edges (3), then the vertical sides and edges (4). When the window is dry, paint the frame (5) including the edges. Leave the sill (6) to the end, to avoid smudging; do the stay last of all, if it needs painting, so that you can use it.

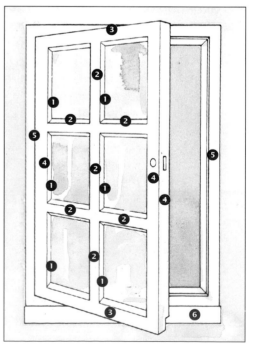

Problem areas

There are some areas in your home that may present some difficulty when it comes to painting – these include high-up awkward corners, stairwells, covings and picture rails.

A stairwell is one of the most difficult areas to decorate, and for some people it is enough to put them right off even attempting to do it themselves. However, with a just bit of planning and taking extra care while you work – because you will have to stand on an elevated platform – it is quite possible to paint this part of the home yourself, even if you are inexperienced.

The first thing you need is some form of scaffolding. The most reliable solution is to hire a staircase platform, which is designed to fit neatly onto stairs by means of adjustable legs. However, if you are not worried by heights then you can construct your own platform. Make frequent checks that the scaffold board is centrally placed and has not slipped out of position, particularly as you climb on and off it. (*See p. 18–19 for more details.*)

By using a roller or a paint pad with an extension pole, you can greatly increase your reach and apply paint overhead on the ceiling and high up on the stairwell walls.

Before painting picture rails, make sure that they are free from dust, dirt and grease, particularly along their top surface. It is usual to work in a similar type of paint as for the walls, which is likely to be emulsion, although you may choose a contrasting colour to pick out the detail of the picture rail. Using a small paintbrush, paint along the run of the rail. Use the same method for shielding the wall as described for painting skirting boards.

With covings, as with picture rails, it is usual to use the same type of paint as for the walls. The paint can either match the walls or the ceiling or be in a contrasting colour, which will help to emphasize any detailing. Use a paint shield or masking tape for a neat finish, as already described above.

ABOVE The creative effects you can achieve with paint are virtually limitless as this rich red bathroom proves. A simple MDF bath panel has been transformed.

Painting skirting boards

When the rest of the room is freshly painted, a discoloured skirting board will mar the overall effect. Painting the skirting is a quick job that is best left until after the walls are completed. Because skirtings are low down and narrow, you should work with a small brush and use a hard-wearing paint that will withstand knocks. Wipe down the skirting with a damp cloth to remove any dust and vacuum along its bottom edge to remove any dirt or fluff in the carpet that may stick to the wet paint. Lay down newspaper to protect the floor. To protect the wall, use a piece of stiff card or a slim offcut of wood and hold it to shield the wall while you brush. If the wall has been dry for some time, then you can use masking tape – but remember to peel away the tape before the gloss paint hardens or the paint may tear. Work the brush following the direction of the skirting, making horizontal strokes and working your way in one direction around the room. When you come to painting close to the floor, ensure that your brush does not pick up dirt or fluff from below the skirting by moving a sheet of card or an offcut of wood along the floor as a shield as you paint.

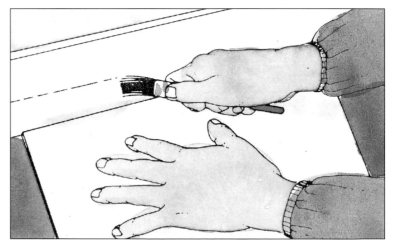

When painting the bottom edge of a skirting board, use a sheet of stiff card or an offcut of wood both to protect the surface of the floor from paint and to prevent the paintbrush picking up dirt or fluff and transferring it to your fresh paintwork. Slide the card or wood along the floor as you proceed. Check from time to time that there is no paint on the inside edge or bottom of the card.

Painting faults

Good-quality modern paints rarely give any trouble, and flaws with the finished results are usually caused by problems with the surface on which the paints are applied. All too often, mistakes occur due to poor surface preparation. Here are some common faults and ways of remedying them.

Blistering occurs when air or water is trapped underneath the paint and the paintwork begins to bubble up. It occurs on wood if the wood is damp or if resin is drawn out of the wood by heat. The only sure remedy is to strip back the paint, ensure that the surface has thoroughly dried out, and begin the whole decorating process once again from scratch.

Flaking occurs when the paint has no grip on the undersurface and does not key on properly. The topcoat of paint lifts and flakes off in dry fragments. Perhaps the surface was too smooth, as with old gloss paint, or maybe it was too chalky. Badly flaking areas are best stripped back, then provide a key and redecorate from scratch.

Wrinkling in oil-based paint is caused by a second coat of paint being applied before the solvent has evaporated out of the first layer. It can also result if a topcoat is applied too thickly. A wrinkled surface shows patches of shrivelled or puckering paint, which is rough to touch. The best remedy is to strip back the surface and redecorate, making sure you allow each coat to harden and dry thoroughly before applying the next; also avoid applying paint too thickly.

Matt patches in the paint can occur where a priming coat has been omitted. Subsequent coats then soak into the wood, which results in a loss of the gloss finish in these areas.

Unfortunately, applying further coats of paint rarely solves the problem, and the only effective solution is to strip the paint back and prime first before repainting.

Staining is often encountered when emulsion paint is applied over a stained area and the stain begins to bleed through. To remedy, allow the emulsion to dry completely and then spray the affected area with a stain-sealer, which will dry in a few minutes. You can then paint over the affected area again.

Crazing forms a pattern of tiny cracks similar in appearance to crazy paving. It occurs either when incompatible paints are used together or when a layer of paint is applied over a previous coat that was not completely dry. The solution is to rub the cracked surface until it is quite smooth, either by hand with a sandpaper block, or using a sanding attachment on a power drill. Repaint when really smooth.

Bleeding is a fault that occurs on wood containing knots that have not been properly sealed. The warmth of sunlight encourages the resin to bleed out of the knots, which damages the paint film. To correct this, strip back the damaged area to bare wood, treat the knot or knots with a suitable sealant, and then repaint.

Poor drying is usually caused when paint is applied over a dirty or greasy surface. You should strip back the paint and thoroughly clean the underlying surface. Remove any traces of grease and particles of dirt or dust before repainting.

Runs are the result of too much paint being applied with an overloaded brush, roller or paint pad. It occurs on vertical surfaces and the descending drips are also known as sagging or curtaining. Use a wide-bladed scraper to scrape off the runs when they are dry. Then rub down the surface by hand or with a sanding attachment on a power drill until the runs are eliminated and the surface feels really smooth when you run your hand over it. Unfortunately, runs can be very obstinate, so a lot of rubbing down may be required before you can repaint.

Colour showing through is most often the result of a lack of undercoat. Bear in mind that a topcoat is really just a protective layer and is not designed to obliterate what lies beneath. To remedy this problem rub down the surface well and apply enough undercoat until the colour is completely hidden, then apply top coat again.

Grittiness happens when dirt that has been picked up on a paintbrush is transferred on to the surface during painting. It is particularly common when painting outside close to masonry. If the paint is still wet, you can simply wipe away the grittiness with a lint-free rag and repaint the area with a clean brush. If the paint has dried, however, you should rub it back with glasspaper and then repaint. If the paint in the can is contaminated with bits of dirt, you must strain it with a nylon stocking or paint strainer (*see p. 104*).

Insects can find their way into newly applied paint all too easily, particularly on a warm, sultry day during the summer months. Insects can also be a problem if there are any plants growing nearby. If the paint is still wet, lift off the insects with the point of a penknife, or a similar implement, and carefully smooth out the paint to erase the imprint, using the paintbrush or a lint-free rag. If the paint is starting to dry, leave it well alone until the paint is hard, and then rub the insect gently free with your finger.

Materials for special effects

The following tools and materials are used in a wide range of applications, and you may find that you have some of them already about the home. Some of the specialist brushes mentioned are expensive, so look for synthetic substitutes which can equally be of excellent quality. Ideally, it is best to use brushes either for paintwork or for varnishing, and not to mix them between the two jobs. It is a good idea to have a range of different grades of glasspaper and some wire wool to hand, too. One golden rule is to clean brushes scrupulously, especially taking care not to leave any paint or varnish near the handle end of the brush. This takes time and effort, but it pays dividends in the long run.

Materials and equipment

Ground chalk Finely powdered chalk is applied to some wood surfaces to fill the grain and provide a smooth background for subsequent painting.

Scumble glaze or transparent oil glaze Thin this liquid glaze with white spirit and brush it over the surface. It can be tinted with a universal stainer or an oil-based paint and creates a see-through film of colour.

White spirit This is also called turpentine substitute. Use it to dilute oil-based paints and varnish and to distress oil-based paints and glazes when they are still wet.

Polyurethane varnish This is an oil-based varnish available in different finishes. It is easy to apply and provides good surface protection.

Universal stainer This is a chemical dye that dissolves in white spirit. Use it to tint emulsion and oil-based paints and glazes.

Acrylic paint Available in tubes in an extensive range of colours. It is water soluble and is useful for tinting emulsion paint. It becomes waterproof when dry and dries very quickly, making it convenient to use.

Mottler A brush made from hair, available in a range of different sizes. It is used primarily for dragging or to simulate wood grain.

Softening brush Use just the tip of the brush to blend oil-based glazes gently after they have been applied but are still wet.

Flogger A horsehair brush made with long, coarse bristles. It is used to tap, or 'flog', a wet glaze to give a finely flecked finish.

Flat fitch A hog's hair brush useful for applying glazes in small or difficult areas.

Jamb duster This is usually used to remove dust before painting a surface. It is also useful as a softening and blending brush instead of a dusting brush.

Artist's brushes Available in various sizes with round or flat bristles. They are used for detailed or delicate work.

Stippling brush A brush with a flat, square head, and with flat-edged bristles on the underside. It is commonly used for stencilling work.

Stencilling brush The stiff bristles hold only a small amount of paint. Designed to produce neat, sharp-edged stencil designs.

Sponge For covering large areas of stencil cut-outs, a small piece of sponge is quicker to use.

1 Mottler 2 Softening brush
3 Stencilling brush
4 Stippling brush
5 Natural sponge 6 Flogger
7 Small artist's brush
8 Flat fitch 9 Graining tool
10 Ground chalk
11 Scumble glaze
12 Acrylic paint

Paint effects

There are various ways of creating colour effects that lend interest to a bland expanse of wall. You can either work with traditional paints commercially prepared, or you can create your own effects with readily available emulsion or eggshell paints, tints and pigments. Traditional techniques include sponging, colourwash, rag-rolling, ragging on, dry-brushing and liming. These methods involve the use of a base coat to cover the wall or ceiling followed by a glaze or tint applied in various different ways. Rollers and pads with textured or broken finishes are available to produce many special effects.

Whichever paint finish you choose, the wall or ceiling must always be properly prepared. None of these fine paint finishes will disguise bad workmanship, like unfilled cracks or dirty walls, so be prepared to spend at least the usual amount of time on surface preparation. The secret of successful paint decoration is to test all the different techniques on odd sheets of lining paper, pieces of wood or hardboard. Then you can see beforehand how the impression looks and whether it is the finish you want. You may need to reduce the amount of pressure on the tool you are using or maybe thin the paint. With practice you will soon build the skills required to achieve the results you want.

RIGHT This subtle colour wash adds depth and warmth to the walls of this room. The vivid colour complements and sets off the decorative Arts and Crafts style iron fireplace.

Colour washes

You can buy ready-made colour wash paint, but you can also create your own finish with emulsion or water-based eggshell paint and a tint or pigment.

To prepare the surface of the wall, paint a base coat of matt or silk emulsion and allow to dry. Either choose the same colour paint or a colour close in tone and mix up a wash of emulsion and water, in equal parts. Gradually increase the water to make a thin colour that will not run down the wall in heavy droplets, but will allow the base colour to show through when it is applied on top. Once you have tested the wash on a sample area continue to apply the remaining colour with a wide decorator's brush using sweeping strokes. Further coats can be applied in a toning colour. For a more durable finish, you can use a thinned glaze as a wash over the whole surface. If you want a hard, protective finish, use a clear, matt polyurethane varnish, or a water-based acrylic varnish.

LEFT A colour wash creates a friendly atmosphere in this country-style dining room. The walls blend in with the woodwork and provide a sympathetic setting for paintings and antiques.

Freehand motif

The technique of colourwashing walls lends itself to the addition of hand painting on the top. It has an individual, crafted look and finish which, particularly in a country setting, gives an individual flourish to any wall, corner or recess.

Before you start your design it is always a good idea to carry out a small trial on a piece of paper. This helps you to establish the colour combination you are going to use, the depth and tone of your paint, and the relationship between the scale of the design and the rest of the room.

Materials

- **Sponges and different-sized paintbrushes**

- **Card, craft knife and pencils**

- **Emulsion paint for walls**

- **Acrylic (water-based) paint, pigment or commercial paint tints**

1 Select the background colour for your wall and apply the paint with a sponge. Leave a generous space around the area where you are planning to paint your tile.

2 Place a cut-out shape of the motif you are going to use on the wall and sponge carefully all round the edges with the background colour of the wall. Take care not to let any paint creep underneath the

cut-out. When the paint is dry, remove the template and you will find a clean area upon which to start work.

3 With a paintbrush, sketch out the outline of your tile in the colour you have chosen, in this case blue.

4 You might find it easier to draw your design on the wall using a soft pencil and then paint over it. With confidence you can work directly with brush and paint and complete your design.

5 Working freehand gives any motif or design that you choose a highly individual look. The variations in paint add to the originality of your work, so do not try to create the same uniform finished effect of a machine-painted tile. This hand-painted tile is both pleasing and eye-catching.

Handy hint

Before taking any fresh-loaded brush or other applicator to the wall, first test out its effect on a spare piece of paper to make sure the brush stroke or imprint is the right size, depth and thickness. Keep a piece of clean rag or paper beside the paint as you work and dab the brush or applicator onto this first to ensure that any excess paint is removed. This will help to prevent unwanted drips.

Sponging

Sponging is one of the easiest decorative paint finishes to achieve. Use closely related colours to give a subtle effect or contrasting colours to achieve a striking mottled finish.

Apply the base coat with matt or silk-finish emulsion and allow to dry. Choose your first topcoat colour and thin with a little water. Dip the flat side of the sponge into the paint, taking care to wipe off any drips, and apply to a test surface. Sponge the wall using a dabbing, twisting movement to achieve an uneven, mottled effect. Cover the whole wall and allow to dry. Then, if required, start at the beginning again and continue to apply more coats of either colour until the wall is evenly covered.

You can experiment with sponging using an oil-based finish or a glaze instead. A transparent glaze sponged over an emulsion base coat will add depth and warmth.

❶ A cool fresh mood can be achieved by using a crisp green as one of the sponged colours. An apricot base coat is applied, allowed to dry, and then sponged with green. Apricot is then sponged over the top.

❷ A warmer feel can be achieved by changing the sponged colour to a deep, earthy red. The base colour is applied and then sponged with a warm red, followed by a sponged coat of apricot, as before.

Handy hints

- Practise each paint finish and colour combination on paper before applying it to the wall.

- Keep a clean cloth to hand to remove any drips that may form.

- Wait for the paint to dry thoroughly before correcting errors or making improvements or additions.

- Dilute ragged-on or sponged-on paint with about 50 per cent water for a paler shade of colour.

- If possible, complete a whole wall before finishing a painting session so there are no visible 'joins' in obvious places.

RIGHT Bag graining creates a broken paint finish with more texture than a plain colour. Here, a paler background colour has been overlaid with a richer green glaze or thinned emulsion which has been 'bagged' while still wet to reveal some of the base colour. The effect is quite subtle from a distance.

Rag-rolling

This soft, mottled paint effect is an excellent technique for disguising bumps or surface irregularities. You can work with water-based or oil-based paints. When applying paint, where possible work in pairs – one person painting on the glaze with a brush, followed by another person working with the rag.

Colour recipe

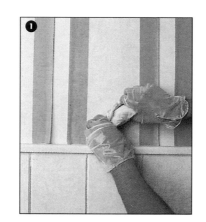

Rag-rolling, as the name implies, is literally rolling a rag over a coat of wet glaze or paint. The crumpled rag leaves its impression in the glaze, removing varying amounts of it to allow the base coat colour to show through. Either match the tone of the top colour with the background, or introduce a slightly darker tone on top.

If using oil-based paint, mix 3 parts of paint with 7 parts of transparent oil glaze. Thin with white spirit. The glaze slows down the paint's drying time, giving you more time to work; it also gives a soft, shining finish.

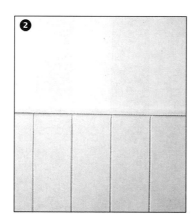

1 Here, a coat of magnolia emulsion has been applied as the background colour. A coat of grey gloss, mixed with an oil glaze, has been applied on top. While the top coat is still wet, a crumpled rag is rolled both down and across the surface to achieve an even, broken effect.

2 To create the stripes, use masking tape to blank out the areas you want left plain. Rag-roll the colour in between the strips of masking tape. Allow to dry before removing the tape.

RIGHT A soft magnolia emulsion is painted on walls and ceiling, then allowed to dry. The walls are then rag-rolled with an antique grey gloss colour to finish. The top coat is applied in stripes to create an elegant finish.

Bag graining

Bag graining gives a traditional broken-paint finish using only the simplest of tools – a plastic bag filled with rags. The result can be beautifully subtle, producing an effect similar to the look of crushed velvet.

1 Working on a small section at a time, use a wide brush to paint on the topcoat glaze or thinned paint in vertical strokes.

2 Half fill a plastic bag with small pieces of rag and secure the top firmly. When each section is completed with the brush, use the plastic bag to press down onto the paint, immediately lifting off and pressing down on the next spot in a dabbing motion. Take care not to smudge the grain as you lift the plastic bag. This will produce a crinkled effect, which should be left to dry. Protect with a glaze.

Handy hints for bag graining

• Overlap each bag-graining slightly as you work along the wall to avoid bands where one section finishes and another starts.

• You can do bag graining either in a pale colour over a darker base coat or vice versa. Experiment first with different colours.

Other broken colour effects

Dry-brushing is another colour effect with a similar finish to sponging and rag-rolling. You can apply a dry-brush technique to walls covered with lining paper as well as bare plaster. Working with a good quality paintbrush, load the paint, a little at a time, at the end of the brush and work with it dry, using a small brushing movement. The paint is spread out over the wall giving a mottled, milky effect. As with other techniques, you are building up colour, layer upon layer, until you have the result you want. If you are working with emulsion paint, add water to thin the paint. Remember, too, that emulsion paints dry more quickly than oil-based paints, so you need to allow for this as you will have less time to work with the paint to create the effect you want.

Materials

- **Emulsion paint, darker colour for background, lighter colour for dry-brushing**

- **Paint brush and paint container**

- **Top coat of eggshell paint, slightly thinned with white spirit**

- **Clean white paper and clean lint-free rags for removing excess paint**

1 Select the paint colour for the background and paint the walls. Next, choose the colour for your top coat. If you are working with an oil-based eggshell paint you will need to thin it (3 parts top colour to 1 part white spirit). Choose a top coat colour that is either close in tone or contrasts with your wall colour. With dry-brushing you can completely cover the background colour, so your top coat is the colour you will see on your finished walls.

2 Take the paint onto the bristles of the brush and wipe off any excess onto a piece of clean paper, until the brush is almost dry.

Ragging on

Materials

- **Emulsion base coat**

- **Emulsion for ragging on**

- **Cotton, lint-free rag or sheeting**

- **A bowl and an old spoon for mixing the paint**

Apply the base colour to the wall and allow to dry thoroughly. Scrunch up a lint-free rag into a ball, and dip into a bowl of paint of a contrasting shade. Remove the excess paint, then dab the rag straight onto the wall. Keep dipping the same side of the rag into the paint and dabbing at the same angle with even pressure to achieve a uniform pattern. For a more random effect, frequently rearrange the painty rag, dabbing with even pressure. Avoid overloading the rag.

With free movements, paint in all directions over the wall. Repeat the dry-brush technique with layers of paint until you have built up the finished effect you want.

3 When you have finished working with the larger paintbrush and the colour is the strength and intensity you want, use a smaller paintbrush to soften the edges of the brush strokes where they are very prominent. If you are using emulsion paint, work quickly as it will dry very fast.

LEFT These dry-brushed walls and cupboards have been painted with large brush strokes for a bold look.

RIGHT A country-style kitchen is enhanced by using the broken colour effect of dry-brushing to draw attention to the rustic quality of the room.

Painting stripes

A simple way of giving a plain painted surface an interesting pattern is by using masking tape to create bold stripes. First paint the walls the colour of the lighter stripe. Decide how wide the stripes are to be (they could be uniform or alternately wide and narrow) and, when the base coat is dry, smooth a length of masking tape along one edge of the proposed stripe and a second length down the other. Press the tape down firmly with the back of a teaspoon to prevent paint seeping underneath. Apply the second stripe colour with a brush, or sponge or cloth if you wish to create a subtle ragged stripe effect. When the paint is dry, peel off the tape slowly and carefully.

The same technique can be used on wooden furniture with acrylic paint, which adheres to most surfaces. If possible turn the piece of furniture over so the surface you will be working on is horizontal.

Choose low-tack masking tape, specially designed for delicate painted surfaces, and remove it carefully as soon as the paint is dry.

LEFT A striped effect created by using masking tape gives this child's bedroom a fresh, attractive finish.

Stencils, stamps, découpage and friezes

The decorative paint finishes described so far offer a variety of attractive effects, but why not use your walls like a canvas to create truly original designs? Stencilling and stamping are fun and easy techniques, and the choice of pre-cut templates has grown to an enormous array of patterns. Cutting your own stencils means there is no limit to the possibilities, and you are not restricted to decorating walls: floor paints and aerosols make floor stencils a fun alternative.

Découpage, popular in Victorian times for adorning small objects or table tops, has also developed into an imaginative technique for decorating walls, with results that can vary from quaint to futuristic. Alternatively, try a repeat-pattern frieze on a wall or a piece of furniture, an opportunity to introduce the originality of freehand painting within a simple design that can be tackled by anyone.

TOP This country feel has been created using a lacy stencil motif which is repeated throughout the walls, corners and sloping ceiling of this delightful attic bedroom. The design is picked up in the deep frill of the muslin curtains at the window. A luxurious quilt in a traditional geometrical design contrasts effectively with a country-check bedspread to complete the look.

ABOVE AND LEFT An example of very bold stencilling used on the walls to create an Oriental look. A large, bold motif runs along the wall below the dado rail and another runs along the top of the wall. The muted yellow, blue and red tones of the stencil contrast and harmonize with the bold, geometric fabrics and ornate furnishings in the room.

Using a stencil

There are a number of ways you can apply colour to pre-cut stencils, and many different effects can be achieved. Tones of colour can be built up in layers or colours can be blended into one another. You might like to experiment to find the method of applying paint which best suits the work you are doing or which you prefer.

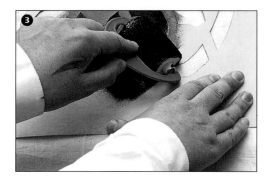

❶ Using a stencil brush with firm bristles, take up a little colour, remove any excess, and apply with a light, dabbing motion.

❷ Using a sponge is a very economical method and gives a distinctive mottled effect. Dampen the sponge slightly, take up a small amount of colour, remove any excess and apply with a light, dabbing motion. Colours can be blended as you work, or left to dry between coats.

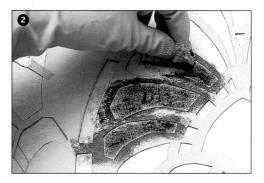

❸ Using a small foam roller is probably the most economical method of achieving a dense, even coverage, especially on fabric. This roller was bought in a toy shop and is ideal for stencilling large motifs.

❹ Aerosol sprays are not ideal for use with all stencils. Not only can the fumes be hazardous, but careful masking with newspaper is essential if you do not want to spray the surrounding area. Seepage of paint

under the edges of the stencil can also be a problem, so apply the paint lightly from above. Sprays are wonderful, however, for working with large areas of flat colour and particularly good if you arc working on fabric.

Repeating patterns

Repeating patterns needs some planning and measuring, but it is equally important to ensure that the visual balance of the room is kept in mind. When placing your stencil on the wall, start from the centre of the wall and work outwards, until you come to a corner or a break. Find the correct position for a horizontal pattern with a spirit level, or use a plumb line to align a vertically repeating stencil correctly and fasten the stencil to the wall with low-tack tape. If a design looks gappy, add extra motifs between existing ones.

STENCILLING MATERIALS 1 Artist's brush to apply tints or paint free-hand 2 Small stencil brush 3 Large stencil brush 4 Artist's acrylic paint to apply tints, details or highlights 5 Oil painting brush 6 Natural sponge to create sponging effect 7 Pre-cut stencil 8 Dish for paint

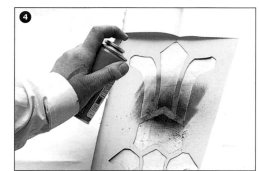

Making and cutting a stencil

When you are looking for patterns for stencils, work out the different elements carefully so that they are joined together by a small 'tie' of stencil paper. When your design is ready, draw it onto tracing paper using a soft pencil; on the reverse of the tracing paper, scribble over the lines with the soft pencil. Lay the tracing paper, right way up, onto your stencil paper or board, secure with masking tape and draw over the lines again with a harder pencil. If you are working with acetate, trace your design direct with a felt tip. Standard stencil paper is good as it is specially treated to resist absorbing paint.

Cut the stencil with a sharp craft knife, taking care to cut away from your free hand and your body in case the knife slips. Work on a cutting board or piece of plywood larger than your work. It is a good idea to mask the edges with tape so that the stencil does not slip and smudge your design work.

When working on a large design or in more than one colour, it will be easier to cut more than one stencil. In the design below, for example, cutting the diamond and the rectangle separately gives a more manageable piece of card or acetate. These templates will be less flimsy if the the central circle is not cut out. Cut it separately from an offcut.

BELOW Bright colours give a modern look to this design. A more subtle effect can be achieved by using pale, toning colours on a pale background.

Multi-colour stencils

There are two important things to remember when working in more than one colour. First, ensure that the first colour is completely dry before you embark on the next colour. Secondly, if you are working with more than one stencil, cut out small alignment marks on each before you start, so that you can see exactly where to match up the pattern.

Handy hints

- Test your design and colours on a piece of hardboard before you start.

- Always ensure that stencils are firmly secured to the wall at corners or edges with masking tape.

- Acetate stencils are ideal for uneven doors or walls. They mould to the surface and prevent paint seeping behind the stencil.

- When accuracy is essential, align your stencil card with a faint pencil line ruled with the aid of a spirit level.

- Make sure the paint is completely dry before untaping the stencil card from the surface.

Materials and equipment

- **Stencil card, craft knife and pencil**

- **Paintbrush, sponges and emulsion**

- **Clean, lint-free rags and masking tape**

- **Matt-finish, clear acrylic varnish (optional)**

1 Copy your pattern onto stencil card. Cut out carefully with a craft knife. You may find it helpful to secure the stencil card with masking tape so that it does not move while you are cutting.

2 Make sure your stencil is straight as the first stencil will set the angle for all the rest. Using a sponge, paint the first colour. Allow to dry. Apply a second coat.

3 Use small cut-out shapes in the corners to position the second stencil.

ABOVE This floor stencil is carried around the edges of the room and the bottom of the banister to create a delightful design.

Stencilling a floor

In an otherwise plainly decorated room, a bold, well-designed stencil pattern used as a border running around the floor can have real impact. Stencils look fantastic on painted or sanded floors. To prevent the paint creeping behind the stencil card and spoiling the design's outline, the floor will have to be sanded and sealed. Once the stencilling is complete, give the design at least three coats of varnish, sanding back between each coat. Make sure that you work in a well ventilated room and wear a vapour mask while you are painting.

Materials and equipment

- **Steel rule or tape measure**

- **Soft pencil**

- **Stencil card**

- **Masking tape**

- **Clean newspaper**

- **Aerosol paint**

1 Measure and mark at regular intervals from the edge of the wall or skirting so that the stencil can be positioned exactly parallel with it. Make small, light pencil marks that will not show afterwards, and then use masking tape for lining up the stencil card. Use further pieces of masking tape to hold the stencil card straight and in position.

2 Use sheets of clean paper to mask all the areas around the stencil, including the

wall, to shield them from paint. Don't forget the strip between the stencil card and the wall. Shake the aerosol thoroughly and spray a light coat of paint from a height of about 20–25cm (8–10in). Leave the paint until it is completely dry.

3 Lift the stencil card and line it up with the pattern on the floor, overlapping the last two elements on the end of each line. Secure the stencil with masking tape; if it does not lie flat use a little double-sided tape on the reverse to increase the contact with the wood.

4 Use fresh sheets of newspaper around the stencil card and continue to work as before, leaving the paint to dry between stencils, until the border is complete. Apply several coats of floor varnish to the boards to protect the design, sanding lightly between each coat.

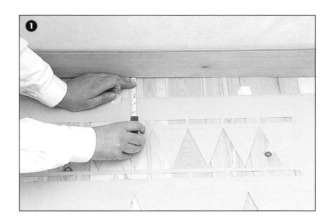

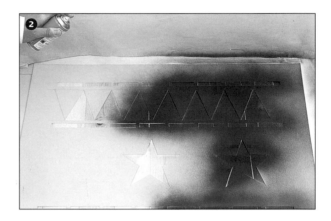

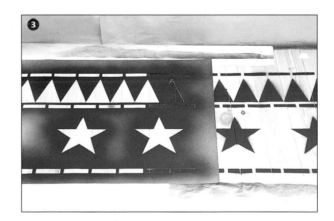

Découpage

Découpage simply means 'cutting out', and is a decorating technique anyone can turn their hand to. Paper images are cut out and stuck on a painted or varnished background – such a basic idea, and yet one that produces many different effects. You could embellish a child's wooden bedhead with a collection of teddies, create a sophisticated 'print wall' with copies of black and white etchings, cut a patterned paper into complex shapes for an abstract mural or make up a border of botanical flower prints to frame an uncurtained window. The possiblities are endless.

There are books available in craft outlets that contain pictures reproduced especially for découpage, or you can find images that appeal to you in magazines, brochures and catalogues, posters or old birthday cards. To create a repeat border, you will need several copies of the same picture – gift-wrapping paper can be a useful source, or experiment with a good colour photocopier.

Stamping

Printing patterns onto fabric, wallpaper or walls is an old art that has never quite been lost. You can still pick up woodblocks quite inexpensively in antique and junk shops and stalls, and many craft shops and mail order firms stock modern wood or rubber stamping blocks and inks: you could use some to print your own unique wallpaper border, for example.

But there is also an ever-widening choice of stamps designed for use with either emulsion or acrylic paint directly onto the walls or ceiling. They are cut in firm foam and are easy to work with, although, like stencilling or sponging, it is worth practising on a spare piece of wood or paper to get the paint loading right. You could quickly create a pleasingly looser, less formal pattern on a wall than with wallpaper, or a larger stamp might provide an eye-catching motif above each door in a corridor.

Materials and equipment

- **Paper pictures for cutting out**

- **Sharp scissors or craft knife for paper cutting**

- **PVA adhesive and applicator**

- **Pencil**

- **Blu-Tack**

- **Clear acrylic varnish**

BELOW A découpage rose garland has been used to decorate a headboard and complete the antique-style look of the bedroom.

1 Once you have planned the effect you want to create, carefully cut out the images you have chosen.

2 Decide on the precise layout (a little Blu-Tack on the back of each will enable you to arrange and rearrange *in situ* until you are satisfied), then lightly draw round the shapes onto the wall or whatever surface you are decorating.

3 Remove the images one by one, apply PVA paste to the back and stick into place, using your pencilled outline as a guide.

4 Finish by covering with several thin coats of varnish for protection (choose a matt finish unless you want glossiness to be a feature of the design).

A wall frieze

This paint effect can be fun to do and has the quality of originality that comes with free-hand painting. Choose a design that you really like, since you will be working closely with it until the frieze is completed!

Materials

- **Emulsion paint**

- **Artist's acrylic colours**

- **Pencils, colours and paper**

- **Artists' brushes of various sizes**

- **Acrylic glaze to finish and protect**

- **For a harder finish and protection, clear polyurethane varnish, matt or satin**

1 Sketch your design on paper before you begin, using coloured pencils to achieve the effect you want to create. When you are happy with the design, prepare your wall thoroughly and paint the background with your chosen colour.

2 Working from your design, mark out the simple, geometric elements (the green straight lines in this case) using a ruler and light pencil marks. For accuracy, you can lay masking tape down either side of the line to get a straight edge. Paint the line freely, with a firm brush and a steady hand.

3 To make a template for the other elements of the design, draw them onto tracing paper, turn it over and draw over the lines on the back of the design using a soft pencil. Place the wrong side of the design against the wall and trace over the lines again. Remove the tracing paper and check

the lines. Paint your design with the size of paintbrush that suits you, using the pencil lines as a guide. If you prefer to work completely free-hand, take a soft pencil and draw in the stalks and leaves directly onto the wall, then paint over the lines as before. Wall friezes can run both horizontally and vertically on walls, ceilings or wooden doors.

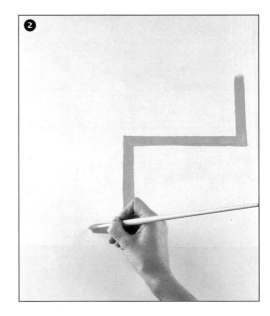

LEFT A delightful effect is created in this part of the room by the wall frieze. Its carefully hand-crafted look adds warmth and liveliness to the area.

Wallcoverings: styles and types

Although the term 'wallpaper' is commonly used, 'wallcovering' is more accurate since many of the patterns and textures now sold for walls and ceilings are made from plastic or fabric. The variety of wallcoverings on the market is enormous, so choosing the right one for your needs can be a daunting task unless you are familiar with what's available.

RIGHT Blacks and whites and tones of grey can form the perfect foil for colour introduced in curtaining, chair fabrics, pictures and ornaments.

BELOW Here, Chinese willow pattern is repeated on the wall, in the furnishing fabric and on the wall frieze.

the adhesive, each length of paper is dipped in a small trough of water and then applied directly to the wall or ceiling.

Relief papers or Anaglypta Available in a range of designs from formal patterns to simulations of such textures as plaster, pebble-dash and brick. Generally, the more heavily embossed the paper, the more expensive it is. Once it is hung and painted it is extremely difficult to strip.

Flocks These expensive papers are available mainly in traditional patterns – they were originally developed to mimic velvet wall-hangings. The designs are made from chopped fibres of rayon or silk stuck to a backing to give the effect of a raised pile. They require expert hanging.

Dry-strippable paper A good choice if you think you will want to redecorate, since it can be removed without soaking or scraping.

Papers

Lining paper A smooth, unpatterned paper designed to cover poor wall or ceiling surfaces before a decorative covering is applied. It is always laid at right angles to the main wallcovering. Textured coverings can disguise poor-quality surfaces without the use of lining paper.

Pulps and woodchip papers Pulps are inexpensive coverings made from a single thickness of printed-pattern paper. When wet with paste, pulps are easily torn. Woodchip

paper has chips of wood bonded to the front surface. It is a cheap form of covering and is often used to disguise less than perfect surfaces. The woodchips are available in a range of grades from fine to coarse.

Duplex papers Made in layers, they are stronger and easier to handle than pulps. There is a vast range of designs, often with matching or toning fabrics. Some duplex papers are also embossed.

Ready-pasted wallpapers This type of product has a dry adhesive on the back. To activate

Washable papers A coating of clear plastic on the surface makes them easy to hang and clean. Use a damp sponge only for cleaning – too much water could weaken the wallpaper paste.

Vinyl wallcoverings These papers have patterns printed with vinyl inks onto a layer of vinyl fused to a paper backing. Textured vinyls are also available – plain coloured but textured to imitate other types of surface. Heavily textured vinyls mimic tiles and such materials as grass cloth and stone, not always very realistically. Roll lengths of these may be less than standard. There are also flock vinyls, in rich or pastel colours in a variety of designs. Metallic vinyls are sophisticated (but expensive), with areas of gold, silver, bronze or copper. Most vinyl papers are dry strippable, ready-pasted or unpasted.

Material wallcoverings

Fabric wallcoverings A wide range of paper-backed fabric wallcoverings is available, either in wallpaper-sized rolls or by the yard or metre. Hessian, for example, is bonded to backing paper and comes in a good range of colours.

Felts and silks Paper-backed felt is often used to deaden sound and to insulate against heat loss to some extent. Paper-backed silks are luxurious, but they are expensive and require expert hanging.

Woollen cloths These offer the choice of a range of natural colours, plus some brightly dyed effects. Textures range from coarse fibres to fine cloths in herringbone and other weaves. Crushed suede and velvet cloths are also available.

Grass cloths This material is sold by the metre. It is made in the Far East by hand and has a unique charm.

Cork Colours include a choice of browns ranging between a light neutral shade to a rich, deep colour. This material is often used as an alternative to cork wall tiles.

Metallic coverings These consist of thin metal foil bonded to a paper backing and need great care in hanging.

ABOVE Textured and patterned wallpaper in an off-white colour harmonizes with cushions and covers.

LEFT Walls can be enlivened by the use of coloured and patterned coverings. The choice is endless.

Preparation

Wait until you have finished painting all the woodwork in a room before applying your ceiling or wallcovering, to avoid drips and splashes ruining it. Give the walls and ceiling a final check for uneven filler or rough areas where any old wallcovering has been removed, and rub down with medium glasspaper where necessary.

Clean the room using a vacuum cleaner to pick up fine dust. Remove any old newspapers you may have spread over the floor while sanding, and wipe skirtings, doors and window frames with a damp rag. Then spread fresh newspaper around the walls to catch any splashes of size. Size prevents too much wallpaper paste being absorbed by the plaster of the walls or ceiling. Size may either be bought as a powder or paste, to be mixed with cold water. Apply it to all the surfaces to be papered and leave it to dry – usually about an hour or two – before papering.

If you are papering the ceiling, do this before the walls. Check how you will reach the highest point of the room before you begin. A short step-stool may be sufficient, otherwise use a small pair of steps. Pairs of steps with a plank between them may be necessary for papering a high ceiling (*see p. 18–19 for further details*).

ABOVE The use of textured wallcoverings can add an extra dimension to a decorative theme. Choose from flocks, Anaglyptas, false plaster effects, woodchip (in various grades), false hessian, grass cloth, cork and many, many others.

Measuring up

As we have seen, the term wallpaper refers to more than just a paper covering applied to a wall. Although wallcoverings do have paper backings they may be faced with a great number of different materials, from silk and hessian to metal and cork (*see p. 122–3*). However, for convenience, the word 'paper' is used here as a generic term for all types of wall and ceiling coverings.

The chart below will help you determine the number of rolls of paper needed for a particular room, but remember to take account of any pattern repeats and roll sizes.

RIGHT When faced with pattern repeats make sure you allow a generous amount of wallpaper. This pattern may appear random, but needs careful matching.

Calculating the number of rolls for walls													
Measurement around room	8.5m (27ft 9in)	9.75m (32ft)	11m (36ft)	12m (39ft 4in)	13.4m (44ft)	14m (46ft)	16m (52ft)	17m (55ft 6in)	18.5m (59ft 5in)	19.5m (63ft 5in)	20.75m (67ft 4in)	22m (72ft)	23m (75ft)
Height from skirting													
2.13–2.29m (7ft–7ft 6in)	4	4	5	5	6	6	7	7	8	8	9	9	9
2.30–2.44m (7ft 6in–8ft)	4	4	5	5	6	6	7	8	8	9	9	10	10
2.45–2.59m (8ft–8ft 6in)	4	5	5	6	6	7	7	8	8	9	9	10	10
2.60–2.74m (8ft 6in–9ft)	4	5	5	6	6	7	8	8	9	9	10	11	11
2.75–2.90m (9ft–9ft 6in)	4	5	6	6	7	7	8	9	9	10	10	11	12
2.91–3.05m (9ft 6in–10ft)	5	5	6	7	7	8	9	9	10	10	11	12	12
3.06–3.20m (10ft–10ft 6in)	5	5	6	7	8	8	9	10	10	11	12	12	13

Calculating the number of rolls for a ceiling										
Measurement around room	9.75m (32ft)	10m (32ft 10in)	11m (36ft)	11.5m (37ft 9in)	12m (39ft 4in)	12.8m (42ft)	13.4m (44ft)	14m (46ft)	14.5m (47ft 6in)	16m (52ft)
Number of rolls required	2	2	2	2	2	3	3	3	3	4
Measurement around room	16.5m (54ft 2in)	17m (55ft 10in)	17.5m (57ft 5in)	18m (59ft)	19m (62ft 4in)	19.5m (64ft)	20m (65ft 8in)	20.5m (67ft 3in)	21m (69ft)	22.5m (73ft 10in)
Number of rolls required	4	4	4	5	5	5	5	6	6	7

Measuring up and calculating

To work out how many rolls of wallpaper you need, you cannot just calculate the area to be covered because you need to work in complete vertical runs or 'drops' – joins halfway down a wall are not good!

First measure your drop, from the ceiling down to the dado or skirting. How many drops you get out of a roll will depend on whether you have a pattern repeat to take into account. A standard roll is 10m (33ft) long. A paper with no repeat would provide 4 drops of up to about 2.4m (8ft) (you will need to allow an overlap top and bottom). Over that and you will only get 3

drops, although the leftovers will be useful for areas over doors and below windows. Allowing for a pattern repeat will increase the wastage, but you should still get 3 drops unless the ceiling is very high. If only papering from dado rail to picture rail you can expect to get 5 or 6 drops per roll.

To see how many drops you need, simply measure all around the room. A standard roll is 53cm (21in) wide, so if your round-the-room measurement comes to 14m (46ft), that's 27 drops. At 4 drops per roll you will need 7 rolls; at 3 drops you will need 9 rolls. If in doubt, over-order, checking that you can return what you do not use.

Roll sizes

A standard roll is 10m x 53cm (33ft x 21in). The paper comes ready trimmed and will usually be wrapped to keep it clean.

The charts for calculating wallpaper quantities (*see left*) are based on the standard roll size. However, some continental papers may be narrower than this, and American papers may be twice as wide. If selecting any of these papers, look in the sample book for guidance on coverage.

Batch numbers

Each roll of paper should be stamped with a production batch number. When selecting rolls, check that all the production numbers

Repeats

Another variable to be aware of when calculating quantities of wallcoverings is the pattern repeat. The larger the pattern repeat, the more likely it is that extra rolls will be required.

Free-match papers have designs that do not require pattern matching, and so involve little wastage. Set-match papers have motifs that repeat in a straight line across the paper. Wastage will depend on the overall size of the pattern repeat, but it is not usually too much.

Drop-match patterns have a repeat in diagonal lines, and so each new length of paper has to be moved either up or down to allow for this. You can minimize wastage with drop-match patterns by cutting alternate lengths from two different rolls.

are the same. If they are not, this means that the rolls have been produced in different batch runs and there may be slight variations in colour and shading. For this reason, it is a good idea to over-order. If you run out and have to buy one or two more rolls at a later date you may be supplied from a different batch. If you do order too many rolls, the supplier will usually allow you to return any that have not been used, provided that the wrappings are intact. If you have to finish off with rolls from a different batch, plan to use this paper in an alcove or recess, or somewhere in the room where any slight differences in colour or shade will not be immediately obvious.

ANTICLOCKWISE FROM TOP Free-match papers have patterns or stripes that don't require matching; set-match papers have patterns that repeat in straight lines across the paper, and so involve little wastage; drop-match designs repeat diagonally across the paper, and these involve most wastage of all.

Pasting and hanging

Before beginning, you need to find the starting point for the first length. To do this, measure out 48cm (19in), or a little less than the width of your roll, from the corner on the wall adjacent to the window wall and make a pencil mark just below picture rail level. Extend a plumb line cord and let the line hang down to just above the skirting board. Have a helper make marks on the wall behind the line. Check the distance between each mark and the corner. If the wall is out of true, and the reading is more than 48cm (19in) at any point, move your plumb line nearer the wall and make a new set of marks. Use the marks to line up the edge of the first piece of wallpaper.

Handy hints

- With coverings such as hessian, silk, cork or foil, check if you paste the wall or ceiling or the back of the material itself.

- If bubbles or blisters appear, you may have left insufficient time for the paper to soak.

- You can often shrink bubbles back into place by wafting the surface of the paper with a hair dryer.

Papering walls

Before you start, set up the pasting table and collect all your tools together (*see p. 14–15*). Double-check your measurements, taking into account pattern matches and an allowance top and bottom, and cut the first few lengths with long-bladed sharp scissors.

❶ Make sure the pasting table is dry and clean. Then, if you are right handed, lay the cut piece of paper on the pasting table, pattern-side down, with the surplus to your left, loosely rolled. If you are left handed, place the spare paper to your right. Load the brush with paste and apply a strip down the middle of the paper (*see* a, *right*). Reload the brush and work out from the middle, herringbone fashion (b *and* c), lifting the brush off as you reach the edge of the paper. Check that the edges are well covered.

❷ Carefully fold the pasted paper back on itself, lift the paper and ask a helper to wipe any paste from the table with a damp cloth. Lower the paper to the table and then slide it to the right, thus bringing the unpasted surplus paper onto the table. Reload the brush and apply paste as before. Fold the paper in on itself so that it almost meets the other fold. The last fold will be the top of the piece. Fold it again to make the length easy to move, and place it out of the way to soak. This is important, since the paper will continue to expand for some minutes. If it does not expand fully you may get bubbles later on. While the paper is soaking, paste one or two more lengths. Wipe the table with a damp cloth each time.

❸ Carry the first length of paper to the wall (*as shown right*).

❹ Unfold the top fold and let the paper drop. Position the left-hand edge against the pencilled line, ensuring that you have about 50mm (2in) spare at the top for trimming. Once the left edge is positioned,

Wallpaper adhesives

Wallpaper paste can be bought either ready-mixed (usually in a handy tub) or as a powder to mix with water. Ready-mixed wallpaper paste is convenient to use and a tub usually contains enough to do about five rolls of wallpaper, but it works out very much more expensive if you have a lot of wallpapering to do. You can also buy tubes of wallpaper paste for very small jobs such as borders or patches. These are often described as strong wallpaper paste. Different papers need different strengths of paste, so check on your paper's requirements before you buy the paste. Some papers come pre-pasted and just need wetting before use.

Ready-pasted paper

Ready-pasted paper will not stretch so there is less chance of it bubbling through

expansion. Before soaking, check the manufacturer's instructions and follow them if they are different from those below.

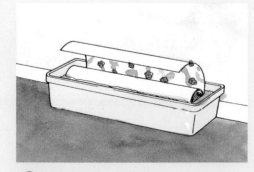

❶ Fill the trough provided two-thirds full with clean, cold water. Measure and cut a length of wallpaper. Loosely roll it, pattern-side in, and submerge it in the trough.

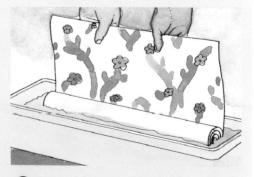

❷ Agitate so that the water makes contact with all of the paper. Lift it slowly from the trough, allowing excess water to drain away. No soaking time is necessary.

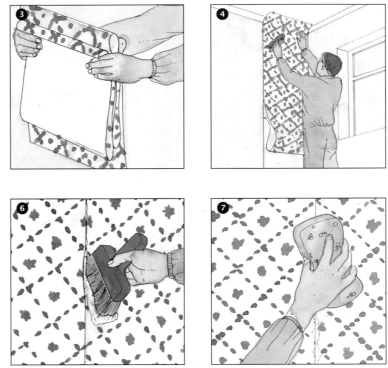

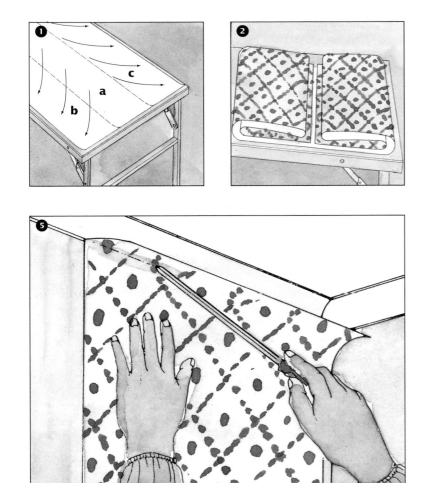

wipe your hand across to the right to secure the top of the paper to the wall. With the paper correctly positioned, take the smoothing brush and run it down the middle of the length, pressing the paper lightly to the wall. Now use the brush in light, outward strokes until the length is in place. About 2.5cm (1in) of paper should have turned onto the window wall. Lightly press this into place, ensuring that there are no wrinkles. Don't force the paper down at the skirting and picture rail in the corner, since you still have to trim the paper. If the turned edge seems dry, apply a little extra paste. Before trimming, smooth the paper again from the middle outward, making sure that the edges are securely stuck down. Lightly dab any bubbles flat. Bubbles will usually disappear as the paper shrinks and tightens.

5 Use the edge of the closed scissors to press the paper firmly but gently into the top edge, under the cornicing or against the ceiling, and into the corner against the skirting board at the bottom. Press very lightly to avoid tearing the damp paper. Use scissors rather than a knife for trimming, again to avoid tearing the paper. Pull the paper away from the wall just far enough to enable you to position the scissors and then cut about 3mm (⅛in) outside the score mark. With the surplus removed,

carefully dab the paper back in place. If the paper is still a little too long, gently pull away from the wall again and trim a little more off. Repeat this at the dado rail and/or skirting board end of the length of paper. The first piece is now complete.

To trim heavy vinyls and heavy papers you can use a very sharp knife and steel straight edge, such as a ruler. Once you have creased the vinyl or paper to form a guideline, place the straight edge just above the crease and cut with the knife.

6 When you have finished the first piece, check that the edges are well stuck down – heavy wallpapers tend to curl at the edges. If so, try dabbing them down with a clean, dry rag; if the paste has dried, smear a little extra under the edge of the paper with the paste brush. Wipe away the surplus and then dab the paper down. This problem occurs most often with smooth vinyls, where the edges frequently seem to curl away from the wall. In this case, apply a special seam adhesive, not extra paste. Use it sparingly under the edge and then press the edge down in place. If you use a clear resin adhesive, take care not to get any on the surface of the vinyl – the adhesive will soften it. With the second length pasted, folded and soaked, carry it to the wall, drop out the top flat, and position the right corner against the wall (assuming that you are working right to left), lining it up with the edge of the first length. Match any pattern by sliding the paper up or down. Then smooth the top of the paper to the wall, run the smoothing brush down the length of the paper and brush outward toward the first length.

7 Check that the seams align perfectly, and then continue adding lengths. As you progress, clean up between each length. Use a damp cloth or sponge to wipe paste from picture rails, skirtings and window and door frames while it is still soft. Keep any trimmed pieces for patching. Wipe the pasting table clean after each length.

Ceilings

When papering a ceiling, it is important to be able to reach it safely and in reasonable comfort. So, the first thing you need to do is secure a platform to stand on so that your head is about 75mm (3in) from the ceiling. (*See p. 18–19.*) Place the platform along the line of the first length of paper that you are planning to hang.

If the ceiling has been newly plastered, you will first have to 'size' it to prevent too much of the wallpaper paste being absorbed by the plaster and weakening the adhesion of the paper (*see p. 123*). An application of size also helps to slide your paper into place, by making the ceiling surface more slippery.

Pendent light fittings

With a ceiling pendent, cut the paper to length and mark it on the back. Allow for trimming. Paste the paper and make a series of star-shaped cuts from the middle of the light position. Hang the

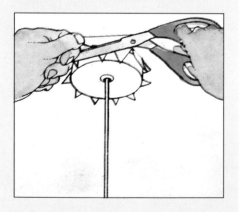

paper normally. Then, when you reach the light fitting, feed the pendant through the hole and press the paper into place around it.

Crease each flap with the blunt edge of the closed scissors and carefully cut off the surplus paper 3mm (⅛in) outside the crease marks. Press the paper into place and wipe the paste from the fitting.

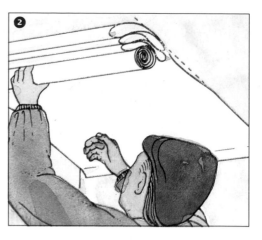

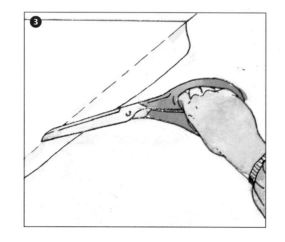

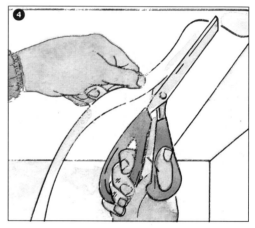

Positioning the first length

The best starting place is parallel with the window wall. This ensures that no shadows will be thrown should any paper overlap. The simplest way to indicate the position for the first length is to mark the ceiling at each end with a pencil, the width of the paper away from the wall.

Rub a length of string with coloured chalk. Secure it to the ceiling at one end, just over the mark you have made. Ask a helper to hold the other end tightly to the other mark while you pluck the string, leaving a line on the ceiling.

① Measure the ceiling for the first length of paper and add 10cm (4in) for trimming. Cut and lay the length on the table with the surplus on the floor to your left (if you are right handed). Paste the paper on the table with a thick paste, covering it evenly, fold over about 50cm (20in), and draw the unpasted paper up onto the table. Paste and fold again then continue until you reach the end of the length.

② Allow the paper to soak and then lay it over a spare roll of paper, with the edge to be stuck first uppermost. Hold the roll in your left hand (if you are right handed), grip the top edge with your right hand, turn it paste-side up, and apply it to the corner where you plan to start. Slide it to the chalk line and smooth it onto the ceiling. Move along the platform releasing the folds as you go. Smooth the paper to the ceiling and get a helper to hold the paper in place with a broom as you move along. Continue until the whole length is in position. Run over it with your smoothing brush, making sure the edges are well stuck down all along the length.

③ Press the paper into the end walls and crease it with your closed scissors.

④ Trim 3mm (⅛in) outside the crease so that the paper just turns onto the wall. Dab the paper back into place. Hang the second length, matching it to the edge of the first.

Problem areas

Papering flat areas of walls is straightforward. However, many rooms present problem areas, especially if you are inexperienced! These may include features such as alcoves, fixed radiator panels, light switches and fireplaces.

Radiators

If you have a central heating system with fixed radiators, it may be possible to swing them away from the walls to allow you to paper behind. Try lifting the radiator. If it rises enough to clear the holding brackets, slightly loosen the pipe nuts either side and lean the radiator forward. If the radiator will not move, you will have to tuck the paper down behind it. Cut two slits corresponding to the holding brackets. Then use a radiator roller – or improvise with a length of wood wrapped in clean rag – to smooth the paper down into place behind the radiator. Do not worry about getting the joins exact as the area is not easily visible.

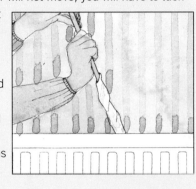

Recesses

Position the unpasted length of paper, that will turn into the recess, to the wall and mark the area of surplus paper. You need to keep enough for the depth of the recess plus about 25mm (1in) for trimming. Continue the strip above the recess, leaving about 25mm (1in) to turn under the ceiling of the recess. Cut away the surplus paper and paste the remainder. If the paper will not reach the full depth of the recess, cut it so that only 25mm (1in) turns the corner and add a further panel of paper later.

1 Make a horizontal cut at the window ledge and then at the top edge of the recess, leaving a 25mm (1in) overhang of paper. Turn the side panel into the recess wall and gently smooth it down flat. Be careful not to stretch or tear the wet paper. Crease and trim the surplus paper with your scissors.

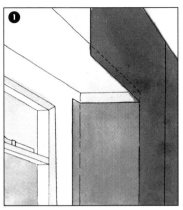

2 Now cut a panel to finish the ceiling recess. Test it for size and pattern match before pasting, remembering to add about an extra 25mm (1in) for trimming at both the window and recess walls. Paste the length as normal, and bring the front edge of the ceiling panel to meet the front edge of the recess. Smooth the paper onto the ceiling and trim the surplus at the window and recess walls.

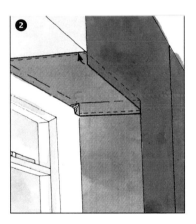

3 Paste your next length of paper as normal and hang it, allowing sufficient paper to reach the full depth of the ceiling recess, plus about an extra 25mm (1in) for trimming. Carefully crease and then trim the surplus paper with your scissors. Cut into the corner of the overhanging paper and fold it back onto the ceiling panel for a neat edge.

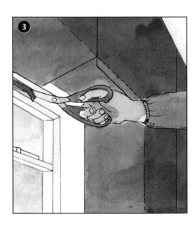

LEFT Coping with pattern matching in window recesses and the angled ceiling in this attic bedroom is not recommended for a novice wallpaper hanger.

Fireplaces

If the fireplace is a feature of the room – and if it is on a chimney breast – it is best to hang a length of paper centrally on the chimney breast, and then paper out in each direction. Then, any slight discrepancy in pattern can be lost around the internal corners of the chimney breast.

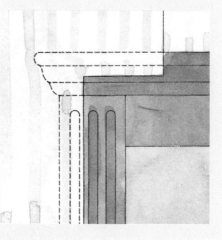

1 At the sides of the surround, cut the paper as if you were tackling a door frame (*see above*). You will also have to make cuts in the paper to let the mantelpiece come through. When measuring, allow extra paper to push into the mouldings.

2 Trim along the crease marks with scissors. With odd shapes, such as those made by a stone fireplace, make small cuts in the paper edge, mould it to the contours and crease it. Trim 3mm (⅛in) outside the creases so that the paper just turns onto the stone.

Wall-mounted light switches

If you need to paper around a light switch that can't be unscrewed from the wall, first drape the pasted length of paper over it. Feel for the middle and press to mark the paper. Now make star cuts in the paper out from the middle of the switch to the edges and then finish hanging the length. Press the cut paper lightly around the switch and mark it with the scissors. Pull each flap away and trim it to overlap about 3mm (⅛in). Dab the pieces back into place and wipe the paste from the switch.

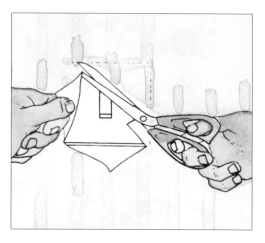

BELOW Bathrooms, which usually have a high percentage of built-in features such as basins, toilets, vanity units, baths and other items, often represent a real problem when wallpapering. Wherever possible, unscrew fixtures from the walls before papering. In the bathroom illustrated here, the towel rails, toilet roll holders, wall light covers, wall vent and the hooks supporting the mirrors were all removed prior to papering and replaced after the paste was dry.

Flush-mounted switch

First of all, cut off the power supply to the circuit. If you are papering around a switch that has a removable faceplate, loosen the screws and ease the plate away from the wall. Drape the paper over the switch, find the middle, and make two diagonal cuts out to the plate corners. Trim the paper 6mm (¼in) inside the switch area and tuck the excess behind the plate. Retighten the screws and wipe away the paste.

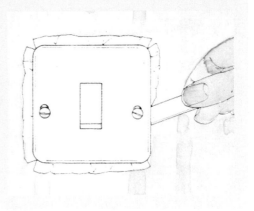

Wallpapering around doors

1 Cut the length of paper to fit around the door, marking a spare 50mm (2in) on the back for trimming top and bottom. Measure the distance from the last hung length to the door frame and add 25mm (1in). Do this near both the top and bottom of the door and mark these distances on the prepared length of paper. Draw a line between them. Measure the height from the skirting to the top of the door frame and deduct 25mm (1in). Mark this point on your drawn line and draw a horizontal line from it to the doorway side of the paper. Cut out the surplus.

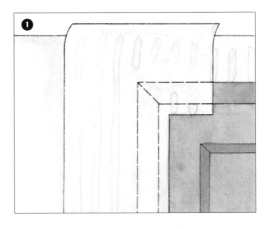

2 Hang the length of paper as normal, running it over the door and pressing it into the frame. Make a diagonal cut at the frame corner to allow the surplus paper to be pressed down.

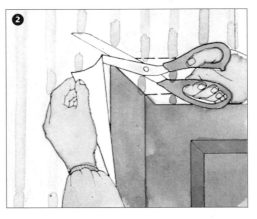

3 Smooth the paper into place as normal, then use closed scissors or a stiff brush edge to score a crease around the door frame to make a cutting guideline.

Gently pull the paper away from the wall around the door and trim it along the crease line. Now work from the other side of the door, and cut your length in the same way if the two pieces will meet above the frame. Even so, it is wise to drop a plumb line to the right-hand edge of this length so that you hang the piece vertically. If the two pieces will not meet, cut an infill piece to go above the door. If there is a pattern to match, cut and hang the infill before the next length is cut. But if pattern matching is no problem, hang the next full length and then the infill piece at the end.

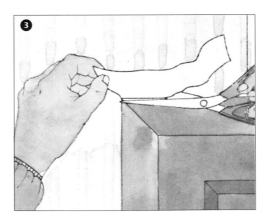

Wallpaper borders

Materials and equipment

- Wooden batten and spirit level

- Soft pencil

- Pasting table and brush

- Tape measure

- Wallpaper or border paste

- Seam roller

- Craft knife and metal rule

A selection of borders

Wallpaper borders are available in a wide range of designs and colours.

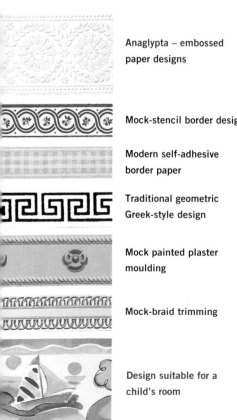

Anaglypta – embossed paper designs

Mock-stencil border design

Modern self-adhesive border paper

Traditional geometric Greek-style design

Mock painted plaster moulding

Mock-braid trimming

Design suitable for a child's room

Many wallpaper manufacturers produce a range of decorative borders to complement their own products. Pattern books, for example, often contain samples of wallpapers with two or three suggested border papers for each included, perhaps in different shadings or designs. Bear in mind that these are only suggestions, however – what looks best in the context of your own home, with your belongings and decorations in place, is an entirely personal decision. As well as plain-edged strips, borders can be shaped on one or both sides. Some manufacturers also make individual appliqué motifs to be arranged in a line as a border, or positioned randomly on the walls or ceiling.

There are two basic types of border paper to choose from: ready-pasted and ordinary. Some people prefer the ease of use and lack of mess of the ready-pasted types, while other decorators feel that they can achieve a better finish with ordinary paper borders. Ready-pasted types are more expensive to buy. But no matter which type you use, the base surface must be completely dry, clean and sound before you stick the border to it.

ABOVE A border placed low on the wall, above the decorative dado rail, draws the focus of the eye to this part of the room. The patterns and colours in the chair covers and cushions pick up particular elements in the border and wallpaper.

Marking and pasting a border

Before cutting or pasting your border paper, first determine the height you want it to run at and then draw a pencil guideline with the help of a straight edge and spirit level. If pasting a border over freshly hung wallpaper, leave at least 48 hours for the base paper to dry out thoroughly. If pasting a border over new paint, wait at least a week.

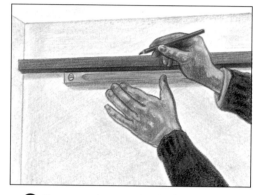

1 To ensure that your border is completely straight and level, use a wooden batten and a spirit level to draw a guideline for the bottom edge of the border.

2 Measure and then cut a length of border paper and paste it carefully, paying particular attention to the edges. Use the appropriate paste for the type of border paper you are working with. Check the manufacturer's recommendations if you are unsure. Vinyl papers require a stronger adhesive than non-vinyl papers, for example. Paste sold by the tube specifically for borders may be convenient if you are not also hanging wallpaper. Align the edge of the paper with the edge of the pasting table to help keep adhesive off the decorative surface. Check that no hairs which have come loose from the pasting brush end up on the back of the paper.

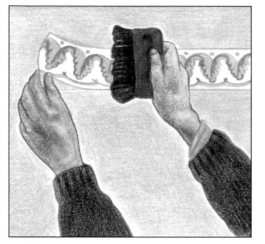

3 Align the edge of the border with your ruled pencil guideline. When you are satisfied that the border paper is straight, brush it onto the wall. Until the paste dries, you can make minor adjustments to the position of the paper, if necessary. Just carefully lift a corner, peel back as much paper as you wish to reposition, and then brush it down in place once more. Don't overstretch the border paper at this stage. By tugging it you may get a perfectly flush fit, only to find that it shrinks back slightly as it dries out. This will leave unsightly gaps that cannot then be rectified.

4 If a join in the middle of a wall is unavoidable, butt up the ends of the pieces very carefully, matching the pattern if necessary. Use a seam roller to press the join neatly into place. Don't use a seam roller on embossed papers, however, because it will flatten the texture and simply draw attention to the join. Carry on measuring, cutting and pasting pieces of paper until you have a continuous border round the room.

Turning corners

Taking a paper border around a corner of a wall (**1**), simply involves overlapping the paper from one wall to the next and then pasting over the overlap with your next strip of paper on the other wall. Take care to line the two up carefully so that the overlap does not show.

Where you want to emphasize the shape of a room feature, however, mitred corners are very effective (**2** and **3**).

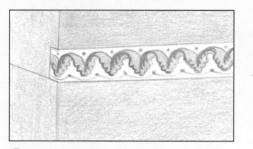

1 When turning a corner, take about 12mm (½in) of border paper around onto the next wall as an overlap. Never cut the paper flush with the corner. Then cut and paste your next length of border and lay it over the overlap you have created.

Creating optical effects

Wallpaper borders can be purely decorative features or they also can serve a more practical purpose, such as disguising an unsightly crack in a wall.

Wallpaper borders are also useful for altering the apparent proportions of a room. By running the border round the room at, say, the height of a traditional dado rail, you can visually break up the dimensions of a room – useful when you want to create an intimate, cosy atmosphere in a large or imposingly proportioned area.

You can also use wallpaper borders to enhance the visual impact of a room's architectural features – stairways can look very stylish, for example, if they are outlined with a suitable border paper. Alternatively you can emphasize the slope of a ceiling or window recess in an attic room by following its line with a strip of border paper.

2 For a 90° bend, overlap the two pieces and cut diagonally through both layers.

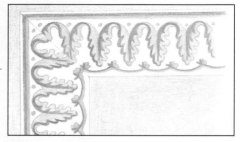

3 Trim off the waste border and ease the edges together to make neat mitred joins. Use this technique to make a frame on a wall, mimicking the decorative plaster frames found on some walls. Press each join lightly with a seam roller.

ABOVE An intricate border around the moulding and door links with the simple star pattern on the walls, and helps to create an optical effect.

Ceramic wall tiles

In use for many centuries, ceramic tiles are highly decorative, hard wearing, hygienic and easily maintained. Manufacturers produce a variety of patterns and colours that can be used for imaginative designs to blend with your existing fittings and furnishings in bathrooms and kitchens.

Ceramic tiles are the perfect protection against water penetration and, therefore, are extensively used to decorate any room where water is in frequent use. But ceramic tiles should not be used only in specific parts of rooms, such as splashbacks behind baths and sinks, they can also link these areas decoratively with the rest of the room – for example by using them as surfaces for bath panels or kitchen worktops to give a coordinated finish.

Ceramic tiles for floors are more robust than those used for walls. They can also be used for kitchen worktops and other surfaces that need to be hard wearing.

ABOVE RIGHT The decorative theme established on the walls can be taken through to the floor.

BELOW Plain tiles can be used on their own or teamed with border tiles or other tiles featuring all kinds of repeating decorative patterns.

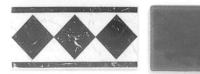

Tile sizes

The best size of tile to use depends on the area to be covered. The 152mm (6in) square size, for example, may be best for large expanses of wall, since you can cover a given area in less time using large tiles than you can with smaller ones. Tiles measuring 108mm (4¼in) square work particularly well in small rooms – such as bathrooms – where the tiles have to coordinate with fittings and may form a major part of the decor. These tiles make for easier cutting and shaping around typical built-in bathroom fixtures – cabinets and sanitary ware – and other awkward areas, such as recesses and window rebates. As well as the area to be covered, however, also consider the effect that different sizes of tile will create in the room. Smaller tiles create a busier look.

Bear in mind that some imported tiles are available only in metric sizes, including 10cm (nearly 4in), 15cm (nearly 6in), and 20cm (nearly 8in). Always check carefully that you know the precise size that you are intending to use before working out the quantity you need.

Smaller than the standard sizes already mentioned are tiny mosaic tiles. These obviously take much longer to fix into position, but they can look extremely attractive as low splashbacks around, say, worktops. Find out the range of colours available and then work out a pattern that uses them to best advantage. You could create a geometric pattern, for example, or simply use graduated shades of the same colour across the area to be covered.

Rectangular tiles are available, too, for creating interesting herringbone and other traditional brickwork patterns, and there are other shapes that interlock for special decorative effects.

You can also choose from ranges of extra-large ceramic tiles. These tend to look best covering very large areas of wall – and perhaps the ceiling, too – and they can produce dramatic, eye-catching effects.

Plain and patterned

It can be difficult to know how to intersperse decorative feature tiles among plain ones to create the best effect. In order to get a feel for the right design balance, first cut out tile-sized squares of paper and tape them to the walls, then move them around until you are happy with the effect. In general, it is best to keep feature tiles at least one tile out from the corners of a room. If you don't, the eye will tend to be drawn to the wall edges and away from the central areas of pattern.

Tile spacing

For a professional-looking finish, it is vital to get the spacing even between the individual tiles, otherwise the grouting will accentuate these irregularities, especially a coloured grouting. To get the spacing correct between tiles, packets of plastic spacers are available. These are left in place and grouted over. Other tiles have sloping edges and are laid so that they abut. The grooves thus formed are then grouted and even tile spacing is assured.

Estimating quantities

When planning a tiling job, draw an accurate room plan on graph paper, using each square to represent one tile. As a general rule, to work out the quantity needed measure the width and height of the area, expressing the dimensions as so many whole tiles, and rounding up as necessary.

Multiply the two figures together, and add 10 per cent extra to allow for cutting and some inevitable breakages. Try to order all the tiles you need for the job at the same time. Variations in the firing process can mean that batches of tiles differ slightly in appearance.

Tiles commonly come in boxes of 25 or 50, or in packs to cover, say, one square metre. Included will be tiles for both main body tiling (unglazed edges) and for external corners (finished edges). Before ordering, work out how many edging tiles are needed, and check there are enough in the pack or box.

Tools and materials

You will need a tile cutter, a spirit level with a vertical vial, a steel rule, a few long, straight timber battens, a serrated adhesive spreader (usually supplied with the adhesive), tile clippers or pincers, a sponge and a soft cloth. Assemble these before you begin.

Basic tiling materials are spacers, if needed (or matches will do), plus adhesive and grout. For condensation-prone areas, or those areas that will get regular soakings – as in a shower cubicle or splashback – use water-resistant adhesive and a good-quality waterproof grout.

ABOVE Tiles are often used in the kitchen, not only because they offer hardwearing floors, but because of their decorative qualities. In this room a combination of plain and decorated tiles are used on the walls.

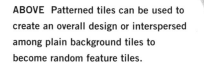

ABOVE Patterned tiles can be used to create an overall design or interspersed among plain background tiles to become random feature tiles.

Cutting and fixing

The principal fact to remember about ceramic tiles is that they are brittle. This means that once you have introduced a line of weakness, by scoring a straight line in the tile, for example, it can be snapped relatively easily. More problematic, however, is shaping a tile to fit around a pipe or the edge of a basin. Here, it is best to nibble away at the tile until you have the shape you need.

When marking tiles for cutting, never be tempted to use a felt pen on the tile's reverse side. The ink from the pen may soak through the tile and appear as a stain under the glaze where you cannot reach it to remove it.

Marking up

❶ To help you position your tiles, mark a long, straight batten with tile widths along its length to act as a gauge stick, allowing gaps for grouting. Next, tape tile-sized paper squares to the walls to remind you where any patterned tiles will be fixed. As well, mark the positions of any special tiles – those carrying a soap dish or towel ring, for example.

Mark out a rough tile grid on the wall, starting on the window wall. Use your gauge stick to get the right balance horizontally, then use the stick vertically to ensure you will get a whole tile at the window sill. Avoid having cut tiles where they will show. If you need to do any tile cutting at floor level, make a pencil mark to indicate the base of the first full tile above floor level. If you are tiling a large area and have several boxes, always take a number

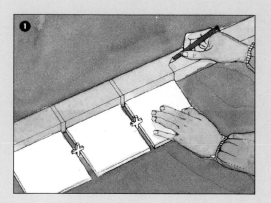

of tiles from each one and mix them up to minimize the effect of any variation in colour between boxes. Place a row on the floor, positioning them to the marks you have made on the walls. Check for balance either side of the window. Look at any pattern on the tiles. Is it really random, or is there a motif that suggests that the tiles should go a certain way up?

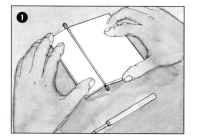
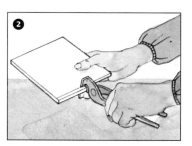
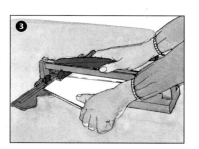

Cutting

❶ Mark the tile on the glazed side with a chinagraph pencil and, once only, run a tungsten-tipped stylus cutter along it, guided by a steel rule. Press hard enough just to penetrate the glaze. Place matchsticks under the score line and press either side to snap the tile.

❷ If shaping tiles with pincers or pliers, mark and score the line with a pencil and stylus first. Support the tile on a flat surface with the area to be shaped overhanging. Hold the tile firmly and start nibbling away from the tile edge, slowly working to the score line.

❸ Use a platform cutter for extra-hard tiles. Set the gauge to the width of tile to be cut; position the tile on the platform and, gripping the cutter arm, use it to push the cutting wheel across the tile. Exert just enough pressure on the tile to leave a score mark. Then snap the tile between the jaws at the end of the arm, or by applying downward pressure on the arm.

❹ A tile saw simplifies the task of cutting irregular tile shapes. The saw has a circular cutting blade, tipped with tungsten carbide, held in a metal frame. The blade cuts

in any direction, and the size of the frame enables you to turn the saw around a tile without obstruction. If you have to cut an irregular shape, pierce holes in the tile to form the desired shape and, using pincers, cut away the excess until the correct shape is formed.

❺ A template former, or profile gauge, is a helpful tool for drawing awkward shapes. It consists of a number of needles or strips of plastic held in a frame. When pressed against a shaped surface, the tool takes up its exact shape, which you can then

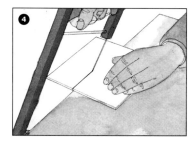
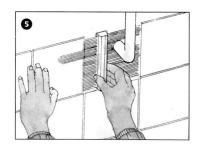

transfer to a tile by following the outline with a chinagraph pencil.

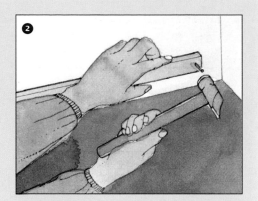

2 Starting on the window wall, look for the pencil mark representing the first full tile above floor level, and position a batten there. Check the batten is horizontal with a spirit level, then secure it to the wall with masonry nails. Position a vertical batten at the outer edge of the first row of full tiles from the corner. Check the batten is vertical and secure it.

Materials and equipment

- **Chinagraph pencil and steel rule**

- **Wooden batten, hammer and nails**

- **Spirit level**

- **Tile adhesive and notched spreader**

- **Tungsten-tipped cutting stylus**

- **Platform cutter**

- **Tile saw**

- **Pincers or pliers**

- **Profile gauge**

- **Tile grout and spacers**

- **Polishing cloth**

Fixing

1 Starting at the batten, apply tile adhesive to the wall with the notched spreader, covering about 1sq m (1sq yard) at a time. The spreader should leave a layer about 3mm (⅛in) thick. Lift away any surplus adhesive.

If you find it easier, you can apply the adhesive to the wall with a small trowel, and then use the notched spreader to get the correct thickness.

2 Place the tiles in the adhesive on the wall, arranging them against the edge of the batten, pressing them firmly in place. Try not to slide the tiles into position, since this forces adhesive up onto the tile edge.

Insert a cross-shaped spacer at the top corner of each tile and position your next tile alongside so that it sits tightly against the spacer.

Continue tiling until the horizontal run is complete, then start on the next line. You can leave cut tiles until later, completing all full tiling in an area of wall first.

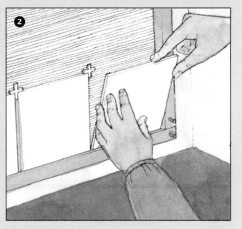

Grouting

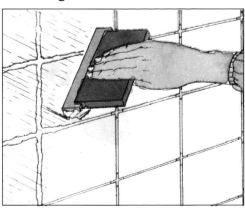

1 If the grout is in powder form, mix it to a thick paste according to its instructions. Grout from a tub is ready-mixed. Force the grout into the gaps between the tiles, making sure no holes are left.

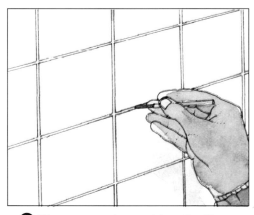

2 Wipe away surplus grout from the tile surface, then smooth the grout with the special grouting tool supplied with tiling kits. Alternatively, make use of an item such as a pen top to smooth the grout.

3 Allow the grout to dry, then rub the surface of the tiles with a cloth. This removes surplus grout and polishes the tiles at the same time.

Awkward spots and fittings

Equipped with good-quality tile cutters and a degree of patience, tiling around tricky shapes and into recesses should be a reasonably straightforward task – provided that you plan for it carefully in advance. As for fittings, remember that many of these, particularly for bathrooms, can be bought integrated with a tile. If you do have to drill to make a fixing, there is a simple technique for avoiding the risk of cracking the tile.

If you are planning a room from scratch, or building partition walls, ledges or recesses in an existing room, take the size of tiles to be used into consideration from the outset to avoid too much tile cutting and shaping later on.

BELOW Bathroom accessories add the finishing touch to a room and are important decorative items. All of these can be drilled and fixed easily to tiled walls and other surfaces using the technique shown opposite.

Tiling round corners, doors, windows and fixtures

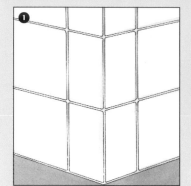

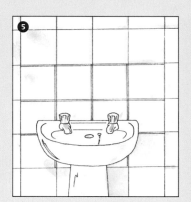

1 Finish external corners with edging tiles, cut to the same size for both oppostite walls. With patterned tiles, it is better to use whole glazed-edged tiles and work away to where a cut tile and a pattern break will be less obvious.

2 Internal corners should, wherever possible, be completed with tiles cut to equal size on both oppostite walls. With patterned tiles, use the offcuts from tiling one wall to begin the opposite wall. This maintains the continuity of the pattern.

3 The door into a room is very much a focal point, so try to maintain a visual balance by tiling round it evenly, using

whole tiles whenever possible. The door frame may not be vertical, so don't use it as a guide for your tiling rows unless it is completely true.

4 A window is an important focal point in a wall, too. For symmetry, position the tiles within the recess either side of

Drilling

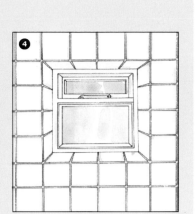

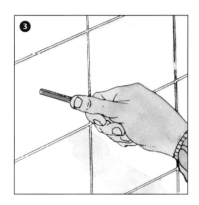

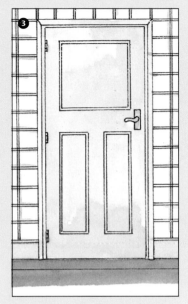

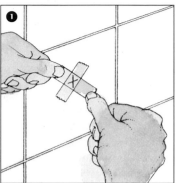

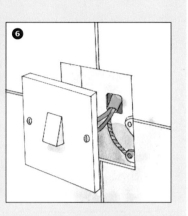

the exact centre line, and make the tiling of the wall as a whole correspond to this.

5 Try to tile round wash basins and other fixtures in a symmetrical fashion. Ideally, plan to use a row of whole tiles above fixtures, since cut tiles can look untidy. Where this is impossible, be sure to fill any gaps with good-quality waterproof sealer.

6 In bathrooms, light fittings must be fitted with a cord pull. To produce a neat finish round a

light switch in another room, turn off the power at the mains, undo the screws in the faceplate and ease the front of the switch clear of the wall. Tile up to the edge of the mounting box so that the faceplate will cover the cut edges of the tiles. Carefully screw the faceplate back into place, hiding the tile edges.

The problem with drilling into ceramic tiles is penetrating the glaze without the drill tip skating over the surface. Use a pointed tile bit or a sharp masonry bit. Don't, however, drill right through the tile into stone or brick with a tile bit. If you have a variable speed power drill, run it at its slowest setting to maximize your control. Never use a power drill set to hammer action – the vibration will shatter the tile.

1 Mark the spot to be drilled with a chinagraph pencil, then apply two strips of clear sticky tape in a cross over the spot. This helps hold the bit in place until the glaze is pierced.

2 Fit a drill bit wide enough to allow the shaft of the screw

to pass comfortably through. Hold the bit firmly against the spot for good purchase. Apply gentle pressure while drilling.

3 Push the wall plug gently into the drilled hole and use a screw that matches the plug for size. Don't attempt to force the screw. If it does not pass through freely, widen the hole with a larger bit.

Tiling a recess

Planning the work carefully in advance is one of the secrets of making a good job of tiling a room, taking into account such architectural features as recesses. For a professional appearance, ensure that the tiles are 'balanced' across a window recess – in other words, that the cut tiles either side of the recess are in symmetry. Tiles which protrude on external corners must have glazed edges.

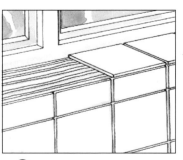

1 To produce the neatest effect, tiles lining a window recess should project to overlap those on the wall. The tiles in the recess should therefore have glazed edges.

2 Make sure the tile spacings in the recess are precisely in line with those on the wall. Use cut tiles with glazed edges at either end of the ledge to finish it off neatly.

3 Start the sides of the recess with a cut, glazed-edge tile so that the spacings remain exactly consistent with those between the horizontal rows on the wall.

Showers, sinks and worktops

Some tiling projects call for attention to particular details, and for the use of specialized materials. This is especially true of showers, when it is vital to seal every gap to prevent water penetration. Also, should you wish to replace the tiles of, say, an existing sink splashback, or anywhere else, it may be possible to leave them *in situ* and simply tile over them.

RIGHT This fully tiled shower enclosure looks dramatic – but it takes a lot of work.

BELOW When tiling splashbacks, always use water-resistant adhesive and grout.

Shower enclosures

In most situations a shower enclosure will involve two walls of the room, but should a third wall need to be constructed, use marine plywood on a framework of pre-treated timber. The plywood will be unaffected by damp. Make sure you use both waterproof adhesive and grout.

The most vital factor with a shower enclosure is to ensure that all gaps are carefully sealed, particularly where tiles meet the shower tray. The tray must be firm and not flex, and meeting edges must be dry before you apply sealant.

Use a silicone rubber sealant, either clear or in a colour to match the tray as closely as possible. Leave the sealant to set before you use the shower. Always follow the manufacturer's instructions.

Sink splashbacks

If you have never tried tiling before, then tackling a small area such as a splashback is a good introduction. Check that the back of the sink or basin is horizontal – if it is, the tiles can follow this line. With a freestanding basin, extend the tiling by one tile either side

of the basin. Place a rule across the back of the basin and mark a pencil line on the wall where the extended tiles will sit. Pin a piece of wooden batten to this line to give the tiles something to rest on while the tile adhesive sets. It can be removed later.

Use water-resistant adhesive to fix the tiles, and waterproof grout to finish. If the wall is papered, apply adhesive to the back of the tiles that overlap the paper, within 3mm (⅛in) of the edges, rather than risk getting adhesive on the paper. If this does happen, wipe off the adhesive immediately.

Preventing water penetration

Sealing gaps is also important behind sinks, basins and baths. Use silicone rubber sealant or a plastic sealing strip, stuck in place with the adhesive supplied or with a clear silicone rubber sealant. Ceramic quadrants, or edging tiles, may be available in matching colours. Stick these to the wall with waterproof adhesive and seal them to the bath or basin with silicone rubber sealant.

Worktops

Tiles for worktops must be tougher than those used on walls. Flooring-grade tiles or special worktop tiles should be used.

Applying sealant

Applying sealant so that gaps are completely filled can be a difficult job. Some dispensers have winged applicators that help to shape the sealant as it leaves the cartridge, but when using a straight nozzle the simplest way of getting a neat result is to run a strip of masking tape either side of the area to be sealed. Apply the sealant between the tape, and then, while it is still soft, wet your finger and run it quickly along the sealant, pressing it home and shaping it precisely. Next, carefully pull the masking tape away from the wall straight away, leaving behind a neat-edged line of sealant.

If any sealant does stray and starts to set, let it harden and then cut it with a sharp blade and peel it away to leave a clean finish.

Since these tiles are tougher than normal, you may find that your existing tile cutter cannot cope. In this case borrow or hire a heavy-duty cutter that can handle tiles of 10mm (just over ⅜in) or more thick.

Try to plan your worktop so that you can use multiples of tiles without the need for cutting. This will also look neater. Shaping can be a problem, however, for although a tile saw will cut hard tiles, its blade will blunt quite quickly.

Some worktop tiles have matching edging strips to give a neat, rounded look to tiling. For many tiles, however, you will need to produce an edging. Plastic trim strips are available designed to sandwich under the row of edge tiles as they are laid, or wooden beading can be cut and used just like a picture frame.

Always use waterproof adhesive, and space the tiles with the larger spacers used for floor tiles. Finish with waterproof grout, and seal the joint between worktop and wall with a silicone rubber sealant or with a plastic edging strip, some of which are self-adhesive.

RIGHT Worktops need to be covered with hard-wearing tiles, such as those made for flooring.

Tiling over old tiles

If you have a room where old tiles are firmly attached to the wall, and removing them could be a problem, you can tile over them provided that the surface is firm and flat and clean.

Start one tile up from the floor, working to a horizontal batten. To save drilling into the old tiles, hold the batten in place using a number of double-sided adhesive pads.

If the walls were previously half-tiled, you will end up with a thick ledge where the tiling ends. Finish this with edging tiles or make a feature of the step by bonding a hardwood strip along the top.

When attaching towel rails and other fittings to a wall tiled in this way, use plugs and screws that are long enough to reach into the wall behind – the old tiles alone will not support the weight of these fittings.(*See p. 139 for details on drilling through tiles.*)

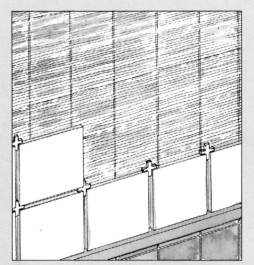

1 If removing existing tiling is likely to cause damage to the wall, you can tile over the top if the tiles are firmly attached. Lay out new tiles so that the joints of the old and new tiles don't align. Use conventional tile adhesive on top of the old tiles.

2 Where the existing tiling finished part way up the wall, you will be left with a wide ledge of double-thickness tiles. Either finish this edge with hardwood strips or use tile edging tiles. Stick and grout edging tiles in the same way as normal tiles.

Creative tiling

Tiles are hardwearing, practical and easy to clean, but it is also possible to have fun when decorating with them. Old tiles can be jazzed up with paint or transfers or you could even try your hand at creating a mosaic with them.

Decorating tiles

Transfers specially designed for adhering to ceramic can enliven an expanse of plain tiles, or you could paint on your own design with glass paint. This does not necessarily need great artistic flair – look in books and magazines for simple patterns to copy. Ensure the tiles are free of grease and follow the manufacturer's instructions.

Ceramic-painting centres are increasingly popular, and offer 'blanks' of all shapes and sizes (tableware and even lamp bases as well as tiles) in their unglazed state, known as bisque. You might paint a few single tiles as incidental motifs to tie in with plain shop-bought tiles, or create a block with a single design for use, for instance, as a splashback. Typically, a centre will have thousands of ideas, helpful advice and usually coffee and snacks on hand. They will glaze and fire your finished work, for collection a few days later.

Mosaics

Mosaics, whether geometric, abstract or pictorial, are all created by impressing small pieces of material such as tile, stone or glass into a bed of cement. The art of mosaic is an ancient one, but you don't need to look to Pompeii or ancient Rome for inspiration.

You can buy bags of individual mosaic fragments (*tesserae*), often in ranges of colours to help with coordinating a design, or you can collect your own. Before selecting your material, consider where it is to be used. Pebbles are extremely hardwearing, but are uncomfortable underfoot and not really suitable for an indoor floor mosaic. Shells can be worked into beautiful and evocative mosaics, but they are fragile, so avoid using them anywhere vulnerable where they may get knocked.

Creating a mosaic is not technically difficult, but it takes patience to arrange all the little *tesserae* into a satisfactory pattern or picture – even an apparently random effect needs to be worked at carefully to get the right balance of pieces.

ABOVE Tiny mosaic tiles in varying colours have been used to cover the walls of this very contemporary bathroom – a lot of work, but well worthwhile.

RIGHT Although small pebble mosaics can be uncomfortable to walk on when used on the floor, they can be fantastic when used on walls as splashbacks for cookers or sinks. This mosaic will have taken considerable time and patience but a similar effect could be created on a much smaller scale.

Quarry tiles

Quarry tiles are usually used on the floor, but they make a handsome alternative to ceramic tiles on the wall.

Although as equally hard wearing as ceramic tiles and requiring similar preparation and fixing, they are unglazed and have more of a casual, country appearance – a look that is emphasized by their warm, earthy colouration. Quarry tiles contain a high proportion of quartz and are not particularly porous, which makes them a suitable choice for kitchens and even bathrooms where they will create a hot, sunny, Mediterranean feel.

There may be slight natural colour variations in quarry tiles, even those from the same batch – a characteristic that you can exploit when planning a colour scheme around them.

If left untreated, quarry tiles have a matt appearance. If, however, you want to produce more of a shiny finish, then you need to treat them with linseed oil and turpentine.

RIGHT Quarry tiles are a natural accompaniment for wood in a country-style kitchen.

Making a mosaic border

Left with a lot of part-tiles to cut to finish off the top of a bathroom wall or shower cubicle? Instead, use the same tiles to create a subtle mosaic border.

Break up sufficient spare tiles into small pieces (use pincers or pliers rather than smashing them, which will damage the glaze and crumble the edges). Lay out lengths of sticky tape of the width you need to fill (parcel tape is usually about right) and make up your 'jigsaw' of *tesserae* on them, sticking them right side down on the tape. Because there is no colour pairing to worry about, it does not matter that you are seeing only the underside of the tiles, and when a length is ready it can be lifted straight into place and pressed into the tiling cement.

FLOORING

Choosing floor coverings

Deciding on a suitable floor covering is not just a matter of cost and taste. You will also need to consider a number of practicalities. What is the function of the room? Who will use it and for what? How much will the floor be used – whether at home or in a work space? What is the condition of the existing subfloor, and what will the maintenance involved be for the new floor?

Choosing the right material and colour for your decorative scheme will also need to be taken into account, since floor covering can be a dominant element in this regard. With so much choice available, you need to take care to plan carefully before you start. Indulging your personal taste can lead to unwelcome expense.

ABOVE RIGHT Coir fibre matting is easy to lay and makes a hardwearing floorcovering. This particular coir has a herringbone weave and natural colouring.

BELOW Wood strip flooring makes a hardwearing, practical surface for a kitchen.

Carpet

Carpet is perhaps the most common floor covering in homes. It is comfortable to walk over and sit on, and can transform any interior instantly. Made from wool, synthetic fibres, or a mixture of the two, carpet is available in a vast range of thicknesses, patterns, colours, textures and prices. Its durability as a floor covering depends on its quality and the wear to which it is subjected.

Fibre matting

Made from plant fibres such as sisal and seagrass, matting is easy to lay, either as a wall-to-wall covering or as loose mats. It is available in a range of patterns and shades from cream through green to brown. It does not show stains, and it is fairly easy to clean. It can be an inexpensive flooring option, although some styles are costly.

Wood

Bare wooden floors are beautiful in their own right. Stripped, carefully stained or coloured if desired, sealed, and decorated with a rug or mat, they can look stunning. If you are not fortunate enough to have an old floor suitable for such treatment, you can buy wood strips or blocks. They are not difficult to put down and can be very reasonably priced.

Vinyl

Vinyl is an excellent choice for kitchens, bathrooms and utility areas. Available in a wide range of colours and patterns – usually textured – this durable material is waterproof, oil- and fat- resistant, and often cushioned for sound and heat insulation, although it will burn or scratch. It is sold as tiles, which are easy to lay, and in sheet form, which is more tricky. It ranges in flexibility from soft and rubbery to rigid and stiff. Prices vary depending on the amount of PVC (polyvinyl chloride) present; the more it contains the more expensive the vinyl. It is essential to follow the manufacturer's cleaning instructions, since the wrong type of cleaner can damage the surface. Most advise warm, soapy water and rinsing.

Cork

Warm and practical, floor-grade cork is a reasonably priced option for kitchens and bathrooms. Usually sold as tiles, it is sometimes available in sheet form, which cuts down on laying time. Unless it is presealed cork, it must be cleaned and sealed with at least three coats of floor-grade polyurethane lacquer or varnish, after which it is durable and easy to clean. Cork is limited in colour, but it can be stained or stencilled before sealing. White cork tiles are now available to suit pale schemes.

Rubber

This is an expensive alternative to vinyl. Anti-slip and resistant to most household spills, rubber is available in primary colours, subtle two-tone effects, and with raised designs. It is sold in sheet or tile form.

Linoleum

The lino of granny's old kitchen has been given a new lease of life under a variety of brand names. Made from natural oils, gums and resins, linoleum is very durable and easy to clean (although it will rot if water seeps under it). Interior designers use it to create unique effects, from impressive marble-effect motifs to toning 'water ripples' across a bathroom floor. The price ranges from economical to expensive.

Slate

Extremely hardwearing, but also hard underfoot, slate comes in many shades and can be smooth or textured. It is not cheap but will last a lifetime if well laid.

Ceramic

Ceramic tiles are available in a truly vast array of styles, finishes, colours and textures. Good looking and easy to wipe clean (unglazed tiles need regular washing and they do absorb oil), they always remain cool no matter how hot it gets. They range from inexpensive to very costly, require a certain amount of skill to lay, and are unsuitable for all but the strongest of subfloors.

Quarry tiles

Made from unrefined silica alumina clay, these rustic tiles are usually in shades of brick red, gold or brown. Although durable, they can become pitted – but this often adds to their charm and appeal. Like ceramic tiles, they are cold and noisy underfoot and range in price from economical to expensive. They may require a lot of cleaning, however. If permitted by the manufacturer, they can be sealed with linseed oil mixed with four parts of turpentine, which should be painted on, covered with brown paper and left for 48 hours before washing.

ABOVE Slate floors are the ultimate in hardwearing durability. Slate can be stained darker with linseed oil before sealing.

BELOW Floorboards can be stripped, sanded, stained, and then sealed to provide a beautiful, easy-care surface for any room in the home.

Wood floors

If you find a wood floor beneath old floor coverings, why not refurbish it? The preparation and finishing involves a lot of physical work but the rewards can be tremendous.

Before starting, check that the boards are in good condition and that the supporting joists and wallplates are sound. Have any serious problems rectified. Make sure, too, that there are not too many gaps between the boards. A few can easily be filled, but if the whole floor needs this treatment, the results will probably be unattractive.

If you are lucky, the floor may need only a light sanding and cleaning by hand, but a floor sander is often necessary to level uneven edges and expose fresh surfaces for treatment. Where the wood is a consistent colour, just seal the surface with polyurethane lacquer or varnish; but to enhance or even change the colour, use a wood stain. Stains are available in natural wood colours or ones designed to harmonize with decorative schemes but still let the grain show through. Boards that are in poor condition or heavily filled can be coated with floor paint. Painting floorboards presents endless possibilities for colour use and design.

Staining

You can alter the colour of timber floors using a wood stain. Since wood can only be darkened with stain and recently applied stain is difficult to remove, first test a small inconspicuous area to check that the shade is right. To lighten timber you must apply bleach.

First, fill any cracks or holes with wood stopper or a filler that will take the colour of the stain. If the wood is open grained but you want a smooth finish, apply grain filler, rubbing it across the grain.

Next, make sure the floor is absolutely dust free and remove any marks with white spirit. Apply the stain with a dry, lint-free rag or brush, working quickly and evenly in the direction of the grain, wiping off excess stain with a clean cloth.

An alternative to staining and then sealing is to use a varnish stain, which combines the two jobs. The varnish must be brushed on very evenly to avoid patchiness, however, and every successive coat of varnish will deepen the colour.

Safety precautions

Before using stains and varnishes on a wood floor, carefully read the manufacturer's instructions on the tin or the accompanying leaflet. Many of these products are highly volatile and give off unpleasant or potentially dangerous fumes. Do not smoke, drink or eat while using them, work in a well-ventilated area, and if you are particularly sensitive wear a face mask and some form of eye protection. Keep these products away from exposed skin. It is best to apply stains and varnishes during the day so that you can keep the windows open. Daylight is also best for critically judging the effects you are creating.

BELOW LEFT Modern wood strip flooring is easy to lay and durable. The small size of the pieces makes it suitable for covering staircases as well as floors.

BELOW RIGHT Old wooden floorboards create an elegant, period look. They can be sanded, if necessary, and stained or painted to suit the decorative scheme.

LEFT This floor is a beautiful example of liming, and indicates just how effective this technique can be. It is particularly striking, since the colour is highlighted in the soft furnishings which add an air of elegant luxury to the room.

Liming

Using lime to alter the colour of wood is a traditional technique stretching back hundreds of years. Like staining (*see opposite*), liming alters the colour of the underlying surface without obliterating its most attractive feature, which is the grain of the wood. It can be applied to a floor which is stained with colour, giving a very attractive finish over blues and greens.

The most typical woods to treat in this way, using either a liming paste or wax, are the hardwoods, since these often have the most decorative figuring. Pine is a softer wood but it is also suitable for liming. The most usual woods to be limed include oak, ash and elm.

Materials and equipment

- Liming wax or paste

- Steel wool

- Liquid floor wax

- Clean, lint-free cotton rags

- Buffing cloth, brush or polishing machine

1 If you have stained the wooden surface to be limed (*see opposite*), allow the stain to dry thoroughly. Open the grain up by brushing with a wire brush. This may be omitted on softwoods such as pine. Make sure that surfaces are clean and dust free before applying the wax.

2 Apply a coat of liming wax and work it well into the grain using extra-fine steel wool. Liming wax dries relatively quickly, so it is better to work in smaller areas in order to achieve an even finish.

3 After about 5 minutes, remove most of the excess liming wax using a pad made up from clean cotton rag. Change to a clean piece of the rag as it becomes clogged with wax. Depending on the area being treated, you may need to make up several fresh pads in order to remove all the wax.

4 To form a protective surface for the newly limed wood, add a coat of liquid floor wax, making sure that it gets well into the grain. Allow a few hours for the wax to dry properly and then buff the surface to a soft

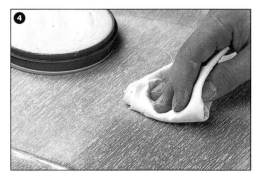

sheen. You can use soft, lint-free rags for this or a soft brush. However, if the area is a large one, such as an entire floor, it is much less effort to use a floor-polishing machine fitted with a soft polishing pad.

Wood stains and varnishes

All articles made of wood need treating with a preservative or finish, not only to preserve and protect the surface but also to bring out the inherent beauty of the grain and the texture of the timber itself.

The finish of the wood is an extremely important factor. Although painting would hide any slight surface defects, any blemish in wood is immediately accentuated when a clear finish, or a stain followed by clear finish, is applied. It is important, therefore, that all woodwork is clean and smooth before decorating work begins.

When a clear finish is to be applied, it is essential that you give the surface a final sanding by hand, following the grain of the wood. If a rotary electric sander has been used at any stage, small circular scratches, resembling fish scales, will be seen in the final coat.

Finishes and their effects on sycamore.
1 Matt polyurethane varnish 2 Tung oil
3 Patinating wax-black 4 Yellow acrylic stain
5 Gloss polyurethane varnish 6 Liming paste
7 Staining varnish.

Non-pigmented finishes

All finishes alter the colour of wood to some extent, and some woods – mahogany and walnut, for example – turn much darker even when a completely clear finish is applied.

An approximate idea of the colour wood will take on when treated with a clear finish can be seen by dampening a small area with ordinary water. If this colour is too light for your needs, then the wood can be stained before finishing. It is only possible to stain wood to a darker colour; for a lighter shade it must be bleached.

When staining wood, it is advisable to test the stain on an off-cut, or on an area that would normally be out of sight. It is notoriously difficult to remove stain, even immediately after it has been applied.

If the wood has an open grain, and a smooth finish is required, then you will need to use a grain-filler to fill the pores. The alternative is to apply extra coats of the finish, rubbing down with an abrasive paper between coats. Fill any cracks or holes in the wood with a wood-stopping material before applying the stain.

The final finish may be of a type that gives a surface film, such as French polish, varnish or polyurethane. The latter two are available in gloss, satin and matt finishes. Varnish stains are also available. These are convenient, since they will colour and finish the wood in a single operation.

Do bear in mind that each extra coat of varnish stain will darken the colour of the wood and, unless brushed out very evenly, the colour will vary with the thickness of the film. When wood is stained with a penetrating dye, the colour will not vary – no matter how many coats of clear finish you later apply.

Don't neglect to treat areas of woodwork that are normally out of sight. For example, when varnishing an external door, it is important that at least one coat is applied to the top and bottom edges, otherwise water may penetrate at these points and eventually cause the varnish to fail.

Oil finishes

Oiled finishes, such as teak oil and Danish oil, are a useful alternative to the finishes mentioned above. They are also easier to apply than polyurethane and other varnishes. On new wood, you will need to apply two coats, either with a brush or a mildly abrasive pad, cleaning off excess oil with a cloth. Teak oil and Danish oil leave the wood with a soft, lustrous finish that is truly resistant to liquids. You can also add stains to them.

When a high-gloss finish is required on exterior woodwork, consider using a yacht varnish. This usually contains tung oil, which has outstanding exterior durability.

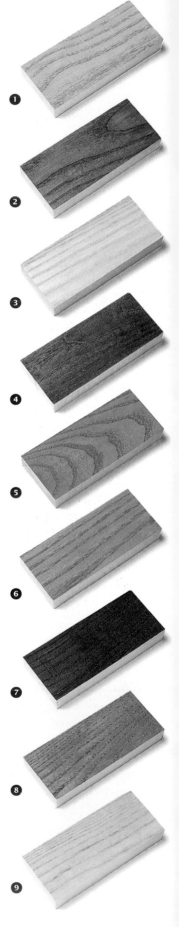

A selection of dyes on sycamore.
1 Ash grey 2 Medium oak 3 Light oak 4 Walnut
5 Bright green 6 Apricot 7 Deep mahogany
8 Mulberry blue 9 Antique pine

Waxing

This is popular for treating newly stripped pine. Some waxes colour the wood a little – improving the bleached-out look of pine that has been immersed in a caustic solution, and giving the surface an 'antiqued' appearance. If you don't wish to alter the look of the pine, make sure the wax you buy is colourless.

Always rub the wood down first with a fine-grade of steel wool. If the wax is applied with a soft cloth, it will produce a natural satin finish. If you want a higher gloss, however, allow the new wax to dry completely and then buff it vigorously with a soft duster or clean, soft shoe brush.

RIGHT When stained to produce the right colour and then treated with a protective top coat of varnish, the true beauty of a natural wood floor is unsurpassed.

Painting floors

Water-based floor paints have hugely increased the repertoire of decorating floorboards. They give a more solid effect than coloured stains and are particularly effective at giving a new lease of life to unattractive boards or where some boards have at some point been replaced and the different age of the woods shows. Just like walls, painted floors can be stippled, dragged or sponged.

If you do not have wooden floorboards, you could try recreating the effect on hardboard. Measure and mark out with a soft pencil boards of the width you wish. Using a metal rule, score heavily down the lines with a sharp, heavy-duty craft knife. (Remember to do some cross cuts too, as real boards seldom span a room without a break.) Study the colours and grain pattern in suitable woods and with a reference alongside, paint the boards, dragging and feathering until you have the result you want. Seal with clear matt varnish.

LEFT Wood stains and coloured varnishes are increasingly available in shades other than browns and can create a very modern look. The more coats that are applied, the deeper the colour attained.

Laying woodstrip and woodblock floors

Woodstrip floors give a more contemporary look to a room than traditional floorboards. They come in solid wood or, more commonly, ply or composite with a veneer of real wood or a laminate simulation. Finishes come in a wide variety from blonde ash to dark oak or rich cherry and different grades are suitable for different areas of the house.

Choosing the right boards

Woodstrip flooring comes in several grades: choose a quality that will stand up to the treatment it will get and check that the thickness will leave sufficient clearance below doors. Most boards are pre-sealed, but some are supplied ready to treat yourself.

Laminate flooring boards are supplied in packs which cover a calculated area, usually in the region of 20sq m (215sq ft). Divide the area of your floor space by the area covered by the pack to give you the

Materials and equipment

In addition to the flooring boards and underlay you will need:

• **Damp-proof membrane, to cover a concrete floor**

• **Quadrant or skirting, to conceal the expansion gap**

• **Spacers to maintain the expansion gap**

• **String, to mark a straight line**

• **Tape measure**

• **Hammer**

• **Tamping block of wood, to protect the strips when being hammered into place**

• **Fine-toothed saw**

• **Adhesive, as recommended by the manufacturer**

Laying a floating floor

First lay the damp-proof membrane, if using, and then lay the underlay. Underlay, which is available in more than one grade, not only cushions the floor but helps deaden sound. It comes in rolls and lengths which can simply be abutted without any need to join them.

1 Begin at the opposite end of the room from the main door. If laying directly onto existing floorboards, the new boards should be laid at right angles to the old ones. Put down the first board in one corner with the tongue facing into the room. Insert spacers on the two wall sides, to establish the expansion gap. Lay the next board or boards in the row, adding spacers against the wall as you go. Cut the last board to fit, again allowing for the expansion gap at the end of the row.

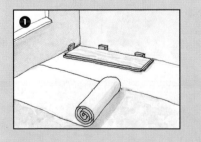

2 Check that this first row is straight by stretching a piece of string taut along the leading edge. If the wall is at all bowed the row of boards will also

curve and you will not get a close fit between boards across the room. Adjust the size of the spacers until the row of boards is straight and still tight against the spacers which are in turn tight against the wall.

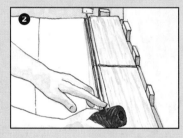

3 When the row is in position, add the second row, beginning either with an offcut of the last part-board in the first row or a half-board. This will have the effect of staggering the joins and avoid lines of board ends running across the room. Insert a spacer at the beginning and end of each row. Check the straightness of the leading edge again and, if the first row was awkward to align, lay a third row to satisfy yourself that there is no distortion.

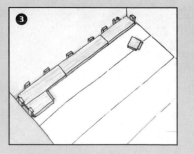

4 Take up all boards except the first row and re-lay, this time with adhesive. Apply glue to the groove and the upper surface of the tongue of each board. Slot back in position then glue the next.

5 Hammer each firmly in place, using a tamping block to protect the board's tongue. Wipe off any excess glue that oozes through the gaps. Use the string line to check once again that the leading edge is straight. When three or four rows are in place, leave them to dry for two hours before gluing the next three or four. Continue until the floor is complete. You may need to saw the boards of the last row lengthways to fit. Finally, fix quadrant to the skirting all the way round to conceal the expansion gap.

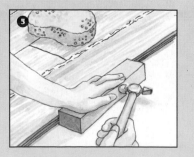

number of packs, but remember to allow for wastage.

Take into account, too, how many lengths you will require to fit a single row. Boards come in a number of lengths up to about 1.8m (6ft). Using 1.8m boards in a room 3.8m (12ft 6in) wide will lead to a lot of awkward small fillers, but 1.5m (5ft) lengths would be less fiddly and probably more economical.

Methods of fixing

The thickest flooring boards are designed to replace existing boards or boarding and are nailed down in a way similar to regular floorboards. Other floorings require a sound, level surface. Thin laminates can be stuck down but the most popular method is the 'floating floor', by which tongue and groove flooring is laid over a thin underlay and the individual boards are glued to each other but not to the surface beneath.

Preparation

The tongue and groove boards can be laid on both solid and wood surfaces, but it is vital to ensure before you begin that the subfloor has no irregularities; only very minor ripples or bumps will be masked by the underlay. Use sheets of hardboard to cover uneven floorboards while a layer of levelling compound can improve the look of a solid floor.

Damp is the enemy of wood. A damp-proof membrane should be laid to provide a barrier to residual moisture in a solid subfloor but must not be used over wooden flooring. If you even think there may be a problem, get joists and floorboards treated for damp first. Most woodstrip floorings are not advised for use in bathrooms – check with the manufacturer.

Atmospheric moisture also affects wood. After buying your flooring, lie it out flat in the room in which it is to be laid for at least a couple of days. Floating floors are laid with a small expansion gap left all the way round the edge to allow for the natural expansion and contraction of the wood. This is concealed either with quadrant attached to the skirting all around the edge of the room or by removing the skirting board and replacing it after laying the floor so that the boards have room to expand below it. To cover the gap the skirting or quadrant should be at least 16 mm (⅝in) thick. Many manufacturers supply quadrant that matches their boards, or you can use your own, painted or stained to match the existing skirting.

Woodblock floors

Provided that the subfloor has been well prepared, and is level, firm, stable and dry, it is relatively easy to lay a woodblock floor. The wood pieces are laid in a pattern onto a self-adhesive hardboard. Allow for an expansion gap at the skirting boards.

1 Remove the self-adhesive membrane after laying the self-adhesive underlay.

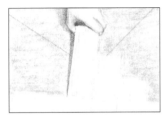

2 Place the blocks of wood in the desired pattern.

3 Gently bond the wood blocks to the adhesive with a soft mallet.

4 Mark the edges, leaving an expansion gap.

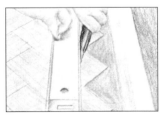

5 Cut off waste wood with a knife and straight edge.

6 Fit the quadrant into place along the skirtings.

LEFT A beautifully laid and polished woodstrip floor is both hard wearing and a pleasure to look at.

Carpet and matting

Whether fitted wall to wall or loose laid as a rug, carpet is hard to equal in terms of sheer comfort and warmth. But as well as being a practical floor covering, carpet is available in such a wide range of styles, colours, patterns and textures that it can be used to complement the decorative theme in any room in the house.

Matting is becoming increasingly popular as a floor covering as the range of colours increases and modern manufacturing techniques make it easier to keep clean. It creates a soft, natural look in a room.

Carpet

A fitted carpet can transform an interior and where it continues through doorways it provides a unifying feature. Carpeting a large room can be difficult and many people prefer to employ professional layers rather than risk spoiling an expensive piece of flooring. Heavily tracked areas such as halls, staircases and landings need heavy-duty carpeting to withstand the extra wear.

When working out how much carpet you need, take exact room measurements. For anything other than an absolutely straight-sided room make a plan and mark on it the precise measurements of every nook and alcove. Alcoves and bays may need extra pieces to be joined to the main carpet. Take the plan to the shop and ask an estimator to calculate quantities.

To give maximum wear, a hessian-backed carpet needs to be stretched into position using a knee-kicker, over grippers, which are nailed to the floor around the room's edges. Carpet should be laid over good-quality underlay of felt, foam or rubber to improve comfort and durability and to minimize dust travelling up from floorboards. Foam and rubber underlay are not suitable for stairs or heavily seamed areas. Rubberized felt and bonded underlays are also available.

Foam-backed carpets are much easier to lay, being simply unrolled in place over a paper underlay to prevent them sticking to the subfloor. They are usually stuck down at the edges, but can be secured over special grippers. Generally cheaper than hessian-backed carpets, foam-backed carpets have a shorter life. They are useful for small rooms with little foot traffic as well as bathrooms as the backing prevents shrinkage.

Carpet tiles

Seal-edged carpet squares come in a range of sizes and colours and are easy to lay. Shades can be mixed to make chequerboard or more complicated patterns. The squares

ABOVE LEFT Carpet tiles can be cut up and joined together in a bright and cheerful mosaic pattern.

LEFT Room-sized matting is durable and hardwearing and provides a wealth of texture.

can be stuck down or laid loose, enabling damaged or heavily worn squares to be replaced or moved around – a boon for children's rooms, dining rooms and even kitchens. Being removable, they also give access to underfloor services with the minimum of disruption.

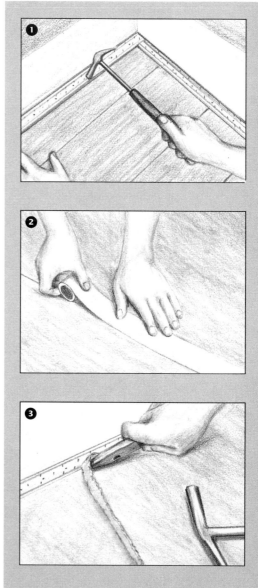

CARPET SWATCHES 1 Wool and synthetic mix
2 Synthetic fibres 3 Long-pile wool 4 Patterned
weave 5 All wool 6 Wool patterned long pile
7 Wool patterned short pile 8 Traditional patterned
wool 9 Short pile wool 10 Modern geometric pattern

Laying carpet

With a lot of determination, you can
make a good job of laying hessian-
backed carpet. First-timers should start
with foam-backed carpet.

Materials and equipment

- **50mm (2in) single-sided tape**

- **Sharp knife and carpet hammer**

- **Knee-kicker carpet stretcher**

- **Bolster**

1 To fit traditional carpet, fix gripper
strips 3mm (⅛in) away from walls or
skirtings around the room.

2 To join seams in rubber underlay,
use a single-side 50mm (2in) carpet or
underlay tape on top of the pieces.

3 Butt the underlay up to the gripper
strips and trim to fit with a sharp knife.

4 Cover the gripper with carpet and
stretch the carpet onto the gripper pins.

5 Cut the carpet 6mm (¼in) oversize.
Tuck it between the gripper and skirting.

ABOVE Light-coloured carpets may need
protecting with a rug where they receive most wear.

Threshold strips

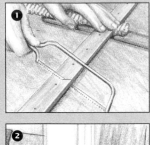

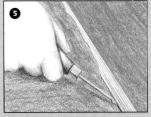

1 To protect carpet in doorways use an edging strip, either in aluminium or wood. Measure and cut the bar to size.
2 Nail the bar down. It can be single or double sided.
3 On a double bar, hook the carpet on both sides and trim with a knife.
4 To seal carpet edges that may fray, apply adhesive to the edges.
5 Tuck the carpet under the edge and hammer down.

Stair carpet

Stair carpet must be laid over underlay, which can be in the form of pads tacked to each tread and overhanging the nosing by 50mm (2in). You can tack the carpet in place, although special staircase grippers will give a better finish.

Start at the bottom, with the pile facing down the stairs. Tack the carpet to the first tread, press the fold into the first gripper and working upwards keep the carpet very taut. When you reach the top riser, tack it under the last nosing so that the landing carpet just overlaps it.

Angled treads (winders) need a series of folds in the carpet to take up the slack. An easier method is to cut the carpet just below the nosing and tack it in place on each winder.

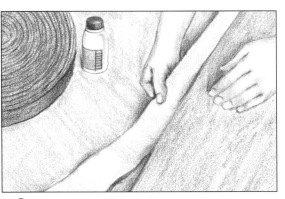

1 Make joins by placing half tape under the carpet edge when tacky.

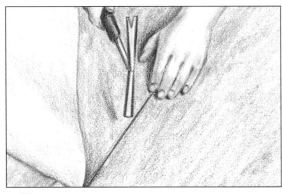

2 Butt up the second piece over the tape and hammer it down to form a good bond.

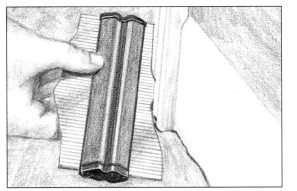

3 Use a template former to trace the contour of any difficult or awkward shapes, such as mouldings.

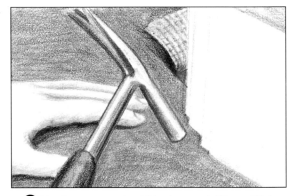

4 Fraying carpets should be hemmed 25mm (1in) at the edges and then tacked down into place.

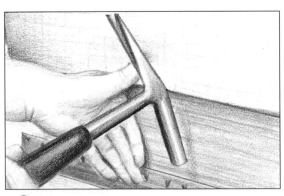

5 Nail a stair strip over the underlay pad at the back of the tread on each stair when fitting a stair carpet. Start work at the bottom of the stairs.

6 The hall carpet should cover the first riser. The landing carpet should cover the tread nosing at the top of the flight and be tacked neatly in place.

Matting

Matting made from sisal (agave leaves) and coir (coconut fibre) is inexpensive, practical and hard wearing and ranges in colour from pale to dark brown. Most coir is honey gold and some sisal is now dyed in other colours. Thought to be uncomfortable and dusty, coir and sisal is now often backed with latex or vinyl, which stops dirt falling through and adds strength. They can be used in almost any area unless food is likely to be dropped.

When laying sisal or coir, it is best to cut it slightly oversize and leave the matting in the room for at least 24 hours to adjust. Broadloom types are best for wall-to-wall use, although you can sew narrow lengths together or butt them over double-sided tape. It can be loose laid, but it is better to secure matting with double-sided tape.

Rush, seagrass and maize matting is more finely textured than sisal or coir, and less robust. Available in different weaves, the squares can be sewn together with fine twine. Since they are liable to dry out and become brittle, they need to be moistened occasionally with a plant mister.

Many mattings are not suitable for stairs so take advice on which may be used.

RIGHT Pieces of loose-laid matting can be used informally to differentiate different activity areas within a large room.

MATTING SWATCHES 1 Coir two-colour basket weave 2 Sisal two-colour bouclé 3 Sisal one-colour bouclé 4 Coir three-colour herringbone 5 Sisal two-colour herringbone 6 Sisal one-colour bouclé 7 Coir three-colour twine weft 8 Coir two-colour bouclé 9 Coir two-colour bouclé 10 Sisal natural basket weave 11 Coir one-colour bouclé 12 Coir two-colour herringbone

Laying tiles

Flexible vinyl tiles are easier to handle and cut than hard tiles, and they are generally easier to lay as well, but the technique to use is much the same for vinyl, ceramic or quarry tiles.

Tiles require a stable, level surface to be laid on. Unless the subfloor is perfect, it is best to put down hardboard or chipboard before laying the tiles. You will have to use a special tile adhesive, although some vinyl tiles are self-adhesive.

RIGHT Bold chequerboard patterns are easy to achieve and look particularly good with otherwise plain decor.

Materials and equipment

- Squared graph paper

- Coloured pencils

- Metal rule

- Marking chalk

- Tile adhesive and spreader

- Heavy-duty craft knife (for vinyl tiles) or tile cutter for ceramic or quarry tiles (*see p. 136–7*)

Planning

1 Make a scale drawing of the room on squared graph paper. Each square represents one tile.

2 Mark all alcoves and other irregularities. In a kitchen where much of the floor may be taken up with fixed units, include these to scale as well. Mark each square as you calculate quantities.

3 Find the total of tiles needed for the room.

4 Shade in the design for pattern and quantities of each colour required.

Laying tiles

Before laying vinyl tiles, remove the packaging and leave them in the room for 24 hours to acclimatize. It is usual to lay tiles from the centre point and work outwards, towards the edges of the room, but in bathrooms and kitchens where much of the floor space is occupied by cupboards, you may have trouble finding the centre of the area to be tiled.

1 Mark the centre line in chalk and check that the edge tiles will be at least a half-tile wide.

2 If not, move the line a half-tile width to one side.

3 Mark a centre line in the other direction. Check as before and move the line if it is necessary to avoid having small strips of tile at the sides of the room.

4 Spread tile adhesive along the floor, on either side of the centre line chalk marks.

5 Lay the marked central tiles first, either side of the chalk line.

6 Continue working outwards from the centre tiles towards the edges until the floor area is completely covered.

7 Lay the border tiles last. Place a border tile that needs cutting squarely on top of the last tile, then place another tile on top of it, arranged against the wall or skirting. Mark a pencil line along the edge of the top tile on the loose tile below. Cut the marked tile to this line: it should fit perfectly in the gap. Apply adhesive and firm into position. Repeat with the other edge tiles.

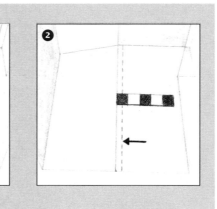

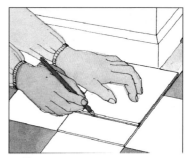

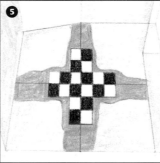

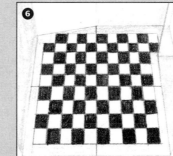

External corners

To cut around an external corner where one tile is involved, use the same technique for cutting border tiles to fit (*see left*).

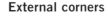

1 Place two full tiles over the last laid tile and slide the top one over to butt up against the skirting or wall. Mark a pencil line on the tile beneath.

2 Move both tiles around the corner, without turning them, and position over the last laid tile on that side. Mark a line as before, cut out the rectangle and glue the tile into place.

Tiling round a pipe

First, cut an edge tile to fit the space, and then push the tile against the pipe and mark the centre. Next, move the tile against the wall and mark the pipe centre on the edge of the tile. Draw light pencil lines from both points and cut a hole where the lines bisect. Finally, make a slit in the tile to allow you to feed it around the pipe.

Sheet flooring

Vinyl sheeting is made in a huge variety of colours and designs: Spanish and Portuguese ceramic tile patterns, marble and parquet effects, and bold designs in strong colours and black and white. It always pays to buy the best you can afford. Cheap sheeting will eventually crack and does not withstand scratching, staining or spills for long. The best type is cushioned by an inner layer of bubbles making it soft and warm underfoot – essential for long standing and tramping around the kitchen. It is also harder wearing.

BELOW The many colours and patterns available in sheet vinyl make it easy to coordinate with the decor of any room, and its easy-clean, hard-wearing, and spill-resistant surface is ideal for kitchens and bathrooms.

Handling sheet vinyl

Although large rolls of vinyl are heavy and awkward to handle, demanding a degree of strength and skill to manoeuvre, vinyl sheeting does have the advantage of covering large areas quickly and with the minimum of seams through which water and other spillages might seep. For large kitchens and bathrooms use 4m (13ft) wide sheet material.

When working out how much vinyl you need, allow an extra 50mm (2in) all round in case walls are uneven or out of square, which is likely to be the case. Decide which way you want the pattern to run and avoid seams in doorways, since this is where foot traffic is heaviest. Laying seams at right angles to windows makes them less noticeable because the light won't cast a shadow.

Cold temperatures make vinyl brittle, so if you are laying it in winter warm it up first. Leaving it in the room overnight with the heating left on will probably be sufficient.

Laying vinyl sheeting

It is best to leave the vinyl loosely rolled in a warm room for 24 hours prior to laying to allow it to become supple.

❶ Cut the vinyl about 50mm (2in) longer at the edges to allow for trimming. Lay the vinyl up against the skirting or wall by 50mm (2in). Sweep over the vinyl with a soft broom to ensure the sheet is in close contact with the floor.

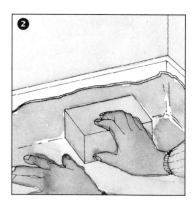

❷ Use a block of wood to press the vinyl firmly into the angle between the floor and skirting. If necessary, make vertical release cuts into the corner flaps. Don't trim or use adhesive until the fitting is complete.

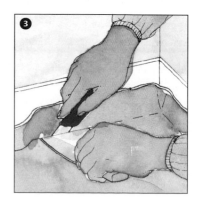

❸ If a second sheet is used, lay it overlapping the first. Cut through both sheets and remove the waste. Use a paint scraper to hold the vinyl hard against the junction of floor and skirting, and trim off the surplus with a craft knife.

Trimming around a door frame

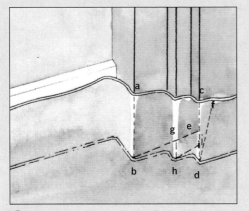

1 Make two 50mm (2in) vertical cuts in the vinyl at the projecting points of the frame (**ab** and **cd**). Next, make diagonal cuts to the same points (**eb** and **fd**). Make another vertical cut around the frame (**gh**) and cut diagonally (**ih**).

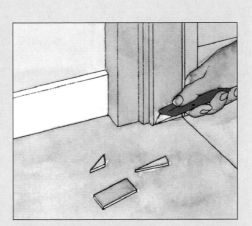

2 Press the vinyl tightly against the frame and trim off the surplus. Take the vinyl into the doorway and trim it so that it will end up halfway under the door. Finish it off later using a metal or wooden edging strip to prevent it lifting.

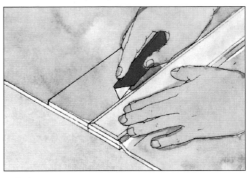

Joins

If at any point adjoining vinyl overlaps, use a straight edge and a sharp craft knife to cut through both thicknesses at the same time. Pull away the waste material and you will be left with a perfect fit.

Applying adhesive

Apply adhesive with a notched spreader. Check how long the adhesive should be left before the vinyl is applied. With solvent adhesive, work in a well-ventilated area and avoid smoking or any form of naked flames.

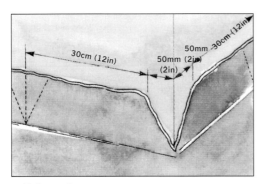

External corners

Lift the vinyl and make a vertical cut at the corner. Take the knife blade just to the floor. Make further diagonal cuts from 50mm (2in) on either side down to the base of the first cut so that the vinyl will rest against each wall. Make other cuts about every 30cm (12in) if necessary.

Hold the vinyl tight against the wall with a block of wood, then position the knife with its point where the wall and floor meet. Cut into the corner holding the blade at 45° as you proceed.

Repeat this process for the remaining flap of vinyl, making sure to get a neat fit on the corner. Bear in mind that it is better to trim away too little rather than too much: you can always pare away a little more if necessary. Finish all the fitting before sticking down the vinyl flooring. It will be too late to make changes once it is stuck into position.

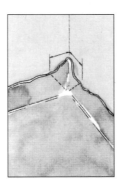

Internal corners

Leave 25mm (1in) of the surplus running up the wall, then cut out a triangle from the corner. This will allow you to press the vinyl against both walls for trimming.

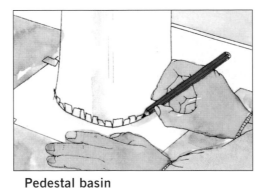

Pedestal basin

With awkward shapes, such as a pedestal basin, it is best to make a paper template first and then transfer the shape onto the vinyl to be cut.

Cutting safely

Sheet vinyl is not easy to cut and care is needed. Keep a sheet of scrap hardboard at hand on which to make cuts: the knife may snag on floorboards. Use a sharp knife with a snap-off blade so that you can maintain a keen edge. Position a steel straight edge along the line to be cut and use the knife so the blade cuts away from your other hand. With thick vinyl, make a number of passes, allowing the knife to follow the cut until it breaks through. If vinyl has to be cut *in situ*, push the blade through the sheet and draw it along the marked line – again making sure that your holding hand is always behind the direction of the cut.

LIGHTING

Types of lighting

Demand for more subtle variations in lighting and a consciousness of saving energy have greatly increased the choice of light bulbs. Think before you buy, to decide which is best for a particular purpose.

Tungsten bulbs

The 'ordinary' light bulb. It comes with either ES or bayonet fitting (*see opposite*) and gives off a warm, slightly yellow-tinted light. The most popular wattages for use around the house are 40, 60 and 100W although tungsten bulbs are available in both lower and higher wattages.

Bulbs can be pear-shaped, squat (mushroom-shaped) or globe (more decorative, if the bulb is going to be on view). As well as clear glass you can choose pearlized for a more diffuse light and pastel-tinted for a softly coloured glow. Strongly coloured bulbs are more for fun for outdoor parties than for everyday use.

Crown-silvered These bulbs are designed for use with a reflector. In a table lamp with an ordinary shade, they have the useful property of casting light downwards only.

Daylight These blue-glassed bulbs give off a light much nearer daylight – useful for working under when seeing colour by near-natural light is important.

Candle and pygmy These bulbs have small versions of bayonet or ES fittings (*see opposite*) and candles come with or without flicker effect. Pygmy bulbs are usually 15W and used inside wardrobes or for small display lighting.

Tungsten filament bulbs, which were once the most common choice throughout the house, are nowadays often being ousted by halogen and new-style fluorescent bulbs. Both these types of bulb are longer lasting and more energy efficient.

Effects on colours

Light, whether artificial or natural, exaggerates the effect of colours. White and pale colours reflect light and so make rooms appear larger. Conversely, dark colours absorb light and tend to make rooms seem smaller. Under most artificial lights, blues become darker while reds and yellow tones become brighter. You will also find that ordinary tungsten filament lamps create a warm reddish light effect, whereas warm-white fluorescent tubes produce yellowish colour effects. These affect the feel in the room.

CLOCKWISE FROM TOP LEFT Natural daylight (as reference); tungsten filament lighting; 'cool' fluorescent lighting.

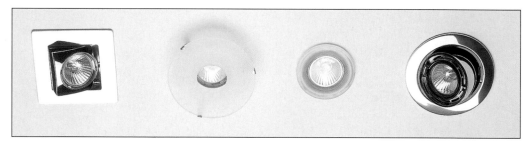

ABOVE Fully recessed spots make effective down-lights, while 'eyeball'-style lights can be swivelled to alter the lighting direction. These are particularly good in a workroom or study.

BELOW Lighting track systems have evolved dramatically over the last 50 years, and they are now available in as many different designs as there are types of room to accommodate them.

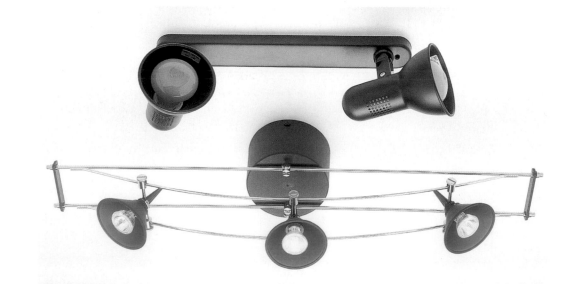

Halogen bulbs

These low-energy bulbs emit a clearer, whiter light than tungsten. They are available in the same standard size as tungsten, but have the advantage, apart from saving energy, of also being capable of being made extremely small. Mains-voltage halogen bulbs look similar to tungsten bulbs and fit ordinary BC fittings, but low-voltage have their own type of fittings and are mostly available in 20 and 50W. As these miniature bulbs run on 12V rather than the standard household 240V, they have to be run via a transformer. This is either integrated into the light fitting (usual in a desk or floor light) or comes as a separate box installed alongside.

Dichroic reflectors Spotlights ranging from small to tiny, these powerful but discreet lights have transformed recessed lighting.

Candle power

Electric lights are not the only form of night light. Candles are a centuries-old alternative and the range of designs available make them a suitable option in virtually any style of room, especially when a romantic atmosphere is called for. As well as table-standing sticks and candelabras, there are also large floor-standing holders and wall-mounted sconces. Many candles are scented to impart a delicate perfume which will linger on after the candle has burnt out.

Linear Looking like miniature fluorescent tube lights, these are used in some desk lights or in display cabinets.

Fluorescent bulbs

Once limited to harsh strip lights, fluorescent lighting has undergone a sea-change. Fluorescent's advantages of low energy consumption and a shadow-free, low-heat light have been developed into compact bulbs which can, increasingly, be used in standard bulb holders. Usual wattages are 9–23W: you need only a quarter or a fifth the output of a standard tungsten bulb to get the equivalent light. They cannot be used with dimmer switches, time switches or other security-activated devices. For lights as focal points rather than for radiating light, track down brightly coloured fluorescent tubes in sinuous or geometric shapes.

To avoid too bright a flame, keep the wick well trimmed. This also ensures that the candle produces the minimum of amount of smoke while it burns. Choose non drip candles to avoid dripping wax over the carpet or furniture.

LEFT A large, floor-standing candelabra is a room feature in its own right. **ABOVE** Candles can also be wall mounted, casting soft light around a dining room, for example.

Bulb fittings or caps

On tungsten, newer compact fluorescent bulbs and high-wattage halogen bulbs:
- **Bayonet Cap (BC)**
- **Edison Screw (ES)**

These each have a small version (labelled SBC and SES respectively)

On low-wattage halogen bulbs:
- **Twist and lock (TAL)**
- **Double pin**

Spotlights and tracks

Spotlights, which project a beam of light rather than giving an all-round radiance, can vary from a narrow pinpoint to a broad flood of perhaps 80°. They can be fixed beam or can swivel, and can be discreetly recessed or make a design statement. The miniaturization available with halogen lamps has greatly broadened the range available.

A lighting track is, in effect, a continuous light socket and can be either mains or low-voltage. Within the limits recommended by the manufacturer, track lights with compatible fixings can be added anywhere along the length of the metal channel. Some systems are straight lengths that can be extended or made to turn corners with connectors, others are curved or flexible. Each system is slightly different and lights from one maker will not usually fit the tracks made by another – particularly annoying if you already a have a track installed and then discover that the lights from a different system would better suit your needs.

Cost and energy efficiency

The cheapest bulbs to buy are standard tungsten and their average life is about 1000 hours. Long-life tungstens are slightly more expensive but should last twice as long. Halogen bulbs are more costly and a low-voltage system is initially more expensive to install because of the need for a transformer. However, they use much less power and should last around 3500 hours. Fluorescent bulbs last even longer – up to10,000 hours – and they only use about a quarter of the power of a tungsten bulb.

Planning a scheme

When you are choosing a colour scheme for any room in your home, the first thing to take into account is how that room will be used and, thus, the type of lighting you will need. Just as natural light from windows will change the appearance of colours at different times of the day, artificial lights also affect the colours in a room, making them look lighter or darker. They can also play tricks with colours, sometimes causing dramatic changes at, literally, the flick of a switch.

Two-way switches

Two-way switches are a small refinement to a system that can add greatly to your convenience. Consider them in particular at the top and bottom of the staircase and beside the bed.

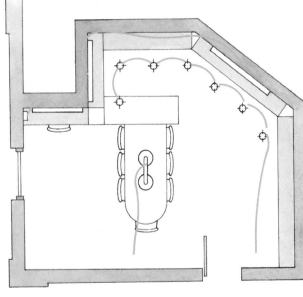

LEFT AND ABOVE In a multipurpose room, such as this spacious kitchen, you will almost certainly need a lighting diagram to ensure that all the different areas of the room are adequately illuminated – especially the dining table and worktops.

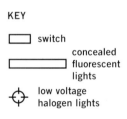

KEY

☐ switch

▭ concealed fluorescent lights

⊕ low voltage halogen lights

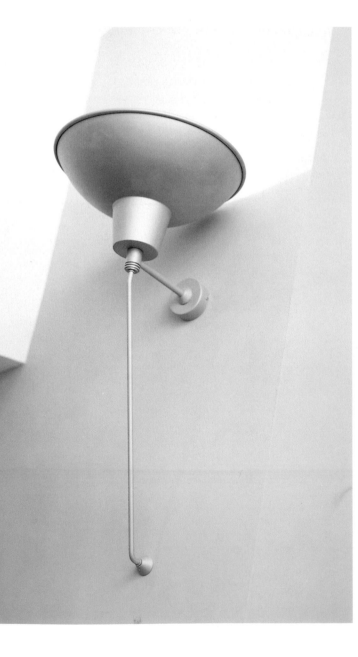

LEFT This minimalist silver uplighter features a halogen bulb which casts bright white light, making it particularly suitable for a kitchen.

Time of day

How you incorporate lighting into your room scheme will probably depend on when and how that area is most used. A bedroom, for example, is usually the easiest room to plan, since it will be used in artificial light for the greater part of the year. A dining room most often used for evening meals is also quite straightforward, but living rooms and kitchens in particular need careful planning and adaptable schemes.

Highlighting features

Lighting can be used to accentuate features in the room in much the same way as colours and patterns can. Strategically positioned wall lights, spotlights, uplighters or ceiling downlighters can be arranged so that they wash a complete wall with a blanket of light, a feature in itself.

They can also be used to good effect to highlight an isolated area, such as a display shelf, or a recess filled with beautiful objects, or to light a work of art such as a sculpture or a painting.

Halls and stairs

Lighting in the entrance or hall is important because it sets the scene for the style and mood you wish to convey; it reflects the atmosphere you wish to create and ensures the entrance to your home is safe and well illuminated. Although the hall should extend a welcome to visitors, you can, if you wish, treat it in a more dramatic way than the other rooms in your home. Since it is a room which people pass through, you can aim for effects that are too theatrical for living rooms.

ABOVE If your hall or stairway is used to display paintings or other pieces of art, then the lighting needs to take this into account. Bright levels of indirect, full-spectrum lighting in this picture-festooned stairway ensure that glare from the glass frames is minimal and colours accurate, without in any way compromising on safety.

RIGHT A good level of general illumination is useful in the hallway near the front door to your home, but this should not be dazzlingly bright. Pockets of brighter lighting to highlight specific areas can then be created with table lamps.

Links and continuity

Halls, and indeed stairs, represent the links between different rooms and areas of your home. In order to create a continuity of style you may, therefore, wish to carry your lighting theme through from one room into the hall or stairway. Many ranges of light fittings now available offer the choice of wall- or ceiling-mounted uplighters and downlighters, as well as freestanding lights, all with the same cosmetic appearance. In this way, you can take continuity of appearance into account while introducing wide-ranging lighting effects, each tailored to the requirements of each individual area.

Stairs are often very badly lit, relying entirely on the overspill of light from hallways or landing areas. From a safety point of view, stairs need to be adequately lit. The light needs to be bright enough for people to move around without fear of tripping or falling. Stairs can be made safer by installing strong directional light that draws attention to the vertical risers and horizontal stair treads. Avoid glaring landing lights and use wall fittings to provide an additional source of light.

Varying lighting intensities

Think carefully about the lighting intensity of different parts of halls and stairs. In an entrance hallway, for example, you will probably want relatively high light levels, since this is where you congregate, at least

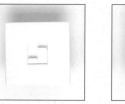

Dimmer switches

One easy way of increasing the range of lighting effects you can create is by replacing your existing on/off switches with dimmer control switches. Although designs differ a little between manufacturers, they all work in much the same way by controlling the amount of voltage reaching the lamps, and hence varying their light output. One-gang dimmers are the most common type, but two-gang versions are also available. All are suitable for two-way switching, and installing one in place of an existing switch simply involves switching off the lighting circuit, then disconnecting the existing switch cable and reconnecting it to the dimmer. If you are not sure which type to choose, check with the retailer that it will be suitable for the combined wattage of the lights it is to control.

briefly, when people enter or leave your home. You may also not want too marked a difference in lighting intensity between, say, the living or family room, which tends to be brightly lit, and the adjacent hall, so that your eyes don't have trouble adjusting. In the upstairs hall, however, or in the area of hall in a single-storey home or apartment adjacent to the bedrooms, it is a good idea to have a reduced level of illumination. This helps create a mood, and also avoids an abrupt change in light level between the bedrooms, which tend to be softly lit, and the adjacent area of hall.

You may also want to differentiate areas by using lights with different colour effects. For example, in an entrance hall you may want a bluer lighting effect – one that closely resembles the qualities of daylight – than that used near the bedrooms, which could be warmer orange in quality to create a more intimate atmosphere.

Living areas

The most difficult room to light in most homes will be the main living room. This is because it may be in use during the day time, as well as at night. Much will depend on whether the room has a bright or gloomy aspect. If it is a sunny room, you can choose cool blues and greens and rely on warm, artificial lighting in the evening. A shady living room, however, may need oranges and yellows to create a feeling of warmth.

RIGHT For a dining or breakfast room table, you often want a good level of illumination directly over the table itself. The ideal solution is an adjustable ceiling-mounted pendent light that can be moved up or down and fixed at the perfect height.

BELOW To show off a collection of ornaments to best advantage, concealed, unobtrusive lights are the answer.

The living and dining areas of the home are often used for many different purposes. A variety of activities take place, from relaxing, talking, reading, sewing, studying and watching television, to daily meals, parties and entertaining. To meet these many and varied activities, you need an effective and extremely adaptable lighting scheme.

Ceiling pendents

Although often not producing the most attractive of lighting effects, ceiling-mounted pendent lights do provide useful general lighting in a living or dining room. The main drawback with pendents is that they rarely light a room evenly, so there will inevitably be pockets of gloomy shadow, especially in the farthest corners.

If mounted over a dining table, however, retractable pendent fittings can be extremely useful, creating a bright highlight just where it is needed most. Be careful, though, that the light is not low enough to dazzle the eyes of the diners. For a long dining room table, you may need more than one pendent light to light the eating area evenly.

Spotlights

Individual spots can be wall mounted, fixed onto or recessed into the ceiling. This form of lighting is highly directional, ideal for reading or sewing, for example. Take care to position spots correctly, however, so that shadows are not cast over your book or work. Spotlights are also ideal for emphasizing things in the room, such as an attractive architectural feature or a plant perhaps. Spotlights can also be mounted on electrical tracks that are available in different lengths. These allow you to fix the light anywhere on the track (*see p. 165*).

Uplighters and downlighters

These lights can produce very dramatic lighting effects, washing walls or ceilings in bright but localized illumination. Depending on the opacity and shape of the hood used, you can create all manner of intensities and shaped areas of light from scallop-edged highlights to relaxing curves. An uplighter on the wall adjacent to the television should provide enough general illumination to reduce any effect of glare from the screen.

Table lights

Depending on the wattage of the bulb itself, as well as the characteristics of the lampshade, table lamps can be used to create very localized pockets of illumination in a room, as well as a more general level of lighting. If a table lamp is to be used as a reading or sewing light, or for any other activity needing visual concentration, make sure it is positioned so that it casts an even light without any annoying shadows that will affect your ability to see well.

The colour of the lampshade is important, too, since strongly coloured lighting can result in eye strain. Like uplighters, table lamps can help to illuminate a room sufficiently to reduce the glare from a television screen. If a central pendent light is failing to light all of the room, then consider strategically positioned table lamps to brighten the more shadowy areas.

Floor lamps

Floorstanding lamps, usually found in a living or dining room, can be interesting decorative features in their own right. And the range of standard lampshades is magnificent! They may harmonize with the lighting scheme by using a fabric in a matching tone, or create a dramatic focus of light by using a material with a bold, contrasting pattern. Being portable, you can move them wherever you want, depending on your activity. The central column of some types can be adjusted to give a range of lighting heights, while others have multilamp heads or lighting arms to increase the range of effects that can be achieved. Standard lamps are usually made from metal or wood.

TOP Table lamps tend to produce isolated areas of lighting. Use them to brighten gloomy corners or, if accurately sited, as activity lights.

ABOVE Use picture lights when you want to make a statement. You will be inviting close inspection of the picture, however, so make sure its quality is good.

LEFT In this area around a hearth, the lighting is pitched at the right level to produce an intimate, welcoming atmosphere.

Kitchens and bathrooms

In most homes, the kitchen is where people congregate and where a lot of the day-to-day work of preparing food and cooking takes place. So the main utility areas – the sink, worktops, cooker and the oven and hobs if separate – need to be particularly well lit.

BELOW Spotlights set into the ceiling have been positioned to give a high level of illumination directly over the main task areas in this kitchen.

BOTTOM Concealed lighting fitted to the undersides of the wall units also gives good light where it is most needed in a kitchen.

Kitchens

Track lighting This versatile form of lighting can work well in a kitchen, provided that the track is carefully positioned. For example, if you fix a track in the middle of the ceiling with the spotlights aimed at the oven or sink, every time you stand in these areas you will be casting a forward-facing shadow. Instead, for shadow-free lighting, mount the track over the area to be illuminated with the spots directed downwards.

Concealed lighting The most usual type of concealed lighting consists of light fittings attached to the undersides of wall cabinets

Pendent lighting A pendent light can provide good background illumination. If it is the only light source, however, it is likely to cast shadows and leave some areas of the kitchen inadequately lit. A pendent light is better used in conjunction with track and concealed cabinet or shelf light fittings.

Pendents can be used in a more versatile fashion, however, if they are removed from the traditional centre-ceiling position and rehung so that they are directly above the main utility areas. If the surface to be lit is long, you may have to install two, three or even four pendent lights to ensure even illumination.

Bathrooms

Any form of plug-in light fitting cannot be used in a bathroom, since regulations forbid the inclusion of power sockets in this room, and all switches situated in the bathroom must be operated by pull-cords. These restrictions are to prevent you coming into contact with the electricity supply with wet hands, but they should not restrict your lighting choices to any significant degree.

Fluorescent lights Most people opt for a gentle, restful form of lighting in a bathroom, which makes fluorescent tubes an unlikely first choice. However, fluorescent tubes mounted behind translucent panels in the ceiling or, indeed, a wall can add a touch of style and panache. Bear in mind that many low-voltage tubes evenly spaced produce a more flattering light than a smaller number of high-voltage tubes. Another advantage of fluorescent tubes is that they produce virtually no heat, making them a safe form of lighting to position near water.

Downlighters Strategically placed downlighters can be used to accentuate different areas of a bathroom, either to illuminate specific task areas or simply to create interesting light and shadow contrasts within the room.

Mirror lights A mirror is an important feature in a bathroom, either for shaving or putting on make-up. The best lighting solution is sidelighting – a row of low-voltage bulbs either side of the mirror which gives you virtually shadow-free illumination.

Shower lights A shower cubicle will probably require its own light. Use a specially sealed lighting unit that is completely protected against all moisture.

LEFT Lights on flexible brackets attached to the shelves of this traditional dresser have been used to highlight the decorative nature of the kitchenware.

BOTTOM LEFT Bulkhead lights either side of this bathroom basin give shadow-free lighting.

BELOW Carefully designed lighting can help to differentiate different task areas in a bathroom.

BOTTOM Large areas of mirror in a room will reflect any available light and boost the overall brightness.

or shelves suspended over the kitchen's worktops. These produce light just where it is needed. But make sure that the light is low enough not to shine directly into your eyes, as this might prove to be dangerous if you are working with sharp knives or hot liquids in the kitchen.

Another type of concealed lighting consists of fluorescent tubes mounted behind translucent panels fixed into the ceiling. Fluorescent fittings are not attractive, but this way you obtain the benefit of bright, energy-efficient lighting without the fittings or tubes being visible. This form of lighting can be very attractive.

Bedrooms

In many homes today, bedrooms have to serve more than one function. Your bedroom may not only house and store your clothes, but may also have to double up as a part-time workroom or study. It may be more like a bed-sitting room, or it may simply be a restful, quiet area in which to relax and retreat for a while.

General lighting

The background lighting for a bedroom can consist of a single pendent light or, in a large room, a series of pendents. Alternatively, consider track lighting or recessed spots. Position these lights so that they illuminate the areas of the room where most light is required. A dimmer switch is also useful, giving you the option of soft, restful lighting or bright, full light for reading.

Special purpose lighting

Bedside lights If you enjoy reading in bed, then some form of bedside lighting is essential. Lights can be mounted on the wall behind the bed, angled so that the light falls directly on the page. Lamps can also be placed on bedside tables, but make sure that sufficient light falls on the page without the lamp itself being visible when you are in your normal reading position. Switches for bedside lights should be ideally located so that you don't have to get out of bed to use them.

Mirror lights A dressing table mirror or a full-length mirror will benefit from being sidelit by a series of lights positioned either side of the glass. If the light output on both sides is exactly matched, then this type of lighting gives out a flattering, shadow-free form of illumination.

Wardrobe/cupboard lights If the general room lighting is not sufficient to illuminate the inside of large cupboards when the doors are open, these should have their own light source. This is practical lighting and does not need to be sophisticated. A simple fluorescent tube is probably the best. These sit close to the surface on which they are mounted, and so are less likely to be knocked or broken. They also produce little heat and will not scorch delicate fabrics that may accidentally touch the tube.

ABOVE A simple table lamp by the bed will be sufficient for late-night reading.

ABOVE LEFT A lighting scheme consisting of uplighters, table lamps, wall-mounted lights and ceiling lights produce a good range of options.

BELOW Lighting controls situated by the side of the bed are most convenient. The wall-mounted light has a flexible stem so that it can be pointed in the direction it is needed.

Workrooms and studies

Tasks such as writing, drawing, working at a computer and sewing all require the right lighting. With your existing lighting set-up, does your body cast a shadow over your work? Is there dazzle, either direct or reflecting back up from your work? Do you find yourself squinting or suffering from headaches? Too little light or light from the wrong direction will cause eyestrain.

Choosing lights

A flexible desk lamp will provide good light in the right place, and counteract any shadows cast by other lighting. Beware of reflection in a computer screen – a task light should light the desk area and the keyboard, not the screen.

Colourwork, such as painting or needlework, is best carried out in natural light where the colours can be judged most effectively. Artists usually favour a north-facing window for the clearest light without the sun's direct rays. However, a daylight-simulation bulb (*see p.166*) will give less colour distortion when additional light is needed, perhaps when the weather is dull or you are working in the evening.

Lighting flexibility

Unless you have a dedicated office or workroom, plan your lighting for maximum flexibility, so that when you are not working, the focus is on other areas of the room, and the level of lighting reverts to, say, the quieter ambient light of a bedroom.

If you do have a dedicated work area, however, the emphasis is off appearance and flexibility and the lighting scheme can be geared much more towards functionality. In this instance, fluorescent lights may be your preferred choice. The bulbs last about 10 times as long as normal tungsten bulbs and they require a fraction of the electricity to run. They also radiate less heat when they are switched on, making them suitable for hobby rooms where a lot of light, but a cool atmosphere is required. Halogen bulbs are also a good choice (*see p. 165*).

BELOW A desk lamp is one of the most useful types of lighting in an office or study as it reduces the shadows cast by shelves and even your body.

STORAGE

Choosing and planning

One of the features of modern life is clutter. The home has never been a materially more complicated place, and the need for attractive and versatile storage never greater.

In the kitchen, typically we find a range of saucepans, dishes, mixers, grinders, graters, extractors, kettles and toasters, not to mention larger items such as cookers, refrigerators, washing machines and dishwashers. And don't forget the table and chairs. In a mixed-activity room, such as the living room, the clutter can be far worse. Where do you move for sofas and settees, coffee tables, ornaments, books, magazines, record collections and hi-fi speakers, television sets, CD players and tape machines?

It would be possible to make a list such as this for every room in the home. Bear in mind, however, that the type of storage option you favour may vary from room to room, depending on the degree of clutter and the type of atmosphere you wish to create.

Awkward spaces

In a narrow galley kitchen, a combination of traditional storage – in the form of a freestanding dresser – and floor- and wall-mounted units, maximizes the amount of standing space in the centre of the room.

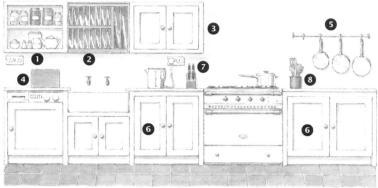

1 **Open shelves for display 2 Plate rack for everyday crockery**
3 **Closed cupboard for things that need to be kept up high, away from children**
4 **Chopping boards close at hand 5 Saucepan rack when shelf space is limited**
6 **Base units are ideal for heavy objects and their tops make good work surfaces**
7 **Knife block 8 Containers for utensils used daily.**

Kitchens

In the kitchen, built-in base and eye-level cupboards are an effective way of keeping things out of sight until they are needed. The range of modern materials, surface finishes and colours available is extraordinarily large, allowing your imagination wide rein.

However, ideas from the past should not be overlooked. In a large family kitchen, or a country-style room, why not consider a traditional dresser? Dressers in traditional designs are still made today, and most offer you a combination of open shelving, on which to display your best and most attractive crockery and ornaments, as well as closed cupboards beneath for all those less eye-catching items that you don't want on permanent show. Perhaps the answer to your kitchen storage problem may be a mixture of the old and the new – in the food-preparation area, built-in, easy-clean units may be best, while in the eating area you may favour the friendly charm of a dresser or a set of open wall shelves.

Mixed-activity rooms

Purpose-made cabinets to accommodate the typical types of home-entertainment equipment – such as televisions and video recorders – are readily available. Modular designs allow you to add on as necessary if you want your hi-fi system in the same area of the room. Many, too, also allow you to extend the units upwards, with purpose-made units for tapes

ABOVE A place for everything, and everything in its place – this is the philosophy behind this immaculately planned kitchen.

and CDs. By choosing the modular components with care, you should be able to put together just the right size and shape to fit into, say, the alcove created between the chimney breast and room wall. These units are often very simple to make, and you should have few problems in building your own if you wish.

Walls are often under-utilized for storage and display, especially hard-to-get-at areas above tables and sofas. Open shelves here may be the perfect place to display ornaments and photographs, since you will only want access to them occasionally. Where books are concerned, however, make sure that you build shelving in an easily accessible part of the room, or you may wish to build or buy freestanding bookshelves instead. With these you have the added flexibility of being able to change the arrangement of the furniture at will without destroying the room's decor.

LEFT If shelves and cupboards do not provide sufficient storage space, then kitchen utensils can make an attractive display suspended above head-height from the ceiling, here on an old-fashioned clothes airer.

ABOVE Practical as well as attractive, this simple unit comprising a wall shelf and drainer is the perfect place to store a few pieces of everyday crockery without restricting access to them.

RIGHT There are lots of ideas for storage of different kinds in this room. In the office section, there are sets of similar storage drawers, while a freestanding unit to house small items, books and a sound system serves as a room divider.

Bathrooms

The main storage requirements in a bathroom are for linen, towels, toiletries and cosmetics. If the hot-water tank is in the bathroom, then building an airing cupboard surrounding it, with slatted shelves to allow warm air to circulate around the towels, sheets, and so on, can be a great boon.

If you have young children, you need to take care with medicines. You could readily build or buy a medicine cabinet, which should then be fixed high on a wall or fitted with a secure lock.

Most modern bathrooms are not large, so there is usually relatively little scope for storage. However, in larger rooms you could include some freestanding furniture – perhaps a small freestanding shelf unit of a square design, or a number of wicker baskets for storing clean towels or dirty linen ready for washing.

Bedrooms

The most obvious need for storage in a bedroom is for clothes and shoes. A good way of utilizing the available space is to build a wardrobe along one wall, taking advantage of the depth offered by the alcoves either side of the chimney breast. After the basic framework is in place, the fascia and doors can be made out of some sort of composite material or wood. A built-in wardrobe can also incorporate a dressing table area and overhead cupboards for spare bedlinen and pillows.

In a child's bedroom, you will more than likely need somewhere for toys and games, as well as clothes and perhaps a study area, too, for an

LEFT A period-style armoire fitted out with shelves is an elegant solution to the need for additional storage in any room of the house.

ABOVE A modern freestanding column of shelves takes up little floor space and can be moved around.

RIGHT An alcove was created in this bathroom to provide lightweight shelving and to support one end of the vanity shelf.

ABOVE A dazzling combination of yellow, green and red has transformed an inexpensive cupboard into a spectacular hideaway for all those odds and ends that accumulate in a child's room.

LEFT Beds with spaces beneath can be utilized as storage areas. Make or buy special boxes on casters.

BELOW Style has not been sacrificed in the pursuit of storage space in this basement kitchen, with a staggered series of storage cubicles moving diagonally up the wall supporting the staircase.

older child or teenager. An attractive storage solution for toys and games, assuming you don't want to use a built-in cupboard, is a toy chest. This is relatively simple to make or buy, or you can adapt an old chest or blanket box for the job, perhaps giving it a coat or two of paint in bright colours and making sure there are no nail heads standing proud of the wood. Where space is tight, modular furniture systems are available that incorporate bunk beds, an integral wardrobe (usually quite small), and a study area for children.

Hallways and stairs

Since the hallways and stairways are often thought of as the connecting bits between the 'real' rooms of the house, their full potential as storage areas is usually not realized. Fixed to the wall above the front door, for example, you could construct an out-of-the-way storage cupboard. Or, if the stairs are comfortably wide, you may be able to build a set of bookshelves on the flank wall, and be able to choose books at different heights as you ascend or descend the stairs. There are usually vast areas of unused wall space around the hallway and stairs.

The largest potential storage area in a hallway, however, is often the space under the stairs. It is a good idea to block in the space to hide the stored contents. In an existing understair cupboard, you may decide to change the internal arrangement of shelves and partitions, as well as the access doors to allow better use to be made of it.

Shelving

Shelves can be strictly utilitarian or attractive enough to be a positive room feature. Shelves are available in a wide range of materials and can be either fixed in one position or adjustable.

An alcove or recess, formed between a chimney breast and a wall, or in a purpose-built niche, is an ideal place for shelves; they can be fitted flush to the walls or uprights where the fixings will be virtually invisible.

Before starting, you need to consider the composition of the supporting walls, since this will determine the size and type of fixing you choose (*see p. 60–1*).

Heavy-duty goods will need strong shelves and supports. Since heavy-duty items are usually stored in garages and workshops, the actual appearance is not so important as strength. The shelving is erected using the same methods as those for indoor shelves, but the fixings may be slightly different. However, bear in mind that a shelf laden with hardback books will also be very heavy and these will need to be stored in the house.

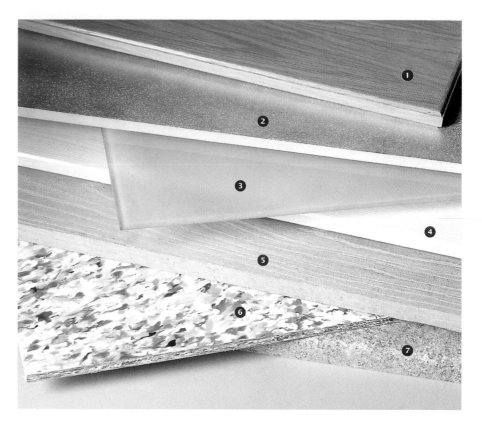

LEFT Adjustable shelving used as a display area for a range of ornaments of different sizes and shapes.

ABOVE 1 Veneered particle board 2 Zinc-covered MDF (medium-density fibreboard) 3 Safety glass 4 Pine 5 Sand-blasted wood 6 Recycled plastic 7 Laminated chipboard

Maximum spans between supports

The following table gives an indication of the distances between supports.

	thickness		span	
Timber	16mm	(⅝in)	50cm	(20in)
	18mm	(¾in)	90cm	(36in)
	30mm	(1¼in)	110cm	(3ft 8in)
Blockboard	12mm	(½in)	45cm	(18in)
Plywood	18mm	(¾in)	80cm	(32in)
	25mm	(1in)	100cm	(3ft 4in)
Veneered chipboard	12mm	(½in)	40cm	(16in)
	18mm	(¾in)	60cm	(24in)
	25mm	(1in)	75cm	(30in)

Shelving brackets

Brackets for fixing shelves to a flat wall come in a range of styles and sizes, made of wood or metal. Wooden brackets are usually bought untreated, and can be varnished, stained or painted to fit in with any decorative theme. Metal brackets may be enamelled in one of a limited range of colours or metallic finishes. Right-angle brackets support shelves in fixed positions, while strip and spur types are more flexible, and allow you to adjust the height of each individual shelf.

Shelving in an alcove

There are many different ways of fixing shelves into an alcove, like the one shown here:

1 Wooden or metal pegs fitted into predrilled holes in the side uprights are a neat type of recess fixing. The supports, fitted along the width of the shelves, are almost invisible.

2 Peg supports are also perfect for glass shelves as they are almost invisible. For glass, use rubber-covered dowels.

3 Simple L-shaped brackets at either end of each shelf, screwed to the uprights, make suitable supports for light-weight shelving such as wicker.

4 When shelves need to be very securely fixed in place, this type of bracket supports the entire width of the shelf.

5 Fixing strips and spur brackets allow you to vary the space between the shelves, and to accommodate different sized items. They do, however, support the entire width of the shelf and are, therefore, more visible than other supports.

6 Simple right-angle brackets are inexpensive to buy and very serviceable. Unlike strip and spur fixings, they do not allow shelf intervals to be varied. Not suitable for very heavy loads.

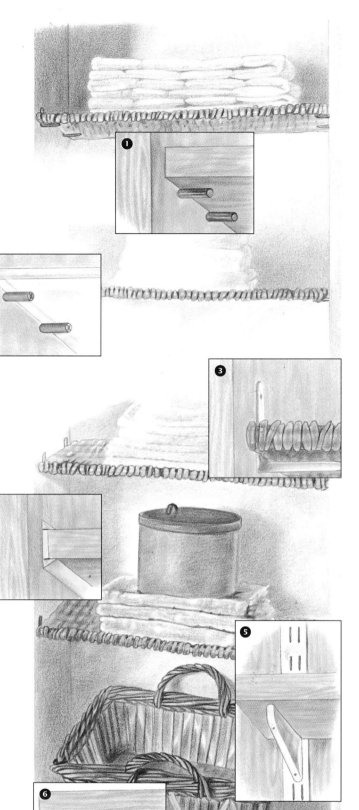

Heavy-duty shelves

1 For heavy loads a wooden upright is plugged and screwed to the wall and a stout bracket screwed to it.

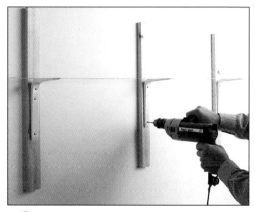

2 The outer brackets are fixed first and the centre ones are positioned using a string-line. Drill a pilot hole first to avoid splitting the timber.

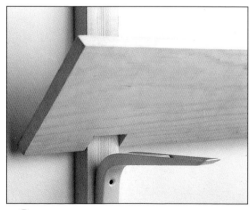

3 For a neat fit, the shelves are notched to fit around the wooden uprights before being screwed into place. This avoids having a gap between the shelf and the wall. To hang a short length of shelving, you can attach the right-angle brackets to the shelf first.

Simple storage

There is an adage that states that possessions expand to fill the available space, and no sooner have you added a cupboard or set of shelves to your home than they seem full to overflowing once more. Simply building or buying more and more freestanding or built-in units all too often results in an uncoordinated, aesthetically unsatisfactory look, as different shapes and styles are slowly incorporated into your rooms. One solution to this dilemma is to devise some sort of modular storage system that you can add to as the need arises. By using the same materials and method of construction, you can increase the overall height or length of the storage unit whenever you choose while maintaining a design consistency within the room. For smaller objects, however, especially those you use frequently and need to find instantly, there will always be a need for simple, convenient, yet attractive, storage solutions.

TOP A lattice of wood makes an instant kitchen tidy.

LEFT Storing foods in jars makes them instantly visible and accessible.

ABOVE Pull-out wicker baskets arranged on drawer runners provide much welcome extra storage in this small kitchen alcove.

Small-scale storage

It is the small-scale storage objects we collect and display that tend to give our homes charm and character and reveal, often unconsciously, much about our personalities. In any room in the house, you have the chance to make a creative statement by including some carefully chosen boxes, a basket, some spoon tidies in the kitchen, or a wine rack in the dining room.

Many of these objects would be suitable as home-build projects, and yet others can be picked up for next to nothing at second-hand shops and charity stores. If the colour is not right, they can be painted or even découpaged to personalize them.

ABOVE LEFT Storage space beneath a basin is attractively hidden by a curtain.

LEFT Shaker-style wooden boxes make charming storage for letters, trinkets and other small items. These boxes come in sets designed to fit inside each other.

TOP An unusual solution to the problem of storing wood for an open fire has been provided by this columnar metal frame. Holding far more wood and kindling than a traditional wicker basket, it takes up very little floor space and looks good too.

ABOVE LEFT AND ABOVE Three ideas for storage systems: stacking vegetable baskets used for toys; open shelves decorated to match a collection of sea shells; and a freestanding wine rack, tucked neatly out of the way on the floor of an alcove.

Unusual storage ideas

Practically every house has some area of under-utilized space that could potentially be used for extra storage; it is just a matter of looking properly. Older houses tend to be better endowed in this respect because they are likely to have more of the recesses, higher ceilings and the types of nooks and crannies you rarely find in modern, formula-built houses and apartments.

Over the years, houses are often added to and adapted to suit the needs of the current generation, and each change brings about its own potential for extra storage space. Look at the storage areas currently in use to see whether you could change the way the doors open or rearrange the internal divisions or shelving. You may find that you can make better use of the space.

BELOW The free space beneath this staircase has been utilized to the full. Racks of shelves running the full depth of the stairs can be pulled out to provide access and, when closed, they produce a flush finish.

The modern home

In the contemporary house or flat, rooms can
be of such meagre dimensions that your
imagination needs to work overtime to find
space for the most modest amount of day-to-
day clutter. In such a situation, the best
solution may be to devote one room, perhaps
a spare bedroom or an accessible loft, to
storage. Clothes can be hung on a series of
open rails, of the type used in shops and
stores, and one wall could be taken up with a
series of modular storage boxes, stacked as
high as necessary, to accommodate less used
objects. Where this is not possible, then look
for unusual ways of utilizing what space is
available – walls, for example, especially in
little-used corridors, can often be pressed
into service, as can the usually wasted space
found underneath beds.

LEFT Any area of flat wall, even the tiny space seen
here sandwiched between two staircases, can be fitted
with bookshelves. The supporting upright then makes
a convenient surface to hang pictures.

BELOW LEFT This unusual storage space
surrounding the fireplace is turned into a feature by
filling it with piles of logs.

ABOVE In true
Shaker tradition, the
lengths of pegboard
running around the
walls of this room have
been used to support a
plain set of shelves
hung on stout cords.

LEFT Older and
traditionally built
houses have interesting
nooks and crannies that
can be pressed into
service as unusual
storage areas.

The Shaker tradition

The Shakers were one of a number of
Utopian sects that migrated to the New
World in the 18th century. The interiors of
Shakers' houses were kept light, plain and
simple. Storage was often built in, and their
clever designs for walls of cupboards and
smoothly fitted drawers have never been
bettered. In fact, copies of traditional Shaker
designs are on sale today and are still
immensely popular. Because Shaker rooms
were also often used as meeting places, any
objects that might clutter the room – hats,
cloaks, tools, chairs, clocks and so on – were
hung on pegboards high on the walls out of
the way. Their storage boxes, which tended
to be made in sets that fitted inside one
another (*see page 183*), were also coded in
cheerful colours depending on their
contents. Many of the practicalities that
shaped these traditions are just as relevant
for us today, especially where space is
limited in modern homes.

Cupboards

Many houses have alcoves and recesses that are often wasted spaces. Fitted cupboards, of the type shown here, not only provide useful storage space for a range of items, but may also enhance the appearance of the room.

The recesses either side of a chimney breast are the obvious places to build in. But since the sides of an alcove are rarely flat and true, even in a new building, it is essential to construct each cupboard as a square, freestanding unit, fractionally smaller than the alcove. To fit it neatly into the recess, join it to a fascia frame. Make the frame very slightly oversized and then plane it to fit snugly into the opening with the top and bottom rails perfectly horizontal.

Materials and equipment

- Timber for fascias, frames, top and bottom boards, sides, shelves and doors (ready-made doors, if preferred)

- Marking gauge, try-square and profile gauge

- Tenon saw, wood saw and cramp

- Smoothing plane

- Powered jig saw or hand coping saw

- Adhesive

- Pins, screws and wallplugs

- Screwdriver and hammer

- Power drill and masonry bit

- Spirit level

- Iron-on veneer (if using blockboard)

- Hinges, handles, magnetic catches and steel corner brackets

MDF

Medium density fibreboard or MDF (also sometimes referred to as particleboard) has been enthusiastically welcomed for DIY construction. Denser and smoother than chipboard and without the sandwiched layers of blockboard, it is also easier to work. It is amenable to being cut into complex shapes with a jig saw or hacksaw and provides a smooth surface for paint. MDF can also be varnished, although it does not have the attractive grain of wood. It is not suitable for outdoor use.

Although its lack of grain means it won't splinter when cut, MDF does give off a very fine, glue-laden dust, so it is necessary to wear a face-mask when sawing. Some suppliers will cut it for you.

The standard sheet size is 244 x 122cm (8 x 4ft), with a choice of thicknesses ranging from 6mm (¼in) to 18mm (¾in). Large suppliers usually stock smaller sizes.

1 Measure and cut 25 x 75mm (1 x 3in) softwood for the upper and lower fascia frames. Mark out halving joints at the corners of the frames, using a try-square and marking gauge, to half the depth of the timber and the width of the adjoining piece. Cut down the shoulder to the centre line with a tenon saw, then remove the waste wood by cutting down from the end.

2 Check the joint for fit and then apply adhesive to the shoulder and face of both parts. Clamp loosely, check the corner with the try-square, and tighten the cramp. Trim all

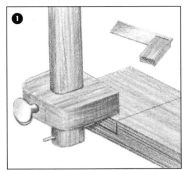

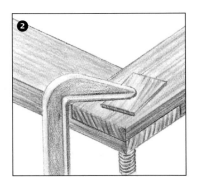

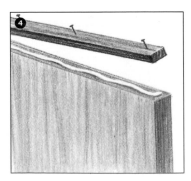

faces with a smoothing plane when the glue is dry and trim the upper frame to fit the alcove.

3 Set a profile gauge to the shape of the skirting at the height of the lower frame, and then transfer the outline to the timber. Carefully cut out and smooth the skirting shape.

4 Measure and cut 18mm (¾in) blockboard or MDF for shelves, top board, doors and foot board. The top board should overlap the finish flush with the lower cupboard fascia. Glue and pin a strip of wood to the front edge of the top board of the lower cupboard.

5 Use 25 x 25mm (1 x 1in) battens to join the cupboard components. Cut to length and drill for fixing screws.

6 Glue the screw battens to the outer edges of the top and bottom panels, and to the front edges of end panels. Join the cupboards and fascia frames by gluing and screwing through the battens on the outside.

7 The cupboard backs are 3mm (⅛in) plywood, glued and pinned into position.

8 Fix brackets into corners of the cupboards. Drill the back through the hole in each one.

9 Cut the foot board from 25mm (1in) thick timber to fit between the skirtings and to reach from the floor to the underside of the bottom panel. Drill and screw to the back of the fascia.

10 Before fixing the cupboards in position, finish the outside with paint or varnish. When dry, position each cupboard and check that it is horizontal, using a spirit level. Mark through the fixing brackets, remove the cupboards, and drill the wall with a masonry bit. Insert wallplugs and screw the cupboards securely into place in the alcove.

11 Exposed edges of block-board on shelves and doors can be edged with narrow wooden moulding or by applying a matching iron-on veneer.

12 Make doors to fit, or buy ready-made doors and adjust them to suit your cupboard dimensions. Screw flush hinges to the backs of the doors and hang them by fixing the flaps of the hinges to the fascia frames of the cupboards.

13 Drill the doors (with scrap wood behind to prevent burst through) and fit the handles. Finally, fit magnetic catches to hold the doors closed.

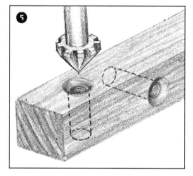

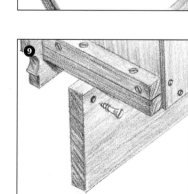

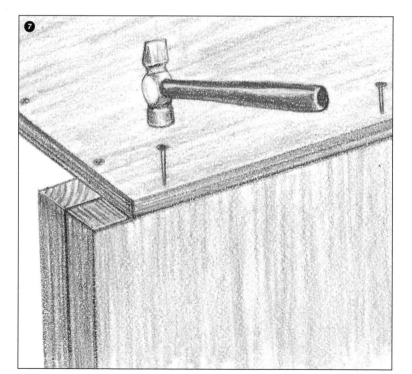

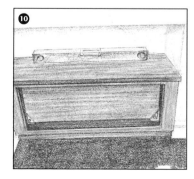

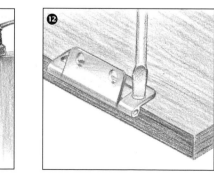

Wardrobes

The major advantage of a fitted wardrobe is that it makes best use of any available space – you can take it right up to the ceiling and wall, sometimes to both walls, to produce wall-to-wall cupboards.

With fitted furniture there is the potential problem of uneven ceilings and out-of-true corners. To overcome this, first fix a framework to the walls, using hardboard or plywood scraps to level out the undulations.

BELOW By building the wardrobe out more from the wall, the chimney breast can be incorporated.

BOTTOM These wardrobes fill out the alcoves, leaving the chimney breast intact.

Wardrobe fitments

Fitted wardrobes help you make the best possible use of space, but they must be fitted out carefully inside or you will end up with a disorderly jumble of clothes.

Interior fittings

It is a good idea to fit an intermediate shelf to the width of the wardrobe just above hanging rail height, with a clearance of 45–65mm (1¾–2½in) to allow space for hangers to be hooked over the rail. Where the wardrobe is not sufficiently deep for a side-to-side rail there are various front-to-back rails that enable you to organize your clothes efficiently.

TOP TO BOTTOM Sliding rail with hanger guides; sliding wardrobe rail; extending wardrobe rail; traditional side-to-side clothes rail.

Hinges

There is a good range of different types of hinge designed to be used by those with little or no carpentry skills.

Lay-on
Screwed to inside surface of door and cabinet side. Concealed when closed.

Flush
Does not need a recess in either the door or the door frame.

Concealed cabinet
Requires a hole to be bored on the inside surface of the door.

Easy hang
This cranked hinge does not need a recess in either the frame or the door.

Butt
Made of pressed steel, this is useful for internal and external doors.

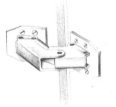

Simple woodworking joints

A well-made joint will increase the strength of the piece of furniture as well as ensuring that it is completely square. There are many different woodworking joints, with many variations, but the ones most useful for cupboards and waredrobes are described here.

Butt joint This is a simple joint but it needs to be carefully prepared in order to be strong and look professional. The square-ended butt joint involves joining two pieces of wood or board together, usually end to side, to form a right-angled corner, or a T-joint. To be successful, a butt joint must be cut squarely and accurately. Trim the cut ends with a plane if necessary and then glue and pin or screw.

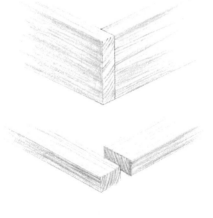

Dowel joint Dowels (hardwood pegs) are an effective means of strengthening a butt joint without resorting to screws or nails, both of which are visible on the surface. Use precut, fluted dowels with chamfered ends, which make a strong joint by allowing glue to escape from the dowel hole, coating the surface of the dowel as the joint is assembled.

Hardwood dowels are an excellent form of invisible

strengthening for a butt joint. The centre points help to align the holes.

Corner-halving joint Halving joints are ideal for joining wood of the same thickness. This joint is formed by measuring and cutting each piece to half its thickness.

To make a corner-halving joint, first saw down to the shoulder line on each side.

Fixings

The range of simple-to-use DIY fixing joints now available makes many building projects very straightforward. These joints require no woodworking skill to use, and all are invisible once the doors are closed.

Block joint

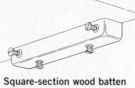

Square-section wood batten

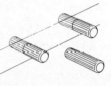

Two-part block joint

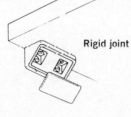

Rigid joint

Traditional dowel joint

Then saw square to the shoulder, and then finally across.

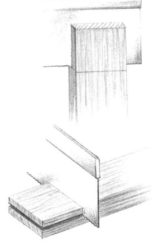

T-halving joint Like the corner-halving joint, this type of joint is also used for joining wood of the same thickness, but this time to form cross rails. Again, you need to measure and cut each piece to half its original thickness.

To make the T-halving joint, saw down to the shoulder line using a series of cuts and then chisel out the waste wood.

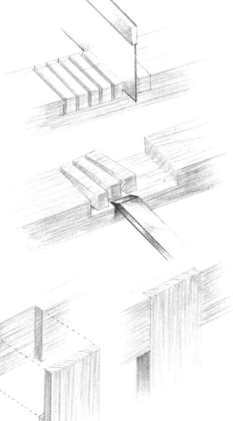

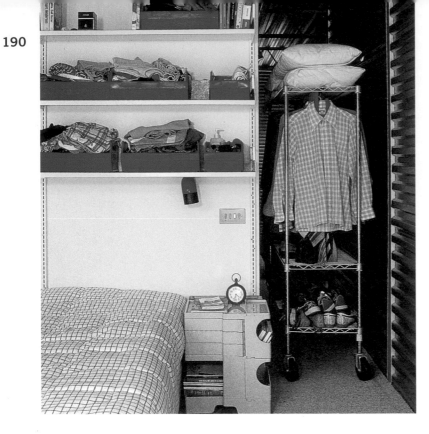

ABOVE Wall-mounted shelves are an obvious storage solution when floor space is limited, but even a space too small for a traditional wardrobe can be adapted by using freestanding racking of the type shown here.

Materials and equipment

- Timber for fascias, battens, shelves and doors

- Ready-made doors, if preferred

- Moulding

- Wood saw

- Tenon saw

- Jig saw

- Spirit level

- Try-square

- Marking gauge

- Smoothing plane

- Power drill and masonry bit

- Cramps

- Adhesive

- Pins, screws and wallplugs

- Hammer and screwdriver

- Chisel

- Angle brackets

- Iron-on veneer (optional)

- Hinges, handles and magnetic catches

- Paint or varnish and brushes

Construction

The best way to approach a recess comprising a chimney breast and alcoves is to construct cupboards as identical units. An ideal width for doors is 60cm (24in) – this allows you to cut them from a 120cm (4ft) sheet of blockboard without wastage (or use ready-made doors). If this width of door is not convenient for the space you have, determine the number and size of doors by measuring the distance from wall to wall and then calculating the number of same-size doors that fit, allowing space for them to open.

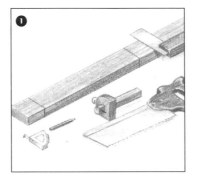

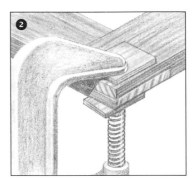

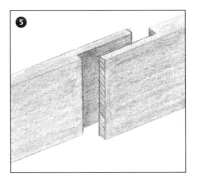

1 Cut to length 75 x 25mm (3 x 1in) softwood for the fascia framework. Mark out and cut T-halving and corner-halving joints using a tenon saw and chisel.

2 Use PVA woodworking adhesive and cramps to complete and secure the joints. Check with a try-square before final tightening. When the glue has set, trim the joints neatly using a smoothing plane.

3 Mark out and then cut 15cm x 25mm (6 x 1in) softwood for the footboard. Screw it to the rear of the bottom frame, 12mm (½in) below the top edge.

4 Cut 12mm (½in) plywood shelves. Screw 25 x 25mm (1 x 1in) battens to the wall and check they are level. Screw battens to the side and rear walls and then fix plywood to the battens with panel pins. Punch the pins below the surface. Fix a batten to the rear of the frame on the horizontal

member. Position the frame. Pin the top shelf to the batten and the lower to the footboard.

5 Cut out the top inner fascia board from 15cm x 25mm (6 x 1in) softwood, using an electric jig saw or tenon saw. You may have to join two pieces.

6 Screw angle brackets to the rear of the fascia board and screw it to the ceiling – use the right fixings for your ceiling. Fix the inner fascia board to the rear of the side frames.

7 Make up the central cupboard frame from 75 x 25mm (3 x 1in) softwood. Fix it in between the side frames using metal brackets. Then screw it to the inner fascia.

8 Screw 25 x 25mm (1 x 1in) battens to the chimney breast wall, with inner edges aligning with those of the fascia.

9 Cut and fix 18mm (¾in)

blockboard to enclose each cupboard. Fix side panels using panel pins.

10 If required, cut the dressing table top from 18mm (¾in) blockboard. Fix 25 x 25mm (1 x 1in) battens to the sides of the cupboards and rear wall.

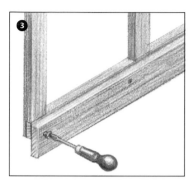

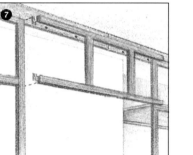

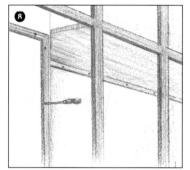

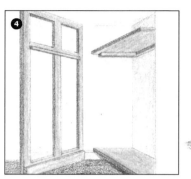

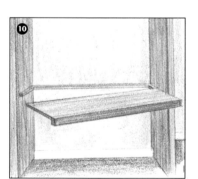

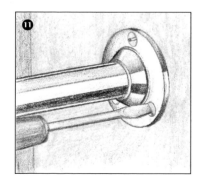

Fix a 50 x 25mm (2 x 1in) batten to the front. Screw the top to the battens.

11 Fix hanging rail brackets to the end wall and the side of the chimney breast. Slot the pole into one bracket before fixing the other.

12 Cut the doors to size from 18mm (¾in) blockboard and add a decorative moulding to give a panelled effect – or use ready-made doors adjusted to fit. If using blockboard, cover all exposed edges with veneer. Screw three 75mm (3in) flush hinges to each door, then fix to the frame. Fit door handles and magnetic catches. Sand down the complete wardrobe ready for painting or varnishing.

COLOUR

Choosing colours

Adding colour, pattern and texture can be one of the most exciting aspects of decorating your home. Through the use of colour, you can express aspects of your personality. Colour also allows you to create precisely the mood and atmosphere that you want, and so, as a result, make your home uniquely yours.

The visible spectrum is huge and the colour possibilities almost limitless. For example, a red scheme can vary from crimson to scarlet, peach to shocking pink, and it can be adapted to very different living areas. In a formal dining room, lit for evening entertaining, rich crimson tones can be very romantic – suffusing the entire decor from tablecloth to patterned fabrics and carpeting. In a sunny family kitchen, the warm tones of terracotta tiles, patterned blinds and a range of accessories can appear to be friendly and inviting. In a bedroom, combining deep and pale tones of rose and peach in the wallpaper, bedspread and curtains can produce a country-style atmosphere. For something different in the bathroom, consider shocking pink carpeting set against wallpaper decorated with a riot of enormous roses.

Colour inspirations

You can build an entire colour scheme around a single item such as a rug or a piece of furniture. For example, your imagination may be inspired by a wooden dresser painted a rough apple green colour. This colour contrasts wonderfully with brown, and so it is ideally suited to a room with a natural wood floor, unpainted brick walls and bare pine furniture. The effect you are trying for can be further heightened with additional touches of the same green – for example, in cushion covers, painted window frames and perhaps a few accessories.

ABOVE Soft pink tones and patterned fabrics look perfect in the context of this charming bedroom, offset by the solidity of dark-stained furniture.

LEFT This bright and airy living room uses soft mint green and dull, rich pink to create a summery feel, enhanced by the French windows to the garden. The colours are picked out in the soft furnishings, including the cushions on the day bed.

RIGHT Highlights of colour and pattern from a floor rug are picked up in the furnishings in this room.

Green is the colour we associate with living things, so it is an easy hue to live with and a popular choice for decorating schemes. Particularly if you live in a city, it makes sense to bring the colours of nature indoors; the varieties of green range from earth green to olive green, emerald to turquoise. Consider enhancing a range of greens with a flush of deep purple for a rich, almost regal effect.

For a colour scheme that is strikingly different, consider decorating areas of your home in bold blocks of primary colours. A spacious and sparsely furnished sunny hallway or living room can look warm and welcoming with a daffodil-yellow ceiling, bleached wood floors, orange curtains and turquoise cushions and accessories set against deep blue-grey walls. This, however, is only one possible colour scheme from the myriad available from which you can choose.

Another way to add bold splashes of colour is to hand-paint or stencil lively motifs on walls and furniture – an ideal treatment for an informal entrance way or kitchen, bedroom or bathroom. The subject of the motif can vary from room to room – to reflect changing uses and activities – or stay consistent throughout, and so act as a unifying decorative element. In this way, you can begin to build bridges between the decorative approaches in different areas of your home.

As you will see in more detail further on, your choice of colours can make a room seem smaller or larger, cramped or spacious, warmer or cooler, brighter or more subdued. Knowing which colours to select to achieve the precise effect you want is not always an easy task. The secret of success lies in the skill with which the fabrics, furniture, wallpaper and decorative objects are selected and mixed. So it is vital to look and learn as much as you can before actually buying anything. Try the colours of different items together first before making your choice.

Developing a colour sense

Everyone can develop an eye for harmonious colour combinations, and so become aware of how colours and patterns work together. To explore your own taste and style, observe colour combinations in window displays, colour magazines and advertising brochures. Make notes of what you like and what you don't like, and even cut out interesting pictures and stick them onto a large sheet of paper. You will soon begin to develop your own personal preferences and discover the combinations you find most pleasing.

There are some broad guidelines to help you choose colour combinations for your home. For example, to emphasize spaciousness, choose a limited range of white, pale pastels or shades of blue. To give a feeling of intimacy, use plenty of deeper tones and bold colours in the warm red range; and include lots of colourful patterns and textures.

Decorating in rich, bright colours will help to enliven a dull, predominantly shady room, while subtle colours and darker tones will subdue a sunny room. Warm bold colours and strong contrasts create a lively and inviting atmosphere, while cool tones and subtle contrasts create more of a calm and relaxed environment.

Despite all these 'rules', using colour is a very personal matter. Colour – like music – varies enormously in the mood and atmosphere it creates, and we all have our own taste. So allow your own style and taste to develop as you plan; have confidence in whatever colours appeal to you, and have fun!

ABOVE Bold blocks of primary colour have been successfully employed here to create fresh and striking decor for this children's room.

BELOW Green is a popular choice for a decorating scheme. This unusual variation on the theme incorporates a suffusion of turquoise.

Bright or dark

When thinking about colours for a decorative scheme, consider what tones they should be to complement the mood and atmosphere of each room. In fact, the tones of a colour can have a greater influence on decor than the basic colour, making a room appear larger or smaller, brighter or duller. This may seem confusing, but by following a few guidelines you can incorporate a variety of tones in your decorating scheme to achieve very precise effects. First, make a list of factors to consider, such as the dimensions of the room to be decorated. If the room is small, using pale tones will make it appear more spacious; if it is large, dark tones will create a feeling of warmth and intimacy.

If you have a sunless room, you may wish to enliven it with light tones, while a sunny room can tolerate a range of darker tones. Consider, too, the major items of furniture, and the carpeting and curtains, that the decor must complement. If you already possess a dark-coloured suite of furniture and want to create a bright, spacious atmosphere in your living room, consider light tones for the rest of the decor. If, however, you have pale carpeting, the room will appear warmer with the addition of deep-toned, rich-coloured furnishings.

BELOW The warm tones of rich pink and bare wood create an intimate atmosphere, ideal for a bedroom, without closing the room in to any significant degree.

RIGHT The pale muted tones in this bathroom provide a perfect atmosphere for long, luxurious bathtimes. Pale tones also maximize the impact of any available natural light.

White

Decorating in white has many advantages. Since white reflects light, it makes poorly lit areas seem brighter, and increases the apparent size of a room – ideal for creating an illusion of spaciousness in a relatively small room. White walls are like a bare canvas, complementing pale-toned furnishings and providing a strong backdrop for dark items without making the room seem cluttered. You can easily and quite dramatically alter the mood of a predominantly white room simply by integrating colourful cushions, pictures, and other accessories, all of which can be easily changed.

One drawback to choosing a completely white decor is that it can make a room appear rather cold and clinical. To offset this, include a few touches of warm tones and textured surfaces.

Pastel shades

Decorating a room in pastel shades allows you a great deal of flexibility when it comes to choosing accessories to match. Pastel shades by themselves can help to create an atmosphere that is bright and spacious – useful for small and well-lit areas. At the same time, pastel shades can impart a feeling of tranquillity and restfulness; this may be ideal

LEFT Large rooms allow you more flexibility when it comes to selecting bright or dark tones as part of your decorative scheme. The almost strident contrast between the rich blue of the chair and sofa coverings and the red of the cushions does not look overpowering in this large, bright, sun-filled room.

BELOW Deep tones of red create a warm and seductive environment for a bedroom, seen here in an opulent bed canopy and Oriental rug. The touches of gold in the bedspread and canopy fabric add a rich accent.

in a bedroom or quiet living room where you like to settle down with a good book. Pastel tones from the blue end of the spectrum give a cool effect; those tinged with red, orange or yellow add warmth.

An easy way to create colour harmony with pastel shades is to choose a couple of basic colours – perhaps a pale blue and a beige, for example – and only add tones that are very slightly lighter and darker versions of them.

Dark tones

Decorating with dark tones is a definite design statement. If you are not used to working with colour, this decision takes a degree of courage. For a start, it can be difficult to visualize the effect beforehand, and if you are not happy with the result it will take several coats of paint to restore a light-toned base to work on.

Dark tones can, however, be very effective in the right environment. They are ideal for

creating a cosy atmosphere in a large, well-proportioned room, one that either has lots of natural light or else relies on well-placed artificial lighting.

Alternatively, painting one wall of a room, or an alcove within a room, in darker tones can be a useful technique for accentuating certain features or adding a sense of depth. However, you need to exercise caution in small or poorly lit areas. Hallways, especially, need to be bright and inviting.

Illusions with tones

- For an illusion of both spaciousness and intimacy, use very pale tones for the ceiling and floor, darker hues for the walls, and fill the room with light-coloured furniture and accessories.

- Special features and shapes in a room can be highlighted by juxtaposing complementary contrasts of light and dark tones.

- Offset the coldness of very pale tones with textured surfaces and touches of red or orange. Blue tones and smooth surfaces accentuate coolness.

Combining colours

When planning colour combinations, you need to consider how bright or dark a decor should be and what range and intensity of colour to use. For lively colour harmony, it helps to know a few basic principles of colour theory and to understand how different colours influence one another when used in interiors.

ABOVE Colour juxtapositions designed to challenge convention have been employed in this imaginative room. The predominant colour here is primary red, which has an enclosing effect on the space. This effect is enhanced by the canopied ceiling, also featuring red, as well as other colours.

RIGHT Although this room looks to be full of colours, it is rather illusory, since apart from white, the predominant shades are all variations on pink or peach.

The colour wheel

Colour designing is based on the spectrum of visible light, which can be visualized as a colour wheel, like that illustrated below. At three equidistant points on the wheel are found the primary colours – red, blue and yellow – from which all other colours are derived. Mixing two primary colours in equal proportion results in the formation of the secondary colours – orange, purple and green. When a primary colour is mixed with an adjacent secondary colour, a tertiary colour – such as red-purple or green-blue – is produced. Seeing colours as spokes of a wheel enables you to see how one colour relates to another.

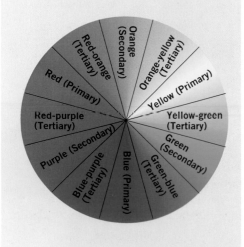

Colour contrasts

Colours that are on opposite sides of the colour wheel, such as blue-green and red, are highly contrasting. Known as comple-mentaries, they will fight for dominance and tend to clash if used in their 'pure' intensities. However, you can incorporate them in your decorating scheme either by using them in extremely unequal proportions or by muting one or both of the colours as lighter or darker tones. You can then enliven the overall colour scheme by introducing just a few hints of strong contrasting colour.

Tonal variations

The pure forms of each of the primary, secondary and tertiary colours can be modified to create an enormous range of tonal variations simply by adding differing amounts of white or black. It is these subtle variations in tone that are most likely to produce colour combinations that blend together successfully in a room's colour

scheme. For example, a range of pale blue-greens and blues will combine happily together, some lighter and some darker.

If you want the striking contrasts of colours on either side of the colour wheel, use lighter or darker tones of one or both colours. As a general rule, lighter tones produce subtle harmonies; darker tones give bolder and more dramatic results.

Warm and cool colours

On one side of the colour wheel are the 'warm' colours – red-purple, red, red-orange, orange, yellow-orange and yellow. On the other side of the wheel are the 'cool' colours – yellow-green, green, blue-green, blue, blue-purple and purple.

Colours from the same side of the colour wheel tend to blend most effectively, whereas a mixture of warm and cool tones may produce jarring results.

Whether you opt for a warm or a cool colour range depends on the mood you wish to create. Warm colours tend to be lively and exciting. Cool colours tend to suggest a relaxed, calm atmosphere. The degree to which you achieve these atmospheric effects depends on the intensity of the colours you choose, and whether you use them in their pure forms or mixed.

RIGHT The brightness of the yellow used on the armchairs and rug is effectively balanced by the white walls and sofa.

ABOVE CENTRE With neutral shades as the background, themes can be established by the accessories used within the room. As fashions change, so, too, can the accessories without major upheaval.

ABOVE Colours from the red/yellow part of the colour wheel produce a warm decorative theme.

Match or mix

Unless you are starting from scratch with an empty room, you will probably have certain basic elements to match with your colour scheme. Do you already have a fitted carpet, a set of curtains or a suite of furniture to be incorporated? Will you paint the walls in a tone that contrasts or complements the existing colours? Will you introduce more colours and, if so, which ones? The question is, what to match and what to mix?

LEFT To create a thoughtful colour scheme for a room, determine which colour is to be your starting point, or source colour. It may, for example, be the dominant colour of the sofa fabric. Next, make up a test card of paint colours that you can use either to harmonize or contrast with it.

ABOVE A predominantly white colour scheme produces a decor that feels bright and spacious, which is ideal in a small room.

Matching a scheme

As a basic rule, choose one colour of an existing item and use it as the cornerstone of your colour scheme. To match, extend tonal variations of this colour – lighter and darker tones – onto the walls and other features.

Alternatively, pick two colours that are very close on the colour wheel (*see p. 198*), such as blue and blue-purple, and then use varying proportions of each. As long as you ensure that there is sufficient continuity of colour to create a consistent atmosphere, you can then introduce touches of black, white or some other colours to avoid a bland result in the overall scheme.

Matching colours

- Carry fabric swatches with you when shopping for new decorative materials. It is surprisingly difficult to remember exactly how light or dark a colour is.

- Colours look different according to the light, so it helps to examine all colours under the same lighting conditions.

- Large expanses of a single colour can look dull. Instead, match a variety of closely related tones with an occasional splash of contrasting colour to create a more lively harmony.

- For successful colour schemes, incorporate a balanced mixture of primary colours, darker tones and lighter tones.

BELOW This simple bedroom colour scheme used shades of blue on the walls, wood panelling and bedlinen. The dark wood furniture adds a contrasting note but the overall effect is one of harmony.

Experimenting with mixing

You can mix strongly contrasting colours to create a pleasing effect as long as you follow a few basic guidelines. Pure primary colours are lively and vibrant, but they can also be over-powering and garish. To avoid problems, use them in unequal proportions and introduce lighter or darker variations of each one. For example, rather than introduce equal amounts of red and yellow in the same colour scheme, select varying proportions of paler and darker red-oranges and yellow-oranges.

Complementary colours – those on opposite sides of the colour wheel – can be mixed successfully, too. Although such combinations usually clash, they can work if they are less 'pure'. For example, juxtaposing tones of warm reddish-green alongside dark, slightly greenish-red can create very pleasing harmonies in a room.

Another way to mix contrasting colours is to start with just a few closely related warm colours and then set them against the

ABOVE This striking scheme features a range of primary colours mixed together for a surprisingly attractive kitchen. The sunny nature of the room helps to make these colours combine.

CENTRE LEFT The starting point for the decorative scheme in this room was the mellow brown of the ceiling and wall beams, the colour of which has been picked up in the curtains, cushions and furniture.

BOTTOM LEFT In a large room, you can be bold in your use of colour and pattern. A restrained colour palette usually works best, however.

opposite cool colours from the colour wheel. For example, mix orange, terracotta and soft yellow with a little rich blue and grey.

Using black and white

White mixes well with any colour scheme. Interspersed with pale colours, it creates subtle harmonies and serves as a backdrop for strong colours or brightens dark ones. Black contrasts with white, yellow and pale tints – ideal for bold and dramatic effects.

Small rooms

Colour influences mood. Whatever main colour you choose for your decorating scheme, it will have greater dramatic impact on a small space than on a large one. In a small room the focus will be on combining simplicity with rich textures, tones and special features.

   With this in mind, choosing the decor for a small room can seem slightly daunting. However, if you abide by a few basic principles, colour can really work to your advantage. Since you can decorate a small room relatively quickly and inexpensively, why not take the chance to experiment? You can try more unusual colour combinations and explore different textures and effects.

Lighting and mirrors

- If you use dark colours in a small room, make sure the lighting is adequate so that they don't look dull and gloomy.

- Experiment with indirect lighting. It influences subtle colours and gives an extra dimension to small spaces, particularly in alcoves and corners.

- Since mirrors reflect both light and space, they can dramatically transform a small room. They are particularly effective in small spaces and corners, where they can be angled to catch interesting features.

Illusion of spaciousness

When you are not very experienced, the simplest way to ensure an uncluttered and restful effect in a small room is to limit the basic decor to white. Very pale colours make surfaces recede and seem less noticeable, thus creating the impression of spaciousness. Conversely, dark colours emphasize surfaces, making them appear to advance toward you.

Incorporating colour

Although white is a good choice for small rooms, if used in its pure form it can be stark and boring. By using just a hint of colour, you can begin to make more of a statement. For a start, walls can be painted in one of an enormous range of almost-whites – from warm peach to soft, cool blue. Texture, too, can add interest and warmth to a predominantly white scheme.

   If bright-toned colours are important to you, incorporate curtains, cushions, small prints or rugs as a way of introducing colours in occasional splashes. When the time comes for a new look, all you need to do is change the accessories. However, if you have a lot of furniture and accessories, it may be better to select plain fabrics and muted tones to avoid a cluttered feeling in the room.

   But don't feel limited to white and the off-whites just because you are decorating in

LEFT A small bedroom with white walls and a white bed has some gentle neutral shades introduced in the soft furnishings to add interest.

a small room. Why not start with a strong colour, such as yellow or purple? There is no basic problem here, as long as you bear one principle in mind – limit your colour scheme to different shades of a single colour. You can even incorporate dark-toned colours in a small room as long as you avoid creating too many colour contrasts or combining them with bright, richly coloured or patterned furnishings. If you include too many colours, a small room may end up looking cramped and cluttered.

Illusion of height

In a small room with a low ceiling, you can use colour to give an illusion of height and space. If the room has no decorative features, simply paint the ceiling white and the walls a single almost-white tone, from skirting boards to ceiling. If the room has traditional mouldings, such as dado or picture rails and cornicing, you can 'shade up' by painting each horizontal 'band' of the wall a subtle tonal variation of white.

As an example, start by painting the ceiling white, the cornice an almost-white tone, then the area above the dado rail with a touch more colour. Carry on like this down to the skirting board. The floor will be the deepest colour, but avoid very dark floor tones, as this will make the room look even smaller than it is.

LEFT In a small room, colour-coordinated furnishings add interest to a plain, pale background. The mood can be changed quickly and without great cost simply by changing accessories, furnishings, cushions and blinds without the need for redecorating.

BELOW In a small kitchen, built-in units have been designed to make best use of the available space. They have been painted in a restful shade of soft blue so that they do not dominate the room.

BOTTOM Although it appears to mix many colours, this room only features related shades of reds and yellows, with a little blue as a contrast.

Rooms within rooms

Many modern houses, as well as older-style, traditional houses, have deep alcoves, recesses or even a box room, that can be modified to make a room within a room. If the area is reasonably large, then an en suite bathroom (*see below*) may be a possibility. If the space is smaller, however, it could be ideal as a walk-in closet. Natural light will probably be restricted, if not absent altogether, so you need to pay particular attention to the colours used and the way they are affected by different types of artificial lighting (*see p. 164*).

Large rooms

Making a small room feel spacious is a familiar decorative challenge. Less frequent, perhaps, but equally challenging is the task of making a large, high-ceilinged room feel warm, intimate and friendly. In both of these situations, colour is a vital tool for producing the particular effect you want to achieve.

Warm-toned surfaces in reds, oranges and yellows give the illusion of advancing towards the viewer, so they are an ideal choice when you want to make distant walls seem nearer and the room cosier. In contrast, cool blue and green tones give a feeling of movement away from the viewer, so they make an already large space seem larger and airier, which is desirable in some situations, but not others.

Deep, rich colours emphasize surfaces, making them appear to advance towards the viewer, and so are another good choice for large rooms. Conversely, pale tones are less conspicuous and have the effect of making surfaces blend into the background. This makes them more suitable for decorating small rooms.

A large room can withstand – and even benefit from – strong, pure colours. In fact, decorating it in a variety of colours, tones and textures is another way of making it appear intimate. All the vivid contrasts break up large expanses of space, creating interest and a feeling of warmth. It is a good idea to link these strong colours with their very pale equivalents – or neutral colours, such as tones of grey – to avoid garish results.

Creating areas of interest

- If you decorate a room in predominantly warm, dark tones, introduce furnishings in pale tones of the same warm colours for harmony and brightness.

- Create two well-defined but linked areas in a large room by decorating one area in subtle warm tones and the other in similarly subtle cool tones.

- Try painting just one wall of a large room in a dark tone to create an area of intimacy.

- Experiment with lighting to create different areas of interest in a large space – recessed lights for soft background effects, spotlights for work surfaces, and display lights for focal points, for example.

Creating zones

In a very large, open-plan room, one way to achieve a feeling of intimacy is to create several clearly marked zones. Each zone can be defined both by its colour scheme and by its furniture. For example, to break up a large living room, choose four complementary tones for each of, say, four areas – perhaps one for a dining corner, another for studying, another by the windows for daytime work, and another for evening relaxation and socializing. Be sure to choose colours that are sufficiently different to provide the desired contrast, but not so far apart in the spectrum that they clash and compete for attention. Link the colours together by interspersing some neutral tones, such as beige or grey.

LEFT The use of different areas of bright colour, tone and pattern attracts the eye and helps to prevent this long room appearing impersonal. The structural timbers also act as visual resting points, so you don't immediately look to the far end of the space.

TOP RIGHT Rather than using a mixture of warm colours to make this sitting room feel more intimate, it has been painted white, with just a few points of colour in the fabrics and wallcoverings. This goes against most of the rules, but creates a stunning space.

RIGHT Large expanses of strong, pure colour help to break up the areas of pale-toned decor in this sitting room. The effect is eye-catching without being garish.

Lowering a high ceiling

There are some simple decorating tricks you can try in order to reduce the apparent height of a high-ceilinged room. One method is to paint the ceiling in a dark, rich tone such as a brick red, possibly matching the floorcovering. Then paint the walls in a complementary pale shade. This will add intimacy and, at the same time, avoid a drab or dull atmosphere.

If the walls of the room have dado rails or other interesting features, paint these in a contrasting lighter tone to create another focal point and further break up the expanse of wall surface. Alternatively, paint both the ceiling and the top of the walls down to the dado rail in one dark tone, the dado rail in the contrasting pale tone, and the lower walls in a medium tone that complements the ceiling and upper walls. This will give the illusion of a much more compact room with a lower ceiling height.

Function and mood

Choice of colours in decorating your home is partly determined by the size and shape of each of the rooms, the existing furnishings, the furniture and the lighting. However, most important of all, your decorating scheme will reflect the mood that you wish to create; and this in turn will be influenced by the function of each of the different areas of your home.

When you are choosing a colour scheme, consider the purpose of each room and how much it is used. For example, do you have a busy living room with a lot of activity in a small space? If so, lots of strong colours may add to the confusion. Instead, plan colour schemes that provide a fairly simple, neutral background. Perhaps you have a clinical-looking bathroom that could benefit from a lively colour treatment, or a room that needs to serve more than one function at different times of the day.

Whatever your colour scheme, think about how frequently you may need to redecorate and how much you may want to spend. If you want to be able to create an entirely different atmosphere at minimal cost, keep the room's basic colour scheme fairly light and simple. Then you can introduce strong colours with curtains, blinds, painted woodwork, prints, plants, accessories and lighting – all of which can be changed with minimal disruption.

Kitchen

Although kitchens vary enormously in basic design, they are working spaces that need to be bright and fresh. Rich yellows, oranges and reds often work well. Cool blues and greens tend to be effective in rooms with lots of early-morning sunlight. Since most kitchens are cluttered places, choose a colour scheme that is easy on the eyes – such as pale, soft tones – and add colour with accessories. If you have a broad expanse of plain-coloured laminate or wood, created by the doors and drawers of fitted units, you will have lots of scope for using a contrasting colour on the walls and floor.

ABOVE The kitchen is often regarded as the heart of the home. This is where meals are prepared and, in a large kitchen, where the family gathers to eat and, often, just to socialize. The colours and patterns in this kitchen radiate a feeling of warmth and the general clutter is welcoming and relaxed.

LEFT The Shaker influence is evident here, with a run of high-level pegs used to keep utensils and other kitchen requisites handy but out of the way. Although essentially a hardworking space, colour has been used to create a sunny atmosphere, while the single concession to comfort is a wicker easy chair.

RIGHT A plain, yet colourful, decorative scheme is perfectly in keeping with the simple, plastered walls and ceiling of this family room.

Living room

The living room is the area of the house for relaxing in, enjoying leisure activities, getting together with the family, and entertaining. And so the ideal colour scheme should reflect all the moods and atmospheres required of this multipurpose space. Personal tastes vary greatly, but one approach would be to decorate a busy living room with plain, pastel walls or small-patterned wallpaper. In a sparsely furnished room, splash out with bold, contrasting colours and patterns to enliven the decoration and perhaps create two or more colour zones.

Workroom/study area

The working environment at home should be decorated in clean, simple tones that offer the least excuse for eyes to wander. Typical schemes are black and white or one using wood and neutral browns.

Bedroom

Although most people aim for an atmosphere that is peaceful, relaxing and comfortable for the bedroom, the choice of colour is a highly subjective one. Some people like the romantic atmosphere of warm pastel shades, for example, while others prefer the cool tranquillity of blues and blue-grey. If you are uncertain, then consider a range of pale harmonies in tones of beige and brown. These are warm yet fairly neutral, and they respond well to small touches of colour.

Child's room

When you plan a child's room, take account of changing needs and tastes over the years – from nursery to play room to teenage study. If you want to keep redecorating costs down to a minimum, consider using a

TOP LEFT A home office needs to have as few distractions as possible, so a simple black and white scheme is a practical choice.

CENTRE LEFT Decorating in tones of blue and white provides a streamlined yet elegant decor for this study/bedroom. The beige carpeting lends warmth to what would otherwise be a cool colour scheme.

LEFT A ship's lantern, a model sail boat and a frieze of frolicking dolphins creates the perfect mood for this country-style bathroom.

basically neutral decor for the walls, ceiling and any built-in furniture, while ringing the changes with new accessories as necessary as the child grows older.

Bathroom

The bathroom tends to be a cool room – made colder by the unyielding enamel, chrome, glass and ceramic surfaces. Unless you are starting from scratch, you will want to work your decorative scheme around the colour of the existing bath, basin, tiles and other fixtures. Warm-toned, off-white walls, brightly coloured accessories, and lots of green plants are a straightforward choice for softening the bathroom environment. But since the bathroom is used for only short periods of time, you could take the opportunity to experiment with more colourful and adventurous options.

Hall

The hall is the first thing visitors see when they enter your home, so it sets the mood for the rest of the house. If the entrance is spacious, consider using vivid colours and large-patterned decorations. However, follow a basic decorating guideline and stick to simple patterns, pale colours and small designs if you want to make a narrow entrance hall seem wider and more inviting. You can also use subtly contrasting colours and textures to add interest to a hallway that is long or narrow.

Collecting samples

Collect samples of existing and proposed wallcoverings, carpeting, upholstery, curtain fabrics and any other major decorative elements. Take them with you when you shop around for each item, and lay them on a flat surface to see how they look next to one another, keeping in mind the expanse of space to be covered by each colour and the type of illumination they will be seen by.

Choosing patterns

Like colour, pattern can serve many functions. Patterned wallcoverings can be a focal point or a backdrop, or they can alter the apparent dimensions of a room. In addition, patterns are more effective than plain surfaces in disguising an odd-shaped room or covering uneven walls. Patterned fabrics can give a new lease of life to old upholstery, and patterned rugs and curtains can be stylish and sophisticated. When choosing, you need to consider how effectively a large area of pattern will complement or contrast with your existing colour schemes.

Patterns influence the mood of a room, much like colours do, so start by considering the function of the room. Large, bold patterns – like deep, rich colours – are intense and active, and work best as focal points in large living areas. Small, subtle patterns – like pale, neutral colours – offer a less-challenging backdrop.

You will also need to consider the basic colour scheme with which the pattern will contrast or harmonize. If the pattern is fairly small, it will take on the appearance of a single tone when seen from a distance. You can then use the principles of colour matching to decide if it works with the rest of the decor.

A common mistake is to choose a pattern that is either too dark or too fussy. Be sure to consider both the lighting and the size of the area you are decorating. If you are not certain what pattern to choose, opt for one with an off-white background and colours subtly contrasting or complementing the colours in the room.

Balance is all important. Too little variety of colour, tone, pattern or texture and the room may seem lifeless. Too much, and it can look chaotic. If you already have a neutral colour scheme, then you have the scope to balance it with a variety of rich patterns. But if you have heavily patterned, richly coloured curtains, consider a plain wallcovering in a muted tone of the predominant colour in the pattern.

RIGHT A limited range of colours – whites and pinks – prevents the intense patterning in the different elements in this room from becoming overpowering.

Collecting ideas

- To collect ideas for colour and pattern combinations, keep a file of samples from magazines and swatches of colour and pattern of your existing and proposed decor. Pay attention to any bold-coloured items that need to be matched, and take all the samples with you when shopping for fabrics and papers.

- Remember that the predominant colours in a pattern influence mood. Reds have a warm, welcoming quality; blues are restful and calming; browns and oranges are warm; yellows are bright and reflective; greens have a natural, cool and spacious feel. Patterns in pale, neutral tones of these colours act like texture to add depth and interest rather than explicit mood.

Size and scale

The scale of patterns that you incorporate into your decorating scheme can vary from enormous repeats that dominate a room to minuscule mini-prints that are hardly visible from a distance. Generally, large patterns have much the same effects and uses as vivid colours, while small patterns function like muted colours. It is easier to have a great variety of colour and pattern if the patterns are detailed and of a fairly similar small size.

Large patterns

Large-scale patterns require careful planning. If the design contrasts highly with its background, it will create a basic colour scheme around which the rest of the decor must revolve. Usually large, bold patterns emphasize form and movement. They look most attractive when used on large areas such as a stairwell, where the design can be seen in its entirety without the interruption of furnishings. Like dark colours, they can also be effective on a single wall of a large room, as a focal point or backdrop to plain

BELOW LEFT Big areas of large-scale patterns, such as the ones in this living room, in vivid primary colours dominate a room. The effect will be overpowering unless the room is well proportioned and balanced with more muted decorative elements, such as a comparatively plain carpet and ceiling.

BELOW A very limited range of colours has been used here, from the blue-purple part of the spectrum. Note that although the patterning is bold, it is all of a consistent size and the background is plain.

RIGHT The striking, bold curtains in this room are neutralized by the otherwise pattern-free décor. The expanse of red of the walls, ceiling and carpet is effectively alleviated by the white woodwork.

Pattern for effect

- Bold, vertically striped wallpaper increases the apparent height of either small or larger rooms.

- Horizontal stripes make the walls appear longer and lower.

- One way to incorporate a large-scale design into a fairly small room is to choose a pattern with muted colours on a background that does not form too vivid a contrast.

furnishings. Large patterns tend to make a small room look smaller, and are less suitable for rooms with lots of windows, doors or alcoves, since the motifs will be constantly interrupted. However, you can emphasize the intensity of a small space by using a large pattern in a small room.

Small patterns

Small patterns – like pale, neutral colours – suit smaller spaces. They are particularly effective in rooms with lots of surfaces at different angles, such as an attic room. Here, miniature designs, such as small floral patterns, can give the illusion of a larger, cohesive space.

Tiny patterns take on a single colour and tone when viewed from a distance, making them the easiest to match to a colour scheme. Whether you allow a small-scale pattern to function as a single tone throughout a room, or coordinate it with areas of plain colour, is a personal decision. In general, however, a balance of plain colour and patterned areas tends to be easy on the eyes. Avoid using small designs in large rooms, since they can look spotty.

ABOVE RIGHT The blue check chair was the starting point for this room's decorative theme. The blue colour, contrasted with white, is repeated in the curtains and wall lamps and, using paler tones, in the wallpaper, too. The yellow background colour of the sofa finds expression in the pot of flowers, and is reflected in the wall frieze.

RIGHT Although this leaf pattern motif is rather large for a small room, it does not appear too dominant because it does not contrast strongly with its background colour, on the curtains, walls or cushion.

Pattern harmony

Contrasting a single pattern with a limited number of plain colours requires thought and planning. The size, style and colours of the pattern all need to be selected carefully so they harmonize with the rest of the decor. When it comes to combining two or more patterns that match or contrast with one another, the challenge is that much greater. However, by following a few guidelines, you will quickly see how to use a variety of patterns to create a strikingly successful decorative scheme.

Making decisions

- Making a sample board is both useful and fun when planning a decorative scheme. Collect samples of the materials you propose to use and see how they look when laid out next to one another when pinned onto a board.

  Include colours from paint charts, swatches of fabrics, pieces of wallcoverings, samples of carpeting and offcuts of any other materials you are planning to use. Cut out the samples into their correct proportion in relation to the scheme and paste them onto the board.

- If you are using a variety of patterns, create visual continuity by relating their predominant colours throughout the house.

- Link areas of the home by limiting the wallcoverings in the halls and stairways to a single pattern and colour, or by having fitted carpeting in a single colour and texture throughout the house.

Size, shape and colour

There are many ways to create a decorative scheme with patterns. So much colour mixing and matching is a matter of personal taste! For example, patterns can be the same size and form but have different colours, such as varied floral designs. Or they can have the same form and colour but be different sizes, such as different types of stripe. Or they can have the same colour and size but have varied forms, such as a mixture of geometrics and florals.

Perhaps the easiest way to match patterns is to pick ones that have the same size and design and differ only in colour. In this context, you then really only have to choose colours that contrast or blend well together, following the guidelines established earlier.

If you want to combine small, regular patterns with large, bold ones, make sure that the two patterns are linked by colour. If the overall colours of each pattern are close to one another on the colour wheel (*see p. 198*), the effect will be successful.

ABOVE In this bedroom, a clever mix of patterns creates a striking yet restful decor. The patterns, varying from plaid and star-shaped to floral, are linked through a limited number of similar colours.

BELOW Two different patterns – one large and geometric, the other small and floral – have been linked through colour. Yellow and white are repeated in the wallpaper, tablecloth and cushions, as well as in the bedposts, chair and table lamp. Even the framed prints are colour coordinated.

RIGHT In this kitchen, two different styles of pattern have been connected through the use of colour.

BELOW Although initially looking discordant, all the colours making up the patterns in this room have been coordinated to produce overall harmony.

BOTTOM The same plant motif has been carried through comprehensively in this room – in the chair and table coverings, curtains, wallpaper and frieze.

Successful contrasts

When you match or mix patterns, if their main colours are complementary they will work well together, and also if they are lightened or darkened in tone, and used in unequal amounts. Common examples of complementary colours that contrast successfully are rust red with dark green and dark blue with orange.

Very different patterns – such as florals and geometrics – can also work together, if their main colours are linked. As a general rule, the more complex the patterns, the simpler the colours should be, to avoid clashes. For good results, choose patterns with a single main colour and small amounts of contrasting accent colours; or patterns with two main colours that are very close in tone; or mix complementaries and link them with neutral tones.

Pleasing results can also be obtained by matching large, bold patterns with small-scale versions of the same or similar designs in the same colour scheme. This can be very effective in a child's bedroom.

Pattern
and texture

Like pattern, texture is often used for decorative effect – adding interesting focal points and variety to a room. Textured surfaces, whether on walls, furnishings or flooring, are also useful as a device for concealing underlying imperfections. Since the texture of a surface has a significant effect on how the final colour looks, it is an important element to consider when planning a scheme.

The same colour appears quite different depending on whether it is applied to a rough or smooth surface. Rough surfaces scatter light and make colours appear darker and duller. They can, in some situations, create interesting shadows. By contrast, smooth surfaces reflect light and make colours look lighter and livelier. Even black or very dark walls reflect some light if decorated with gloss paint rather than one with a matt finish.

Texture and lighting

Imagine a well-lit room with ceramic-tiled floors, shiny plastic furniture, venetian blinds and gloss walls. Painted in primary colours, these smooth, shiny surfaces would reflect all the light, and the resulting glare would be overbearing. Yet in a poorly lit area, such colours and textures could serve a valuable function.

Now imagine the same room with thick-pile carpeting, wood furniture, lace curtains and hessian wallcovering. In strong light, these textures would modify even the palest colours and prevent glare. Yet in poor light, even a white colour scheme could look drab.

Creating a mood

Smooth surfaces create a cold, clean, sparse mood – especially when combined with black or white. Such a scheme may be ideal for the bathroom, and it could also work well for a business-like study. However, for a bedroom or candle-lit dining area, textured surfaces, such as brick, wood, cork and coarse fabrics, can create a softer mood. And when used with a combination of muted colours and tones, they impart warmth and intimacy to the overall scheme.

Combining colour, pattern and texture

Just as the predominance of a single colour can be overwhelming or dull, so too can the use of a single texture or pattern. However, it is best to limit the variety of textures and patterns if you have a complicated colour scheme. Otherwise, the effect can be cluttered and confusing. For example, if you have a range of textured surfaces in tones of, say, brown and beige, it is a good idea to limit the patterns and stick to smooth surfaces for the other colours in the room.

Tricks with textures

- Create visual continuity by linking interconnecting rooms with the same carpeting or by repeating a fabric.

- Break up large areas into more intimate areas by using different textured hangings, drapes and rugs.

- Create contrasts by interspersing textures and patterns with areas of plain, smooth colour.

ABOVE Texture and pattern dominate in this child's bedroom, giving an enclosed and comforting, yet visually stimulating, effect.

TOP LEFT The pattern of a tiled floor, overlaid with a brightly patterned rug, anchors interest firmly at ground level in this attic bedroom.

FAR LEFT Visual continuity has been assured here through the use of repeated colour – the red, blue and purple of the walls, ceiling and furniture are echoed in the patterning of the rugs and bedspread.

LEFT When small areas only of pattern are used they immediately become a focal point for a room.

Focal patterns

If the room you are decorating has a special feature you might like to emphasize it and treat it as a focal point. The most obvious focal points are fireplaces, large bay windows and unusual recesses. Any of these could be accentuated by applying pattern to the surface. For example, to highlight a fireplace, use a wallcovering in a warm-toned complementary style, or turn an alcove or wall into a focal point with a splash of colourful pattern; offset these by keeping the adjacent walls plain. You could enhance a bay window with richly patterned floor-to-ceiling curtains.

The opposite can also work successfully. For example, you could decorate most of the room in subtle patterns, leaving an expanse of plain colour in a featured alcove, as a backdrop to shelves of attractive ornaments or a display of framed pictures.

In general, select smaller and more subtle patterns for small areas; larger, bolder patterns work better in more spacious areas. Strong patterns tend to dominate and should be used thoughtfully. In a narrow room, horizontal stripes make the space look wider. Regular geometric patterns are more static and formal, while repetitive floral patterns give a sense of movement and flow.

ABOVE The curved shape of this bathroom wall is subtly emphasized by the pattern of terracotta squares running along its base. The horizontal wall stripes continue the geometric theme and make the room seem wider.

BELOW In this attic, attention is drawn towards the boldly coloured, patterned rug, sensibly combined with plain walls. By limiting the range of colours and forms, the room looks more spacious than it really is.

Planning

- Warm, rich colours and hard, shiny surfaces appear to come towards you. Cool colours and soft, matt textures give the appearance of receding more into the background. Bear this in mind when you want to alter the apparent size of a room.

- Draw a sketch of the room and indicate areas of contrasting colour, texture and pattern. When selecting a focal point, keep in mind a balance of activity in order to avoid making one area busy with pattern and colour and another area relatively quiet and plain, unless you want to visually separate these areas.

Planning the framework

At the planning stage, you will have lots of decorating ideas about incorporating light and dark tones, contrasting and harmonizing colours, and using textures and patterns. However, what seems like a good idea in theory may not be very appealing once you see the finished result. And what works for each room on a small scale may be jarring as an overall scheme. In order to avoid disappointment, it is a good idea to think through a variety of decorating possibilities before starting.

Begin by listing the main colours, tones, patterns and textures you are considering for each room. Draw a rough plan of the rooms involved and mark the existing features you do not intend to change. Make several copies, and colour in different decorative schemes and colour combinations. Attach samples of the wallcoverings and fabrics for both the new and the existing ones.

When looking at your plans, make sure there are some decorative elements that link different areas to create visual harmony. You could, for example, use the same colour for the ceiling, dado rail or carpet throughout the house, or leave all doors or door frames as unpainted wood. With just a little careful planning, you will be able to achieve a harmonious decorative scheme and a balance of moods and styles for your own home.

ABOVE The simple device of using the same colours in the rugs leads the eye easily and naturally from one room to the other, creating a sense of unity.

LEFT The focus in this room is created by the fireplace. A play of colour, tone and line is set up between the ceiling, beams and walls, the floor rugs and the sofa.

SOFT FURNISHING

Fabrics

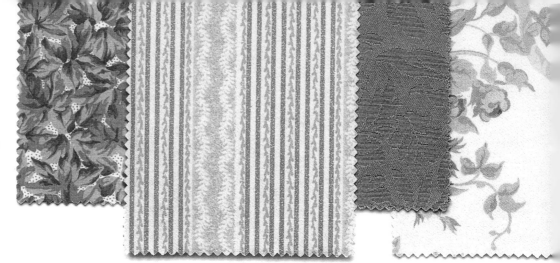

Decorating your home involves far more than selecting the most pleasing combination of wall and floor coverings. By incorporating fabrics – curtains, blinds, furniture covers and cushions – you can change the decor from plain, drab and lifeless to one that has softness, warmth and vitality.

Fabrics are available in an enormous range of colours, patterns, textures and weights. They vary from fine to coarse weaves, shiny to rough surfaced, flimsy to heavyweight. Each is best suited to a particular range of uses and creates its own special effects. Heavy fabrics – primarily used for curtains and fitted upholstery – give a feeling of solidity, while sheer ones have a graceful movement that is ideal for loosely draped furnishings and curtains. Strongly patterned or textured fabrics can be used as a focal point for your decor. Those with subtle designs and colours can complement your chosen colour scheme or work as splashes of contrast.

Fabrics in the home

The range of possibilities for using fabrics in the home is enormous. By making your own soft furnishings, you can select the colours, designs and textures that best complement or contrast with your scheme. If you have to make do with old furniture, you can give it new life by making slip covers, tablecloths or throws in your choice of fabric. Selecting the right cloth for your needs can be a daunting task, but, by following a few guidelines, you will soon be familiar with the fabrics and their relative merits.

Fabrics that are sold for soft furnishing should have a guide as to whether they are suitable for upholstery or only for lighter jobs such as curtains or bedcovers. Many other fabrics – from fun fake furs to delicate silks and heavy medieval-style tapestry – can be used around the house, but do check on things like washability and colour-fastness.

Natural fabrics

Cotton is the most widely used natural textile. Its fibres are thin, fairly smooth and very strong, and the material is economic to buy and easy to sew. A huge variety of cottons is available, varying in quality, thickness, weave and design. Some have a single-coloured patterned weave, others have a printed design. Some have a shiny surface, others are plain.

LEFT The weave of a fabric – its coarseness or fineness – largely affects its textural appearance. All woven fabrics have warp and weft threads. The warp threads run the length of the material, from top to bottom, while the weft threads run across.

Slub silk has more texture than other types of silk. The silk yarn used is a little like unevenly spun cotton thread.

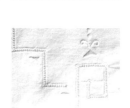

Watered silk often seems to shimmer in different colours, depending on how the light strikes it.

The long, strong fibres of cotton make it an easy material to sew – ideal for embroidered patterns.

The unevenly spun fibres of slub cotton give the material a random, self-patterned effect.

Machine-woven lace became popular in the 19th century. Most was used for making lace curtains.

Made from the fibres of the flax plant, linen is strong and stiffer than cotton. It can be smooth or nubbed.

LEFT The use of pattern and colour dictates the mood of a room. Large, bold patterns and strong colours are more suitable for large areas. More restrained colours and patterns make an ideal background for other decorative items and themes.

Of the self-patterned fabrics, cotton moiré is a good choice for a multi-coloured, light-to-medium weight, economical fabric, while damask is a single-colour, medium weight fabric that is a little more costly.

Many velvets are 100% cotton. They vary enormously in quality and cost, and can be plain cut or have a looped weave – known as chenille. They have a soft texture but can be hard to sew as bits of pile tend to accumulate.

Inexpensive cottons in checks and stripes often have a mix of English and Indian fibres. Check carefully as some are not colourfast or durable.

Chintz is a closely woven, lightweight, durable cotton fabric with a shiny, glazed finish. It usually comes in plain colours or a floral print and is generally used for furnishings in informal décor.

Linen, an ancient fabric, is another popular natural textile. It has a slightly uneven, coarse texture and dull appearance. Although expensive, linen's long fibres make it very strong and durable.

For many washable natural fabrics you may have to allow for shrinkage. Buy 10% extra and wash according to the instructions before you make up the fabric.

Synthetic fabrics

Fabrics with synthetic mixes are also extremely popular and versatile. They are strong, hard-wearing and usually inexpensive. Their main disadvantage is that they tend to attract dirt particles.

Synthetic dupion is lightweight, hangs well and looks like silk. Cheap and easy to sew, it comes in a range of plain colours.

Brocades are a heavier, better-quality synthetic mix of dull and shiny yarns in matching or contrasting colours. They come in a range of colours, patterns and thicknesses that make them an exciting choice for home furnishings.

Choosing fabrics

With so many fabrics to choose from, it is important to look at a selection in a large department store. Compare how they look, feel and hang. Crush a corner of the fabric in your hand to see if it creases easily. Hold it up to the light to examine the weave – the closer the weave, the more durable the fabric. Examine the raw edge to see how readily it frays.

It helps to bring along sample swatches of any wall or floorcoverings that you are trying to match. Keep in mind a balance of colour, pattern, texture and weight. If in doubt, ask for fabric samples and examine them at home before making any final decisions. The way the light interacts with the fabric is an important consideration, so don't make up your mind until you see the samples in your own home environment.

A rough room plan allows you to visualize the proportions of colour, pattern and texture of different fabrics before making any purchases.

Materials and equipment

- **Hand-sewing needles – a comprehensive collection**

- **Upholstery needles**

- **Steel dressmaker's pins**

- **Pin cushion**

- **Stitch unpicker**

- **Tape measure**

- **Polyester or cotton thread in assorted colours and weights according to fabric used**

- **Tailor's chalk or pencil marker**

- **Basting cotton**

- **Dressmaker's scissors**

- **Small embroidery scissors**

- **Cutting-out shears**

- **Pinking shears for finishing seams**

- **Sewing machine**

- **Steam iron and ironing board**

Curtain styles

Everyone is aware that curtains serve a practical function – offering privacy and insulation from draughts. However, the role that they can play in a decorative scheme is frequently underrated. Varying enormously in size, style and material, curtains can have a striking influence on the mood and atmosphere of any room in your home. Floral cotton curtains, reaching to the windowsill, create a fresh, casual atmosphere, while elaborate floor-length velvet drapes give a stately formality.

The kind of curtains you choose depends on your personal preferences, your need for warmth and privacy and the kind of atmosphere you are trying to convey visually. Your choice also reflects the physical characteristics of the room – the height of the ceiling, the dimensions of the window and the amount of available light entering the room.

RIGHT Softly coloured fabric drapes can be used to partition off part of a room. The same considerations are used to select the styles and fabrics for these as for curtains at windows. The soft colours enhance the bright room.

BELOW A sheer curtain hangs on a simple pole. This curtain is used to create privacy, so it is rarely pulled back. This means it does not need complicated fixings, the fabric has simply been sewn over at the top to create a hole for the pole.

This curtain heading uses pencil pleat tape and simple hooks attached to rings hanging from an iron pole.

A pleated curtain is made with triple-pleat heading tape and pronged hooks hanging from a simple track.

Hand-sewn curtain headings, made from fabric loops secured with a button, suspend curtains from an iron pole.

Colours and patterns

Your choice of curtain colours will be based largely on the atmosphere you want to create and whether the effect is to be warm or cool. Generally, colours in the red range are warm and lively; those in the blue range cool and relaxed. Colours become softer when muted with black or white.

Rich colours and strong patterns are better for large rooms, where there is space to make them a dominant feature. Smaller rooms look less overwhelmed with curtains in gentler tones and small, subtle patterns. Pale-coloured curtains are a good choice for dark rooms, reflecting the maximum available light. If the decor is bland, you can make a feature of the curtains with highly contrasting colours and patterns. It is best to match the size of any pattern to the size of the windows. To unify a room, use matching or complementary colours.

LEFT A bold fabric has been chosen for this curtain in an otherwise plain room. Because the curtain is not very gathered, the strong geometric pattern can be appreciated. The contemporary metal curtain rings and clip fastenings make for very little sewing. The curtain is a simple rectangular panel, hemmed at the edges.

ABOVE RIGHT Cool colours combine with fine iron work to create an elegant atmosphere to this room. An eastern look is achieved by softly draping the window with a sheer Oriental fabric and covering the chair seat with the same material.

RIGHT This ornate pelmet is shown to best advantage by the plain white curtains. Curtains with strong colour or pattern would have taken the emphasis off this fine feature.

FAR RIGHT The unusual pattern and shades of the curtains and bed cover reflect the wood in the room. The subtle pastel shades of the window curtains harmonize with the bed furnishings. Iron curtain fittings and fixtures create a rustic feel to the room and work together with the wooden beams, floor and furniture.

Tracks, poles and pelmets

Windows are functional parts of a room's structure, but if they are left unadorned they can look stark and uninviting. Curtains and drapes can greatly influence the visual impact of a room and the type of track or curtain pole on which they hang can make a big difference to the style they achieve. Gathered curtains look very different from flat fabric panels and wooden curtain poles create a very different look to hidden curtain tracks.

Track and pole types

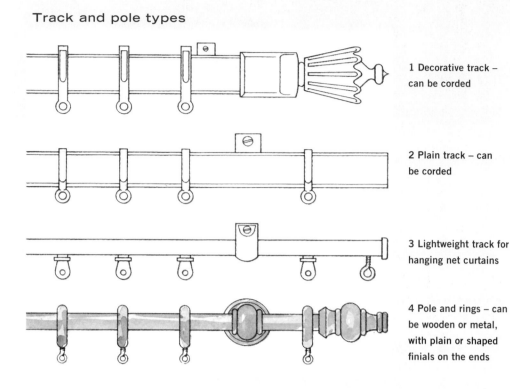

1 Decorative track – can be corded

2 Plain track – can be corded

3 Lightweight track for hanging net curtains

4 Pole and rings – can be wooden or metal, with plain or shaped finials on the ends

BELOW A decorative wrought-iron curtain pole adds a graphic element to this otherwise flouncy curtain, creating a good balance. Poles like this come in many different designs and sizes.

Tracks and poles

Curtains and drapes are hung from rails (tracks) or poles, and there are literally dozens of different styles from which to choose. The type of heading will determine how the top of the curtain will pleat and fold and whether it will hang below a track or hide it when drawn.

Poles can be much more attractive but curtains pull along them less smoothly. If the top of the curtain will be hidden by a pelmet, a track is all that is needed. Tracks are usually available in PVC or aluminium, both of which are flexible enough to be bent into curves or awkward shapes. The simplest type of track has visible sliders that clip over the rail. Others have the sliders inserted in grooves along the back or in a recess below it. Whatever the type, treat tracks regularly with a grease-free lubricant to keep curtains and drapes running smoothly.

More expensive rails have cording sets that enable the curtains to be opened and closed by pulling on a cord.

Poles are usually made of timber, brass or wrought iron. The curtains hang from rings that simply slide along the pole.

Wherever possible, screw the holding brackets for tracks and poles directly to the

wall. Battens are useful in some situations to help the curtains clear the window frame, but they can look clumsy. To allow a full-length curtain drop, some tracks can be screwed to the ceiling. If you want this effect, make sure you can fix the brackets into the joists, or fix timber between the joists to provide a secure fixing.

Pelmets

A well-fitted pelmet has a threefold effect – it forms part of the window dressing, hides the curtain track, and protects the head of the curtains and the track from dust and dirt.

Pelmets, such as the one shown opposite, are simple to make. The front edge of the pelmet can be given an ornate shape before assembly. To do this, make a pattern half the width of the front board, trace it onto the wood, turn the pattern over and trace the other side to match exactly, and then cut out the shape with a jig saw. The pelmet can be painted or covered with a fabric to match or contrast with the curtains.

Fabric pelmets can be made from stiffened material or from frilled or pleated curtain material mounted on a valance rail that clips onto a matching curtain track. The valance may be curved to fit a bay window.

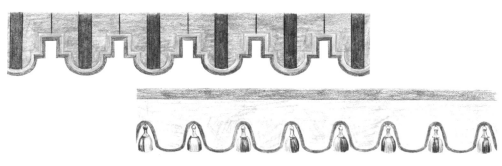

Lambrequins

Popular in Victorian times, the lambrequin is experiencing a comeback. It is constructed in much the same way as a pelmet, but its sides extend all the way down the window. The front can be simply squared off or shaped in a variety of styles. Because of the extra weight it may need supporting with brackets. Padding the frame with wadding glued to the wood will make covering easier and give the finished lambrequin a more rounded outline. A lambrequin can frame curtains but is especially effective at softening the surround of a blind.

ABOVE A mock-heraldic mood is represented by these two examples of fringed pelmets. The stripes represented by the top pelmet, if repeated in the associated curtains, would tend to emphasize the vertical nature of the window area. The stripes are colourful and bold and so would perhaps be most suitable in a generously proportioned room. The single coloured pelmet (below) with its discreet tassels along the lower edge, would be easier to accommodate in most room settings.

RIGHT This eye-catching pelmet with its zig-zag border makes a stylish finish for the matching floor-length curtains in this bedroom with its gentle muted colour scheme.

Making a pelmet

To install the holding batten, drill holes, plug them and screw the batten to the wall; it should represent the top of the pelmet less the thickness of piece **1**. If drilling into concrete, use a drill with a hammer action and a sharp masonry bit.

Cut all the lengths to size, smooth them with glasspaper, and then glue and pin them together. Allow the glue to dry thoroughly, then partly insert two or more screws into the top of the wall batten and cut off their heads with a hacksaw.

Position the pelmet on the wall batten and tap it with a hammer to make indentations where the pins are located. Drill holes into the pelmet top at these marks so that the pelmet can slip over the headless screws to secure it in place.

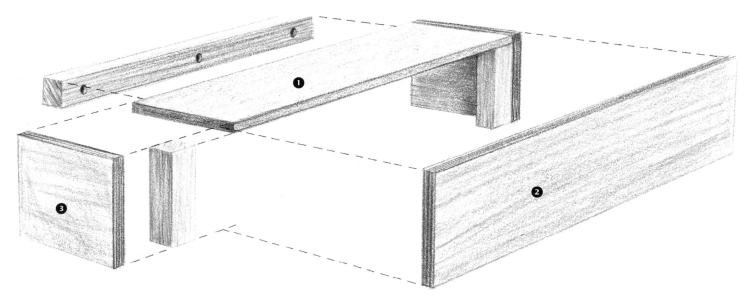

The front piece **2** should overlap the end pieces **3** for a stronger construction and better appearance.

Lace and voiles

Translucent window dressings have come a long way from the old net curtains. Draping windows with sheer curtains has many advantages. They give a room daytime privacy, screen it from unpleasant views beyond the window, and at the same time let in plenty of softly diffused light. They can form a contrast with heavier fabrics or can be used alone for an airy, romantic look.

Choosing a style

Think about the effect you want to create. If privacy is a priority and you want the window covered most of the time, choose white or coloured voiles with a light pattern. Or consider a pretty lace panel, hung without gathering, so you can see its intricacy.

When choosing ultra-light fabrics for effect rather than practicality, the choices expand. Jewel-coloured sari silks shot through with gold or silver can be made up or simply draped around a metal pole; voiles come in many colours both bright and pastel, some incorporating pockets to hold whatever appeals to your individuality – dried flowers, lightweight mementoes, fabric swatches in contrasting colours, etc. Most voiles and muslins are inexpensive, but look best used in generous amounts, so don't stint.

ABOVE Hazy muslin drapes with a blue printed pattern that reflects the deep blue of the walls.

LEFT The texture of layers of lace is brought out by the strong sunlight pouring through the window.

Making sheers and voiles

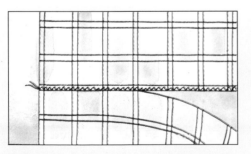

1 When cutting the fabric, carefully follow the line of the weave to ensure that the edge is even. Some weaves are prone to fraying. To prevent fraying, sew zigzag stitches along the cutting line, using a sewing machine, before you cut it.

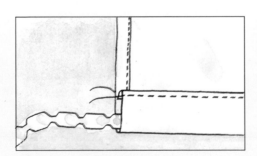

2 Sew the side and bottom hems in exactly the same way as for simple unlined curtains. Lightweight fabrics hang better if the bottom hem is weighted down with flexible, lead-weighted tapes available in haberdashers.

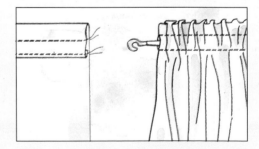

3 To make a heading for a spring wire, thin brass rod or wooden dowel, allow about 50mm (2in) of extra fabric. Turn under and fold again to make a 38mm (1½in) hem. Sew two rows of stitches to make a channel for the wire or rod to go through.

Measuring up

First select the style and decide the length of curtain – either to the sill or the floor. Once you have fixed the curtain track or pole in position, select your curtain heading – always choose this before buying your fabric.

Curtain fittings – tracks and poles

Choose tracks or poles that are strong enough to support the weight of the curtains. They must also be long enough to overhang either side of the windows by 25–30cm (10–12in), depending on the fullness of the curtains. It is advisable to install tracks and poles before measuring up for curtains because the shape of the window or the style of curtains intended will govern where the fixings are placed. Curtains can also hang from ceilings, and in front of shelves.

Gathering tape

Gathering tape with holes for detachable lining

Metal-pronged hook for pinch pleats

Standard hooks

Pin hook

Measuring for curtains and blinds

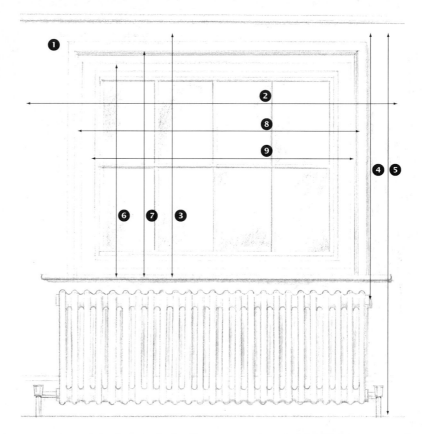

You can make curtains to hang to the floor, level with the top of the radiator, or to the sill. Remember to measure the width of the track, not the window frame itself. Take note of the measurements in the diagram above when planning curtains or blinds. For over-length curtains, add 10–15cm (4–6in) to measurement 9.

CURTAINS 1 Proposed level for curtain track 2 Measurement of track width 3 Drop from track to sill 4 Drop from track to top of radiator 5 Drop from track to floor.

BLINDS 6 Height inside recess 7 Height outside recess 8 Width, no recess 9 Width inside recess.

Making the calculations

First measure the width of the track or pole and multiply by the number of widths the type of heading requires (usually a minimum of 1½ times for simple gathers to 3 times for pencil or box pleats). Divide the width of the fabric you have chosen into this total width and round up to the next whole number. Even if you don't usually do so, it will be easier to measure up in metric, because fabrics are seldom still sold by imperial widths or lengths. The most common widths are 122cm, 135cm and 150cm. As an example, a track width

of 160cm x 2½ for gathering would give you a total width of 400cm. This means 4 widths at 122cm and 3 at 135 or 150cm.

Next, measure the drop you need, add an allowance for any pattern repeat and add 20–40cm (8–16in) for heading turnings and hems. For example, if the finished curtain is to be 190cm long, and your chosen fabric has a 15cm repeat, you will need 195cm (to allow for a complete number of pattern repeats) + about 30cm for headings and hems = 225cm per drop.

Finally, multiply the drop by the number of widths for the total amount you will need.

Curtains

Almost any furnishing fabrics may be used for curtains, from heavy velvets to the lightest of cottons. The fabric should drape well to ensure the curtains hang in balanced, graceful folds from the gathered headings. Furnishing fabrics are normally wider than dress fabrics, so check the width of the fabric you intend to use before measuring up and calculating.

Lining fabrics specially designed for curtains are available in a range of colours, as well as white and off-white. If you wish to use coloured lining, check the effect with the fabric you intend to use, to see that the colour of the lining does not affect that of the curtains when they are hung together with the light behind. Curtain lining fabrics are usually slighter narrower than curtain fabrics: when calculating quantities simply use the same number of widths of fabric.

The lining

Curtains do not need to have a lining, but it is worth including one. Linings increase the life of the curtains by protecting them from sunlight, adding insulation and giving a fuller, more luxurious finish.

Once you know how much fabric you will need for the curtains, it is a straightforward matter to work out how much you will need for the lining. Since the lining is slightly smaller than the curtain, simply allow 15cm (6in) less in the length and 12.5cm (5in) less in the width. Unless you are planning a highly decorative lining, you will not need to allow for pattern repeats.

Materials and equipment

- Curtain and lining fabric

- Curtain tape and hooks or rings

- Sewing thread in predominant colour of the fabric

- Needle – of length and thicknesses according to weight of fabric

- Long dressmaker's pins

- Marking pencil

- Strong thread and larger needle for making gathers

Making unlined curtains

Unless curtains are sheer, they will hang better when lined. However, there can be occasions when unlined ones are preferable and the technique for making them is basic to making any curtain.

Begin by matching patterns where necessary. Join the widths and any half widths using a flat seam. Trim off selvedges or notch in order to prevent puckering. Press the seams open.

1 Turn in and press the fabric 50mm (2in) on each side edge. Make a 25mm (1in) double hem, pin, and baste to within 65mm (2½in) of the top edge and 15cm (6in) of the lower edge.

2 Press in the mitre at each corner (*see p. 236*), then turn in and press the raw edge to make the double 75mm (3in) hem. Use a loose slip stitch to sew the side hems for a more professional finish. Stitch the mitre then stitch the hem.

3 Turn down and press 65mm (2½ in) along the top of the curtain.Tack. Cut tape to the width of the curtain plus 50mm (2in). Pull out about 50mm (2in) of cords at each end of the tape. Knot the cords together on the wrong side at one end of the tape and loosely on the right side at the other end. Turn the tape under 25mm (1in) at each end, pin and tack the tape to the wrong side of the curtain with the top edge along the line of tacking. Machine stitch the tape top and bottom. Start each row of stitching from the same end so the tape is not distorted.

4 Draw up the cord from the loosely knotted end until the curtain fits the track or rod, and space the gathers evenly. Knot the cords to hold them in position, then tie the ends and hide them behind the curtain with a stitch if necessary. Insert the hooks, and hang the curtains. Check the length and then make a 15cm (6in) hem and slipstitch it in place.

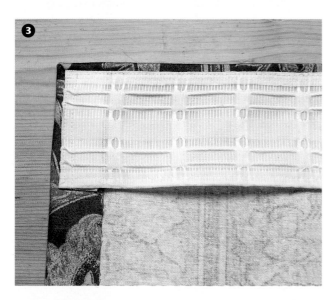

Making machine-stitched linings

Unless curtains are specifically intended to filter light and create a semi-sheer effect, it is best to line them. This will give insulation and protect the main fabric from dirt and from perishing in strong sunlight.

❶ The lining should be cut out to the size of the finished curtain. The curtain, made up, should be 12cm (5in) wider and 22.5cm (9in) longer than the lining. Position the lining on the curtain, right sides facing, with the top edge of the lining 75mm (3in) below the top of the main fabric, with the side edges matching.

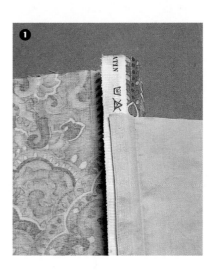

❷ It is a good idea to secure the lining to the curtain as this helps the two layers to hang well together. With the lining facing you, work long catch stitches down the centre of the lining, from top to bottom.

❸ Adjust the two layers. Pin the side edges together. Machine stitch and press. Remove the selvedges or notch the seam allowance. Turn a 15cm (6in) hem along the lower edge of the curtain, and a 50mm (2in) hem along the lower edge of the lining (which should be 50mm (2in) shorter than the main curtain). Press. Turn the lining and the fabric right sides out. Slip stitch the remaining edges of the lining to the curtain.

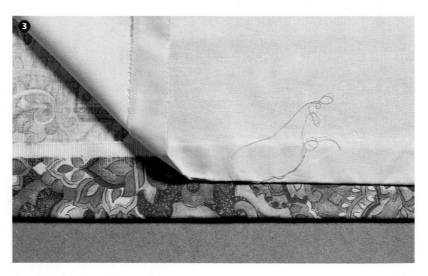

Blinds

Blinds are an inexpensive alternative to curtains, and easy to make yourself. Be sure to balance the colour, pattern and style of your blinds with the rest of the decor in the room.

In general, elaborate blind styles look better with plain fabrics, while simpler styles can benefit from colourful patterns. You can purchase kits to make blinds and match the fabric with your own colour scheme. When not in use, blinds can be rolled up out of the way to allow light and air to enter the room. Blinds made of paper with bamboo struts are delicate and allow the light to filter through.

BELOW A simple straight blind is given a more dressy finish by making a scalloped edge, with binding, and a colourful contrasting pelmet.

Fixings and fittings

Roller blinds have a flat pin at one end for the slotted bracket and a round pin at the other end – incorporating the spring – for the drilled bracket. To fix the blind level, first screw one end bracket into position. Then slot in the appropriate end of the roller.

Use a spirit level to check that the roller is horizontal, and then you can fix the other end bracket into the correct position on the wall.

Styles of blinds

The simplest and cheapest type of blind is the plain roller blind, made from stiffened fabric attached to a sprung roller. It requires a minimum of sewing and is widely available in kit form. The flat surface lends itself to almost any colour, pattern or design. You can add your own trim to complement the style of the rest of the decor or you can make a pelmet, covered with matching or complementary fabric.

Roman blinds have sewn-in vertical pull-cords that enable them to be pulled up into evenly spaced deep pleats. They can be lined or unlined, as long as you use fabric with an even weave. Roman blinds look best in a solid colour or simple geometric pattern that follows the weave of the fabric. They can be trimmed with braid for extra interest. Austrian and festoon blinds are constructed in a similar way, but they are gathered at the top and pull up in a series of soft scallops.

RIGHT This striking blind, set in a very white window frame, is outstanding for its bold, dark pattern which is echoed in the clear lines of stripes in the room.

Making Austrian blinds

Austrian blinds are made from fabrics such as silk or chintz and gathered at the top like curtains, with or without a lining.

❶ Fix the blind track in position in the window recess. Measure the dimensions of the window and make up one piece of fabric to twice the width measurement and the length measurement plus 45cm (18in) for the heading and bottom hem. Hem the sides of the blind and fix vertical rows of looped tapes to the reverse of the fabric. The outer rows should be 10cm (4in) from the hemmed edges. The inner rows should be at intervals of 30cm (12in).

For an optional frill at the bottom, cut a 16cm (6½in) wide strip of fabric to twice the width of the blind. Hem the bottom edge and work two rows of gathering stitches along the upper edge.

Measuring up

Decide where you want to fix the blinds – either inside or outside the window recess. If the recess is deep, position the blind inside it, close to the window (*see p. 227*). Then measure across the recess and deduct 16mm (⅝in) on one side for the pin end and the same amount on the other side for the spring mechanism.

Next, position the blind brackets 30mm (1¼in) from the top of the recess to allow room for the full roller. The brackets must be level for the blind to roll neatly. Measure the drop of the blind from the roller to the bottom of the recess, add an allowance of 75mm (3in) both top and bottom.

If you are fixing your blind outside the window recess, decide on the amount of fabric overlap on each side, and measure the total width of the blind.

For windows without recesses, the fixings will have to be mounted on supports above the window.

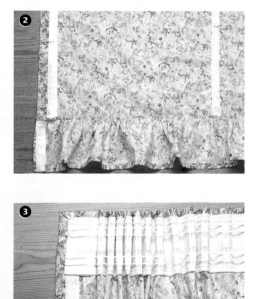

2 Pull the gathers evenly and then pin, tack and sew the frill in position.

3 Make the headings as for curtains, fit gathering tape and curtain hooks, and hang the blinds in position. Fit a screw eye into the window surround at the top of each row of looped tapes. Cut some lengths of cord – one for each row of loops. Make each cord twice the length of the blind, plus one width.

4 Tie a cord end to the lowest loop in each row. Pass each length of cord up through all loops in its row. Then pass all the cords to the right through the screw eyes along the track. All the cords will hang on the same side of the window. Knot them together and trim the ends level with the sill.

Table linens

With a little imagination and a minimum of expense, the most worn out of tables can be transformed into a decorative feature when draped with an eye-catching tablecloth. And you can turn any meal into a sense of occasion by displaying your own personalized tablemats and napkins as well.

It takes only the simplest sewing stitches to make a basic tablecloth, tablemat or napkin. And you can easily make them more special by adorning them in one of a variety of ways. For example, you can make the table linens from several different-coloured fabrics – cut in strips, squares or other shapes and sewn in patterns much like a quilt. Alternatively, you can adorn them with embroidery or appliqué, or edge the border in satin ribbon, frills or scallops.

Tablecloths give scope for all kinds of imaginative effects. You can superimpose layer upon layer of translucent fabric, put lace over darker contrasts, or drape and knot soft fabrics. You can knot the corners of a very large square tablecloth and, if you have a round tablecloth, you could catch up the sides to make flounces.

BELOW A simple round table is transformed into a dining feature with a flowing circular table cloth covered with a washable half-length gingham cloth.

Rectangular tablecloths

Rectangular tablecloths require the least effort to make – and with a large expanse of fabric there's plenty scope for creativity. They look best with a drop of no more than 30cm (12in). When joining up lengths of fabric, position the seams so they create a central panel or else fall along the overhang. Alternatively, you can take advantage of the shape of the tablecloth and make the separate sections of fabric an integral part of the design – especially if you are incorporating material in more than one colour or pattern.

Some tables are suited to covering in heavier fabric such as tapestry or damask. The fabric can hang in rich folds that show off their pattern and texture. Or it can be a simple panel, revealing the edges of the table.

Circular tablecloths

Small occasional tables can be covered with a floor-length cloth. However, circular dining tables, like rectangular ones, usually look best with tablecloths that have a drop of no more than 30cm (12in). The tablecloth will look better if you can make it from a single piece of fabric rather than joined panels.

Placemats

Individual placemats are often used instead of tablecloths, saving on laundering and adding to the festive mood of any occasion. They can look very attractive, especially if made in sets with matching or contrasting napkins. When planning the colour and design of your placemats, think in terms of the presentation of the entire table display – including plates, cutlery, napkin rings, glasses, flowers and, of course, the food you will be eating!

Making a rectangular tablecloth

- Before measuring, decide on the length of the overhang. The width of material you will need is the width of the tabletop plus twice the overhang you want for your cloth. Add an allowance of 18mm (¾in) on each side if the cloth is to be edged with lace, frills or other decorations, or is floor-length. Add 50mm (2in) to each side if it is to be plain hemmed. The length of material can be calculated in exactly the same way: the length of the tabletop plus allowances for overhangs and hems.

- If the fabric is not wide enough to make the tablecloth from a single piece, add side panels to the centre (top) one, making sure to match any patterns.

- When sewing plain hems on a tablecloth, fold the corners neatly and finish by hand. The corners look neater if they are mitred (*see p. 236*).

Making a circular tablecloth

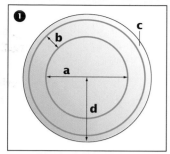

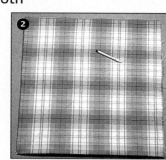

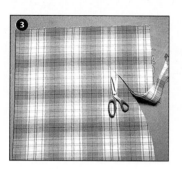

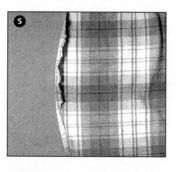

Circular table cloths are not difficult to make and can transform a simple, or even worn, table into an object of interest and delight.

1 Measure the diameter of the table top (**a**) and add twice the desired overhang, (**b**) plus 18mm (¾in) on each side for the hem (**c**).

2 Start with a square piece of fabric. Fold the fabric in half lengthways and then again crossways to make a smaller square. Make sure the edges are all perfectly aligned. Pin one end of a piece of string to the central, most folded corner of the fabric square and tie a pencil or piece of chalk to the other end, adjusting the length of the string to exactly the radius of your tablecloth (**d**). Draw an arc on the fabric with the pencil or chalk, taking care not to ruck up the surface as you draw.

3 Holding the layers of fabric firmly together, cut along the curved line, cutting through all the layers at once. Open out the fabric to a single layer and you should have a neat circle.

4 To prepare a plain hem, cut small v-shaped notches along the edge of the cloth, no deeper than 12mm (½in), and spacing them about 25mm (1in) apart.

5 Turn in an 18mm (¾in) hem, folding the fabric over twice, and stitch in place. If you wish, decorate the border with braid, tassels or a fringe.

Napkins

To finish off the table display, you can easily make your own napkins. Traditionally, cotton, gingham or seersucker are ideal fabrics for napkins. Napkins are usually square, and range in size from 30 x 30cm (12 x 12in) to 60 x 60cm (24 x 24in). When marking up the fabric, allow at least 18mm (¾in) all round for double hems. For the neatest finish, mitre the corners (*see p. 236*). Handstitch, or disguise the machine stitching line with close zigzag stitching, or finish with a braid.

ABOVE A tapestry table runner, fringed on all sides, sets off an old wooden table and complements the curtains used to divide the two rooms. The runner can be left on all day, or removed when the table is used for a meal.

RIGHT A small occasional table in a bedroom is greatly enhanced by a quilted tablecloth, made like a traditional patchwork quilt. The cloth reaches right to the floor and makes the table into a distinctive feature in its own right.

Cushions

Cushions mean comfort! Scattered plentifully or piled high, casually strewn or carefully placed, cushions create a welcoming atmosphere. Cushions vary from soft, small shapes and downy pillows, to foam pads and firm bolsters. With creative use of fabric, you can add a touch of surprise with cushions, by changing the covers according to your mood or the season of the year.

Quick Cover

This is an easy-to-make flapped cover.

1 Cut a strip of material 50mm (2in) wider and two-and-a-half times the length of the cushion. Turn both short edges under by 25mm (1in), baste and press. Turn both edges under another 25mm (1in) to make double hems. Baste, press and slip hem or machine on the wrong side.

2 Centre the cushion on the right side of the fabric, marking the corners of the cushion with pins. Remove the cushion and fold over both hemmed ends so that they overlap each other with two pins on each folded edge. When the raw edges are level, baste and stitch both seams, leaving 25mm (1in) seam allowances at each side. Turn the cover right side out and insert the cushion through the overlapped opening.

Frills

An attractive finish to a cushion, frills can be made in a plain colour which tones with the main fabric. You can repeat a colour used for curtains, or reverse the main fabric and trim.

Allow three times as much fabric as the length round the edge of the cushion, and double the depth of the frill, plus seam allowances. Fold the fabric in half, wrong sides together and press. Gather by hand or machine, or fold into knife pleats or box pleats. Insert the frill into the cushion before the main seams are sewn up, as for piping.

Cushion pads, stuffing and trimmings

You can buy ready-made pads in a variety of shapes and sizes, stuffed with feathers, down or synthetic fillings.

If you want to make your own pads you will need to make your own casing. This can be made from a lining material, old cotton sheeting, calico or ticking. When you have decided on the size and shape of your cushion, make the casing following the instructions for making square or rectangular cushion covers (*see opposite*).

Stuffing materials include foam chips, synthetic fibres, kapok (a vegetable fibre) and pieces of foam cut to size.

Cushions may be trimmed in a variety of ways. You can simply sew on bought braid or trimming (either by hand or with a sewing machine). However a more tailored finish can be achieved by using piping or a pleated frill, while the cushion is being made.

ABOVE   These cushion covers have been made using small pieces of Indian embroidered fabric.

BELOW   These cushions bring pattern and rich texture to a neutral room setting.

FAR LEFT The pillows are trimmed with corded piping and the bolsters are knotted or tied with frayed tassel.

LEFT Beautiful, elegant pillows tied and finished with ribbons, tassels and bows.

BELOW Smart cushions and bolsters in elegant shades of green and grey offer a comfortable place to recline on this day bed.

BOTTOM This tapestry cushion, with its pattern of fruits and leaves in warm but gentle colours blends well with a wide range of interior decoration schemes.

Square and rectangular cushion covers

Measuring

Make the cushion cover the same size as the pad. Measure with a tape from end to end and side to side of the pad. Add a 25mm (1in) seam allowance to each measurement.

Materials

- **Fabric (if the fabric has a large pattern, allow extra material)**

- **Cushion pad**

- **Zip fastener if required – this should be 10cm (4in) shorter than the shortest edge of the cushion**

- **Piping cord and braids to fit round the edge of the cushion, plus an extra 25mm (1in)**

Method

Lay the fabric out and draw on the cutting lines with tailor's chalk. Cut out the two squares or rectangles, following the grain of the fabric as far as possible.

1 Place the two pieces of fabric together, right sides facing and raw edges matching. Pin, baste and stitch round three sides. Neaten the raw edges. Stitch the seams up to about 50mm (2in) from each end of

the fourth side towards the centre. Clip the corners, press all the seams and open out the edges.

2 Turn the cover right side out and put the cushion pad in it. Poke the pad right into the corners. Finish the cover by hand sewing (slipstitch) the opening. If a zip fastening is required, insert before the side seams are sewn up.

Piping

Piping is made by covering a purchased piping cord with bias strips of fabric which is stitched into a flat seam to give a tailored finish. The cord is available in different thicknesses, so choose the size according to the scale of the item you wish to pipe. Shrink cotton cord before use or it will cause the piping to pucker during washing. To do this, boil the cord in water for 5 minutes and allow to dry thoroughly.

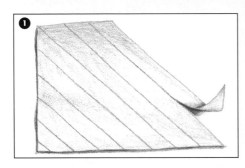

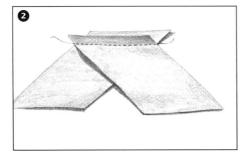

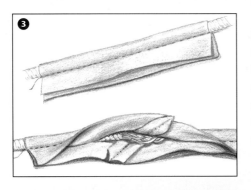

1 Mark the bias line of the fabric and cut out strips according to the width you require. The most usual width is 38mm (1½in).

2 Join the strips by placing two strips together at right angles to each other with right sides facing. This will form a triangle. Pin and machine firmly across the width, leaving a 6mm (¼in) seam allowance. Open flat and press firmly.

3 Work out the length of piping required and join enough bias strips together to cover the cord. Arrange the binding strip on a work surface, right side down. Position the piping cord in the middle and wrap the binding with wrong sides facing to enclose the cord. Baste close to the cord. Machine stitch to secure. Remove the basting stitches.

4 Place the panel of the main fabric wrong side down and lay piping on top of it so that the raw edges of the binding face outwards and align with the raw edges of the seam allowance of the main cushion fabric. Place the second panel of the main fabric right side down over the top with the raw edges

aligning with the others, and baste. Machine stitch the four layers together along the seamline. Remove the basting. When you turn the fabric right side out the piping will neatly edge the seam. You can neaten a raw edge with bias binding by hand or machine. Ready-made bias binding has pre-folded edges and can be bought in at least two different widths and a wide range of different colours.

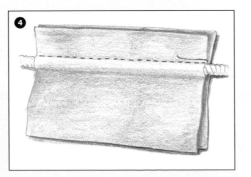

Mitring corners

1 With the fabric wrong side up, turn in about 6mm (¼in) along each edge and press. Fold along the hemlines (marked below with dotted lines).

2 Press and unfold the hems. Fold in the corner so the diagonal fold aligns with the straight fold lines of the hem. Trim the surplus triangle of fabric, leaving 6mm (¼in) seam allowance.

3 Turn in one hem along the hemline crease. Press and pin. Turn in the other hem along the hemline crease to form a neat corner. Pin and hem stitch.

4 Slipstitch along the diagonal at the corner to secure.

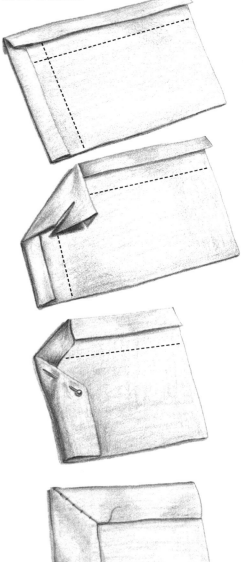

Bed linens

The bedroom is a personal haven for calm and relaxation. Whether you prefer to decorate it in a style that is romantic, exotic, elegant or flamboyant, the decor will include soft furnishings – bedlinens, pillows, covers, drapes and perhaps even wall hangings or a bed canopy. There is no better way to be sure that these items are in the fabrics, colours, patterns and styles that reflect your personal taste than by making them yourself.

Bedroom furnishings can be as simple or as adventurous as you want. You can choose silk for elegance, a floral cotton for a country-style look, or voile for softness and diffused light. If your bedroom doubles as a study or sitting room during the day, you can camouflage the bed with a close-fitting, functional cover.

TOP RIGHT There is nothing better than crisp white linen sheets. This softly quilted bedspread adds to the elegant appeal with its old-fashioned crimson roses.

ABOVE These extremely simple bed canopies are made from basic pine frames. The fabric is used without gathering for a bright, crisp look.

LEFT A child's bed is draped with a soft voile canopy which is contrasted with bold coloured bedlinen.

Bedspreads

Bedspreads can be made in two basic styles – throw-over or fitted. Either style can be floor length and edged with pleats, fringes or braiding. Alternatively, it can be made to come half way down the sides of the bed over a contrasting valance. You can use almost any type of fabric, as long as it is crease-resistant and has enough body to hang well.

Throw-over bedspreads are the easiest type to make, consisting simply of a plain rectangle of fabric that covers the bed from head to foot and hangs down the sides to the desired length. You can make the corners square or curved, and you can leave the hem plain or trim it with edging in contrasting fabric.

A fitted bedspread is made from five pieces: a top panel and a skirt consisting of four side panels of fabric. One of the long side panels should be made in two pieces incorporating a flap opening so the cover is easy to put on the bed.

Bed canopies

It is a straightforward project to transform an ordinary bed into one that is unusual and mysterious with the addition of a fabric-covered canopy, which can be as simple or dramatic as you like.

Canopies can be bought in a variety of styles, from a simple corona to a full four-poster, or you can make your own supports for the drapes with four lightweight, wooden curtain poles. Simply fix them to the ceiling above the head, sides and foot of the bed, making sure they overlap at the corners.

Select lengths of soft, fine-woven material for the canopy cover. Loosely drape it around the poles, or make up the lengths into curtains with deep-cased heading through which the poles can be inserted. Add ribbons or cord to tie back the canopy if you wish.

Materials of different weights, weaves and colours produce very different effects, so experiment before settling on a particular fabric. Be generous with the amount of material you use as a feeling of fullness can add to the effect, unless you want a chic, minimalist feel.

Furniture covers

When you are decorating your home, changing the entire décor can be extremely costly, and it's likely that you'll have to incorporate some existing furniture into your scheme. You may have a couch or armchair that is structurally sound but dull and threadbare in appearance. However, do not despair! Making your own furniture covers in a fabric that harmonizes with the colours and patterns of your decorating scheme is not as complicated as you may think – and it is an extremely effective and inexpensive way to bring new life and interest to a room.

RIGHT This beautiful cover looks elegant and is simple to achieve. Follow the method for a simple loose cover, and finish with self-colour bows.

BELOW A classic style, fitted loose cover with box pleats. This cover will need tucks and darts to achieve an excellent fit over the arms and back.

Selecting the fabric

There is a wide range of upholstery materials available, from which to select the one that best fits your scheme. Linen, chintz, velveteen and many synthetic fabrics are all suitable. Make sure that you choose a strong, firmly woven fabric that will hold its shape. For some fabrics, a fire-retardant interlining may be required.

Plain colours are easiest to work with, since there is no pattern matching. However, fabrics with very small patterns are the most practical choice for a family home since they disguise marks – and may not need matching. Fabrics with bold patterns are very popular but need extra care when cutting out as the motifs must be carefully centred and matched.

Hints and tips

- It's easy to mix up the pieces for your loose cover since they all look similar after cutting out. So, as you cut out each piece of fabric, add a small sticky label to the wrong side indicating its intended position and direction, or number with white tailor's chalk

- To join widths of fabric as inconspicuously as possible, sew them together so the seams correspond with the edges of the seat cushions.

Draped furniture covers

The easiest solution to revitalizing a couch or armchair is to buy a length of attractive fabric and drape it over the furniture. How much you want it to overhang and how much you tuck it in depends of the style of the rest of the decor in the room. You can finish the cover with a fringe, or a bought trim or braid. A lovely drape can be achieved with an Indian bedspread or a beautiful woven rug.

One way of breaking up the expanse of loosely draped material is to cover it with an array of brightly coloured cushions. This is especially effective if you use off-cuts or remnants of expensive fabrics such as plain silk or brocade, and make small cushions in different sizes and shapes.

RIGHT This loosely draped cover is finished with a large knot tied in the soft fabric. An exquisite plain silk cushion is placed on the chair.

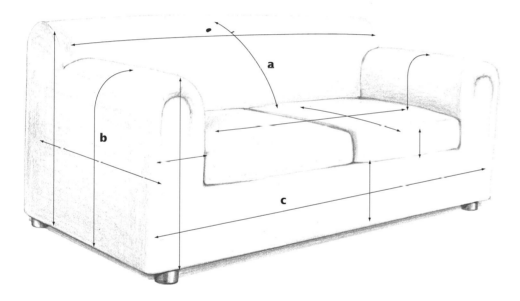

Loose furniture covers

Loose furniture covers are not hard to make, and with this method, the trick is to work directly onto the couch or chair. Working with the fabric inside out, so you can adjust the seams easily, mark the main lines with tailor's chalk and then simply cut out the main pieces as large rectangles (**a**, **b**, **c**). Depending on the shape of your sofa, allow a generous amount of material, and sit on the sofa before trimming the material to the correct size and shape. Remember to allow extra material if you have a pattern that needs matching.

1 First make a rough sketch of the sofa, and indicate the dimensions of each section as you measure it, as marked on the diagram. Always take measurements at the widest point widthways and lengthways, and add an allowance of 50mm (2 inches) for all the seams. If necessary, also include extra fabric for tucking in around the seat. Add an allowance for pattern matching.

2 Cut out all the panels on the straight grain of the fabric and position over the couch with the wrong sides outwards. Pin to fit and then mark the seamlines. Remove the fabric, baste with large, firm stitches and take out the pins. Before machine stitching the seams, sit on the sofa to make sure you have allowed enough material for a generous, comfortable finish.

3 You can attach braid or cord to emphasize the shape of the couch. Measure the length of the seams that give definition to the edges of the furniture and hand sew the braid or cord over the seams. Alternatively you could incorporate covered piping into the seams (*see p. 236*). You can also use concealed piping to make a false hem. Trim the lower unfinished edge all round and baste the piping to the right side of the fabric. Remove the cover and machine sew the piping in place. Press the piping down and stitch the seam to the wrong side of the fabric.

THE EXTERIOR

Roof coverings

Tiles and slates are the most widely used and durable coverings for pitched roofs. They are laid in overlapping rows, or courses, from the eaves to the ridge of the roof, the bottom of each tile or slate overlapping the top of the one in the course below. The joints are staggered on alternate courses, like brickwork. Most tiles and slates are attached to roof battens with clips or nails, although some tiles are shaped so as to interlock with those around them and are held in place, hooked over the battens, only by their own weight.

Roofing tools and materials

- Ladder with stand-off bracket, or scaffold tower

- Roof ladder

- Slater's ripper

- Wooden wedges — for propping up tiles

- Builder's trowel

- Hammer and nails

- Club hammer and plugging chisel or cold chisel

- Ready-mixed dry mortar

- Mortar board (commonly called a hawk)

- Pointing trowel

- Hot-air gun, residual current device (RCD) and extension lead

- Stripping knife

- Wire brush

- Stanley knife

- Roof repair tape, primer, roof-and-gutter sealant

Flat roofs in domestic use are most often found on porches, house extensions and garages. The most widely used materials for covering these roofs are asphalt, heated until melted and spread over the roof, and bituminous felt sheeting. This comes in different grades, is applied in layers and bonded with hot or cold bitumen.

Other types of roofing, not covered here, include rigid sheet roofing, such as corrugated plastic or fibre cement, which is usually used for outbuildings such as garden sheds or lean-to extensions.

Potential problems

Failure of any roof covering allows rainwater to seep through, resulting in damage inside the house to structural timbers and interior plasterwork. Roofs must therefore be kept sound and weatherproof, and regular checks of the roof – from both inside and out – are advisable to pre-empt any problems. All roof coverings have a limited life and while occasional patch repairs are possible, when too much of the roof needs attention, it makes sense to have the roof completely re-covered by roofing professionals.

Tiles and slates The odd tile or slate, damaged or out of place – as a result of high winds, snow or ice, or because of a broken tile lip (nib) or corroded holding nail – can be dealt with fairly easily. Repairs should be undertaken as soon as possible (*see pp. 244–245*), especially with a slipped slate or tile, which could be

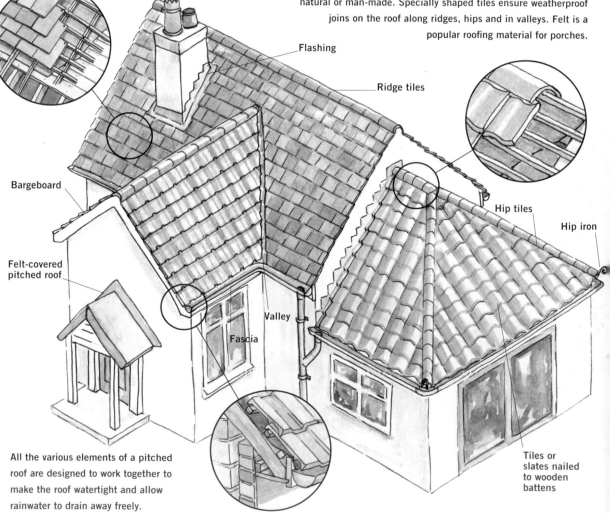

Roof tiles are made of moulding clay or concrete while slates can be natural or man-made. Specially shaped tiles ensure weatherproof joins on the roof along ridges, hips and in valleys. Felt is a popular roofing material for porches.

Flashing

Ridge tiles

Bargeboard

Felt-covered pitched roof

Valley

Fascia

Hip tiles

Hip iron

Tiles or slates nailed to wooden battens

All the various elements of a pitched roof are designed to work together to make the roof watertight and allow rainwater to drain away freely.

Ladder dos and don'ts

- Check a ladder, especially a wooden one, for damaged stiles or rungs before use.

- Never attempt to use a ladder in a high wind. Do not place it in front of an outward opening door or window.

- Use a stand-off bracket (stay) so that the ladder leans against a wall, rather than against guttering or any other flimsy attachment, and it clears overhanging eaves.

- Never lean to the side on a ladder – move the ladder if something is out of reach.

- Never have more than one person on a ladder.

- Never leave a ladder unattended, particularly with children around. Do not allow them to play under ladders or scaffolding.

completely removed by a high wind and cause someone below a serious injury.

Ridge and hip tiles are the rounded or angular-shaped tiles that sit along the ridges and hips of a roof and are held in place with mortar. Mortar crumbles and disintegrates over time. Where this has happened – most likely on older properties – it may be that the tiles are loose and kept in place only by their own weight. Ridge or hip tiles can become dislodged or suffer damage in the same way as ordinary tiles and slates and will need replacing or re-embedding in mortar.

Flat roof coverings There is more potential for water damage to flat roofs than pitched roofs, since rainwater (and snow) drains away less easily and may collect in puddles. Sun and frost can also cause damage to the covering. Splits in the covering may be caused by movement

in the roof structure, usually as a result of expansion and contraction in the sun. Blisters are caused by trapped moisture or air. Both splits and blisters can be patched using a proprietary repair kit comprising special tape and adhesive. For the best results, make any repairs during dry weather and clean the roof covering well first, using fungicide or a bleach solution to kill any traces of lichen or moss.

Flashings These are seals made of lead (especially in older properties), aluminium, zinc, roofing felt or mortar fillets, used to stop water penetrating at the point where the roof meets a chimney, an adjoining roof or wall. Problems can occur when the flashing material corrodes with age, or cracks or shrinks due to slight structural movement. Equally, sound metal flashings tucked into brickwork may have worked loose simply because the old mortar has worn away.

Using a ladder

Use an ordinary ladder that reaches at least three rungs above the eaves to access the bottom of the roof. Set it at an angle of about 70°. Before you climb the ladder, make sure it is stable and securely fixed.

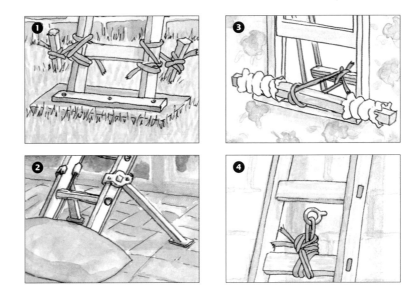

❶ On soft or uneven ground, rest the ladder on a stout board with a batten in front to stop the ladder sliding off. Lash the bottom of the ladder to pegs driven into the ground either side of it.

❷ On hard ground ensure both feet of the ladder are capped with rubber to prevent slipping and clip stabilizers on either side. A sandbag laid across the base of the ladder will also prevent slipping.

❸ Secure the ladder to a length of wood braced against the inside of a window frame, its ends covered to prevent damage to interior paintwork.

❹ Drive a strong metal screw eye or ring bolt into the masonry under the eaves. Anchor a rung towards the top of the ladder to this, using rope.

Roof and ladder safety

Only ever work on a roof when there is someone within calling distance. Access the eaves with a conventional ladder (see above), then use a roof ladder that reaches the distance from the eaves to the ridge of the roof. A roof ladder has rubber wheels for pushing it up the sloping roof and a large hook for looping over the ridge to hold it firm. Purpose-designed rails keep the treads clear of the roof surface and help spread the load.

ABOVE A roof ladder is designed to be wheeled up the slope, then turned over and hooked over the ridge of the roof.

Roof repairs

Check the state of your roof from time to time, looking closely at coverings, flashings, chimney and brickwork. Broken, slipped or missing tiles or slates are fairly easy to spot from ground level; chinks of daylight seen from inside an unlined roof also indicate breaks in the roof covering. You will probably need to climb on to a flat roof to inspect it for damage. Don't wait for signs of penetrating damp inside the house to indicate water coming in through the roof. This is a costly way to discover a problem that might have been avoided with vigilance.

Removing a damaged slate

Insert a slater's ripper under the damaged slate and hook one of its barbs around a fixing nail. Tug downwards hard to extract or cut through the nail. Remove the second nail in the same way. Even if a slate has gone completely the nails must be removed so that you can insert the replacement slate.

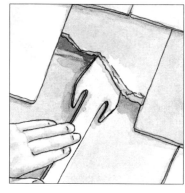

ABOVE A slater's ripper is used to cut through the fixing nails holding a slate to the roof batten, without disturbing the slates in the course above.

Replacing a slate

A new slate cannot be nailed in place because of the overlapping slates in the course above. You therefore need a flexible, 25mm (1in) wide strip of lead, zinc or aluminium, a little longer than the slate.

❶ Hold the metal strip against the gap between the two slates in the course directly below the missing slate; nail it to the roof batten using a galvanized clout nail.

❷ Slide the new slate up into position, aligning it with the others in the course. Turn up the end of the metal strip (double it on itself for extra strength) over the bottom of the slate to hold it in place.

Removing and replacing a tile

If the new tile is a different colour from the originals, which will have weathered since being laid, use a tile from an unobtrusive place on the roof as the replacement and place the oddly coloured tile here.

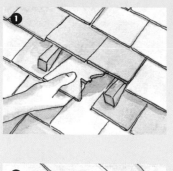

❶ Remove a broken plain tile by lifting it at a slight angle to clear the nib that is hooked over the roof batten. This is made easier by using small wedges of wood to lift the overlapping tiles in the course above. If the tile is nailed, try rocking it loose or break it out carefully, then use a slater's ripper to remove or break any nails left in the batten (*see left*).

❷ Slide the replacement tile, supported on a builder's trowel, upwards beneath the overlapping tiles, until its nibs hook over the batten. Even if the original tile was nailed in place there is no need to nail this new tile down – a few unfastened tiles on the roof will not matter.

❸ Tiles that interlock with each other can also be awkward to remove. Again, use small wedges where necessary to help.

Short-term repairs for a cracked slate or tile

❶ Use small wooden wedges (*see above*) to raise the tiles or slates that overlap the cracked one so that you can make the repair more easily. Clean the surface around the crack thoroughly using a wire brush.

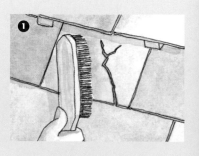

❷ Using self-adhesive flashing tape and flashing tape primer, follow the manufacturer's instructions and brush the primer into and around the crack, across an area that matches the width of the flashing tape. Press the

flashing tape into place over the crack and smooth it down well, using an old rag or a small wallpaper seam roller.

❸ Alternatively, for a very fine crack, use a gun-applied bituminous sealant instead.

Replacing a ridge or hip tile

Defective ridge and hip tiles need replacing or simply re-embedding in fresh mortar. Remove the damaged or loose tile and clear all loose mortar from the ridge or hip of the roof and from the underside of the tile itself. Soak this tile or a replacement one well in water before laying it.

1 Make a stiff mortar using ready-mixed dry mortar. Wet a large paintbrush with water and liberally dampen the uppermost courses of tiles or slates along the ridge of the roof or those on both sides of the hip. Use a builder's trowel to lay a thick bed of mortar on each side of the ridge or hip, following the line of the old mortar. Use sufficient mortar to fix the tiles securely but do not be too heavy-handed with it and block gaps where air needs to circulate to keep the timber in the roof in good condition. Where there is more than one tile to be replaced, work by laying enough mortar for one or two tiles at a time.

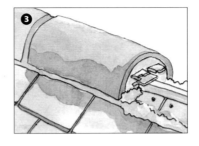

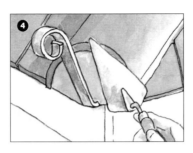

2 Press a water-soaked tile firmly into the mortar, align it with the other ridge or hip tiles and remove any excess mortar with a trowel.

3 Where a ridge or hip tile meets its neighbour, build up a bed of mortar to fill the hollow end of each tile, inserting a small piece of tile or slate into the mortar to stop it slumping and falling through the gap. (Build a mortar join between ridge or hip tiles and a wall or

chimney stack in the same way.) Press the next tile into place, smoothing the mortar in the joint.

4 When replacing the tile at the end of a ridge, seal the open end with thin pieces of tile or slate bedded in mortar and smooth the end so that rainwater will flow off easily. Treat the lowest tile on a hip similarly, making sure that the projecting hip iron remains soundly bedded in mortar.

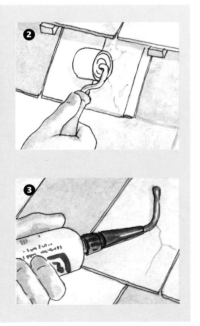

Patching a flat roof

You might need to remove a covering of chippings before you begin. Scrape them away using a wire brush or builder's trowel; if necessary, use a blowtorch or hot-air gun to soften the bitumen. Be very careful not to set fire to the roof covering.

Splits Splits in all types of roof coverings can be patched using self-adhesive repair tape. First clean the split and surrounding area thoroughly. Fill a wide split with a bitumen compound before patching. Following the manufacturer's instructions, brush the primer supplied with the repair tape over the area to be covered and leave it for 1 hour. Apply the tape to the primed area and press down firmly, treading it into place as you work.

Blisters Only repair a blister if it contains water or is causing a leak, otherwise leave it alone. To repair a

Mending defective flashing

Shrinkage cracks can be repaired fairly easily. Use a gun-applied bituminous sealant or other roof-and-gutter sealant for fine cracks in metal flashing, and a gun-applied flexible caulking compound to fill gaps where cement fillets have shrunk away from walls. Clear surfaces of any loose material before you start filling.

Use self-adhesive flashing tape and flashing tape primer for patching small holes in metal flashings or an area of slight corrosion.

If metal flashing is defective simply because the mortar holding it in place has worn away, the joint needs repointing. Remove all loose and crumbling mortar, wedge the flashing in place between the brick courses with nails or strips of lead and repoint the mortar joint (*see p. 252*).

blister in an asphalt roof, first soften the asphalt using a hot-air gun, then try to press the blister flat using a block of wood or a stripping knife. If water is present, cut into the asphalt to open up the blister and let it dry out. Apply gentle heat then press the asphalt back into place, filling with bitumen compound before pressing it down. Cover with a length of repair tape, pressing down firmly to make sure the edges are well sealed.

On a felted roof, make two intersecting cuts across the blister and peel back the four flaps – this will be easier if you first heat the felt. Clean out the opening and allow it to dry out. Apply cold bitumen adhesive to the hole and, when it is tacky, press the covering back into place in the adhesive. Nail down with galvanized clout nails. Cover the patch with self-adhesive repair tape or with a patch of roofing felt a little larger than the damaged area and stick in place with more bitumen adhesive.

Gutters and downpipes

The external drainage system of a house involves disposing of the rainwater that runs off roofs by collecting it in gutters and directing it via downpipes to the drains. Efficient removal of the rainwater prevents water damage to external timbers and paintwork, pointing and brickwork, which would otherwise eventually lead to penetrating damp (*see p. 251*).

The system comprises lengths of gutter and downpipe – usually 1.8–3m (6–10ft) long – and various angled components, which allow the pipes to run around corners, over eaves and into gullies. Assorted screws, clips and brackets secure the pipes to walls or fascias. Guttering varies in width, depending on the area of the roof draining into it, and in cross-section – it may be plain half-rounded, ogee, moulded or square.

Guttering can be made of cast iron, cast aluminium, fibre cement or rigid plastic (unplasticized PVC, or uPVC). UPVC is the most widely used guttering today. It is used on all new buildings and for replacing old guttering systems. It comes in many profiles and sizes, and in black, brown, grey or white; it is lightweight and durable, easy to cut and fit, and requires no painting.

Potential problems

There can be various reasons for an overflowing or leaking gutter or downpipe, but the result is the same – water soaks through the exterior walls, causing damp inside the house. Outside, continually dripping or splashing water results in unattractive water stains or algae growth on external paintwork and masonry.

Guttering blocked with dirt or leaves causes water to overflow; a gutter set at an incorrect angle (known as the fall) – perhaps due to incorrect installation or to rusted and slipped holding screws or brackets – can also cause water to spill over. A sagging gutter

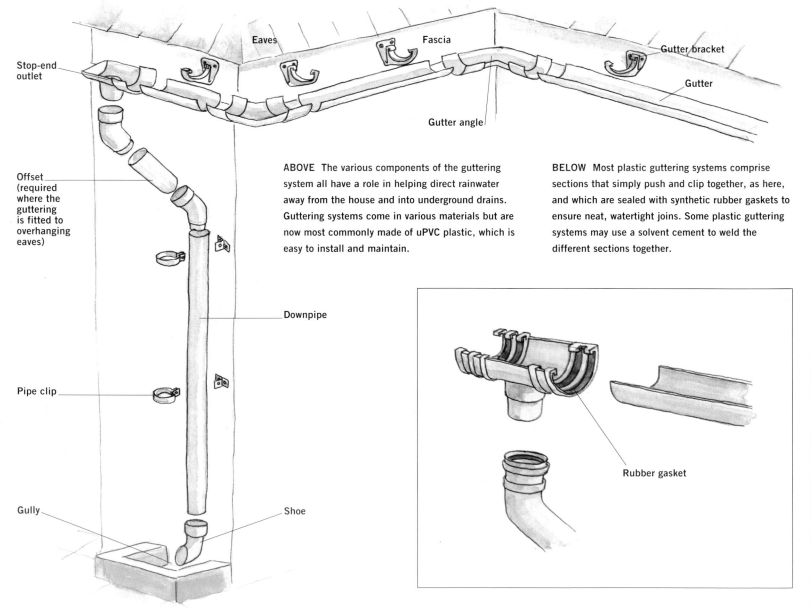

ABOVE The various components of the guttering system all have a role in helping direct rainwater away from the house and into underground drains. Guttering systems come in various materials but are now most commonly made of uPVC plastic, which is easy to install and maintain.

BELOW Most plastic guttering systems comprise sections that simply push and clip together, as here, and which are sealed with synthetic rubber gaskets to ensure neat, watertight joins. Some plastic guttering systems may use a solvent cement to weld the different sections together.

means that water does not run away properly. Water unable to drain away can build up, and its sheer weight can distort the gutter further; it can also collect on a flat roof and damage the roof covering.

Leaks can occur at the joints between sections of guttering. In plastic guttering this may be due to ill-fitting components (*see right*); in cast-iron guttering, the putty sealing the joint may have disintegrated and perhaps the bolt rusted and dropped out. An external blow to guttering can cause it to crack and leak, as can damp obstructed material or trapped water in a downpipe that freezes and expands.

Snow and ice If either is allowed to build up in gutters, it can distort and break them – particularly plastic ones. To prevent problems with snow and ice dislodge any build-up using a broom from an upstairs window or via a ladder. If snow and ice are a regular occurrence, fit a snowboard made from softwood to stand just above the eaves. This prevents frozen snow on the roof from sliding down *en masse* into the gutter.

Building up a chipped metal gutter

Mask off the undamaged areas of the metal gutter around the chip before you start the repair.

Using masking tape, stick a waxed, lightly oiled or polythene-lined piece of thin card across the outside of the broken edge of the piece of metal gutter. Bend it to follow the contour of the gutter and stick it down securely so as to make a temporary support for the putty.

Following the manufacturer's instructions, mix up some two-part epoxy putty and use it to fill the gap in the gutter, moulding and sculpting it to shape before it dries, using a filling knife. You need to make sure you have a smooth finish so that debris cannot collect against the putty when set and cause an overflow in the gutter.

Leave the putty to set before removing the cardboard, which should then easily peel away from the metal gutter.

Good gutter maintenance

Annual inspection for damage and regularly cleaning out gutters helps prevent blockages and potential problems. It is best to do this in autumn after the leaves have fallen. Dirt, sand washed down off the tiles and birds' nests can also build up in gutters. Make sure your ladder or scaffold tower is secure (*see p. 243*) when accessing the gutter and take care not to knock any debris into the downpipe, which could cause an obstruction (*see p. 248*). Wear protective gloves for clearing gutters as the edges of tiles and slates are often sharp.

Preventing blockages You can take certain measures to try and prevent blockages occurring. Fit suitably sized wire or plastic covers in the mouths of downpipes to prevent debris being washed down. If falling leaves are a real problem, tie strips of plastic netting over the gutters with twine. However, you must check regularly that wet leaves have not built up on top of this netting, which could create a further problem by stopping rainwater passing through into the guttering system.

Painting guttering Cast-iron guttering needs regular painting and a bituminous paint applied inside gutters helps preserve the metal. Left unprotected, cast iron will rust and could eventually cause the guttering to collapse. Other types of guttering do not have to be painted and therefore require less maintenance.

Guttering repairs

You can repair minor damage to gutters and downpipes, although this is really only a short-term measure and replacement of the damaged section is the better option.

Mending a crack For a minor crack in metal guttering, self-adhesive flashing tape is a repair option, while any type of guttering with a small split or crack can be easily repaired with a sprayable asphalt mastic.

Brush away any loose material and wipe the damaged area with white spirit to remove any grease or oil. Allow to evaporate and dry. Use old newspaper or card to mask the surrounding area so that the sprayable asphalt does not mark the sound areas.

Repairing a leaking plastic gutter joint

Where plastic gutter sections meet, they are sealed with gaskets (*see opposite*). The joint may leak if dirt has forced the seal slightly apart, and it might simply need a clean. Squeeze the sides of the gutter to release it from the clips of the union piece. If there is no dirt, it may be that the gaskets need removing and renewing. Alternatively, remove the gaskets and fill the gasket grooves with sealant, before replacing the gutter sections in the union piece.

Shake the spray can of asphalt mastic well before using it. For a fine crack, spray one or two coats of mastic on to the damaged area, following the manufacturer's instructions.

For a large crack, apply one coat of asphalt mastic then cover it with a patch of fine glass fibre matting or gauze before it dries and press down. When the first coat has dried, spray on a second coating of mastic to complete the repair.

Repairing a leaking metal gutter joint If the nut and bolt have rusted and are difficult to take apart, try stopping the leak simply with a gun-applied roof-and-gutter sealant. First scrape the joint clean and dry it with a hot-air gun before applying the sealant. If the leak persists, however, you will need to dismantle the joint.

Undo the nut and bolt securing the joint, or cut through the bolt with a hacksaw if necessary, and tap out the shank using a nail punch and hammer.

Separate the joint piece from the two gutter sections, by carefully tapping it with a hammer.

Once dismantled, chisel away all the old putty and scrub the pieces with a wire brush to remove the rust. Brush metal primer over the ends of the two gutter sections and the joint piece and leave to dry.

Using a putty knife, spread roof-and-gutter sealant on to the joint piece and reposition the gutter sections on it. Secure the joint with a new nut and bolt.

Drainage problems

There are various places within a house's external drainage system where blockages can occur; some are easier to clear than others, but all should be dealt with urgently to avoid damp setting in. Removing a blockage in a gutter is relatively easy once you have reached the eaves, but finding and removing the obstruction in enclosed pipes is more difficult.

Unblocking a downpipe

Downpipes are most usually blocked by leaves or similar material lodged in the mouth of the downpipe, particularly in a pipe with a swan-necked section at the top. Obstructions further down the pipe are often identified fairly easily because the sections of a downpipe are loosely slotted into one another and the joints not sealed.

Consequently, during heavy rain water will seep out of the joint above a blockage.

Obstructions near the top (or the bottom) of a downpipe can usually be cleared by prodding with a flexible length of wire or with a cane tightly wrapped at the end with rags (depending on whether the pipe is straight or swan-necked). First cover the drain at the bottom of the downpipe to prevent any debris falling into it. Hook out any debris if possible; if not, probe until you can break it up and flush it downwards with a hose or bucket of water.

For obstructions further down the pipe and out of reach hire a flexible drain rod (*see opposite*) to clear the blockage. As a last resort, dismantle the lower part of the downpipe, working from the bottom upwards, removing screws and clips until you reach

the joint from which water is seeping. Lift each section away from the wall and push a long stick through the pipes to remove any obstruction. Reassemble the downpipe, working from the top downwards and fastening it back on the wall.

Unblocking a drain

For the majority of homes, underground pipes carry water and waste from the house to the main drain. Rainwater may be directed separately into the drain or into a soakaway. Where a house is drained individually, the whole system up to where it joins the public sewer is the responsibility of the householder. First indications of a blocked underground drain are failure of a WC or bath to drain efficiently, or an unpleasant smell from an inspection chamber; more

Clearing a gully

A gully is an underground U-trap at the foot of a downpipe, from which water runs away to the drains. A build-up of leaves, silt or other material in the gully can prevent water from draining away easily. Sometimes it is simply the case of a choked grid cover causing the problem.

To clear a flooded gully, remove the grid cover. Wearing rubber gloves, lower your arm into the gully and bail out some of the water trapped in it. Scoop up the debris from the trap until the remaining water disperses.

Rinse the gully with clean water using a hose and clean it well with household disinfectant. Scrub the grid cover as clean as possible.

If a flooded gully appears to be clear of debris yet water is still not draining away, the blockage is obviously elsewhere in the drainage system and you will need to try and locate it by investigating the nearest inspection chamber (*see opposite*).

serious signs are sewage overflowing from a gully or an inspection chamber. To clear the blockage yourself, you will need to hire a set of drain rods.

Locating the blockage Wearing rubber gloves, lift the cover of the inspection chamber nearest the house, prising it up with a garden spade if necessary. If the chamber contains water, the blockage must be beyond this, so check the inspection chamber nearer the road or boundary (which will be just before the house drain joins the main drain). If the second chamber is dry, the blockage must be between these two. If this chamber is also full, the blockage must be beyond it – in the interceptor trap or in the pipe that leads to the sewer. If both inspection chambers are dry yet the yard gully or a downstairs WC will not empty, the blockage must be earlier in the drainage system – probably in the branch drains that run from the house to the first inspection chamber.

The rodding eye

In the last inspection chamber on your property, the drain drops through a U-trap (the interceptor trap), through which you cannot push the rods. To clear a blockage between this chamber and the main drain, you will have to push the drain rods through the rodding eye. This is a short pipe with a sealing plug in it, which projects above the mouth of the interceptor trap. Remove this stopper, taking care not to let it drop in the channel and block the trap. Pass the rods through this rodding eye and into the drain leading to the sewer.

Use the drain rods fitted with the rubber plunger head to clear a blockage in the interceptor trap. When the chamber and trap are clear and have emptied of water, hose them out thoroughly before replacing the stopper and cover.

RIGHT A rubber plunger is used to clear a blockage in the U-shaped interceptor trap.

Using drain rods

Made of plastic or wire, these short, flexible rods can be screwed end to end to make up the length required to meet the blockage. Various heads (for example, corkscrew, scraper or plunger heads) can be fitted on to the rods, for moving and breaking up the obstruction.

Screw a few drain rods together and attach a corkscrew fitting to the end. Insert the rods into the drain at the bottom of the inspection chamber in the direction of the suspected blockage. If you cannot see the drain opening because of the water in the chamber, use the end of the rod to find the open channel running along the bottom of the chamber, which will direct you to the mouth of the drain.

Feed the rods into the drain, attaching more of the lengths as you work and always twisting the rods clockwise to engage the screw. (Never twist the rods anti-clockwise or they will become detached and cause further problems!)

When you feel the rods come up against the obstruction, pull and push at it until the obstruction breaks up and the water starts draining away.

Extract the rods, use a hose to flush the chamber with clean water and replace the manhole cover. Hose down the rods and clean with disinfectant.

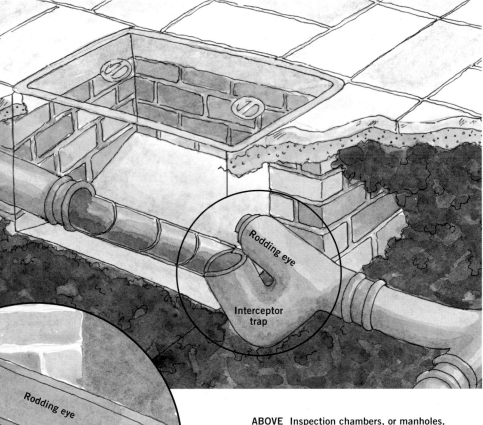

ABOVE Inspection chambers, or manholes, allow access to the underground drains for clearing any blockages that occur. In the last inspection chamber before the house drain meets the main sewer, the drain drops through a U-trap called the interceptor trap. Access to the drain beyond this point is via a rodding eye above the mouth of the interceptor trap, through which the drain rods can be pushed.

Treating damp

Damp that has developed in the fabric of your house and been left untreated is not only unsightly and damaging to the interior plasterwork, timber and decoration, it also creates an unhealthy environment for you and your family to live in. Many causes of damp can be treated successfully by a competent home handyman, but some require specialist professional attention. The three main categories of damp to watch out for in buildings, and which should be eliminated as quickly as possible, are rising damp, penetrating damp and condensation.

Rising damp

This is caused by water soaking up from the ground into the floors and walls of the house. Most houses are protected by a damp-proof course (DPC), a layer of impervious material built into walls and under concrete floors, above which water cannot permeate.

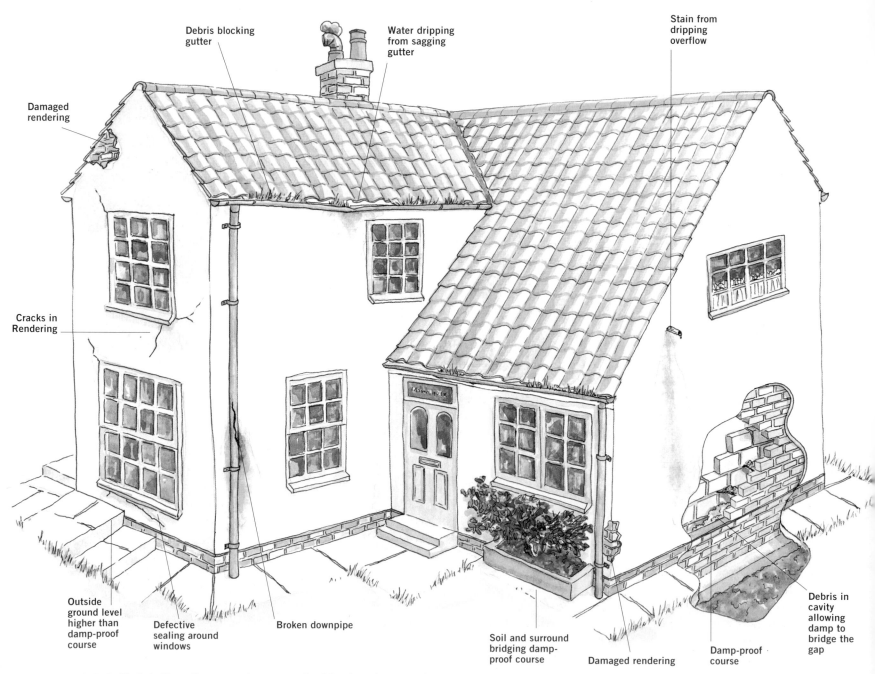

Debris blocking gutter

Water dripping from sagging gutter

Stain from dripping overflow

Damaged rendering

Cracks in Rendering

Outside ground level higher than damp-proof course

Defective sealing around windows

Broken downpipe

Soil and surround bridging damp-proof course

Damaged rendering

Damp-proof course

Debris in cavity allowing damp to bridge the gap

ABOVE As illustrated here, there are various reasons for rising damp (water soaking up from the ground) and penetrating damp (water permeating the building's structure). Some damp problems are resolved more easily than others.

Traditionally, a DPC is built into the wall at about 15cm (6in), or two to three brick courses, above ground level. If the DPC is inadequate, has broken down or is obstructed outside the house by a flowerbed or building material, water seeps upwards and is a continuous problem – even in dry weather. Rising damp occurs mostly in solid walls, and is indicated inside the house by damp patches at skirting board level or by a 'tidemark' on the walls, up to 1m (3ft) above the floor.

Installing a damp-proof course The only certain remedy for a collapsed or absent DPC is to insert a new one. Of the various options available, injection of a water-repellent chemical is perhaps the only one you might consider doing yourself, using hired equipment. However, even this is probably best left to experienced professionals who can provide a guarantee for the work. DPC injection entails drilling a series of holes in the wall through which the chemical is injected into bricks or stones until they are saturated and become impervious to water.

Lowering the ground level The level of the ground outside the house must be at least 15cm (6in) below the level of the DPC, so that heavy rain hitting the ground cannot splash above it. If it is problematic to lower the ground level because of a path or driveway, cut a deep trench, 15cm (6in) wide, along the foot of the wall of the house and fill it with gravel, which allows rapid drainage.

Penetrating damp

This is caused by water permeating the structure of the house. Broken guttering, a leaking downpipe, missing roof tiles, damaged flashing, old overporous bricks, weathered pointing and cracked masonry or render are just some of the many reasons for penetrating damp. This is why keeping up with the maintenance jobs outside the house is so important.

Penetrating damp is more common in older properties because they have solid walls. Problems can arise in modern properties with cavity walls, however, when the wall ties that link the outer and inner leaves have been bridged by, for example,

a piece of mortar dropped during the construction of the house. The mortar acts as a wick, carrying moisture across the cavity to form damp patches on the interior walls. In most cases, treating the external face of the wall with a silicone water repellent (*see right*) will cure the damp problem.

Sealing door and window frames Areas that are particularly vulnerable to penetration by rainwater are any joints between timber or brick, for example door and window frames. The rigid mortar in these joints tends to fail when there is the inevitable structural movement, and the gaps created should be filled instead with a gun-applied flexible mastic sealant.

Condensation

Condensation is a problem inside the house, due to the fact that air carries moisture as water vapour. As air becomes warmer, it absorbs more water. When water-laden air comes into contact with a surface colder than itself, it cools until it can no longer hold the water it has absorbed and deposits it on the cool surface. The most obvious example is when warm air inside the house, added to by steam from cooking or bathing condenses on a pane of glass, made cool by the outside temperature.

Condensation can be prevented in a number of ways. Fitting an extractor fan improves ventilation, allowing fresh air to replace the humid air before it condenses. Raising the temperature of an interior wall affected by condensation – by lining it with thermal board or cork wall tiles – takes the chill off its surface and makes condensation less likely. Installing double glazing also helps reduce condensation as the air trapped between the layers of glass acts as an insulator, preventing cold air passing from the outermost layer of glass to the inner.

Rotten timber

Timber that becomes damp and never dries out can result in wet rot, dry rot or mould. To prevent fungi forming, deal with any damp as soon as you find it.

Wet rot This fungus is found outside the house – commonly at the foot of doors and

Applying silicone water repellent

This fluid is designed to make masonry impervious to water without colouring it or stopping it from breathing.

- Prepare the surface of the exterior wall thoroughly, as though for painting (*see p. 254*), then allow it to dry out completely. Mask windows – both glass and woodwork – and cover up paths or driveways adjoining the wall being treated.

- Using a large paintbrush, brush the fluid generously over the masonry and stipple it into the joints. Apply a second coat as soon as the first has been absorbed to ensure all-over coverage and to make sure there are no bare patches where water could seep through.

- If you accidentally splash any of the sealant on woodwork, wash it down at once with a cloth dampened with white spirit.

around window frames. It spreads over damp timber surfaces only, and is comparatively easy to eradicate. First deal with the cause of the damp since when the wood dries the wet rot will die. Treat the damaged wood with a proprietary wood repair product or replace with well-seasoned wood, drill small holes in the new wood and insert wood preservative tablets (*see pp. 96–97*). Protect any woodwork, new or old, which is liable to damage from wet rot, with regularly applied coats of wood preservative or paint.

Dry rot This very serious problem occurs inside the house and is caused by damp, unventilated conditions. (The area beneath a suspended timber floor where there are not enough airbricks in exterior walls or the airbricks are obstructed or clogged with soil, is a prime spot.) The fungus spreads rapidly, reaching across masonry or metalwork looking for timber. It is difficult to eradicate and its treatment is a specialist job.

Exterior walls and minor repairs

Exterior house walls, solid or cavity, are generally built of bricks, natural stone or concrete blocks bonded with mortar. This masonry can be left bare or given extra protection from the elements by an application of render in one of its various forms. Any of these wall types can suffer damage – particularly from driving rain and seeping water – and some are easier to repair than others.

Masonry (brick, block or stone)

Mortar is designed to be weaker than the masonry it holds and is the first element to crack under any stress or strain to a wall. A single crack in a wall that is confined to mortar joints only could be nothing more serious than some slight settling of the soil and can be repaired simply by repointing. A crack that runs through mortar and more than the odd brick, however, could indicate a more serious strain on the foundations and should always be checked by a professional.

A severe blow can cause a single brick or stone to crack, which can be replaced. Another reason for replacing one or more bricks or stones in a section of wall is a patch of localized spalling. This occurs where moisture has penetrated into soft masonry, expanded during icy weather conditions and caused the outer face of the brick or stone to flake off.

Render

Render is a relatively thin layer of cement, lime and sand applied to masonry to provide a smooth or textured, decorative and

Safety

Wear safety goggles and a dust mask when hacking out render and mortar to prevent debris flying up and injuring you. Protective gloves are practical, too.

weather-resistant finish. Repairing render is not difficult, but it can be hard to match the colour of new work to old. A repaired rendered wall is therefore best painted. Fine hairline cracks can be ignored if the wall is to be painted with a reinforced masonry paint (*see p. 254*). Larger cracks and holes created where large slabs of render have fallen away from the wall need filling to keep the wall watertight (*see opposite*).

Pebbledash, rough-cast and Tyrolean A pebbledash wall comprises a thick base coat of render, topped by a thinner coat to which small stones, up to 12mm (½in) in diameter, have been thrown and stuck. Where water has seeped behind an area of pebbledash, one or both layers of render may fall off. Any repairs to a pebbledash wall will probably be obvious as the original pebbles and render will have weathered and changed colour. You will need about 5kg (11lb) pebbles to repair a 1sq m (1sq yd) area (*see opposite*).

A rough-cast wall is created with a sand–cement render that includes small stones or stone chippings, 8mm (⅜in) in diameter. A wall with a Tyrolean finish has a deep, rough texture, formed by a special 'Tyrolean machine' flinging a fine cement mix on to a dry undercoat of render.

Repointing masonry

General weathering, especially frost, causes the mortar between bricks and stones to break down over time. The mortar cracks and crumbles and eventually falls out, exposing the open joints to wind and rain and resulting in damp on the internal walls.

Repointing is a straightforward job. Work on a small area at a time, using a mix of 1 part cement to 1 part lime to 6 parts builder's sand. Alternatively, buy a bag of ready-mixed dry brick-laying mortar, a convenient although more expensive option. Matching the colour of the new mortar to the old can be problematic. Experiment with

ABOVE Before repointing masonry, first rake out the old mortar using the appropriate tools and wearing protective gloves and safety goggles

different mortar mixes, repointing a few joints at a time and leaving the mortar for 1–2 weeks to dry to its final colour. Liquid or powder additives can be used to change the colour of the mortar.

Rake out the old existing mortar to a depth of about 12mm (½in), using a raking out tool or a plugging or cold chisel and club hammer.

Remove all debris and dust from the joints with a stiff brush. Brush water into the joints to help delay the drying time of the new mortar. Cracks will occur if mortar dries too quickly.

Mix up some mortar in a bucket and transfer it to a hawk (mortar board). Pick up a small slice of mortar on the back of a small pointing trowel and push it firmly into the vertical joints between the bricks. Hold the hawk underneath to catch the mortar that will inevitably drop off as you work. Try not to smear the brickwork with mortar as it will stain. Repeat the process in the same way for the horizontal joints.

Once the mortar is firm enough to retain a thumbprint, the joints need shaping for a neat appearance and to help shed rainwater. Shape the new mortar to match the pointing of the existing brickwork – this could be concave (rubbed), raked, flush or weather-struck (sloping outwards).

When the mortar has almost hardened, brush the wall to remove any traces of surplus mortar.

Repairing render

To repair a small crack, rake it out using a filling knife or a cold chisel and club hammer. Brush out the dust and wet the cavity with water using a sponge. Paint a PVA adhesive inside the cavity to aid adhesion, if liked, before pressing an exterior filler into the crack using a filling knife. Smooth the filler level with the surface. For larger cracks use a ready-mixed dry render or mix your own.

Repairing a large hole Hack away loose render to leave a sound edge around the area to be patched. Rake out any crumbling joints in the masonry behind. Brush out all debris; wet the area well.

① Using a plasterer's trowel, apply the first coat of render (called the floating coat), mixed from cement, lime and plastering sand, or a bag of ready-mixed dry render. Spread it on the wall, working from the bottom of the patch upwards, pressing the lowered edge of the trowel hard against the wall as you sweep it smoothly upwards.

Continue to spread render until it is smooth and about 6mm (¼in) below the level of the surrounding original render. Mix up more render as required.

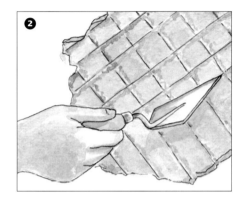

② After about 20 minutes, as the fresh render begins to stiffen, scratch lines across its surface using an old pointed tool. This gives the render a key to which the next coat can adhere. Leave this first coat of render to dry for at least 14 hours.

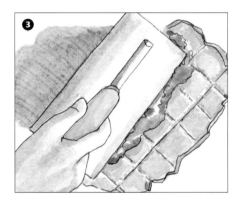

③ Next, apply the finishing coat of render, mixed to the same proportions. Sweep the trowel loaded with render lightly across the patch, this time working down the patch from left to right to spread the render over the area. Leave the render slightly proud of the surrounding surface.

After about 15 minutes, just before the render begins to set, draw a straight-edged piece of wood evenly upwards over the render to level it with the original render.

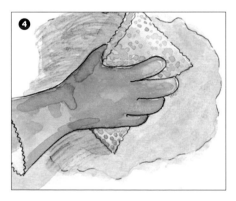

④ After a few minutes, just as the render starts to set, spray a little water over it and smooth its surface gently with a damp sponge or damp wooden float, rinsing it frequently as you work.

Patching pebbledash

Hack away the blown section to leave a sound area to be patched. If necessary, repair the base coat of render (*see left*), leaving it about 12mm (½in) below the level of the surrounding original surface. Wash and drain any of the original pebbles that can be reused.

Mix the render for the top coat, known as the butter coat. This has a lower sand content, which makes it slightly softer than the first coat and ensures that it remains soft for when you apply the pebbles. Spread the butter coat over the base coat. If repairing a large area, work in small sections that can be completed within 20 minutes before the coat starts to set.

While the butter coat is still wet, lay an old sheet on the ground beneath it and fling small scoops of pebbles from a dustpan hard at the drying butter coat until the patch is evenly covered. Press a wooden float lightly over the pebbles to press them into the surface.

Replacing a brick or stone

Chip away the mortar around a loose or damaged brick or stone, then chop out the brick or stone. Brush out all debris and dust, then wet the cavity generously with water and spread fresh mortar at the bottom of the hole, using a pointing trowel.

Dampen the replacement brick or stone equally well and spread its top and sides with mortar. Slot it into the cavity and tap it home with the trowel handle. Remove excess mortar and shape the joint to match the others around it.

If you cannot find a suitably coloured replacement to match, it may be possible, if the old brick or stone is not too damaged, simply to turn it around and replace it with its other face outermost.

Painting the outside of the house

Regularly redecorate the necessary areas on the outside of your house to keep it looking good and help protect it from the elements. Exterior wall paint deteriorates at different rates depending on its exposure to various weather conditions and the initial surface preparation, but will probably need repainting roughly every five years. Choose colours that will blend in well with neighbouring houses. Sound masonry is weatherproof and should not need painting; however, smooth render and pebbledash are often painted.

Weather considerations

Consider the weather when planning exterior decorating, since the surfaces to be painted must be dry. Do not paint when it is damp and cold, frosty, raining or windy – the wind will blow dust on to the wet paint. Ideally, paint the outside of the house during a dry but not really hot spell. The end of summer, when the fabric of the building will have dried out is ideal.

Preparing exterior walls

As with all painting, thorough preparation of surfaces is the key to trouble-free exterior decorating; although it is time-consuming, you cannot afford to neglect it.

Carry out any necessary repairs to guttering and walls (*see pp. 247 and 252–253*), and treatment such as removing organic growth or stabilizing loose surfaces (*see below*). Protect porous walls with a colourless silicone water repellent (*see p. 251*). New walls may suffer from efflorescence (*see below*) and should be left for about three months until completely dry. Never try to paint a wall that is efflorescing since this means that it is damp.

Remove all loose paint and dirt from the walls using a stiff brush. Wearing safety goggles and a dust mask, always brush away from you to avoid flicking up loose debris into your face.

Removing organic growth Organic growth needs treating with a fungicide. The damp problem encouraging the growth of moulds and lichen should be dealt with first (*see p. 251*). It may simply be a case of cutting back any overhanging trees so as to reduce the shady conditions favoured by fungus.

Scrape any thick growths of mould from the wall. Using a large old paintbrush, brush a solution of 1 part household bleach to 4 parts warm water or a proprietary fungicide over the wall. Leave the bleach solution on the wall for 48 hours, the fungicide according to the manufacturer's instructions. Wash the wall well with clean water and leave to dry thoroughly before proceeding.

Removing efflorescence Efflorescence is a deposit of white crystals found on the surfaces of damp walls, as a result of soluble salts within cement, brick, stone and plaster gradually migrating to the surface with water as the wall dries out. Efflorescence is common on newly built walls, which simply need time to dry out, but it can also occur on old masonry where the cause of the damp will need attention.

Regularly brush the crystals from the wall. Do not try to wash them off since introducing water would cause the crystals to dissolve and soak back into the wall.

When the wall is completely dry, paint the surface with an alkali-resistant primer if a solvent-based masonry paint is to be used on top. Water-based masonry paints and clear sealants can be used without a primer since they let the wall breathe and are not affected by the alkali content of the masonry.

Stabilizing a surface New walls or those with a powdery or chalky surface – test the wall by running your hand over it – need sealing with one or two coats of a stabilizing solution. This binds the loose material to the wall and provides a good surface on which to paint.

Preparing woodwork

Prepare sound, previously painted woodwork by first washing it then lightly rubbing it down with abrasive paper to provide a key for the new paint.

Strip any flaking paintwork back to bare wood – this is most easily achieved with a hot-air gun (*see p. 87*), although this should not be used if the paint contains lead. Sand the stripped surfaces smooth. Fill any cracks and dents in the wood with flexible exterior filler and repair any decayed wood, using a proprietary wood repair product (*see p. 96*).

Replace any loose, cracked or missing window putty (only after the window's wooden glazing bars have been primed) and leave the putty to harden for at least two weeks before painting.

Types of exterior paint

The paints used for exterior walls have additives to discourage mould growth. Masonry paint can be water- or solvent-based and smooth or textured; it is usually strengthened with silica or nylon for a durable finish. Smooth masonry paint goes further and is easier to apply, but textured paint is more durable and better for covering hairline cracks.

Exterior grade emulsion is a hard-wearing water-based paint, which dries faster than solvent-based paint. As with any water-based paint, it is also less odorous and less harmful to the environment.

Buying paint

Calculate the quantity of paint required just as you do for painting interior walls (*see p. 102*), remembering that textured rendered surfaces will require more paint than smooth ones. To make your calculations, determine the total surface area of the exterior walls to be painted, and deduct from this figure the combined area of doors and windows. These will need painting with the appropriate exterior primers, undercoats and top coat paints, as will metal guttering. Calculate the surface area for the latter by multiplying the circumference of the pipes by the total length of guttering.

Painting exterior walls

Paint the house, working from the top down. Try to follow the sun around the house, so that the sun dries out the area ahead of you, and by the time you get there it won't be in the full sun. You will find a paint kettle lighter and easier to hold than a can of paint, especially when painting from a ladder. Ensure your ladder is secure (*see p. 243*).

Wrap newspaper or thin card around drainpipes to protect them from splatters of paint, and cover porches or flat roofs liable to be affected. Untie any plants climbing up the wall and cover them with paper or lightweight dust sheets. If necessary, damp down any dust on the ground likely to be churned up as you work, which could ruin your wet paintwork.

Divide each wall into small sections that you can complete in a single painting session, using features such as windows, downpipes and mouldings as natural places to stop, since joins in the paintwork here will be less noticeable.

Start painting at the top of a section, applying the paint in a criss-cross fashion to coat the wall evenly. Use an exterior grade long-pile roller or a 100mm or 150mm (4in or 6in) coarse-bristled paintbrush, plus a smaller brush for working near door and window frames. Use a stippling action on textured surfaces, dabbing the ends of the bristles against the wall. It may help to water down the first coat for a heavily textured

BELOW Work from the top down when painting the outside of the house. Using existing features such as windows and downpipes as 'boundaries', divide each wall into small sections that you can complete in a single painting session.

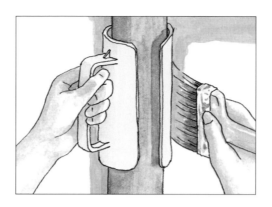

ABOVE Use a purpose-made plastic sleeve or wrap lengths of newspaper or thin card around downpipes to protect them from wall paint. Slide the protective sleeve down the pipe as you work down the wall.

surface, which is quite difficult to paint. Apply a second coat of paint when the first has completely dried.

Remove any unwanted splashes of paint using a cloth dampened with either white spirit or water, depending on the type of paint being used.

Painting exterior woodwork

Remove all dust from the surfaces to be painted. Mask panes of glass before painting exterior window frames and panel doors in the same order as for interior doors and windows (*see p. 106*). Use good-quality brushes in various sizes – probably 50mm and 25mm (2in and 1in) for the main work and 12mm (½in) for window frames.

Prime new or stripped wood, having first sealed any knots with shellac knotting to prevent resin from bleeding through the primer. Use a solvent-based or fast-drying acrylic primer or, for oily woods, use an aluminium wood primer.

The normal procedure for painting woodwork is to apply a wood primer, one or two coats of good quality undercoat, followed by a gloss top coat. (Use the same brand for the different types of paint to ensure good compatibility.) Lightly rub down each dried coat of primer and undercoat with abrasive paper then wipe off the dust before applying the next coat.

Painting metal guttering

Wash the metalwork well and leave to dry. Wearing safety goggles and a dust mask, remove rust and flaking paint with a wire brush. Wipe the surface clean.

Hold a piece of cardboard behind pipes when painting them to protect the wall or fascia behind. Apply either one coat of bitumen paint, or a metal or rust-inhibiting primer plus undercoat and top coat. (To apply a different type of paint over a pipe previously painted with bitumen paint, you will need to seal the old bituminous coat first with an aluminium primer.)

Varnishes and stains

Instead of painting window and door frames you could use an exterior grade woodstain or varnish on stripped or new wood. Water-repellent woodstains resist mould and come in a wide range of colours. Exterior grade varnish has a water-repellent, protective, high-gloss finish and is long-lasting, but deteriorates in strong sunlight. Apply the number of coats according to the manufacturer's instructions.

Order of work for exterior painting

1 Barge boards and fascias

2 Gutters

3 Walls

4 Downpipes

5 Windows and doors

Commissioning professionals

Having decided on a repair or improvement project for your home, the next decision is whether to do the job yourself or to call in a professional. Complicated or long projects may require expertise or time which you may not have but that does not mean that the whole job has to be turned over to a contractor. A compromise could be to do most of the groundwork yourself and call in specialists, such as plasterers, plumbers or electricians, where necessary. Working much faster than an amateur is able to, skilled professionals can save a lot of time and worry. If you decide that hiring a professional is the answer, whether an architect, general builder or specialist craftsman, going about it in a businesslike manner will help ensure you get what you want and avoid potential pitfalls.

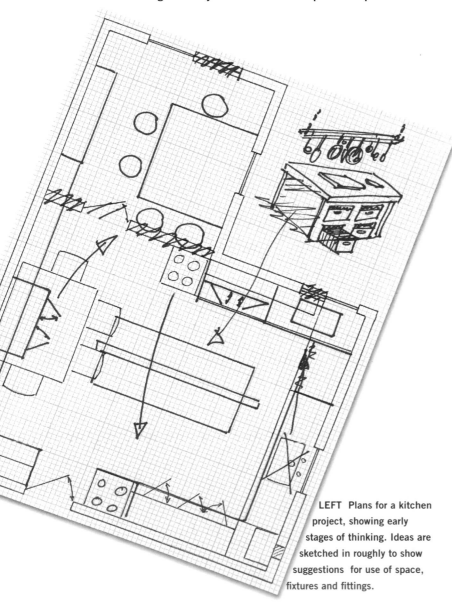

LEFT Plans for a kitchen project, showing early stages of thinking. Ideas are sketched in roughly to show suggestions for use of space, fixtures and fittings.

Choosing the right professional for the job

For large scale projects, such as major structural alteration or building an extension, it is wise to consult an architect. An architect will discuss your plans with you, be able to make constructive suggestions you had not considered and produce structurally sound designs that also look good. In addition, he or she can submit the necessary planning applications and, if desired, hire the building contractor and supervise the work to ensure it meets the specifications.

When hiring a builder yourself it is essential to choose a reliable and reputable person who understands your requirements and can do the job competently within a specified time and according to a budget. Finding such a builder can be a daunting prospect but thankfully, and in spite of the many horror stories of shoddy work and unexplained absences, there are many reliable ones about.

Personal recommendation is a good place to start. If you know someone who has recently engaged a builder, ask to see their work and enquire about how they conducted the job. Failing that, the names of builders can be found in telephone directories and local newspapers. Not all builders do all kinds of work, however, so be prepared for some refusals. Look for contractors who are members of a trade association. Although membership does not necessarily guarantee the work, it is usually dependent on a having a sound reputation as well as bank and insurance references. A good tradesman is proud of his work and will be pleased to supply you with references for you to follow up where you can inspect examples of his workmanship.

Ask more than one contractor for an estimate so that you can compare costs. Estimates will be based on current prices, and may have to change if you do not decide to go ahead with the work straightaway. Cost will not be the only criterion in deciding which builder to use. Their attitude and your confidence in their ability to do the job are equally important.

Establishing the brief

Disagreements between builder and client often arise from a misundertanding as the result of inadequate briefing. The builder may be working to the best of his understanding which, unfortunately, is not what the client had intended. The best way to avoid this problem is to provide the builder with a written specification – a list of the work to be done, the materials to be used and an indication of the required completion date. Many details will need to be revised, but this will give the builder a good idea of your requirements and can form the basis of his estimate for the cost. Before writing a specification, read the relevant chapter in this book to get an idea of the amount and type of work involved.

A quotation is a fixed price for a job. Before asking a builder to start work, ask for a firm quotation with a breakdown of the costs based on all the points you have discussed; provide a revised specification if necessary. There may be grey areas in the quotation, for example estimated costs for sub-contractors such as plumbers or electricians; you can try to get these firmed up before the job begins or you must be prepared to accept the charges. Make sure that all rubble and debris are to be removed and the site left clean and tidy. If you require any making good and decoration, make sure that these are included in the costs.

You also need to agree in advance how you will pay for the job. A small job can be paid for on or soon after completion. But where a job is going to take several weeks or months, and involves the purchase of a large amount of materials, it is reasonable for the builder to ask for interim payments to cover delivered materials and completed work; never pay for anything in advance. You can arrange to hold back 5 to 10 per cent of the costs on completion for a specified amount of time until you are sure that there is no faulty workmanship, but you must agree this with the contractor before the work starts.

Dealing with the unexpected

One can never guarantee, especially with a large project, that there will not be any unforeseen problems as the work progresses. If something unexpected has to be dealt with in the course of the work, ask for an estimate before agreeing to the work. The same applies if you change your mind in the course of the job or you ask for extra work to be done.

For large jobs, it is a good idea to ask the builder to provide a schedule list; if an architect is overseeing the job, he or she will draw one up and ask the builder to fill it in. It sets out the stages of work such as building a blockwork wall, installing new wiring, plastering, fitting a sink, etc.

As well as his own work, the builder is responsible for the quality of workmanship provided by any specialists he needs to employ. If you have any concerns over the work supplied by a sub-contractor, discuss these with the builder rather than the person concerned. To avoid confusion, a sub-contractor should be directed by one person only – the person who employed him.

If you are hiring individual specialists yourself, to help with specific jobs as and when you need them, brief these people as carefully and precisely as you would a general builder, and also ask for estimates or quotations for the work. Again, personal recommendation is the best thing to go by and inspecting examples of their work will convince you of their ability.

Good relations always make for better results in all fields of work. Try to understand the builder's requirements and problems. Provide the builder with access to electricity and water, if required, and storage space for tools. Be prepared for a certain amount of mess where the work is being carried out; good workmen will clear up as best they can each night before leaving for home. Without interrupting the work, monitor progress and inspect work at night after the workers have gone home. If you are unhappy about any aspect of workmanship or the progress of the job, discuss it with the builder in the morning. If you cannot be there, leave a note or telephone to discuss what is worrying you.

Finally, if you are around during working hours, an occasional cup of tea, without holding up the proceedings, works wonders.

RIGHT You can make a copy of this checklist and tick off the tasks as they are completed.

Working Contract

Set out your requirements and know exactly what a builder intends to supply. This provides the basis of a workable contract between the parties concerned.

Finding a contractor	Approach several contractors, personally recommended if possible. Ensure they have good references and ask to see examples of their work.	✓
Specifications	Give prospective contractors a clear and precise outline of the job before asking for estimates and quotations.	
Estimates	Ask several contractors for an estimate. This will give you an idea of costs and help you narrow down your choice. An estimate may be written or verbal and is a guide only to the envisaged costs; the job itself may cost more, or less.	
Quotations	A written quotation is a fixed price for the job and should detail how the job is to be done and the materials to be used; it may or may not include provision for unforeseen problems. It is usually recommended that you get quotations from three contractors.	
Schedule list	If a job is large, a schedule list sets out all the stages of work. It is a good way of keeping track of all the jobs to be done, especially where more than one contractor is involved.	
Access	You must provide the builder with reasonable access to electricity and water if these are required for the job.	
Payment	Before work starts, agree exactly when payment is to be made and whether there are any conditions applying.	

Glossary

Abrasive paper Paper coated with abrasive particles for smoothing wood. Graded by grit size and spacing.

Adhesive Powerful bonding agent. Many types available for specific materials.

Adjustable spanner Open-ended spanner with a movable jaw to adapt to a wide range of sizes.

Bag graining A traditional paint finish created by dabbing the freshly painted surface with a bag full of old rags.

Ballvalve Valve operated by a float that rises and falls with the water level in wc and cold water cisterns.

Basin wrench Long-handled wrench designed for working in awkward spaces.

Belt sander Machine for removing old paint or finishing wood and metal.

Bending spring Long spring that fits inside or over copper pipes so they can be bent without collapsing the walls.

Bevel-edge chisel Bevel-bladed chisel suitable for light woodworking.

Blowlamp Hand-held propane or butane gas canister with flame used for soldering work and softening old paint ready for stripping.

Bolster Wide, spade-shaped cold chisel designed for cutting bricks but often used for lifting floorboards.

Bradawl Small tool used to make starting holes for screws and nails and for piercing leather.

Cable Thick insulated wire for the fixed wiring of electrical systems.

Chipboard Board made from bonded softwood chips, sold in several grades.

Chisel Sharp-tipped wood-cutting tool used with a mallet.

Circuit Complete pass of wiring through which electric current flows.

Circuit breaker Incorporated into the consumer unit or added on, cuts electricity supply if an overload, fault or leakage of electricity occurs.

Cold chisel Steel tool with double-ground edge for rough cutting cold metal.

Colour washing Application of thin glaze washes over a ground coat to create subtle veils of colour.

Compression joint Dismantleable joint made with a compression fitting on plastic or copper pipe.

Consumer unit Wall-hung box housing fixed wiring fuses.

Continuity (circuit) tester Device for testing faults on electrical circuits.

Countersink attachment Power drill fitting for cutting recesses to take screw heads.

Coving Decorative plaster or expanded polystyrene moulding between walls and ceiling.

Craft knife Handle fitted with sharp replaceable blades useful for cutting sheet materials and other items.

Damp-proof membrane Layer of impervious material in concrete floors to prevent moisture rising up.

Dowel Short lengths of dowelling (tubular-shaped wood, sometimes grooved) used for joining wood.

Dry brushing Process in which a glaze is applied over a previously painted colour and stippled with a dry brush and then lightly brushed with a dusting brush while still wet.

File Rough-bladed tool for smoothing metal and wood, removing burrs and other irregularities.

Flex Short for flexible cord; insulated wire used to connect plugs to electrical appliances and pendent light fittings to ceiling roses.

Floor sander One of two types of machine used together for sanding floors: the large drum sander sands the main area and the smaller disc sander cleans the edges.

Flux Paste added to solder to make it run easily when it is heated for joining pipework.

Fuse Rewirable or cartridge devices designed to interrupt a circuit if a fault, overload or leakage of electricity occurs.

G-clamp G-shaped clamp with large screw for securing wood or metal to a workbench.

Glue gun Gun-shaped device loaded with glue sticks, which it heats. The glue dries instantly on application.

Hardboard Fibre building board generally used for covering framework. Standard hardboard has a smooth finish on one side and a textured finish on the other.

Hot air stripper Electric device for softening paint ready for stripping.

Jig saw Power saw for making curved cuts in timber and man-made boards.

Joist Timber or metal beam used to support a structure such as a floor, ceiling or wall.

Junction box Housing for cable connections, usually on lighting circuits of old wiring systems.

Limewashing Dry-brushing technique used to create a mottled effect, traditionally achieved using authentic limewash but today with modern paints.

Liming Process of whitening the grain of hardwood using a proprietary paste or matt emulsion instead of the original lime.

Linoleum Flooring material made from natural fibres, linseed oil and resins. Durable and easy to clean, it is available in a wide variety of finishes.

Lump hammer Double-faced heavy hammer for driving steel chisels and demolishing masonry.

Mallet Wood or rubber-headed implement used for driving sharp instruments that would be damaged by metal hammers.

Marking gauge Sliding device fitted with a pin for scratching lines parallel to edge of the workpiece.

Matting Woven natural fibres used as flooring materials.

MCB Miniature circuit breaker.

Metal-detecting device Device for detecting hidden metal such as wiring or pipework.

Milk paint Traditional paint, made by mixing earth-coloured pigments into buttermilk or skimmed milk and a little lime, which dries to a smooth, flat finish.

Mitre To cut two mating surfaces, each to a 45° angle, so that the components form a right angle when joined.

Nail punch Pointed steel shaft used with a hammer for driving nail heads just below the surface of wood without damaging it.

Newel Post at top and bottom of staircase supporting the handrail.

Oak graining Technique for painting woodwork to give it the appearance of high-quality wood.

Orbital sander Power sander that smooths wood surfaces finely by making a series of tiny high speed cuts.

Padsaw Tapered narrow bladed saw for cutting openings; a small starting hole must be drilled first.

Paint kettle Metal container with a handle for holding paint.

Pasting table Lightweight folding table for laying wallpaper on to paste it.

Pincers Jawed tool for extracting nails and tacks from wood.

Pin hammer Lightweight hammer for driving small pins or tacks.

Plasterboard Ready-plastered sheet with a different surface on each side: grey for plastering, beige for painting.

Plumb line Weight centrally attached to a line for checking verticals.

Plywood Strong sheet material made from bonded layers of veneer, available in a number of grades and thicknesses.

Portable workbench Folding lightweight bench with a central grip feature that can be moved to the site of work.

Power drill Designed for drilling holes, the many accessories and attachments available turn this versatile instrument into any number of useful tools.

Preservative Chemical formulation painted or sprayed onto wood to prevent decay.

Profile gauge Tightly packed sliding needles held together by a centre bar which take on the outline of any object they are pressed against.

PTFE tape Pliable tape used with threaded plumbing fittings to seal joints.

PVA adhesive General purpose liquid adhesive that makes a good primer and sealer when diluted.

Rag rolling Glazed finish resembling fine taffeta or watered silk, achieved by applying a glaze over a base colour then rolling a wet cotton rag over it. A quick way to achieve a decorative finish.

RCCB A residual current circuit breaker monitors the current passing through live and neutral wires of a circuit and cuts off the supply if earth leakage occurs.

Roller Fabric sleeve on a frame for applying paint. Can be made from a number of different materials.

Rose Ornamental plasterwork ceiling centrepiece or fitting through which a pendent light is wired to fixed cable in the ceiling.

Safety glasses or goggles Protective eyewear that should be worn for any work that produces dust or particles at high speed.

Sanding block Shape for holding abrasive paper during sanding.

Scaffold tower Sectional scaffold frames built up to provide a stable working platform.

Scraper Tool designed for removing unwanted finishes or coverings on wood or walls. Narrow-bladed scrapers are for paint, wide-bladed ones for wallpaper.

Screed Thin layer of mortar spread over a solid floor to give a smooth, level finish.

Sealant Paste squeezed into crevices to form a waterproof seal, such as around a bath.

Self-grip wrench Also known as a mole grip, this has jaws controlled by an adjuster to exert great force on objects.

Shave hook A scraper shaped for removing old paint from mouldings. The head can be triangular, pear-shaped or a combination of the two.

Skarsten scraper Tool for smoothing wood surfaces or removing paint, available in long- and short-handled versions with a selection of blades.

Sleeving Yellow-and-green insulation tubing for slipping over the bare earth wire of cable at connections.

Solid floor Concrete slab laid over a bed of compacted hardcore. Modern solid floors incorporate a damp-proof membrane.

Spirit level Vial containing liquid and an air bubble fitted into a holder, which can be of a number of designs and sizes, for checking levels.

Splattering Speckled effect achieved by splattering one or more colours onto a previously painted surface.

Sponging Process of dabbing a sponge onto wet paint to create an effect.

Steel rule Accurate tool for measuring and laying out. Can also be used as a straight edge.

Steel wool Matted steel strands used as an abrasive for smoothing metal and wood.

Stencilling Process of painting a design through a cut-out which allows the shape to be repeated in any pattern.

Stillson wrench Heavy-duty wrench with a moving jaw operated by a nut, for gripping round objects.

Stippling Antique effect achieved by applying a stippling brush to a wet top coat of paint to break it up into a mass of tiny dots.

Stopcock Brass tap fitted on a mains pipe to enable water supply to be switched off.

Straight edge Parallel-sided steel strip, up to 2m (6ft) long, used for scribbling against and checking surfaces are level.

String Board running at each side of a staircase to hold the treads and risers.

Tenon saw Straight-edged saw with a reinforced back for rigidity, used for cutting joints.

Transparent oil glaze Also known as 'scumble' glaze, this is thinned with white spirit before being brushed over a surface. It can be tinted with stain or an oil-based paint.

Try square Parallel-sided metal blade set at a right angle in a stock for accurate marking and checking of 90° angles.

Varnish Clear protective coating for timber. Those made with polyurethane give a waterproof, heat- and scratch-resistant finish.

Veneer A thin layer of attractive timber fixed to a thick core of a less appealing wood.

Vinyl Hardwearing all-purpose material used for sheet flooring and tiles. Available in a multitude of designs.

White spirit Colourless liquid derived from petroleum used as a thinner for oil paints.

Wire brush Handbrush with steel wire bristles for removing paint and rust particles from metal.

Wire strippers Tool for cutting through the sheathing of flex and cable to expose the wires.

Index

Acknowledgments

The publishers would like to thank all those who supplied photographs for use in this book. We are particularly grateful to Kerry Davis from Sage Interiors, High Street, Ripley, Surrey GU23 6BB (tel: 01483 224396) and Claire Gouldstone for their help with this project.

Sunday Times DIY & Decorating Picture Acknowledgements

Crown Back cover right, **Crowson Fabrics** Front Cover top right, **Anna French Ltd**/Avignon Collection Front Cover top centre, **Octopus Publishing Group Ltd**/Di Lewis Front Cover bottom right, /Peter Myers Front Cover bottom centre, /Shona Wood Front cover centre left, Front Cover bottom left, Back Cover top left, Back Cover bottom left, /Polly Wreford Front Cover top left.

The Alternative Flooring Company 146 Top, 154 Bottom, **Arc Linea** 170 Top, **Artisan** 219 Top Left, 226 right, **Laura Ashley** 124–125, 198–199 Bottom, 199 Bottom Right, 206 Top, **B&Q plc** 160, **The Blinds Company** 230 Top Left, **Coloroll** 129, **Cotteswood of Oxfordshire** 135 left, **Crabtree Kitchens** 182 Bottom Right, 185 Top, 206 Bottom, **Crown** 68 right, 110 Top, 112 Top, 112 Bottom, 113, 133, 151 Bottom, 155 Centre Right, 173, 201 Top Left, 208 Bottom, 216 Bottom, /88 shade.po9 158, /Anaglypta pattern RD383 123 left, **Crowson Fabrics** 151 Top, 194 Bottom Left, 215 Top Right, 222 Bottom Right, 235 Centre Right, **Crucial Trading Ltd** 145 right, **Czech and Speake** 52, **Designers Guild** 237 Bottom Left, **Dulux** 99 Centre Right, 111, 114 Top, 115, 116 Bottom Left, 116 Bottom Right, 121, 141, 147 Bottom, 149 Top, 157 Main Picture, 194 Top, 195 Bottom, 198 Top, 203 Centre Left, 215 Bottom Left, 216 Top, 232, **Elizabeth Whiting Associates** 74, 119 Top Left, 143 Top, 148 left, 148 right, 166 Top, 170 Bottom, 176, 178 Top Left, 199 Top Right, 201 Centre Left, /Michael Dunne 167 left, 171 Centre Right, 185 Bottom, 225, /Andreas V. Einsiedel 62, 130–131, 184 Bottom Left, /Brian Harrison 82 left, 184 Top Right, /Clive Helm 171 Centre Left, /Rodney Hyett 67 left, 72 left, 143 Bottom, 153 Bottom, 171 Bottom Right, 179 Bottom, 183 Top Right, 203 Centre Right, 204 Bottom, /Ed Ironside 99 Bottom Left, 140 Top, /Di Lewis 116 Top Right, 171 Top Left, /Neil Lorimer 172 Bottom Right, 201 Bottom Left, 230 Bottom Right, /Nadia

MacKenzie 152, 194 Bottom Right, /Michael Nicholson 153 Top, 190, /Tim Street-Porter 67 right, 175 Bottom Left, 184 Bottom Right, /Spike Powell 183 Bottom Right, /Ron Sutherland 72 Top Centre, /Jerry Tubby 188 Bottom, /Simon Upton 110 Bottom Left, 196 Bottom, /Peter Woloszynski 72 Top Right, 193 Bottom Right, 217 Top, **Fired Earth** 57 Bottom Right, 81 Top Left, 142, 169 Bottom Left, 204, **Anna French Ltd** 132 right, 70, 205 Top, **GE Lighting/Mazda** 163 Bottom Left, 168 Top, 169 Top, 169 Bottom Right, **Grange** 214 Top, **Habitat UK** 82 right, 177 Bottom Left, 178 Bottom Left, 193 Centre Right, 197 Top, 205 Bottom, 217 Bottom, **Robert Harding Picture Library** 237 Centre Left, /Jan Baldwin/IPC Magazines Ltd 219 Centre, 238 Top, 238 Bottom, /Brad Simmons Photography/O'Neill 167 Bottom Right, /Peo Eriksson 239, /Brian Harrison 207, /Mann & Man/IPC Magazines 182 Top Right, **Harlequin** 203 Bottom, 223 Bottom Right, 233 Top Right, **Heuga** 154 Top, 199 Centre Right, **The Holding Company** 175 Top Left, 179 Top Right, 183 Centre, **Houses and Interiors**/Simon Butcher 241 Top, 244 Centre Left, 244 Bottom Left, /David Markson 5 Bottom Right, 240–241, **Ideal Standard Ltd** 140 bottom, **IKEA Ltd** 163 Centre Left, 172 left, 177 Bottom Right, 196–197 Top, 214 bottom, **Junckers** 145 Top Left, 146 Bottom, **Liberty** 234 bottom, **Liberon Waxes Ltd** 149 Bottom, **London's Georgian Houses** 76, **Marie Claire**/Gilles de Chabaneix 178 Bottom Right, **Next** 58, 65 Bottom, 193 Top Left, 195 Top, 203 Top Left, 210 right, 223 Top, **Octopus Publishing Group Ltd**. 86, 87, 105, /Bill Batten 2–3, 219 Bottom Left, 223 Centre, 226 left, 231 Top Right, 235 Top Left, 235 Top Right, 235 Bottom Right, /Jon Bouchier 34, 44–45, 47, 48–49, 54, /John Cook 102, /Paul Forrester 4–5, 8–9, 9 left, 9 right, 10–11, 12–13, 14–15, 16–17, 20–21, 24–25, 26–27 Bottom, 32, 38–39, 56–57, 57 Right, 60, 68 left, 69, 75, 78–79, 84–85, 90, 97, 98–99, 100–101, 108–109, 117 Bottom Right, 122 Top, 122–123 Bottom, 123 right, 125 Bottom Right, 132 left, 134 left, 135 right, 138, 144–145, 150, 155 Background, 157 Background, 162–163, 164 Top, 164 Bottom, 165 left, 167 Top Right, 174–175, 180 right, 200 left, 215 Top Left, 215 Bottom Right, 218–219, 220–221, 228–229, 230 Bottom Left, 231 bottom, 233 Top Left, /Mark Gatehouse 117, 118, 119 right, /Di Lewis 120, 165 right, /Peter Marshall 208 Top, 212 Bottom, /Bill McLaughlin 180 left, /James Merrell 193 right, /Kelvin Murray 1, /Peter Myers 77, 81

Bottom Right, 114 Bottom, 166 Bottom, 172 Top Right, 209, 223 Bottom Left, 233 Bottom Right, 234 Top, 237 Top, /Andrew Twort 192–193, /Simon de Courcy Wheeler 27 Top Right, /Simon Wheeler 181, /Polly Wreford 107, 122, 179 Top Left, 182 Bottom Left, 183 Top Left, 197 Bottom Right, 201 Top Right, 222 Bottom Left, **Osborne & Little plc**/Galatea 222–223, /Lundy 202, 211 Bottom Right, **The Pier** 183 Bottom Left, 183 Bottom Centre, **Pilkington Glass** 57 Top Left, 65 Top, **Sanderson** 122 left, 211 Top Right, **Sharps Bedrooms** 188 Top, 200 Top Right, 208 Centre, 212 Top, **Shand Kydd** 193 Centre Left, 210 left, **Storeys** 134 Right, **Warner Fabrics plc** 81 Top Right, **Wellington Tile Company** 147 Top, **John Wilman Fabrics & Wallpapers** 177 Top Left, 211 Top Left

The publishers would also like to thank Laura Bangert, Tel: 020–7276 3811, for her tireless prop hunting and styling.

Thanks is also due to all those companies and individuals who supplied props for photography and in particular:

Brent Carpet Company Ltd, 60 Craven Park Road, Harlesden, London NW10 4AE, Tel: 020–8961 4030. **Bryon & Bryon Ltd**, 4 Hanover Yard, off Noel Road, Islington, London N1 8BE, Tel: 020–7704 9290. Sean Gilpin, **The Decorative Fabrics Gallery**, 278–280 Brompton Road, London SW3 2AS, Tel: 020–7589 4778. **Foxell & James Ltd**, 57 Farringdon Road, London EC1M 3JB, Tel: 020–7405 0152/2487. **Hamiltons Acorns Ltd**, Halford Road, Attleborough, Norfolk NR17 2HZ, Tel: 01953 453201. **LG Harris & Co Ltd**, Stoke Prior, Bromsgrove, Worcester B60 4AE, Tel: 01527 575441. **Ikea**, 2 Drury Way, North Circular Road, London NW10 0TH, Tel: 020–7451 5566. **The London Lighting Company**, 135 Fulham Road, London SW3, Tel: 020–7589 3612. **Olympic Tiles CTD**, Unit 7, East Ham Industrial Estate, 1000 Newham Way, East Ham, London E6 4JL, Tel: 020–7511 5831. **Plastercraft**, 314 Wandsworth Road, Fulham, London SW6, Tel: 020–7736 5146. **Simeon Oliver**, Tel: 020–7713 1852. **The Stencil Store Company Ltd**, 20–21 Heronsgate Road, Chorleywood, Hertfordshire WD3 5BN, Tel: 01923 285577. **A Touch of Brass**, 210 Fulham Road, London SW10 9PJ, Tel: 020–7351 2255.

First published in Great Britain in 2000 by
Hamlyn, a division of Octopus Publishing Group Ltd
2–4 Heron Quays, London E14 4JP

Copyright © 2000 Octopus Publishing Group Limited

ISBN 0 600 60248 6

A CIP catalogue record for this book is available from the British Library.

Some material included in this volume has been previously published by Hamlyn.

Printed in Italy

10 9 8 7 6 5 4 3 2

Designer: Mark Stevens
Editors: Sarah Ford, Jo Smith and Anne Crane
Contributors: Ned Halley, Judith Devons, Jackie Matthews, Caroline Ball and Jo Lethaby
Photography: Paul Forrester, Colin Bowling and Hugh Johnson
Illustrators: Kevin Hart, Kevin Jones Associates, Paul Webb and Jane Hughes
Picture Researchers: Claire Gouldstone, Liz Fowler and Emily Hedges
Production Controller: Lee Sargent

We would like to thank Leslie Davies and Matthew Hampton for their contributions and Parry Tyzack, 329 Old Street, London, EC1 for their assistance with tools and equipment.

In describing all the projects in this book, every care has been taken to recommend the safest methods of working. Before starting any task, you should be confident that you know what you are doing, and that you know how to use all tools and equipment safely. The Publishers cannot accept any legal responsibility or liability for accidents or damage arising from the use of any items mentioned, or in the carrying out of any of the projects described.